The Politics of Major Policy Reform in Postwar America

The Politics of Major Policy Reform in Postwar America examines the politics of recent landmark policy in areas such as homeland security, civil rights, health care, immigration, and trade, and it does so within a broad theoretical and historical context. By considering the politics of major programmatic reforms in the United States since the Second World War – specifically, courses of action aimed at dealing with perceived public problems – a group of distinguished scholars sheds light on not only significant efforts to ameliorate widely recognized ills in domestic and foreign affairs but also on systemic developments in American politics and government. In sum, this volume provides a comprehensive understanding of how major policy breakthroughs are achieved, stifled, or compromised in a political system conventionally understood as resistant to major change.

Jeffery A. Jenkins is a Professor in the Department of Politics and Faculty Associate in the Miller Center at the University of Virginia. He has published more than thirty articles in peer-reviewed journals, such as the *American Journal of Political Science*, the *Journal of Politics*, *Legislative Studies Quarterly*, and *Studies in American Political Development*. He is also the author (with Charles Stewart III) of *Fighting for the Speakership: The House and the Rise of Party Government* (2013) and the editor (with Eric M. Patashnik) of *Living Legislation: Durability, Change, and the Politics of American Lawmaking* (2012).

Sidney M. Milkis is the White Burkett Miller Professor in the Department of Politics and Faculty Associate in the Miller Center at the University of Virginia. He has written extensively on political history and American politics, with special attention to the presidency, political parties, and social movements. His books include *The President and the Parties: The Transformation of the American Party System Since the New Deal* (1993); *Political Parties and Constitutional Government: Remaking American Democracy* (1999); *Presidential Greatness* (2000), coauthored with Marc Landy; *The American Presidency: Origins and Development, 1776–2011*, sixth edition (2011), coauthored with Michael Nelson; and *Theodore Roosevelt, the Progressive Party, and the Transformation of American Democracy* (2009). He is the coeditor (with Jerome Mileur) of three volumes on twentieth-century political reform: *Progressivism and the New Democracy* (1999), *The New Deal and the Triumph of Liberalism* (2002), and *The Great Society and the High Tide of Liberalism* (2005). His articles have been published in *Perspectives on Politics, Presidential Studies Quarterly, Political Science Quarterly*, the *Journal of Policy History, Studies in American Political Development*, and numerous edited volumes.

The Politics of Major Policy Reform in Postwar America

Edited by

JEFFERY A. JENKINS
University of Virginia

SIDNEY M. MILKIS
University of Virginia

CAMBRIDGE
UNIVERSITY PRESS

CAMBRIDGE
UNIVERSITY PRESS

32 Avenue of the Americas, New York, NY 10013-2473, USA

Cambridge University Press is part of the University of Cambridge.

It furthers the University's mission by disseminating knowledge in the pursuit of education, learning, and research at the highest international levels of excellence.

www.cambridge.org
Information on this title: www.cambridge.org/9781107668485

© Cambridge University Press 2014

First published 2014

A catalog record for this publication is available from the British Library.

Library of Congress Cataloging in Publication Data
The politics of major policy reform in postwar America / edited by Jeffery A. Jenkins, University of Virginia; Sidney M. Milkis, University of Virginia.
    pages   cm
ISBN 978-1-107-03498-3 (hardback)
    1. Political planning – United States.   2. Policy sciences – United States.   3. United States – Politics and government – 1945-1989.   4. United States – Politics and government – 1989–   I. Jenkins, Jeffery A., editor of compilation.   II. Milkis, Sidney M., editor of compilation.
JK468.P64P66   2014
320.60973–dc23   2014005137

ISBN 978-1-107-03498-3 Hardback
ISBN 978-1-107-66848-5 Paperback

Contents

Contributors   *page* vii

Acknowledgements   ix

1 Introduction: The Rise of a Policy State?   1
   Jeffery A. Jenkins and Sidney M. Milkis

2 The Long 1950s as a Policy Era   27
   David R. Mayhew

3 Regulation, Litigation, and Reform   48
   Sean Farhang

4 Courts and Agencies in the American Civil Rights State   77
   R. Shep Melnick

5 The Politics of Labor Policy Reform   103
   Dorian T. Warren

6 Teachers Unions and American Education Reform:
   The Power of Vested Interests   129
   Terry M. Moe

7 Progressive Federalism and the Contested Implementation of
   Obama's Health Reform   157
   Lawrence R. Jacobs and Theda Skocpol

8 Federalism and the Politics of Immigration Reform   179
   Carol M. Swain and Virginia M. Yetter

9 Trade Politics and Reform   203
   Judith Goldstein

10 The Politics of Intelligence Reform   227
   Richard H. Immerman

11 Follow the Leader: Major Changes to Homeland Security
     and Terrorism Policy   253
     Jennifer L. Merolla and Paul Pulido

12 Conclusion: Madison Upside Down: The Policy Roots of Our
     Polarized Politics   282
     Paul Pierson

Index   303

Contributors

Sean Farhang, University of California, Berkeley

Judith Goldstein, Stanford University

Richard H. Immerman, Temple University

Lawrence R. Jacobs, University of Minnesota

Jeffery A. Jenkins, University of Virginia

David R. Mayhew, Yale University

R. Shep Melnick, Boston College

Jennifer L. Merolla, Claremont Graduate University

Sidney M. Milkis, University of Virginia

Terry M. Moe, Stanford University

Paul Pierson, University of California, Berkeley

Paul Pulido, Claremont Graduate University

Theda Skocpol, Harvard University

Carol M. Swain, Vanderbilt University

Dorian T. Warren, Columbia University

Virginia M. Yetter, Bass Berry and Simms

Acknowledgements

This volume grew out the William and Carol Stevenson Conference, which was held at the University of Virginia's Miller Center on November 11 and 12, 2011. The William and Carol Stevenson Conference is a biennial event that explores domestic and international issues of national importance. We are deeply grateful to the Stevenson family for their generous and passionate commitment to scholarship that joins rigorous analysis and public affairs. We also would like to thank Governor Gerald Baliles, Director of the Miller Center, for his support of the conference and enthusiastic engagement with its participants during two days of lively and wide-ranging discussion of public policy. We convened a distinguished group of scholars from political science and history in the hope that they might help us better understand the philosophical, historical, and institutional factors that have contributed to the success or failure of major policy reform in United States since the Second World War. The authors probing attention to policies spanning health care and homeland security met, indeed exceeded our expectations. Thanks to their efforts this volume offers new and interesting insights into how contests over public policy are at the heart of contemporary developments in American politics and government.

Introduction: The Rise of a Policy State?

Jeffery A. Jenkins and Sidney M. Milkis

This book grew out of a major conference at the University of Virginia's Miller Center of Public Affairs. Seeking to place scholarly attention to, and partisan disputes over, recent landmark policy in areas such as homeland security, health care, and financial markets in a broad theoretical and historical context, we convened a group of distinguished scholars to consider the politics of major programmatic reforms – specifically, courses of action aimed at dealing with perceived public problems – since the Second World War. The chapters that follow shed light not only on significant efforts to ameliorate perceived ills in domestic and foreign affairs, but also on systemic developments in American politics and government.

This time period corresponds with the emergence of what Karren Orren and Stephen Skowronek have termed a "policy state" – that is, a political order where policy choice has become a principal dimension of American government and politics.[1] Of course, policy clashes have always been an important part of American politics. But the explosion of government responsibilities in foreign and domestic affairs, the emergence of programmatic political parties, and the formation of a dense network of advocacy groups and think tanks have made conflict over competing policies a defining feature of contemporary American politics.

Given the fragmented nature of public policy during the past sixty years, the concept of an "emergent state" – suggesting a centralized, purposeful deployment of power and an autonomous bureaucracy – might deflect attention from the variety and complexity of programmatic developments during this period. Nevertheless, as Hugh Heclo has pointed out, the leading characteristic of American politics since the 1960s has been what he terms "policy mindedness," that is, the emergence of an outlook that considers "everything in public life besides policy [to be] secondary."[2] This volume suggests that policy mindedness began prior to the 1960s, and the case studies that follow, even as they illustrate powerful centrifugal forces, when considered together represent major developments in ideas and institutions, originating during the 1930s, that dramatically changed the politics of public policy by the end of the Second World War.

Although the volume does not presume to cover all important policy arenas, it includes discussion of nine critical issues – spanning civil rights, social welfare, trade, immigration, and national security – that offer a comprehensive understanding of how major breakthroughs are achieved, stifled, or compromised in a political system conventionally understood as resistant to major changes. As David Mayhew's Chapter 2 on the "long 1950s" (1949–1963) shows, distinguishing policy *reform* from policy *change* or even policy *stasis* is no easy task. But the basic premise that inspires this volume is that policy reforms involve nonincremental change that addresses what policy makers and advocates regard as a major public problem. How something becomes defined as a critical public problem and what constitutes non-incremental change are thorny questions. It is intriguing, for example, that scholars, indeed the authors of this volume, disagree about whether the Patient Protection and Affordable Care Act and No Child Left Behind act were significant policy breakthroughs. Similarly, some of the big-ticket items of the long 1950s, such as the creation of the Interstate Highway System – which Daniel Patrick Moynihan called "the largest public works program in history" and had an immense effect on the economy and society – would be condemned as reactionary by reformers during the late 1960s and 1970s and become the target of programmatic initiatives dedicated to ameliorating the "negative externalities" they created. Mayhew suggests that the post–Second World War years mark an ongoing contest between conservative and liberal policy advocates, neither of whom has been able to forge a consensus on the role of government.

Our central point is that a massive health care initiative, the overhaul of education policy, and the creation of a vast network of interstate highways are just the sorts of major programs, seeking to address what had come to be perceived as substantial public problems, that prima facie have defied policy stasis and marked a substantial departure from existing policies. Whether these policies imposed positive or negative externalities on the economy and society is an important question left unresolved by this volume; however, there is little doubt in our view that these programs marked a substantial departure from prevailing government action.

POLICY REFORM AND AMERICAN POLITICAL DEVELOPMENT

This volume adds a new dimension to the growing attention that scholars have paid over the past decade to the relationship between American political development and public policy. Building on the seminal contributions of scholars such as E.E. Schattschneider, Theodore Lowi, Grant McConnell, and James Q. Wilson on the politics that attended different types of policy,[3] more recent work has sought to discover the logic by which policies have endured and changed throughout history.[4] Placing programs, in time, has aroused a healthy debate over whether the policy process privileges inertia or development,[5] and has fostered important theoretical insights into how enduring policy "paths" have been interrupted by "critical junctures."[6] Like the chapters that follow, this scholarship has posed hard challenges to the shibboleth that American politics remains tightly bound by cultural constraints and constitutional veto points. Policy-mindedness, Heclo argues, has smitten Democrats and Republicans, Liberals and Conservatives alike. Although rancorous politics divide them, both Democrats and Republicans have their own ambitious visions for policy reform in some arenas even as they staunchly defend the policy status quo in other domains.

In fact, the politics of postwar policy reform has often stirred liberals, moderates, and conservatives to propose different solutions to commonly perceived crises. Dwight Eisenhower, a self-styled "new" (read moderate) Republican, responded to the New Deal not by rolling back the national state that it forged, but, rather, as Mayhew shows in Chapter 2, by pursuing policies such as the Interstate Highway System and the Upper Colorado River Storage Project that would promote economic growth. Far less accommodating to New Deal liberalism, Barry Goldwater – the first major American politician to embrace the conservative label – represented important policy aspirations from the political right that began to emerge in the 1950s, most notably a rejection of détente and the embrace of a less-flexible anticommunism.[7] Similarly, the Republican-controlled 104th Congress (1995–1996), led by House Speaker Newt Gingrich, did not propose eliminating welfare policy, but, rather, *reforming* it by linking public assistance to strict time limits and work requirements.

This is not to suggest that the timeless question of whether the federal government has the authority to devise policy solutions to social, economic, and international problems has become a nonissue. Indeed, a major theme of this volume is that the Republican Party has grown more conservative since Ronald Reagan's presidency, a development that crested with the rise of the grassroots Tea Party movement. Militant Tea Party members of Congress, ensconced in the conservative House caucus, the Republican Study Group (RSG), have sought the repeal of the major reforms enacted during Obama's first term, especially the Patient Protection and Affordable Care Act; moreover, the RSG defied Speaker John Boehner's negotiations with the president to reach a "Grand Bargain" that would have overcome partisan gridlock in fiscal policy through a combination of entitlement savings and tax increases.[8]

As Paul Pierson suggests in Chapter 12, the very legitimacy of the policy state, then, has become a flashpoint for partisan rancor. But given how entrenched and expansive policy commitments have become, contemporary "conservative policy" presupposes that comprehensive tax and entitlement reform are necessary to remedy the pathologies of American politics. Moreover, many of those who are active in, or identify with, the Tea Party support middle class entitlements and strengthening America's armed forces.[9] Finally, as Carol Swain and Virginia Yetter show in Chapter 8, many insurgent conservatives promote comprehensive immigration reform, which has been incubating in states such as Arizona, that would establish a stronger role for the national government in cracking down on illegal aliens.

The "legitimacy barrier," as Wilson described the wall of separation between the public and private, has thus been lowered considerably. Since the Second World War, there has been a great expansion of problems, once considered beyond the scope of government action, that are now viewed as legitimate issues on the national agenda.[10] From this perspective, the long 1950s described by Mayhew in Chapter 2 might have paved the way for, rather than been the target of, this breakthrough. By the 1960s, Americans were on what Wilson calls an "Eisenhower High": "a plateau of self-confidence and enthusiasm produced by successfully overcoming a great depression, winning a world war, and establishing this nation as the undisputed economic and military power house of the world."[11] It was not Eisenhower, however, but rather Kennedy who most inspired the sense of national glory that resonated with the historical experience of postwar America. Roosevelt's New Deal, Kennedy said in his acceptance speech at the Democratic convention, had "promised security and succor to those in need." But more prosperous times called for a New Frontier that was "not a set of promises" but a "set of challenges." The New Frontier "sums up not what I intend to offer the American people, but what I intend to ask of them," he declared. "It appeals to their pride, not their pocketbook – it holds out the promise of more sacrifice instead of security."[12] The giftedness or charisma of the young president matched America's feelings that it could solve the world's problems and break through the ancient barriers that had previously limited humankind – even, Kennedy pledged, "landing a man on the moon and returning him safely to earth."[13]

After Kennedy's assassination, it fell to Lyndon Johnson (LBJ) to join this sense of pride to the most nettlesome problems left undone by the national policy advances of the 1950s and early 1960s. He transmuted the New Frontier into the Great Society, trumpeted in the signature speech of his administration on May 22, 1964: a commencement address at the University of Michigan. "The Great Society," Johnson told the graduating seniors and their families, "demand[ed] an end to poverty and racial justice," but this was "just the beginning." Challenging the students and their parents to embrace more ambitious goals for America, LBJ described his vision of a "great society" as a place

where every child can find knowledge to enrich his mind and to enlarge his talents. It is a place where leisure is a welcome chance to build and reflect, not a feared cause of boredom and restlessness. It is a place where the city of man serves not only the needs of the body and the demands of commerce but the desire of beauty and the hunger for community.[14]

This was not merely rhetorical flourish; Johnson's exalted vision would take programmatic form through the 1960s and 1970s, making policy reform, hitherto a rare political commodity, a rather common occurrence. As Wilson points out,

Until the mid-1960s, Washington was not held responsible for the problems of crime, drug abuse, schooling, or the environment, and it had no meaningful policy on civil rights. ... During the Johnson and Nixon administrations, all that began to change. The government embraced new goals – improving education, delivering health care, combatting crime, eliminating racial injustice – that had only their lofty moral appeal to compensate for the manifest difficulty of achieving them.[15]

The wayward path of transportation policy reveals how an expansive and controversial policy state was layered atop, and transformed, the programmatic innovations of the 1950s. In 1956, the Federal Highway Act codified the interstate highway system in twenty-eight pages. Thirty-five years later, the Intermodal Surface Transportation Efficiency Act (dubbed "Ice-Tea") reauthorized that program, but did it in a complex bill of 293 pages with goals that went well beyond the building of roads:

In 1956, we wanted to build a highway system; by 1991, we also wanted to aid mass transit, reduce air pollution, encourage the use of seat belts and motorcycle helmets, preserve historic sites, control erosion and outdoor advertising, use recycled rubber in making asphalt, buy iron and steel from U.S. manufacturers, define women as disadvantaged individuals, and protect native American reservations.[16]

THE POLICY STATE AND THE CONSTITUTION

The path of transportation policy highlights how the new policy regime operated within a highly contentious but pluralistic politics; by the same token, the new policy state emerged within the broad contours of an old constitutional order. The case studies of this volume reveal that the expansion of public policy has been superimposed on constitutional institutions, so that each branch of government and the states have become active in the development of national public policy. As Orren and Skoronek describe this phenomenon,

The hallmarks of this new state of affairs are imprinted in the now-common indictments levelled against each of the old players: that judges routinely make law rather than simply find it; that presidents routinely declare law rather than simply execute it, that bureaucrats routinely give content to law rather than simply administer it; that Congress routinely delegates rather than legislates; that the several states routinely serve objectives promulgated at the center at the expense of local self-rule.[17]

Of course, the blending of constitutional institutional powers and responsibilities begins in an important sense with the Founding. Madison argued in *Federalist* 48 that "a mere demarcation on parchment of constitutional limits of the several departments is not a sufficient guard against those encroachments which lead to a tyrannical concentration of all the powers of government in the same hands."[18] Instead, as he argued in a well-known phrase in *Federalist* 51,

"The great security against a gradual concentration of the several powers in the same department consists in giving to those who administer each department the necessary constitutional means and personal motives to resist encroachments of the others." Constructing a system where "ambition counteracts ambition" necessarily required a complex mixing of powers. Indeed, observing the conventional wisdom that "in republican government, the legislative authority necessarily predominates," Madison proposed that the president and Senate might forge an alliance from time to time, drawing the chief executive into the details of lawmaking, to buttress the integrity of national administration.[19] Similarly, during the Constitutional Convention, he had proposed formally joining the executive and judicial powers in exercising the veto, so that the authority of the president and the Supreme Court might be allied in moderating the important role that Congress would invariably play in shaping executive power and defining rights.

Just as the aggrandizement of congressional power was the principal concern of the architects of the Constitution – a fear that reverberated throughout the nineteenth century – so the breach of the legitimacy barrier aroused fears of centralized administration, grounded in a powerful, if not imperial, presidency. The "conceit" that, as Franklin Roosevelt put it, "the day of enlightened administration has come," underlay most New Deal and Great Society programs. Paradoxically, however, the expansion of "big policy" during the late 1960s and 1970s went hand in hand with the distrust in government.[20] According to James Patterson, this popular disenchantment followed from the overselling of policy reforms that began in the 1950s and reached a crescendo during the Great Society. The "optimists ... underestimated the formidable divisions – of race, class, and region that persisted in the United States." Although Johnson's liberal faith was attractive and well-meaning, Patterson argues, it contributed to the strong alienation from government that abetted the rise of conservatism.[21]

Yet a number of scholars who have probed the deep roots of the new politics of public policy have argued that faith in public policy and distrust in government were not sequential; rather, there was a singularity to this symbiotic relationship. Of course, fear of centralized power is a signature feature of American political culture. But Heclo argues that there was something novel about the animus to public authority that arose in the 1960s. The emphasis shifted from traditional suspicion of power to a defiance of all authority.[22] As Brian Balogh has observed, this pervasive distrust of authority "became embedded in the very relations between students and teachers, doctors and patients, elected officials and constituents."[23] Clearly, Vietnam and Watergate were important contributing factors, but animus toward public authority went well beyond these troubling episodes. The vision of the Great Society itself – the shift from "quantitative" to "qualitative" liberalism – held that an active and energetic national state was no less dangerous than it was necessary. At the core of the New Deal state stood the modern presidency – centered in the White House Office and Executive Office of the President. Even as LBJ extended this institution's legacy, his rhetoric and programs – celebrating a "desire for beauty," "hunger for community," and "participatory democracy" – presupposed limiting the discretion of presidents, bureaucrats, and policy experts. Significantly, between 1965 and 1975, trust in government fell furthest among those who described themselves as liberal Democrats. By the early 1970s, surveys showed, liberals were more opposed to big government than were conservatives.[24]

Teaching Americans both to expect more from government and trust it less, the Great Society was the fulcrum on which the decline of liberalism and the rise of conservatism tilted. But conservatives, too, were complicit in the rise of a policy state that combined the expansion of public programs and profound cynicism toward public authority. The Tea Party's ambivalent orientation to government – expressed in its support for Social Security and Medicare as well as its positions on Homeland Security and immigration – has its origins in the rise of modern conservatism. As Goldwater's messianic campaign foretold, in the wake of the Great Society's sweeping new commitments to activist government self-styled conservatives were no longer content with the policy of forbearance. Nor was conservative policy activism limited to foreign affairs. Rather than seeking a balanced budget, for example, Republicans since the late 1970s have embraced a form of conservative Keynesianism, dubbed "supply side" economics, advanced by innovative thinkers such as Arthur Laffer and Paul Craig Roberts, who argued that a large tax cut would stimulate productivity so much that tax revenues would actually increase and allow the budget to be balanced. Moreover, no less than liberals, conservatives practice an activist politics that expects government to solve national problems. Ronald Reagan, the apostle of contemporary conservatism, promised to "get government off the backs of the American people," but his administration became committed not only to expanding the national government's role in containing communism, but also to preserving "family values." George W. Bush (GWB), a self-professed Reagan disciple, sought solutions to society's ills in government-supported "faith based" groups (a conservative version of community action), educational reforms that would ensure that "no child was left behind," and the creation of a Department of Homeland Security.

THE CONTOURS OF POLICY REFORM IN POSTWAR AMERICA

At the dawn of the twenty-first century, then, both liberals and conservatives had developed an Ibsenesque love-hate relationship with the policy state. A major question addressed by this volume is how this mixture of yearning and dread have affected politics, especially collective efforts aimed at ameliorating problems such as economic insecurity at home and terrorism abroad. Not surprisingly, given the complexity of contemporary American politics, the chapters of this book do not offer a simple answer to this question. The authors differ significantly, for example, in their understanding of the roles that interest groups and the bureaucracy play in policy reform. Whereas Sean Farhang in Chapter 3 and R. Shep Melnick in Chapter 4 reveal how institutional partnerships between interest groups, Congress, and the courts have resulted in significant reform of civil rights and regulatory policy, Terry Moe in Chapter 6 has identified "vested interests" that have thwarted meaningful change in education. Just as Judith Goldstein argues in Chapter 9 that bureaucratic autonomy abetted the liberalization of international trade after the Second World War, and Jennifer Merolla and Paul Paludo in Chapter 11 find that the public and Congress willingly delegate substantial authority to the president and executive agencies to protect the homeland from terrorism, so Richard Immerman shows in Chapter 10 how departmental and agency turf protection has thwarted intelligence reform.

Moreover, the authors of this book offer competing views on the policy effect of constitutional checks and balances. In Chapter 5, Dorian Warren argues that the federal characteristics of the Constitution, made effective at the national level by the Senate filibuster, have severely weakened the labor movement. Similarly, Moe shows in Chapter 6 how teachers unions' powerful influence on state and local governments has obstructed educational reform. In contrast, in Chapter 7, Lawrence Jacobs and Theda Skocpol, in their examination of the Patient Protection and Affordable Care Act, and Carol Swain and Virginia Yetter in their study of immigration reform in Chapter 8, spy a new stage of federalism, where the states play an important role in advancing national reform.

In the first instance, these distinctive tales show the need to transcend longstanding debates about the course of American government in the twentieth and twenty-first centuries. The politics of public policy in post–Second World War America is neither susceptible nor intractably resistant to reform; and when it does come, reform takes many forms, often directly through landmark legislation, sometimes through the autonomy of administrative agencies, other times as a result of judges who overcome bureaucratic intransigence, occasionally through the states filling the void left by policy deadlock in the nation's capital.

The question remains, however, whether the chapters of this volume point to any broader insights into reform politics in the policy-minded polity. Tentatively, we suggest that some order can be discerned among the disparate policy paths traced in our authors' chapters. First, rights are still central to the rhetoric and institutional arrangements of American politics. At the same time, as Chapters 3 and 4 by Farhang and Melnick respectively, demonstrate, new rights – related to race, gender, and consumer and environmental protection – have profoundly transformed education and the workplace. Indeed, the Kennedy administration described what would become the 1964 civil rights legislation as "constitutional policy," suggesting that the idea of natural rights presupposing a wall of separation between government and society had been modified by a new understanding of rights that was embodied in programs. Although this "rights revolution" began during the New Deal with programs such as Social Security and the National Labor Relations Act, it was greatly expanded during the 1960s and 1970s, when the courts became extensively involved in the details of policy reform. As Warren shows in Chapter 5, new rights did not trump old rights. In labor politics the "right to work," codified by the Taft-Hartley Act, has seriously constrained the right to bargain collectively established by the National Labor Relations Act. Indeed, as Moe observes in Chapter 6, the combination of the Great Recession and the success of Tea Party and other conservative activists in the 2010 state and local elections led many states, most notably Wisconsin, to limit the collective bargaining rights of public workers. Even more telling, toward the end of 2012, Michigan, the home of the United Auto Workers, became the twenty-fourth state in the Union to enact a right-to-work law under the auspices of Taft-Hartley, a dramatic sign of just how great a threat current conditions pose to worker solidarity.

Traditional battles regarding the national government's power thus still have cultural resonance and political consequences. But unlike the fault line that divided America during the 1930s – when Liberals and Conservatives fought over whether or not to expand the responsibilities of the national government – both of the competing rights that currently roil labor politics (one invoking the "natural" right of property, the other the collective right of workers) have increasingly taken on the attributes of policy. To a point, Democrats and Republicans battle over the legitimacy of national government action; but many of the chapters of this volume make clear that the real fight is for command of the sprawling, regnant policy state that has formed in the postwar years.

Second, just as the growth of policy-mindedness has been intertwined with rights talks, so the merging of rights and policy has modified, but not overcome, the division and separation of powers. The leading paradigm for reform has been drawn from the New Deal realignment, when a major transformation of parties joined, for a time, the usually separated branches of government to bring about major changes in domestic and foreign policy. But Mayhew's Chapter 2 demonstrates that major policy breakthroughs, such as the emergence of the interstate highway system and the establishment of the National Aeronautics and Space Administration, also occurred under conditions of divided government.[25] Bipartisan agreements to seek ambitious policy initiatives in the service of growth, development, productivity, and efficiency, he argues, "allowed a more or less consensual ticket out of the polarizing and exhausting class politics inherited from the 1930s." By the twilight of the Great Society, however, divided partisan realms were grounded in the cultural and institutional changes that shaped the policy state: paradoxically, the expansion of government programs was allied to distrust of centralized power that encouraged aggressive oversight of executive administration and insurgent assaults on the "Washington establishment." Rather than pursuing solutions to the nation's problems with New Deal-style executive-centered and pragmatic policy solutions, political activists began to engage in ideological confrontation that defied consensus and diminished the public's trust in government. As Farhang shows in Chapter 3, the combination of partisan contestation and divided government that has prevailed since the late 1960s has spawned a regime of private litigation that transformed civil rights regulatory policy – converting "theoretical statutory rights into practical substantive benefits." Of course, the courts established important precedents that challenged the legal ramparts of Jim Crow during the 1940s and 1950s in landmark decisions such as *Smith v. Allwright* (1944), which declared the all-white primary unconstitutional, and a decade later, in the famous *Brown v. Board of Education of Topeka, Kansas* (1954), which forbade "separate but equal" school systems. But such constitutional decrees had a limited impact on forced segregation until they were transformed into public *policy*, formulated and administered by institutional alliances that joined judicial authority to reform advocates in Congress, administrative agencies, and public interest groups. The civil rights regulatory regime, Farhang shows, was greatly expanded by the development of a network of private for-profit attorneys who benefited from legislation that authorized court-appointed lawyers' fees, which made public interest law attractive to regular commercial firms. Private enforcement soon became a model for other areas of social regulation, such as environmental and consumer protection, housing, education, and health care.

Similarly, Melnick shows in Chapter 4 that far-reaching civil rights reform in education and employment were achieved through an institutional partnership of the courts and bureaucratic agencies that he and other public law scholars have defined as "adversarial legalism." In this process, courts and litigation have strengthened the American state by combining an "expansion of the responsibilities of the central government with a decentralized, party-driven form of decision making." This odd but effective combination, Melnick adds, "arises from a fundamental tension between a culture that expects and demands comprehensive governmental protection from serious harm, injustice, and environmental dangers – and hence a powerful, activist government – and a set of government structures that reflects mistrust of concentrated power and hence that limits and fragments political and government authority." So enduring and strong did this court-centered approach to reform become, Melnick argues, that contentious litigation became "our home grown alternative to bureaucratic centralization and thus an essential element of the contemporary American 'state.'"[26]

At the same time that the courts – long considered an obstacle to national reform – emerged as a vanguard of civil rights, environmentalism, and consumer protection during the 1960s and 1970s, the states also became surprisingly engaged in the policy state. Madison argued that federalism would complement the separation of powers; competition between the national government and States would become, he envisaged, the second pillar of a "compound republic" – a "double security [arising] to the rights of the people."[27] The conventional wisdom of most examinations of federalism is that states retard national policy reform – competition among them, as Louis Brandeis feared, has more often than not led to a "race to the bottom" that empowers private interests and weakens social welfare policies such as Medicaid and unemployment benefits.

And yet, the rise of a new policy regime after the Second World War went hand in hand with a "cooperative federalism," as LBJ termed it, which gave states financial incentives and authority to administer and in some cases promote social welfare and regulatory measures. Chapters 7 and 8 by Jacobs and Skocpol and Swain and Yetter, respectively, confirm that the states may sometimes act, to use Louis Brandeis's more hopeful formulation, as "laboratories of democracy." Jacobs and Skocpol go so far as to suggest the Patient Protection and Affordable Care Act has brought to a culmination what they term "progressive federalism." Although depicted by its political enemies as a national takeover of health care, the act (especially as modified by the Supreme Court case that challenged its constitutionality) gives states a critical role in administering the law. More interesting, Jacobs and Skocpol argue that Obama officials and health reform advocates have tempered the harsh partisanship generated by health care reform by offering bonuses to states that are most resistant to implementing the health care act and by "grafting" the programs authorized by the new law onto administrative institutions that had been constructed to participate in the Medicaid program, one of the most significant Great Society reforms.

To this point, as the fierce battle over the implementation of "Obamacare" shows, the fate of progressive federalism hangs in the balance[28]; so policy entrepreneurs have faced major obstacles in creating a cooperative federal framework in immigration policy. Comprehensive immigration reform that reconciled the objectives of border security and more expeditious pathways to citizenship for illegal aliens was thwarted by partisan gridlock in George W. Bush's second term and Barack Obama's first four years in office. But challenging the common assumption that states filled this vacuum by enacting reactionary immigration measures, Swain and Yetter argue that sharp partisan rancor within the Washington beltway encouraged reformers to seek redress at the state level. They report, for example, that the enactment of welfare reform in 1996, which granted states the authority to determine immigrant eligibility requirements for federal benefits programs, has had some counterintuitive results. Although it was "expected [that] most states would use this authority to enforce stricter limits on access to benefits, states were commonly more generous than the federal government had been."[29] To be sure, the policy state has hardly led to a race to the top in health care or immigration policy, but as the noted federalism scholar, Richard Nathan, has argued, since the 1960s American federalism has tended to expand rather than retard the welfare state.[30]

Thus, with the emergence of a new politics of public policy, traditional veto points in American politics, such as the courts and states, have increasingly become alternative sites of opportunity for important policy reform. Self-styled public interest groups and tort lawyers have venue shopped, seeking out the areas of traditional constitutional government that are most susceptible to policy reform. In truth, Warren's depiction of the Senate as the graveyard of labor reform reveals that powerful inertial forces still exist; by the 1990s, in fact, the minority party in the Senate began making regular use of filibusters and other anti-majoritarian mechanisms to block policy reform.[31] Moe argues in Chapter 6, moreover, that rent-seeking by teachers unions in state and local politics has thwarted educational reform. Nonetheless, whether reform efforts have been successful or failed, the constitutional system of checks and balance no longer, as was the case prior to the New Deal, appear to constrain national policy innovation. That Moe and Swain and Yetter view certain states and localities as the vanguard of *national* reform in education and immigration policy, respectively, suggest as much. So does the view of Jacobs and Skocpol that the States have become deeply engaged in implementing The Patient Protection and Affordable Care Act, even as partisan rancor over its legitimacy sharply divided Congress and the Supreme Court.

POLICY REFORM AND AMERICAN DEMOCRACY

Finally, the chapters that follow suggest how the politics of policy reform over the past six decades has transformed the character of self-government in the United States. Although critics of the welfare and national security states that emerged by the 1940s have warned that these institutions have spawned, as Lowi famously put it, "a nightmare of bureaucratic boredom,"[32] the advent of policy minded-ness has not subordinated politics to administration. Administrative politics are certainly important in the areas of intelligence, national security, and trade; however, even these more executive-centered policy arenas have not fostered bureaucratic autonomy.

Of the case studies that follow, Immerman's account of intelligence reform in Chapter 10 describes the most insular example of reform politics. He argues, in fact, that efforts to strengthen intelligence policy – to bring more order to the "confederate" intelligence institutions – have been continually thwarted by the key agencies' unwillingness or inability to work together. Yet Immerman's analysis of the sixties and seventies parallels those of Farhang and Melnick in Chapters 3 and 4, respectively. During these years, the Central Intelligence Agency (CIA), the most recalcitrant national security institution since its crea-tion by the 1947 National Security Act, saw its "veil of secrecy and protective shield" disintegrate. The Church hearings led to the creation of intelligence committees in the House and Senate dedicated to strengthening legislative over-sight as well as strict procedures for electronic surveillance and other methods of collecting information on suspected agents of foreign powers operating on U.S. soil.[33] Animated by the exposure of CIA abuses during the Vietnam War and Watergate, the impetus for "litany reform" that reverberated through the 1970s was "not the [agency's] inefficiency and mixed record of addressing [external threats]." Instead, the reform impulse reflected contentious domestic politics: "The revelations of CIA abuses and the polarized politics that were so inter-twined with them." By the same token, it was not the intelligence community's failures and threat of future attacks that was the primary motivation for reform in the wake of the terrorist attacks on the World Trade Center and Pentagon.

"Rather, it was political finger pointing and blame game that attended the Iraq War." From this perspective, the politicization of national security, both after Vietnam and September 11, 2001, not conventional bureaucratic pathologies undermined "the normative drivers of intelligence reform."

Immerman laments the failure to ameliorate the national security confederation in Chapter 10, one he acknowledges signalled the resistance – deeply rooted in American political culture – to centralized administration. Still, from the vantage point of Merolla and Pulido in Chapter 11, who fear that the war on terror and the creation of the Department of Homeland Security have created a permanent condition of crisis that threatens civil liberties and the rule of law, institutional clashes between the executive and Congress, even when harshened by divided partisan realms, might be a welcome development. "Before 9–11," they observe, "no one had even conceived of the notion of 'homeland security,' [but] the term rapidly became ubiquitous and the publicized focus on intelligence failure and the need for vigilance made sacrifices for the sake of security more palatable." This profound cultural shift, they argue, embodied by the creation of a new executive department that signalled an ongoing obligation of the federal government, fused domestic and foreign policy. An important institutional consequence followed: the blurring of the boundary between the "two presidencies" that has long separated the president's prerogatives in foreign affairs and the more limited authority the White House exercised in domestic matters.[34]

This fusion of domestic and foreign executive power has been reinforced, and made more dangerous, Merolla and Pulido conclude in Chapter 11, by the "war on terrorism" – a struggle against an intractable and elusive enemy that has no clear end. The Obama administration has banished the term war on terror. Nevertheless, the president pursued a "surge" strategy in Afghanistan and expanded deployment of Special Forces and armed drones in counterterrorism missions – policies that resembled more than contrasted with those of his predecessor. Even after American soldiers killed Osama bin Laden and the country began disengaging from Iraq and Afghanistan, Obama initiated measures toward the end of his first term to imbed his administration's "Overseas Contingency Operation" in the national security apparatus, with the expectation that "targeted killings" would continue for at least another decade.[35] The most visible signs of this seemingly permanent struggle, Merrola and Pulido observe, are evident on the home front, where "almost all of the changes to airport security have remained on the books, and have become . . . more invasive of personal privacy." Revelations during the summer of 2013 that the National Security Agency (NSA) and the FBI had been tapping directly into the central servers of nine leading U.S. Internet companies, including Microsoft, Google, and Facebook, and extracting audio and video chats, photographs, e-mails, documents, and connection logs so that analysts can track foreign targets dramatically confirm the intrusion of homeland security on Americans' privacy. The program, code-named PRISM, is not totally unprecedented – the NSA prides itself on stealing secrets and breaking codes, and has often formed

corporate partnerships to sidestep legal barriers. But the alliance between the
NSA and Silicon Valley supports Merolla and Pulido's argument that homeland
security marks a novel and troublesome blurring of the separation between the
government's authority in foreign and domestic affairs.[36]

Given the way homeland security has resulted in another profoundly important breach of the legitimacy barrier, renewed partisan debate and institutional
conflict over national and homeland security may be viewed not as an obstacle to
effective change, but, rather, as an important step in rebinding the changes
wrought by intelligence reforms enacted in the aftershock of September 11,
2001 and the American democratic tradition.[37] Indeed, several of the chapters
in this volume, especially Pierson's conclusion in Chapter 12, show how party
politics has been shaped by the battle between Democrats and Republicans over
the appropriate course of public policy. Goldstein in Chapter 9 praises the free
trade reforms that have defied narrow interest group and provincial partisan
politics. At the same time, she considers on going partisan debates over whether
"government should redistribute the gains from trade in order to compensate for
job loss that results from opening the US market" to be an important factor in
"taking into account the changing nature of politics both at home and abroad."
Just as Jefferson and Hamilton carried on a principled disagreement about the
effect of international trade on economic equality, so the parties continue to
differ on the appropriate relationship between government regulation and economic prosperity. With regard to job losses resulting from foreign competition,
the Democratic Party advocates Trade Adjustment Assistance to both compensate and retrain workers, whereas the Republican Party has been more reticent in
subscribing to such measures that restrain markets in the service of economic
security.

In contrast to the rather civil and deliberative partisan conflict Goldstein
describes with respect to trade policy, many contemporary issues sharply divide
the parties. It remains to be seen, of course, whether contemporary parties,
which are far more centralized and doctrinaire than were the decentralized,
patronage-based parties that shaped American politics from the 1830s to the
1940s, can vitally connect with voters. As Pierson observes, the emergence of
national programmatic parties appears to represent "a stunning reversal" of
Madison's hopeful prediction in *Federalist* 10 that "the creation of a national
polity would provide an institutional foundation for pluralism and diminish the
prospects for the formation of broad and durable coalitions." Although Pierson
attributes harsh partisanship to Manichean Republican politics, both parties
have engaged the country in passionate struggles over the war on terror, health
care reform, business regulation, and fiscal policy that have alienated many
voters and raised concerns that partisan rancor has led to dangerous brinksmanship that denigrates serious efforts to solve the profound economic and
national security problems the country currently faces.

The Patient Protection and Affordable Care Act has been an especially polarizing issue. Health care has divided the parties for decades, representing the holy

grail of the Democrats since the New Deal and the final, most dangerous piece of a full-blown entitlement state to Republicans. And yet, although Lyndon Johnson and the Democratic Party were the main architects of the Medicare and Medicaid programs enacted in 1965, many Republicans supported these reforms[38]; and even many conservative contemporary Republicans, with close ties to the Tea Party movement, consider Medicare a programmatic right that stands above partisan rancor. Indeed, President George W. Bush and a Republican-controlled Congress enacted legislation in 2003 that added a pre-scription drug benefit to the Medicare program – the largest entitlement expansion since 1965. Given this historical consensus, the fight over health care reform from 2009 to 2010, which saw the Democrats create a new middle class entitlement without a *single* Republican vote, marked a critical step in the development of national programmatic parties. Clearly, Republicans' unwillingness to work with Democrats to seek a compromise solution on health care gave eloquent testimony to their militant partisan approach to legislating. But Obama's leadership throughout the health care debate – and his acceptance of the use of the reconciliation process, which circumvented the filibuster rules of the Senate, to pass the Patient Protection and Affordable Care Act – also showed a strong partisan streak.

In Chapter 7 Jacobs and Skocpol may very well offer a prescient view of how the raw partisan conflict over the health care law will be constrained by more pragmatic administrative maneuvers at the state and local level. Nonetheless, the party system has been so nationalized that many of battles fought in the 111th Congress (2009–2010) have been transported to the state capitals. The struggles over the Medicaid program have been especially harsh. The health care legislation mandated a substantial expansion of eligibility for this program, which provides benefits to the most disadvantaged Americans, but the Supreme Court, although it approved most of the law's provisions, invoked the Tenth Amendment to declare that the expansion was an option for, rather than a requirement of, the states. At this writing, twenty-five states, mainly with Republican governors and state legislatures, have rejected Medicaid expansion, in part due to concern about the future costs of the program. Some Republican governors – for example, Rick Scott of Florida, Jan Brewer of Arizona, John Kasich of Ohio, and Rick Snyder of Michigan – noting the federal government's commitment to cover the cost of expansion and the obligation to help America's poorest citizens, have tried to persuade their states' Republican-controlled legislatures to accept the broadening of Medicaid eligibility. These state leaders, however, have faced staunch resistance from GOP legislatures, which express the same ideological opposition to comprehensive health care reform as their partisan brethren in Congress.[39]

As such, the maturing of the policy regime that has emerged since the Second World War might have spawned a novel form of partisanship that defies the sort of resolution and consensus that once characterized major programmatic breakthroughs in American politics. Tellingly, polarization seems to be penetrating society. As political commentator Bill Schneider has observed, *public* opinion may be transforming into *partisan* opinion.[40] For example, the Kaiser Foundation found that Democrats and Republicans deeply divided over the Supreme Court decision that found most provisions of the health care law constitutional: 80 percent of Democrats approved of the decision and 80 percent of the Republicans opposed it; moreover, although an overwhelming number of Democrats proclaimed that in the wake of the Court's ruling it was time to "move on to other problems," Republicans were just as determined to support continued efforts to block the legislation.[41] This transformation is not surprising in light of electoral campaigns and policy debates during the Bush and Obama years that emphasize *mobilization* rather than *persuasion*. Although polarization was a critical filter during the Bush administration, it has taken another huge leap during Obama's presidency: A May, 2013, poll showed Obama getting 87 percent support from Democrats and 15 percent from Republicans – an unprecedented 72 percent division.[42]

Many scholars have probed the dynamics of American political culture and public opinion to demonstrate that the election of the nation's first African-American president has aggravated partisan conflict.[43] Although Melnick's chapter argues persuasively that civil rights reforms are now deeply imbedded in American political institutions, Democrats and Republicans strongly disagree about whether government programs should be "color blind" or designed to assist designated racial minorities.[44] These partisan differences over racial policies, Randall Kennedy has argued, expose a persistent "color line" in America that underlies the "stark polarization that characterizes the racial demographics of support for and opposition to Obama."[45] Racial sentiments, however, have proven very difficult to isolate from other factors that have fueled partisan polarization; more to the point, the chapters of this volume make clear that polarization is a long-term development – part and parcel of the emergence of a national programmatic party system, joined inextricably to contentious policy advocacy.

Chapters 7 and 12 by Jacobs and Skocpol and Pierson, respectively, suggest that harsh party conflict, especially the Republicans' militant resistance to healthcare reform and taxes, marks an unfortunate turn in the politics of public policy, a view shared by many scholars and political commentators.[46] It may be, however, that the battle over health care policy reflects the harsh realities of democracy in the twenty-first century. As the intellectual historian Robert Wiebe has written, "Although [democracy] has some theoretical affinity for doctrines of liberty, equality and farness – hence the frequency with which these terms show up in discussions of democracy – it does not provide reliable, concrete support for any these grand concepts. Democracy, in other words, reveals our humanity, not our salvation. We may not like it."[47] For all the controversy attending it, the health care battle, fueled by lively, sometimes vitriolic town meetings throughout the country, confirmed that the partisan battles for the services of the policy state has renewed interest in politics.[48] Polarization, in fact, offers a potential response, not only to Merolla and Paludo's warning in Chapter 11 that the war on terror has established a permanent state of crisis that risks executive aggrandizement in matters of homeland security, but also to the tendency of Congress to delegate substantial policy responsibility to the courts in domestic policy. Farhang's persuasive argument in Chapter 3 that a private litigation regime is now deeply embedded in regulatory policy does not point to judicial imperialism; rather, his analysis suggests how contemporary policy battles have displaced limited constitutional government with the feverish and partisan pursuit of ambitious policy.

WITHER THE POLICY STATE

In taking account of these changing patterns of public policy and the politics associated with them, perhaps the most important conclusion that might be drawn from this volume is that the politics of policy reform has been interwoven into the fabric of constitutional government so that foundational principles and institutions now serve rather than constrain programmatic ambition. Given this constitutional transformation, it is not surprising that one of the fault lines underneath the new policy regime is fiscal policy.[49] As Melnick has written, since the 1980s, "our political institutions are surprisingly good at innovation, but depressingly bad at coordinating the many responsibilities we have taken on. Nowhere is this more apparent than in our inability to bring taxing and spending into line."[50] Although this lack of fiscal discipline can be attributed partly to partisan combat between one party wedded to entitlements and the other unalterably opposed to paying for them, the perfect storm first hit when George W. Bush was in office and Republicans controlled both houses of Congress. The Republicans simultaneously pursued an aggressive advance of supply-side economics – passing tax cuts in 2001, 2003, and 2004 that composed the largest in history – and a substantial increase in the national government's programmatic responsibilities: the expansion of Medicare, launching of wars in Afghanistan and Iraq, and creation of a new major department of government (Homeland Security). Bush's two terms in office thus marked a critical turning point that saw adventurous policy at home and abroad decisively trump fiscal restraint.[51] GWB's political implosion and the rise of the Tea Party has made the prospects for conservative statism less sanguine; but its demise has only sharpened the clash of parties and given rise to partisan maneuvers on the edge of a "fiscal cliff" – a treacherous contest that has resulted in the reduction of the country's bond rating during Obama's first term and automatic sequestrations during his second that have slowed the fragile economic recovery from the Great Recession.

The partisan brinksmanship over fiscal policy has not led to "gridlock," however. Instead, it has instigated an institutional arms race. After Obama and congressional Republicans reached an impasse on fiscal policy that almost brought the government into default, the White House launched a "We Can't

Wait" initiative, dedicated to advancing policies that the president and his Democratic allies supported through unilateral executive action. During the final two years of his first term, Obama took measures that authorized the Environmental Protection Agency to implement greenhouse gas regulations that were stalled in the Senate; issued waivers that released states from many of the requirements of No Child Left Behind, which Congress had failed to reauthorize, only to bind them to the administration's own education policies; and bypassed the usual confirmation process to make four recess appointments that Senate Republicans had been filibustering. Finally, confirming the adage that policy makes politics, Obama announced in June 2012 that the Department of Homeland Security was setting up an administrative procedure that granted relief to an entire category of young immigrants, as many as 1.7 million people, who would otherwise have been subject to deportation. Obama thus elided Republican opposition to the Dream Act, the administration's bill designed to provide a conditional pathway to citizenship for immigrants who were brought to America illegally as children. This adroit administrative strategy not only contributed to the president's successful reelection campaign, which saw Hispanics support him by an overwhelming margin, but also, given the importance of the Latino vote to the future of American politics, may have contributed significantly to the development of a new Democratic majority.[52] The political consequences of this executive action, in turn, have encouraged Republicans such as Florida Senator Marco Rubio to work with Democrats since the election in crafting comprehensive immigration legislation.

The arc of immigration policy might thus defy the conventional wisdom that the system is "broken" or "gridlocked"; when viewed in a larger context, however, the We Can't Wait initiative may illustrate the emergence of an executive-centered party system that weakens the role Congress has traditionally played in policy reform. Of course, the "administrative presidency" has been an important feature of policymaking since the consolidation of the executive office during the New Deal.[53] But recent policy stalemates in Congress, instigated by escalating partisan polarization, have encouraged the White House to deploy executive power more often. Indeed, the Obama administration not only defended, but also celebrated, the We Can't Wait initiative as a justifiable response to congressional Republicans' obstructive tactics that went far beyond constitutional limits to thwart representative government. Although the minority party in the Senate has utilized aggressive partisan tactics since the Clinton administration, these tactics spiked during Obama's first term. Exercising the filibuster and other dilatory measures, Republicans blocked presidential appointments to the courts and the executive branch as well as legislation from reaching the floor of the Senate at unprecedented rates. For example, during the three legislative sessions of Congress from 2007 (when the Democrats captured the upper chamber during George W. Bush's second term) to 2012, Republicans threatened to filibuster on 385 occasions – equalling, in five years, the total number of filibuster threats to grip the Senate during the seven decades from the start of World War I until the end of the Reagan administration.[54]

Although partisan rancor and institutional combat are important factors in more habitual executive action in seeking to address critical domestic issues, evidence also suggests that the Obama administration occasionally resorted to unilateral action as a *first* resort in bringing about non-incremental policy change. For example, Bruce Oppenheimer's study examining the Obama administration's reform of the rules that govern the Corporate Average Fuel Economy, or CAFÉ, program shows that the White House had decided to circumvent Congress right from the start.[55] According to Oppenheimer, "Having struggled with Congress over a stimulus package immediately upon taking office, anticipating great difficulty in enacting health care legislation, and concerned with the potential of unified Republican opposition to most of its domestic policy initiatives, the Obama administration chose to sidestep Congress to make significant increases in CAFÉ standards well beyond those [for which existing legislation] provided." The Energy Independence and Security Act, passed in 2007 as a result of difficult but ultimately fruitful negotiations between a Democratic Congress and Republican White House, called for manufacturers of cars and small trucks to meet a CAFÉ standard of 30 miles per gallon by 2020. The new rules, announced with much fanfare by Obama in a May 19, 2009, Rose Garden Ceremony, mandated an average fuel economy of 35.5 miles per gallon for the 2016 model year, a substantial victory for environmental groups and an important policy achievement for a president dedicated to reducing greenhouse gases.

Furthermore, Obama's preemption of the legislative process with respect to energy policy was part of a broader pattern. Although Obama waited until June 2012 to announce the Homeland Security Department's new deportation policy, four senior officials in Citizenship and Immigration Services wrote a blueprint for this action well before Congress reached an impasse on the Dream Act.[56] In fact, some critics claimed that Obama's announcement of a new administrative framework for processing applications from immigrants who met the Dream Act criteria might have short circuited overtures that Senator Rubio had been making for months to Republicans, Democrats, Dream activists, and various other stakeholders in an effort to craft a revised version of the bill that had failed to achieve a cloture vote in December 2010.[57]

Oppenheimer and other scholars have raised legitimate concerns about whether the remaking of constitutional principles and institutions in response to the country's state of policy-mindedness has thrust the presidency and the courts into de facto lawmaking and forging consensus among interest groups that might better be left to Congress. Similarly, there are good reasons to lament the way policy advocacy and institutional combat have encouraged Democrats and Republicans – liberals and conservatives – to work within a fiscal system that, according to a *Washington Post* editorial, makes American government "look less and less like a mighty ship of state and more and more like a leaky, patched-together political rowboat."[58] And yet, proponents of a more programmatic constitutional order might argue that given the many obstacles to actual policy change in the United States, existing policies – entrenched by vested interests – should be subject to on going efforts to challenge them. Moe in Chapter 6 shows, for example, that the problem of education might not be too much policy; instead, public schools might suffer from the frozen nature of existing policies, many of which are protected by an unhealthy partnership between public unions and state and local governments. In contrast, Warren in Chapter 5 argues that powerful business interests and their allies in the Senate have exploited the filibuster to undermine the role unions have played in protecting the economic security of American workers.

Moe and Warren do not directly contradict each other, as the former stresses public sector unions whose influence has grown steadily over the past decades, and the latter analyzes the failure to reform labor policy that affects private unions, which have fallen on very hard times. Moreover, both the decline of public education and the demise of private labor organizations have been identified as important factors in the growing problem of equality in the United States. As Paul Frymer has noted, economic inequality is more pronounced than it has been in nearly a century: the last time that the wealthiest 1 percent of Americans held more total income was in 1928, just before the Great Depression.[59] Since the early days of the republic, as Alexis de Tocqueville observed, Americans have expressed "a profound scorn for the theory of permanent equality of goods" – the current controversy over the expansion of Medicaid is only the most recent example of American "mores" that resist redistributive policies. At the same time, Americans have long believed that the United States provides a reasonably fair "race of life," as Abraham Lincoln put it, and that their children will have the opportunity to move up the economic ladder. Alarmingly, however, as Paul Pierson and Jacob Hacker have shown, intergenerational mobility has declined in the United States for the past several decades, and is now lower for native-born Americans than for citizens of many other advanced industrial democracies.[60]

For all the excellent work found in this volume, it remains unclear how the politics of policy reform since the Second World War has affected the economic welfare of the American people. Certainly some of the policies discussed, especially civil rights, have better enabled individual men and women to pursue the promise of American life. But the new sense of rights interwoven into the fabric constitutional government during the New Deal era and advanced during the 1960s and 1970s – the commitment to protect all Americans from the terrifying uncertainties of the market place – seems badly frayed at the dawn of the twenty-first century. Indeed, as Judith Goldstein shows in Chapter 9, even certain policies widely recognized as "enlightened," such as free trade laws, have contributed to the decline of economic security. Given that the growth of imports from low-wage countries has grown significantly over the past three decades, Goldstein's importunity that free trade policy must be joined to the problem of job loss should not go unnoticed. "Trade works best," she writes, "when government does the least in terms of border controls and concentrates instead on ameliorating, not ignoring, a domestic dislocation that follows from this most efficient policy."

Similarly, Warren's Chapter 5 raises the question of whether the American economy can be revitalized while the conditions of laborers in the workplace decline. As Ken Kersch has observed, the Wagner Act, dubbed "labor's magna carta," was considered a constitutional achievement no less significant than the enactment of the Social Security program; but, in 1947, the year that Taft-Hartley became law, the American Heritage Foundation, which organized the famous Freedom Train tour with foundational documents, forced the removal of the Wagner Act from the hallowed touring collection that included the Declaration of Independence, Mayflower Compact, and Gettysburg Address.[61] The recent court decision striking down a National Labor Relations Board ruling that would have required millions of businesses to put up posters informing workers of their right to form a union – arguing that it violated the right of employers not to publish such a government poster – reveals just what a critical turning point 1947 proved to be.[62] Warren's depiction of the failure to redress the effects of the Taft-Hartley, in the face of dramatic political assaults on the right of collective bargaining, is a telling commentary on how the deeply contested politics of policy reform will not easily redress the widely recognized problem of economic inequality.

The authors of this volume certainly do not shy away from the controversies and continuing disputes that roil the politics of policy reform, but resolving them is not the principal objective of this volume. Our hope is that scholars, students, and engaged citizens will find the excellent social science and history that fill these pages both interesting and important, and come up with their own judgments of how the postwar politics of policy reform has affected representative constitutional government.

Notes

1. Karen Orren and Stephen Skowronek, "The Policy State: A Developmental Synthesis," Paper presented at the 2011 Annual Meeting of the American Political Science Association, Seattle Washington, September 1–4. See also, Sidney M. Milkis, "The Politics of the Policymaking State," in Jeffery A. Jenkins and Eric M. Patashnik, eds, *Living Legislation: Durability, Change, and the Politics of American Lawmaking* (Chicago: University of Chicago Press, 2012): 265–280.
2. Hugh Heclo, "Sixties Civics," in *The Great Society and the High Tide of Liberalism*, Sidney M. Milkis and Jerome Mileur, ed. (Amherst: University of Massachusetts Press, 2005), 60.
3. E. E. Schattschneider, *Politics, Pressures and the Tariff* (New York: Prentice Hall, 1935); Theodore Lowi, "American Business, Public Policy, Case-Studies, and Political Theory" (1964), *World Politics* 16(4): 677–715; Grant McConnell, *Private Power in American Democracy* (New York: Vintage Books, 1967); James Q. Wilson, *Political Organization* (Princeton: Princeton University Press, 1974).

4. For a good overview of the work devoted to this question, see Jenkins and Patashnik, *Living Legislation*.

5. For example, see Paul Pierson, *Politics in Time: History, Institutions and Social Analysis* (Princeton: Princeton University Press, 2004); and Karen Orren and Stephen Skowronek, *The Search for American Political Development* (New York: Cambridge University Press, 2004).

6. For example, Martha Derthick and Paul Quirk, *The Politics of Deregulation* (Washington, DC: Brookings Institution, 1985); Frank Baumgartner and Bryan Jones, *Agendas and Instability in American Politics* (Chicago: University of Chicago Press, 2009).

7. Heclo, "Sixties Civics," 62. The current division between progressives and conservatives can be traced back to the 1912 election, and in particular, to William Howard Taft's efforts to fend off the insurgency of Theodore Roosevelt, whose attack on the incumbent president ultimately led to the formation of the Progressive Party. But Taft's conservatism proscribed populism and championed the rule of law. Moreover, he favored the sort of moderate reforms Roosevelt had pursued during his presidency, such as the Hepburn Act, which strengthened the Interstate Commerce Commission's authority to regulate the railroads. Taft's was a "progressive conservatism": his desire to subordinate private power to law made him a progressive; his insistence that public power respect the law made him a conservative. Wilson Carey McWilliams, "Commentary on The President and His Powers," in *The Collected Works of William Howard Taft*, David H. Burton, ed. (Athens: Ohio University Press, 2003), vol. 6, 8–9 (3–10); see also, Jonathan Lurie, *The Travails of a Progressive Conservative* (New York: Cambridge University Press, 2012). Goldwater's nomination in 1964 and Ronald Reagan's election in 1980, calling for a more aggressive and populist assault on the liberal administrative state, marked the demise of this pragmatic conservatism. See Sidney M. Milkis, *Theodore Roosevelt, the Progressive Party and the Transformation of American Democracy* (Lawrence, KS: University Press of Kansas, 2009).

8. Tim Alberta, "The Cabal that Quietly Took Over the House," *National Journal*, May 26, 2013, retrieved from http://www.nationaljournal.com/magazine/the-cabal-that-quietly-took-over-the-house-20130523.

9. Vanessa Williamson, Theda Skocpol, and John Coggin, "The Tea Party and the Remaking of Republican Conservatism," *Perspectives on Politics*, vol. 9, No. 1 (March 2011): 25–43.

10. James Q. Wilson, "New Politics, New Elites, and Old Politics," in *The New Politics of Public Policy,* ed. Marc Landy and Martin Levin (Baltimore: Johns Hopkins University Press, 1995), 249–267.

11. James Q. Wilson, "Reinventing Public Administration," *PS: Political Science and Politics*, vol. 27, no. 4 (December 1994), 669.

12. "John F. Kennedy, Acceptance of Presidential Nomination," Democratic National Convention, Los Angeles, California, July 15, 1960, in Theodore Sorenson, ed. *"Let the Word Go Forth": The Speeches, Statements and Writings of John F. Kennedy* (New York: Delacorte, 1988), 101.

13. "John F. Kennedy's Inaugural Address," in Michael Nelson, ed. *The Evolving Presidency: Landmark Documents, 1787–2010*, 4th edition (Washington, DC: CQ Press, 2012), 187–191.

14. *Public Papers of the Presidents of the United States: Lyndon Baines Johnson, 1963–1964*, 2 vols. (Washington, DC: Government Printing Office, 1965), 1:704.

15. Wilson, "Reinventing Public Administration," 669.
16. Ibid., 673.
17. Orren and Skowronek, "The Policy State."
18. Alexander Hamilton, James Madison, and John Jay, *The Federalist Papers*, ed. Clinton Rossiter, with an introduction and notes by Charles R. Kesler (New York: New American Library, 1999), 310.
19. Ibid., 319–320.
20. James Patterson, *Grand Expectations: The United States, 1945–1974* (New York: Oxford University Press).
21. Ibid., 592.
22. Heclo, "Sixties Civics," 64.
23. Brian Balogh, "Making Pluralism Great: Beyond a Recycled History of the Great Society," in Milkis and Mileur, *The Great Society and the High Tide of Liberalism*, 160.
24. R. Shep Melnick, "From Tax and Spend to Mandate and Sue," in Ibid., 403–404. By the late 1960s, "big government" was leveled, not only against traditional liberal bastions as the Department of Education, but also against the CIA and FBI. See Norman Nie, Sidney Verba, and John Petrocik, *The New American Voter* (Cambridge, MA: Harvard University Press, 1976), 127.
25. For Mayhew's broader argument on how divided government does not obstruct major policy breakthroughs, see David R. Mayhew, *Divided We Govern: Party Control, Lawmaking and Investigations, 1946–2002* (New Haven: Yale University Press, 2005). Sarah Binder offers a critique of Mayhew's approach, arguing that his emphasis on counting major policy breakthroughs overlooks the range of landmark policy enactments that were *possible*; she finds that the *percent* of major policies enacted into law (those that occurred relative to those that were possible) has been significantly lower under divided government. See Binder, *Stalemate: Causes and Consequences of Legislative Gridlock* (Washington, DC: Brookings Institution Press, 2003).
26. As Melnick observes, Robert Lieberman has demonstrated that the "weak" American state has been more energetic and efficacious in enforcing antidiscrimination law than the more centralized regimes of Great Britain and France. See Lieberman, *Shaping Race Policy: The United States in Comparative Perspective* (Princeton: Princeton University Press, 2005). The concept of adversarial legalism was pioneered by Robert Kagan. See Kagan, *Adversarial Legalism: The American Way of Law* (Cambridge, MA: Harvard University Press, 2001).
27. Hamilton, Madison and Jay, *The Federalist Papers*, Number 51, 320.
28. In October 2013, the Republican-controlled House forced a government shutdown in an unsuccessful effort to delay the implementation of the Patient Protection and Affordable Care Act for a year.
29. For a defense of the states playing an important role in immigration reform, See Peter H. Schuck, "Taking Federalism Seriously," Yale Law School Faculty Scholarship Series, Paper 1675, retrieved from http://digitalcommons.law.yale.edu/cgi/viewcontent.cgi?article=2656&context=fss_papers.
30. Richard Nathan, "Federalism and Health Policy," *Health Affairs*, November 2005, retrieved from http://content.healthaffairs.org/content/24/6/1458.full.
31. Sarah A. Binder and Steven S. Smith, "Politics or Principle: Filibustering in the United States Senate" (Washington, DC: Brookings Institution, 1996); and Barbara Sinclair,

Party Wars: Polarization and the Politics of National Policy Making (Norman: University of Oklahoma Press, 2006), especially Chapter 8.

32. Theodore Lowi, *The End of Liberalism: The Second Republic of the United States,* 2nd edition (New York: Norton, 1979), 313.

33. The Church hearings were held by the Senate Select Committee to Study Government Operations with Respect to Intelligence Activities, an investigative body formed in January 1975. The Committee, chaired by Democratic Senator Frank Church of Idaho, dramatically confirmed earlier press accounts of CIA abuses.

34. The "two presidencies" concept was first formulated by Aaron Wildavsky, "The Two Presidencies," *Society*, January/February 1998, 24–31 (first published in 1966).

35. Greg Miller, "Plan for Hunting Terrorists Signals U.S. Intends to Keep Adding Names to Kill Lists," *Washington Post*, October 23, 2012, retrieved from http://articles.washingtonpost.com/2012-10-23/world/35500278_1_drone-campaign-obama-administration-matrix.

36. Barton Gellman and Laura Poitras, "U.S., British Intelligence Mining Data from Nine U.S. Internet Companies in Broad Secret Program," *Washington Post*, June 7, 2013, retrieved from http://www.washingtonpost.com/investigations/us-intelligence-mining-data-from-nine-us-internet-companies-in-broad-secret-program/2013/06/06/3a0coda8-cebf-11e2-8845-d970ccb04497_story.html.

37. For an argument that partisan conflict has been integral to the vitality of representative constitutional government, see David R. Mayhew, *Partisan Balance: Why Political Parties Don't Kill the U.S. Constitutional System* (Princeton: Princeton University Press, 2011).

38. In the final vote on the legislation (H.R. 6675, The Social Security Amendments of 1965), Democratic Senators voted 57-7 in favor, whereas Republicans broke 17-13 against it. Both parties supported the legislation in the House: Democrats by a 237-48 margin; Republicans by a more divided 70-68 vote, retrieved from http://www.ssa.gov/history/tally65.html.

39. Robert Pear, "States' Policies on Health Care Exclude Some of the Poorest," *New York Times*, May 24, 2013, retrieved from http://mobile.nytimes.com/2013/05/25/us/states-policies-on-health-care-exclude-poorest.html; Sandhya Somashekhar, "GOP's Rift Over Medicaid Deepens," *Washington Post*, June 3, 2013, retrieved from http://www.washingtonpost.com/national/health-science/gop-governors-endorsements-of-medicaid-expansion-deepen-rifts-within-party/2013/06/02/b4a42eb8-c7b9-11e2-9245-773c0123c027_story.html.

40. Bill Schneider, "Party Opinion Usurps Public Opinion," May 21, 2013, retrieved from http://blogs.reuters.com/great-debate/2013/05/21/party-opinion-usurps-public-opinion/.

41. Kaiser Health Tracking Poll, Early Reaction to the Supreme Court Decision on ACA, retrieved from http://kaiserfamilyfoundation.files.wordpress.com/2013/01/8329-f.pdf.

42. Schneider, "Party Opinion Usurps Public Opinion." Gary Jacobson's study of George W. Bush's administration reveals how presidents can affect party divisions in Congress and the public. See Jacobson, *A Divider Not a Uniter: George W. Bush and the American People*, 2nd edition. (Boston: Pearson, 2007).

43. For example, see Spencer Piston, "How Explicit Racial Prejudice Hurt Obama in the 2008 Election," *Political Behavior*, vol. 32 (December): 433–451; Thomas J. Sugrue, *Not Even Past: Barack Obama and the Burden of Race* (Princeton: Princeton

University Press, 2010); Alan Abramowitz, *The Disappearing Center: Engaged Citizens, Polarization, and American Democracy* (New Haven, CT: Yale University Press, 2010); Randall Kennedy, *The Persistence of the Color Line: Racial Politics and the Obama Presidency* (New York: Pantheon Books, 2011); Desmond Smith and Rogers Smith, *Still A House Divided: Race and Politics in Obama's America* (Princeton: Princeton University Press, 2011).

44. A pew survey of June 12, 2012, found that 52 percent of Democrats, as compared with 12 percent of Republicans, agree that "we should make every effort to improve the position of blacks and other minorities, even if it means giving them preferential treatment." Since 1987, the gap between the parties on this issue has more than doubled, from 18 percent to 40 percent: retrieved from http://www.people-press.org/files/legacy-pdf/06-04-12%20Values%20Release.pdf.

45. Kennedy, *The Persistence of the Color Line*, 7.

46. See, for example, Thomas Mann and Norman Ornstein, *It's Even Worse than It Looks: How the American Constitutional System Collided with the New Politics of Extremism* (New York: Basic Books, 2012); and Mike Lofgren, *The Party Is Over: How Republicans Went Crazy, Democrats Became Useless, and the Middle Class Got Shafted* (New York: Viking, 2012).

47. Robert Wiebe, *Self-Rule: A Cultural History of American Democracy* (Chicago: University of Chicago Press, 1995), 9.

48. Abramowitz, *The Disappearing Center*.

49. On the relationship between politics and financial crises more generally, see Nolan McCarty, Keith T. Poole, and Howard Rosenthal, *Political Bubbles: Financial Crises and the Failure of American Democracy* (Princeton: Princeton University Press, 2013).

50. R. Shep Melnick, "The Gridlock Illusion," *The Wilson Quarterly*, Winter 2013, retrieved from http://www.wilsonquarterly.com/article.cfm?AID=2239.

51. Christopher DeMuth, "The Real Cliff: The Staggering Debt from Decades of Continuous Government Debt is About to Come Due," *The Weekly Standard*, December 24, 2012, retrieved from http://www.weeklystandard.com/articles/real-cliff_666593.html.

52. David Klaidman and Andrew Romano, "President Obama's Executive Power Grab," *The Daily Beast*, October 22, 2012, retrieved from www.thedailybeast.com/newsweek/2012/10/21/president-obama-s-executive-power-grab.html; and Ryan Lizza, "The Party Next Time: The GOP's Demographic Dilemma," *The New Yorker*, September 2012, http://www.newyorker.com/reporting/2012/11/19/121119fa_fact_lizza. According to exit polls, Obama won about 70 percent of the Hispanic vote. For example, see Mark Hugo Lopez and Paul Taylor, "Latino Voters in the 2012 Election," Pew Research Hispanic Center, November 7, 2012, www.pewhispanic.org/2012/11/07/latino-voters-in-the-2012-election/.

53. Richard Nathan, *The Administrative Presidency* (New York: John Wiley, 1983); Sidney M. Milkis, *The President and the Parties: The Transformation of the American Party System Since the New Deal* (New York: Oxford University Press, 1993).

54. Klaidman and Romano, "President Obama's Executive Power Grab." In November 2013, Democrats used their 55-45 majority to overturn decades of Senate filibuster traditions and allow simple majority votes on most presidential appointments, although an exception was made for Supreme Court nominees.

55. Bruce I. Oppenheimer, "It's Hard to Get Mileage out of Congress: Struggling over CAFÉ Standards, 1973–2013," Paper presented at the Conference on Congress and Policymaking in the 21st Century, University of Virginia, June 3–4, 2013.
56. Ibid.
57. Romano and Klaidman, "President Obama's Executive Power Bag."
58. "A Government by Extension: No Way to Run a Country," *Washington Post*, January 3, 2013, retrieved from http://articles.washingtonpost.com/2013-01-03/opinions/36211206_1_farm-bill-debt-limit-short-term-bill.
59. Paul Frymer, "Labor and American Politics," *Perspectives on Politics*, vol. 8, no. 2: 609–616.
60. Jacob Hacker and Paul Pierson, *Winner Take All Politics: How Washington Made the Rich Richer and Turned Its Back on the Middle Class* (New York: Simon and Schuster, 2011).
61. Ken I. Kersch, "The New Deal Triumph as the End of History? The Judicial Negotiation of Labor Rights and Civil Rights," in Ronald Kahn and Kersch eds., *The Supreme Court and American Political Development* (Lawrence: University Press of Kansas, 2006), 190.
62. Sam Hananel, "Union Notice Rule Losses in Appeals Court," *Washington Post*, May 23, 2013, retrieved from http://www.washingtonpost.com/politics/union-notice-rule-loses-in-appeals-court/2013/05/09/22d1b850-b8e3-11e2-92f3-f29180 1936b8_story.html.

2

The Long 1950s as a Policy Era

David R. Mayhew*

If policy reform amounts to nonincremental change, what can we say about postwar America before the mid-1960s? Those early years are often dismissed as the doldrums and as a time of *Deadlock of Democracy*.[1] I argue here that this judgment is quite wrong.

Discernible in those days is a policy era, with its own kind of content and integrity. By the term "policy era" I do not mean anything fancy. I mean a time span of policy enterprises, all involving congressional action, that can be apprehended using reasonable empirical care, that share an animation and direction, and that amount to a major cumulative policy record. For political context, think of Frank D. Baumgartner and Bryan D. Jones's "waves of enthusiasm" or John W. Kingdon's "national moods" that can pry open "policy windows."[2]

I use a particular empirical wedge in my discussion. I am wary of labels like the New Deal, the Fair Deal, and the New Frontier as guides to policy eras. Politicians promote such labels for their own purposes, and they coast into usages that are both ideologically freighted and gauzy. They can become impediments to understanding. They can dominate and obscure the contents of their presumed packages.[3] Possibly better is a nominalistic course of examining actual policy moves one by one, leaving aside any assumptions about lumping or labels, to see what they are and what they add up to.[4] A good instance is the sequence of new regulatory legislation from the mid-1960s through the mid-1970s. That went from the Traffic Safety Act of 1966 through the Truth in Lending Act of 1968, the Clean Air Act of 1970, the Occupational Safety and Health Act of 1970, the Water Pollution Control Act of 1972, the Consumer Product Safety Act of 1972, the Endangered Species Act of 1973, the Federal Election Campaign Act of 1974, and the Toxic Substances Control Act of 1976. This is far from an exhaustive list. For a decade, the beat went on.[5] At issue is pattern recognition. Through a one-by-one identification of items – not through an overarching label such as "the Great Society" – we can see a major policy era centering on increases in government regulation.

My pitch here is for the long 1950s as an era showing a particular policy content. By the long 1950s I mean chiefly the Eisenhower years of 1953–61, but also before that, to a lesser degree, the last years of the Truman presidency, and to a greater degree, the full Kennedy presidency of 1961–63. In focus are parts, at least, of those three presidential spans. This longish stretch of history has a reputation of being, in domestic policy terms, rather fallow. The Fair Deal legislative agenda of Truman's second term did not go far.[6] At the other end, Kennedy's legislative program faltered.[7] As for the Eisenhower years, those are often seen in policy terms as a forgettable interlude – a kind of a time-out. Not much was happening under the former general, who was often dismissed as a centrist placeholder. For political scientists of a certain vintage, the dominant image of the Eisenhower years may still be that supplied by James L. Sundquist in his engaging 1968 book, *Politics and Policy: The Eisenhower, Kennedy, and Johnson Years*, which presents a drama, a teleology.[8] Sundquist, focusing on unemployment, poverty, education, civil rights, health care, and the environment – the standard liberal agenda of that time – saw the 1950s as a scanty preface to the glorious and productive 1960s, particularly beyond 1963.

Yet that view of the 1950s is really quite wrong. The era was enormously busy and consequential in policy terms. We might like or dislike the policies, but that is another matter. In play from 1949 or so through 1963 was a family of interrelated policy goals involving the economy, aiming for growth, development, efficiency,[9] and productivity. These four nouns or their cognates keep appearing in the accounts. These goals invested Congress as well as the presidency and crossed party lines, making many of the policy drives of the era bipartisan in texture. In general, private enterprise was favored over government control in pursuing these aims, for reasons of presumed economic efficiency as well as basic ideology. But the matter was complicated. It could be more urgent to do something big, as opposed to doing nothing at all, than to favor private enterprise over government. (These two dimensions could be haphazardly related to each other.) One way or another, an explosion of economic inducement or development was what the policy entrepreneurs of the era drove at.

A body of ideological principle, irrespective of whatever else was going on, seems to have fostered and shaped this era. In the wake of World War II, Charles S. Maier has written, "United States spokesmen came to emphasize economic productivity as a principle of political settlement in its own right." A "theme of productivity" took on life.[10] Foreign policy – conducting the Cold War, funding defense, reconstructing allied countries, and keeping ahead of the Soviet Union economically – was one reason. But the memory of the harsh unemployment of the 1930s was there, too. Growth and development – what was not to like? Also, in Maier's view, the theme of productivity served as a kind of solvent: It allowed a more or less consensual ticket out of the polarizing and exhausting class politics inherited from the 1930s.

Such economic ideas drove both the Eisenhower and Kennedy presidencies, according to an analysis by M. Stephen Weatherford and Lorraine

M. McDonnell.[11] That role of the economic ideas has been underappreciated. Those presidents' "economic ideologies" are said to have guided their behavior. Eisenhower's approach was "mostly distinctively characterized by its orientation toward the long-term condition of the economy."[12] The country's future was at stake. Tax cuts, steady prices, and spurs to private investment would pay off in time. Priming the economy for just the next election could take a pass: "Conditions were ripe for a political business cycle in 1954, 1958, and 1960, yet [Eisenhower] explicitly abjured the temptation."[13] He was against such priming.[14] Concerns for growth, development, productivity, and efficiency pervade the president's autobiographical account of his first term in 1953–57.[15] Generally speaking, productivity called for markets rather than bureaucracies: "To stimulate that productivity, I [Eisenhower] dwelt on the need for removing political controls over the American economy."[16] Efficiency called for, among other things, state and local rather than national government action: "Underlying [Eisenhower's] preference for decentralized government was [his] confidence that citizens could be relied on to deal with local problems more economically and, in general, more constructively than could the federal government, acting alone and from a distance."[17] That is an efficiency argument. Stock or anodyne as these causal stories may be, there does not seem to be a good reason to doubt their seriousness.

The case for Kennedy is less familiar. There, too, Weatherford and McDonnell find "a clearly articulated ideology." Economic growth was the motif – "a strong belief that government should play an active role in stimulating long-term, stable growth." For both Cold War and domestic reasons, "a long-term expansion in capacity" was needed – a hoped-for annual growth rate of 4.5 percent, a high bar. "Kennedy's ideology led him to focus on augmenting economic growth and to make redistributive issues secondary."[18] According to Allen J. Matusow, "The president's economic policies ... would be framed above all to create a stable environment for corporate prosperity and corporate expansion. What was good for the corporate system would be good for the country."[19] Interestingly, *both* the Eisenhower and Kennedy presidencies seem to have leaned to austerity in a study by Nathaniel Beck mapping immediate unemployment rates from Truman through Carter by individual president, not by party. In conventional Democratic Party terms, the Kennedy presidency underperformed on unemployment. On this front, the advance from Eisenhower to Kennedy was apparently seamless.[20]

Matching these economic ideologies is an era-long record of particulars, the exhibit of this chapter. It is a story of twenty-one statutes enacted between 1949 (yes, late Truman) and 1964. The list has two foundations. First, in the spirit of my own *Divided We Govern* work, and of 1965 through 1975 as a regulatory era, it is a presentation of a sequence of events. Second, through various reading I have become increasingly fascinated by the policy production of the 1950s.[21] Certain of the most thought-provoking works on that era are recent. I used my own

judgment to choose these twenty-one statutes. No doubt there are omissions, some
of the choices are uneasy fits, and some of them fit into 1949 through 1963
without their thrusts being exclusive to that time span. But all of the enactments
pertain somehow to some mix of growth, development, efficiency, and productivity as aims. There seems to be a gestalt. The statutes appear in Table 2.1. Many
of them, in an interesting pattern, seem to have *unstuck* various policy realms of
the mid-twentieth century. Deadlock, stalemate, logjams, conflict, and even
embarrassment had stacked up during the long years of chiefly Democratic control
of the government in the 1930s and 1940s, and now, in a fresh climate, policy

TABLE 2.1. *Enactments during 1949–1963*

Presidency	Enactment	Year	Final Passage Vote	
			House	Senate
Truman	Housing Act	1949	227–186	57–13
	National Science Foundation	1950	247–126	voice
Eisenhower 1	Submerged Lands Act	1953	278–116	voice
	Outer Continental Shelf Lands Act	1953	309–91	45–43
	Saint Lawrence Seaway	1954	241–158	51–33
	Atomic Energy Act	1954	231–154	59–17
	Agriculture Act	1954	voice	44–28
	Housing Act	1954	358–30	59–21
	Revenue Act	1954	315–77	61–26
	Reciprocal Trade Agreements Act Extension	1955	374–54	75–13
	Upper Colorado River Storage Project	1956	256–136	58–23
	Interstate Highway System	1956	388–19	89–1
Eisenhower 2	Reciprocal Trade Agreements Act Extension	1958	317–98	72–18
	Agriculture Act	1958	voice	62–11
	National Aeronautics and Space Administration	1958	voice	voice
	National Defense Education Act	1958	212–85	66–15
Kennedy	Area Redevelopment Act	1961	224–193	63–27
	Communications Satellite Act	1962	372–10	66–11
	Investment Tax Credit	1962	219–196	56–22
	Trade Expansion Act	1962	256–91	78–8
	Kennedy Tax Cut	1963–1964	326–83	74–19

Final passage means, for either house, the roll-call vote on a measure's "final passage" as that term is
conventionally defined (with a voice vote counting as a unanimous vote), unless the house in question
recorded a later roll call on a conference report, a move to accept the other house's version of the
measure, or a veto override. In that event, the last of the later roll calls was used. Voice votes from
such later rounds were never used.

action could come about – often through inventive designs that attracted cross-party coalitions and steered around sticky troubles.

HOUSING ACT OF 1949

Early in Truman's second term, this enactment was framed and passed under Democratic Party auspices. That is clear enough. Authorizing as it did a large stock of public housing units, it is often seen as a victory for a long-skimped-on liberal aim of direct government provision of housing, a redistributive program. In fact, it was a turning point. On Capitol Hill, support for public housing had been and remained precarious. Conflict on the matter was unending. Most of the units authorized in 1949 were, in fact, never built. Here was a cause going politically stale. The future of the cities pointed elsewhere in the enactment of 1949, a hammered-out compromise. A "progrowth coalition," in John Mollenkopf's phrase, was rising to power at that time in both the cities and Congress, and the new measure reflected that rise. "Largely giving up any emphasis on aiding the urban poor," Congress now wrote an act that was "clearly designed to benefit private development." Federal money and plans would spark that development. From now on, the lexicon of federal urban policy would feature such phrases as "blight," "central business districts," "redevelopment agencies," "slum clearance," and "urban renewal." Bulldozers would roar.[22] Mayors and their business communities would join in visions of renovation. New Haven, Connecticut, under Mayor Richard C. Lee would become a showcase example.[23]

CREATION OF THE NATIONAL SCIENCE FOUNDATION – 1950

This is an uneasy fit. It was World War II that triggered federal support for science, and a good deal was under way by 1950. But there is a point. For five years, deadlock had persisted over the institutional design of a general program. Congressional liberals and President Truman, who vetoed one plan, leaned toward a model of central bureaucratic control. This idea was a hard sell on Capitol Hill. After drawn-out contention and bargaining, the legislation of 1950 enacted the plan of individual application, peer review, and discretionary funding with which we are familiar today. It was an efficiency design, of a sort, offering a widely dispersed decision process as a route to scientific development.[24]

SUBMERGED LANDS ACT OF 1953

Better known as the "tidelands oil" act, this measure followed offshore discoveries of oil and rising demand for it, yet there had been years of explosive controversy about how to proceed. At issue was public versus private development. A tangle of court decisions, presidential vetoes, and failed congressional initiatives left an impasse as of 1952 in which virtually no oil was being taken from the Gulf of Mexico.[25] Cheered on by oil companies, certain coastal states with their eyes on royalties kept campaigning for legal title to lands immediately off their shores. In this 1953 enactment, with the Republicans now controlling the government, they got what they wanted. A supportive House committee "stressed the 'vital necessity' of legislation to promote the exploitation and development of oil deposits in the submerged lands."[26]

OUTER CONTINENTAL SHELF LANDS ACT OF 1953

A lesser-known companion to the tidelands act, this measure was in fact more consequential. It was the "drill baby drill" initiative of its time. At stake was oil exploration beyond the immediate coastal areas. Little was happening out there, either. A legal basis was needed. This enactment supplied it, empowering the interior secretary to lease oil and gas deposits in outer waters to private firms, charging royalties. Some 12 million acres thus came to be leased during the next quarter-century.[27]

AUTHORIZATION OF THE SAINT LAWRENCE SEAWAY – 1954

Here the gridlock went back decades, thanks chiefly to various U.S. regional interests that feared the economic downside of competing with Great Lakes transportation. In 1954, authorization finally occurred. The White House and Canada's government weighed in, Capitol Hill stirred to action, and an agreeable plan was developed.[28] Eisenhower saw the seaway as "an economic necessity" and "a vital addition to our economic and national security."[29] In defense terms, it would offer a way to move iron ore from Labrador to the Great Lakes industries in an emergency.[30] Navigation channels, seven new locks, and a key New York hydroelectric plant were approved. User fees would pay the bill. This was a gigantic enterprise. The country would gain a "fourth seacoast," it was said.[31] In the end, 210 million cubic yards of earth would be dug up and moved – twice the volume removed in building the Suez Canal.[32]

ATOMIC ENERGY ACT OF 1954

Atomic energy dated to 1945, but what to do with it stayed in question as of the early 1950s. Legally, a government monopoly existed. Public versus private development framed a debate. In the general public, a go-go enthusiasm pushed toward action of some kind.[33] The enactment of 1954 brought a private-side solution – in Eisenhower's words, "a program for harnessing atomic energy for the commercial production of electricity," featuring "the private manufacture, ownership, and operation of atomic reactors."[34] This was a tricky blueprint. It involved heavy regulation and some subsidy as well as the statutory design of an industry that could thrive in the private market. Several nuclear plants were online or under construction by 1960.[35]

AGRICULTURE ACT OF 1954

Here also there was impasse, to the point of embarrassment. Neither the Truman administration, with its imaginative Brannan Plan defeated in 1949, nor free-market advocates had been able to dent the high "parity" crop prices guaranteed to farmers during World War II and protected by organized agriculture since then. To assure those prices, the government kept buying up crops. "Wasteful, extravagant, and ineffective" was said to be Eisenhower's take on the situation.[36] The 1954 enactment was a private-side efficiency move using a mechanism of "flexible prices" to lead producers toward market constraints.[37] In general, according to a recent analysis that ends up appreciative, the Eisenhower farm programs "took cognizance of technological advances, the need for American agricultural products to compete in world markets, and the fact that farmers should be reacting to consumer preferences rather than producing for government warehouses."[38]

HOUSING ACT OF 1954

In this measure, the second shoe dropped. The Housing Act of 1949 had brought a compromise between public housing and urban redevelopment. Now with Eisenhower and a Republican Congress came a clear switch. The 1954 act "transcended the acrimonious divide between liberals and conservatives, forging a new consensus that employed commercial redevelopment instead of public housing as the answer to central-city decline. ... The class politics of the New Deal yielded to a new model." In consequence, public housing kept tailing off. Federally supported urban renewal projects grew from 260 in 1953 to 1,210 in 1962.[39] Many more bulldozers would roar. For its mechanisms, "the 1954 act was hailed by large builders as 'an aid to private enterprise,'" not least in the suburbs.[40] Related tax changes in 1954 (see the following section) helped with the construction of malls, roadside strips, office parks, and industrial parks.[41]

REVENUE ACT OF 1954

This was a mammoth overhaul of the tax code wrung from Capitol Hill compromise and laden with many provisions. For our purposes here, it is said that Eisenhower saw the measure as "a cornerstone of his economic program ... a means of stimulating growth while maintaining price stability." Tucked in were depreciation allowances, a credit for shareholder dividends, and a modest tax cut for individuals.[42] "Substantial stimulants to economic activity" were seen as the aim.[43] This was standard Republican fare.

RECIPROCAL TRADE AGREEMENTS ACT EXTENSION OF 1955

Here is another measure keyed to efficient use of resources. It fits snugly into the policy era under discussion, but it was not exclusive to it. A regime of tariff reduction through presidential authority began in 1934 and (notwithstanding certain gaps) continues today. A classic of political science, *American Business and Public Policy*, centers on the complex enactment of 1955.[44] With Eisenhower, leadership on the Republican side joined the cause of tariff reduction, although a Democratic Congress in 1955 proved more enthusiastic on the question than a Republican Congress was in 1953–54. "The advantages to the United States of increasing two-way trade" – a textbook economics case – figured in Eisenhower's reasoning, as well as a need to prop up the economies of U.S. allies.[45] The president won three-year authority to cut duties by 15 percent.[46]

AUTHORIZATION OF UPPER COLORADO RIVER STORAGE PROJECT – 1956

Closing out (nearly: central Arizona was to get its share of Colorado River water in 1968) a half-century-long reclamation drive in the U.S. West, this was a big one. It was "the largest reclamation project ever authorized in a single piece of legislation," claimed Eisenhower. Through a complex of dams, including a gigantic one at Glen Canyon, coaxing into existence today's 186-mile-long Lake Powell, it "would bring light and power and irrigation water and flood-control benefits to five mountain states in the growing West": Colorado, Utah, Wyoming, New Mexico, and a slice of Arizona.[47] Utah's agriculture would benefit. Vast resources of coal, uranium, and oil shale became tappable as a result of this construction, which in turn "ensured industrial growth in the West." A delicate congressional compromise clinched the measure, which was to be paid for by using Glen Canyon Dam as a "cash register" to tax electricity generated there.[48] "And so the list of great projects goes on and on," it was commented later on in the 1970s, "fostering new cities and desert-land agriculture."[49]

THE INTERSTATE HIGHWAY SYSTEM – 1956

Another logjam broken. A congressional act in 1944 had promised a national highway system, but a decade later only 1 percent of it was built. Financing was the hitch. Eisenhower took a vigorous interest. He had seen the poor American roads during an army tour in 1919 and Hitler's Autobahn system as allied armies entered Germany in 1945.[50] As of the 1950s, the slow level of U.S. construction had "failed to solve the traffic crisis and failed to serve as a long-range foundation for economic growth."[51] Congress was ready, too. The 1956 measure, which followed considerable dickering but then passed nearly unanimously, hinged on a congressional scheme for a trust fund into which user taxes could be poured.[52] A total of $31.5 billion was thus committed to build 41,000 miles of roads.[53] It was, Eisenhower wrote, "the biggest peacetime construction project of any description ever undertaken by the United States or any other country." It would "move enough dirt and rock to bury all of Connecticut two feet deep."[54] "The largest public works program in history," Daniel Patrick Moynihan denominated it.[55] Its effects on the American economy and society would be immense.[56]

RECIPROCAL TRADE AGREEMENT ACT EXTENSION – 1958

Here was another trade act extension. This time, four-year authority went to the president to cut duties by 20 percent.[57]

AGRICULTURE ACT OF 1958

Another move away from crop subsidies.[58]

ESTABLISHMENT OF THE NATIONAL AERONAUTICS AND SPACE ADMINISTRATION (NASA) – 1958

This act committed the nation to development on a new front – space. It was a quick reaction to the Soviet launch of Sputnik. On this measure, Eisenhower stood back as Senator Lyndon B. Johnson took the legislative lead. With NASA, American satellites would go up. Kennedy's pledge of a moon landing would come three years later. With luck, spinoff benefits would accrue to the U.S. economy and society.[59] Eisenhower, once on board, foresaw "a new system of global communications through television, radio, and telephone."[60]

NATIONAL DEFENSE EDUCATION ACT OF 1958

Not until 1965 did the U.S. government commit general funds to elementary and secondary schools. However, improvement of high-end human capital to compete with the Soviet Union was something else. That came in this 1958 measure. At stake was scientific development. On offer would be loans to students and schools to perk up science and math education.[61]

AREA REDEVELOPMENT ACT OF 1961

In the 1950s, both parties had hatched plans to combat "structural unemployment" in chiefly rural areas, but the plans clashed, and two Eisenhower vetoes left the policy shelf bare. Enter Kennedy, who had witnessed appalling poverty in West Virginia during his election campaign in 1960. He made the matter a priority. The 1961 act, generally liberal-tilting in various ways, targeted development money to areas of high unemployment. The Department of Commerce would preside. Some $400 million in loans would go for new public and industrial facilities. Rural renewal, so to speak, was the goal.[62]

COMMUNICATIONS SATELLITE (COMSAT) ACT OF 1962

A large battle took place in 1962 over what to do with the new satellite technology. A design was needed. Public versus private framed the terms of debate. In the end, the Kennedy administration and Congress approved a private-tilting compromise that yielded COMSAT – in effect, a consortium of private firms authorized to establish, own, and operate a new system.[63]

INVESTMENT TAX CREDIT – 1962

A Kennedy priority, this was a standard boost to business in tax credits and depreciation allowances.[64]

TRADE EXPANSION ACT OF 1962

Another bow to freer international trade, this measure trumped those of the 1950s in importance. Kennedy threw himself into it. In 1962, he "proclaimed it his number-one legislative priority."[65] It became "the centerpiece of all that year's efforts," entailing speeches, pep talks, other political spectacles, and intense White House lobbying.[66] Foreign policy and the domestic economy were seen as benefiting. The president pretty much got what he wanted, including five-year authority to cut all tariffs by as much as 50 percent; in compensation, there would be "adjustment assistance" for adversely impacted sectors of the economy.[67] This trade act is said to have been the first "modern" one in "complexity and comprehensiveness."[68]

THE KENNEDY TAX CUT – 1963–1964

This was Kennedy's project, his signature domestic policy aim going into 1963, although it did not reach final passage until Johnson became president after Kennedy's assassination. A huge tax cut, this measure, among other things, cut the top-bracket personal income tax rate from a war-level 91 percent down to 70 percent.[69] It is indicative to see how the Kennedy administration put the plan together. In a long run-up of economic and political calculation, economic growth crystallized among politicians and advisers as the unifying policy goal.[70] Other aims got shorter shrift. In the end, some liberals had misgivings: Various liberal tax reforms fell away; redistribution of income was largely sidelined; the American Federation of Labor and Congress of Industrial Organizations (AFL-CIO) would have preferred a stimulus of public works spending; permanent, as opposed to temporary, tax reduction raised questions in theoretical Keynesian terms. The liberal economist John Kenneth Galbraith called Kennedy's speech pitching the measure to the Economic Club of New York "the most Republican speech since McKinley." "New Dealers," it is reported, "preferring public spending, called the President's basic premise contrary to thirty years of Democratic philosophy." (Eisenhower, on another note, back at his farm in Pennsylvania, saw "fiscal recklessness.") In a nutshell, the measure was a large, permanent, more or less across-the-board tax cut to spur economic growth.[71]

That completes the list of statutes. It goes without saying that legislative drives on other subjects, some successful, some not, took place during the long era of 1949–63. Civil rights, Medicare, and comprehensive aid to education, to cite some examples, continued to be pursued.[72] I have selected here on the cues of growth, development, efficiency, and productivity. But, in general, that is where the successful legislative action was. That case is easy enough to see for the Eisenhower years, but it holds for the Kennedy years, too. Generally speaking, it is questionable to see the Kennedy years as act one of the redistributive and regulatory politics of the Johnson and Nixon years (often due, in the Nixon case, to leverage by Democratic Congresses).[73] Kennedy's aims lay largely elsewhere, and the final legislative product of his years, once it ground through the coalitional politics on Capitol Hill, which always seemed to feature the pivotal House Ways and Means Chairman Wilbur D. Mills of Arkansas, lay decisively elsewhere. Free trade and tax reduction were the standout emphases.

The bent for the private side shared by Eisenhower and Kennedy drew fire in an intense, if sporadic, opposition in the Senate. A bloc of senators in the groove of Progressive antimonopolism took great alarm at the "giveaways" seen to inhere in the tidelands act of 1953, atomic energy act of 1954, and COMSAT in 1962 – all favored by the Eisenhower or Kennedy White House.[74] The public domain was being frittered away to private capitalism, it was argued. Voters needed to be alerted. Civil rights aside, rhetorical resistance to these measures seems to have brought the most prominent use of the Senate filibuster during 1949–63. It was filibustering from the left. Night sessions were scheduled, the sleeping cots came out, the senators talked on. Senator Wayne Morse of Oregon, a loquacious would-be blocker of all three of these legislative drives, set a chamber record with a twenty-two-hour, twenty-six-minute speech against the tidelands act in 1953. All three measures passed. On COMSAT in 1962, the Senate voted cloture for the first time on any question since 1927.[75]

What did this long era amount to? In policy terms, many of the tangible deposits of its lawmaking are common knowledge – the space rockets, dams, drill platforms, the shopping malls, industrial parks, nuclear plants, urban belt-ways, and the rest. The new highway system revolutionized the urban and rural landscape.[76] Many were the kinds of change that came about. For self-congratulatory testimony, it is interesting to witness Eisenhower's boasting, which I have supplied instances of. The president was thrilled by material improvement. Chapter 15 of his memoirs, "Power – Electrical and Political" – reads like a bulletin from the Kremlin in the 1930s. In January 1953, he writes, the United States had "a total installed capacity of 97.3 million kilowatts. By January of 1960 that figure had soared to 175 million – almost twice as much." During his presidency, power facilities were built "on a scale historically unprecedented."[77] The Russians were being left in the dust.[78]

How did this collection of policy moves affect the U.S. economy in the long run? That I do not know. A deep answer would require a different project and a different author. Certain clues are available. The Kennedy tax cut is often celebrated for its growth impact. The Saint Lawrence Seaway seems to have boomed during the 1970s but then lost its zing due to, among other things, competition from truckers using the new interstate highway system.[79] Regarding those highways, a new scholarship on "infrastructure investment" that took shape in the 1990s seems relevant. To economists, a prominent puzzle was and is: Why did the productivity of the U.S. economy fall off in the early 1970s? "After averaging 2.0% during the two decades from 1950 to 1970, the annual growth rate of total factor productivity in the private business economy slumped to 0.8% per year during the period 1971 to 1985." The new scholarship says, in one diagnostic report: "The data seem consistent with a story in which the massive road-building of the 1950's and 1960's offered a one-time boost to the level of productivity." But after that, the bulldozers idled. Investment in public capital stock, the general argument goes, has been an overlooked ingredient in the ups and downs of the overall productivity of the economy.[80]

But of course another key question arises. How about the politics? How did these policy moves play out politically in the long run, or even the medium run? Immense kickback, it is fair to say, has been a leading theme. Grist for decades of angst, regret, critical scholarship, mobilizing activity, and corrective lawmaking were supplied by this policy production of the long 1950s. The demolishing of city neighborhoods soon came into question, as did government-fostered suburbanization. In retrospect, were the strips and malls a great idea?[81] The long, fast roads brought a new specter of freeway murderers.[82] The new dams and highways destroyed natural landscapes. Air pollution surged. The Saint Lawrence Seaway brought pollution, zebra mussels, and an upending of native populations.[83] The atomic plant at Three Mile Island ended in a spectacular nuclear meltdown. Gooey oceanic oil spills became a fact of life. In general terms, the country's heavy dependence on oil and automobiles drew ceaseless fire. As the decades wore on, public interest in space development flagged, and the teleology of free trade lost its luster as older industries folded and U.S. jobs went abroad. And why slash taxes on the rich? The whole preceding era became a violation of, by later standards, political correctness.

To put it another way, the stage was set by the mid-1960s for reaction and repudiation, which indeed did come. What was the vehicle for it? One line of analysis owing to Arthur M. Schlesinger, Jr. and Samuel P. Huntington points to reform waves, or periods of public-spirited passion, that have emerged now and then in American history in the wake of spans of contrasting tendency.[84] In the present case, the private-minded 1950s hit the wall in the public-minded, movement-driven 1960s and 1970s. Certainly the latter era is exhibit A for movement activity. The many statutes regulating business were a product of it.[85] Nothing exceeded the force and prominence of the era's surging environmental movement, which had plenty to chew on. Already in 1956, the drive for the Upper Colorado Project had stirred mobilization among environmentalists who managed to kill one of its dams at Echo Park.[86] By the mid-1960s it was full steam ahead for the environmentalists. Many, perhaps most, of the policy achievements of the long 1950s fed into their cause.

For Schlesinger and Huntington, things go back and forth. There is homeostasis. History motors in and out of contrasting and compensating eras. Similar is a recent interpretation based in opinion data offered by Robert S. Erikson, Michael B. MacKuen, and James A. Stimson.[87] The government shifts policy to the left, voters react after a while and elect a conservative government, which in turn shifts policy to right, voters react again, and so on. The effect is of "decade-long swings in the fortunes of ideology and party."[88] The progression from Eisenhower to Johnson is a plausible instance.

But homeostatic interpretations have a drawback. They lack a developmental theme. They tend to skimp on path dependence.[89] For the history under inspection here, dialectical change seems to be a better conceptual fit than homeostasis taken straight. In general, the initiatives of the 1950s were pretty well laid. Returning to square one was a scarce option. To creations embedded in the countryside such as the new highway system, the Saint Lawrence Seaway, or Lake Powell, the familiar process tropes of "reform, "repeal," "retrench," or "amend" have an awkward fit. How could the highways or the seaway be retrenched or repealed? The financing schemes for the highways, dams, and seaway were models of credible government commitment.[90] NASA, COMSAT, and the National Science Foundation (NSF) were sturdily built. New Haven's old slum neighborhoods were gone forever. The high top-bracket tax rates that preceded the Kennedy tax cut were unlikely to come back absent a major war, and they have not. Yes, there was Three Mile Island. And yes, in general a distinct thrust toward reaction or repudiation did come about. But in process terms it diffused into a complicated mix of railing, reform, adaptation, letting things run their course, inventive workarounds, and changing the subject. Much of the American scene today is a deposit of the policy drives of the long 1950s blended with, somehow, reaction to them.

Another take on the long 1950s is that it was just plain *different* from what came later. Perhaps it sampled the past better than the future, at least in its big-projects emphasis. Robert D. Leighninger, Jr., writing from the perspective of 2007, drops an interesting comment in his book on the ample public investment during the New Deal:

> Since the 1930s, there have been only two comparable public works programs of national scope: the interstate highways program of the Eisenhower administration and the space program launched by John F. Kennedy. Both of these received broad support. Both were justified as matters of national defense. No other program of public building since then has involved the nation as a whole and taken place in the public eye.[91]

At any rate, it is well to see that the long 1950s as I have characterized it (convincingly, I hope) was indeed a time of major policy enterprises. For Eisenhower, think highways. For Johnson, think Medicare. Which of these creations has had more impact on American life? The case for the policy punch of especially the Eisenhower years is uncanonical, even in light of Fred I. Greenstein's revisionism about that president,[92] and it is worth asking why. Why have we missed this punch? I can see at least three reasons, each entailing a branch of scholarship.

First, the themes of mainstream political science have not been much help. Analysis of summary roll call data, which among other things ordinarily hinges on ideological unidimensionality, can fall short of illuminating what is actually going on in policymaking. There is not enough flesh, not enough content. Moods and impulses specific to eras can be missed. Policy inventiveness, as seen here in trade adjustment assistance, NSF peer review, highway trust funds, and the COMSAT consortium, has no place in conventional scatterplots. The privileging of conflict, which often occurs in roll call analysis and otherwise, can take the spotlight off productive non-conflict. Laws that pass unanimously or virtually so, such as NASA, may bypass datasets. Of the twenty-one statutes taken up here, all but one – the Saint Lawrence Seaway – passed with at least two-thirds support (or by voice vote) in at least one chamber, and all but nine in both chambers. (See Table 2.1.) All but one – area redevelopment – passed with the backing of majorities of both parties (or by voice vote) in at least one chamber, and all but eight in both chambers. Inventive cross-party coalitions, as on agriculture and trade measures, the Saint Lawrence Seaway, and the Colorado project, can fall between the cracks. Overreliance on the formalities of politics – for example, the configurations of Democrats and Republicans in the various branches – can cloud the picture. There is no good substitute for inspecting and characterizing what actually happened.

Second, much work that I have located on the economics of this long era – especially the Eisenhower years – has dwelt on short-term stimulation of the economy or its absence. Did the government perk up the economy during this or that two-year or four-year interval? There is a strong flavor of the managerial Keynesianism of the 1950s and 1960s, of near-horizon macroeconomics.[93]

Less evident is an emphasis on the direct government investment, inducement of private investment, creation of institutions, or shaping of societal incentives that might have affected the economy in the long run.[94]

Third, the scholarship in policy studies and history has likely had an ideological skew. Moynihan wrote in 1970, in prefacing his against-the-grain remarks on the interstate highway program, "One of the received truths of contemporary liberal history is that no domestic initiatives of any consequence occurred during the Eisenhower Presidency."[95] The reference is to liberal history, but that is where the main U.S. narrative has been crafted. In the absence of initiatives to foster entitlements or government regulation, it has been easy to slip into a mindset that nothing is happening at all. But promotion of the economy is policymaking, too. It is in a long line starting with Alexander Hamilton.

Notes

*   Many thanks to Cecilia Paris for her assistance on this project.
1.   James MacGregor Burns, *The Deadlock of Democracy: Four-Party Politics in America* (Englewood Cliffs, NJ: Prentice-Hall, 1963).
2.   Frank R. Baumgartner and Bryan D. Jones, *Agendas and Instability in American Politics* (Chicago: University of Chicago Press, 1993), p. 5; John W. Kingdon, *Agendas, Alternatives, and Public Policies* (New York: Longman, 2nd ed., 2003), pp. 146–49, ch. 8.
3.   There is confusion, for example, about whether the New Deal era encompasses Franklin D. Roosevelt's policy moves of 1944–45. See David R. Mayhew, "Wars and American Politics," *Perspectives on Politics* 3:3 (September 2005), 473–93 at 478–80.
4.   One workout of this methodology is David R. Mayhew, *Divided We Govern: Party Control, Lawmaking, and Investigations, 1946–2002* (New Haven, CT: Yale University Press, 2nd ed., 2005), ch. 3.
5.   See David Vogel, "The 'New' Social Regulation in Historical and Comparative Perspective," in Thomas K. McCraw (ed.), *Regulation in Perspective: Historical Essays* (Cambridge, MA: Harvard University Press, 1981), p. 157; Richard A. Harris, "A Decade of Reform," ch. 1 in Harris and Sidney M. Milkis (eds.), *Remaking American Politics* (Boulder, CO: Westview Press, 1989); Robert Higgs, *Crisis and Leviathan: Critical Episodes in the Growth of American Government* (New York: Oxford University Press, 1987), pp. 246–54; Mayhew, *Divided We Govern*, pp. 85–89.
6.   See, for example, Richard E. Neustadt, "Congress and the Fair Deal: A Legislative Balance Sheet," in Alonzo E. Hamby (ed.), *Harry S. Truman and the Fair Deal* (Lexington, MA: D.C. Heath, 1974), pp. 15–42.
7.   See, for example, Arthur M. Schlesinger, Jr., *A Thousand Days: John F. Kennedy in the White House* (Cambridge, MA: Houghton Mifflin, 1965), pp. 708, 712; Theodore C. Sorensen, *Kennedy* (New York: Harper and Row, 1965), p. 339; Richard Bolling, *Power in the House: A History of the Leadership of the House of Representatives* (New York: E.P. Dutton, 1968), pp. 204–17.
8.   James L. Sundquist, *Politics and Policy: The Eisenhower, Kennedy, and Johnson Years* (Washington, DC: Brookings Institution, 1968).
9.   Efficiency in the sense of optimal use of resources, minimizing waste.

10. Charles S. Maier, "The Politics of Productivity: Foundations of American International Economic Policy after World War II," *International Organization* 31:4 (Autumn 1977), 607–33, quotations at 609, 613. See also Robert M. Collins, *More: The Politics of Economic Growth in Postwar America* (New York: Oxford University Press, 2000), chs. 1, 2.

11. M. Stephen Weatherford and Lorraine M. McDonnell, "Macroeconomic Policy Making Beyond the Electoral Constraint," in George C. Edwards III, Steven A. Shull, and Norman C. Thomas (eds.), *The Presidency and Public Policy Making* (Pittsburgh: University of Pittsburgh Press, 1985), pp. 95–113. See also M. Stephen Weatherford and Lorraine M. McDonnell, "The Role of Presidential Ideology in Economic Policymaking," *Policy Studies Journal* 12:4 (June 1984), 691–702.

12. Weatherford and McDonnell, "Macroeconomic Policy Making," p. 105. See also Grant Madison, "The International Origins of Dwight D. Eisenhower's Political Economy," *Journal of Policy History* 24:4 (2012), 675–708.

13. M. Stephen Weatherford, "The Interplay of Ideology and Advice in Economic Policy-Making: The Case of Political Business Cycles," *Journal of Politics* 49:4 (November 1987), 925–52, quotation at 932.

14. To the despair of Nixon in 1960, who needed a better economy for his presidential run that year.

15. Dwight D. Eisenhower, *The White House Years: Mandate for Change, 1953–1956* (Garden City, NY: Doubleday, 1963), pp. 12, 121, 122, 124, 208, 287–90, 294, 297, 301, 305, 386–90, 499, 501–02, 547–48. See also Chester J. Pach, Jr., and Elmo Richardson, *The Presidency of Dwight D. Eisenhower* (Lawrence: University Press of Kansas, 1991 rev. ed.), pp. 32, 54–57; Iwan W. Morgan, *Eisenhower versus 'the Spenders': The Eisenhower Administration, the Democrats and the Budget, 1953–60* (London: Pinter Publishers, 1990), pp. 17–18; Merlo J. Pusey, *Eisenhower the President* (New York: Macmillan, 1956), chs. 11–12; Raymond J. Saulnier, *Constructive Years: The U.S. Economy under Eisenhower* (Lanham, MD: University Press of America, 1991), pp. 1–2.

16. Eisenhower, *White House Years: Mandate for Change*, p. 124.

17. Saulnier, *Constructive Years*, p. 5.

18. Weatherford and McDonnell, "Macroeconomic Policy Making," quotations at pp. 106, 109; Allen J. Matusow, *The Unraveling of America: A History of Liberalism in the 1960s* (New York: Harper and Row, 1986), p. 18. The 4.5 percent figure is from Ronald F. King, "Continuity and Change: Fiscal Policy in the Kennedy Administration," ch. 11 in Paul Harper and Joann P. Krieg (eds.), *John F. Kennedy: The Promise Revisited* (Westport, CT: Greenwood, 1988), p. 173.

19. Matusow, *Unraveling of America*, p. 33. This book is the New American Nation Series volume on the 1960s.

20. Nathaniel Beck, "Parties, Administrations, and American Macroeconomic Outcomes," *American Political Science Review* 76:1 (March 1982), 83–93. In this study, Truman and Johnson emerge as the star performers regarding unemployment levels. Kennedy and Carter were laggards. Only the Republican Ford underperformed those two Democrats.

21. One probe into that production appears in David R. Mayhew, *Partisan Balance: Why Political Parties Don't Kill the U.S. Constitutional System* (Princeton: Princeton University Press, 2011), chs. 2–4.

22. John H. Mollenkopf, *The Contested City* (Princeton: Princeton University Press, 1983), introduction and ch. 2, quotations at pp. 3, 74, 78. See also Ashley A. Foard and Hilbert Fefferman, "Federal Urban Renewal Legislation," ch. 4 in James Q. Wilson (ed.), *Urban Renewal: The Record and the Controversy* (Cambridge, MA: MIT Press, 1966); *Congressional Quarterly Almanac 1949*, pp. 273–86.

23. See Robert A. Dahl, *Who Governs? Democracy and Power in an American City* (New Haven: Yale University Press, 1961), pp. 116–18.

24. Bruce L. R. Smith, *American Science Policy since World War II* (Washington, DC: Brookings Institution, 1990), pp. 36–52; Nelson W. Polsby, *Political Innovation in America: The Politics of Policy Initiation* (New Haven, CT: Yale University Press, 1984), pp. 35–55; *Congressional Quarterly Almanac 1950*, pp. 183–86.

25. California was pumping somewhat more.

26. Ernest R. Bartley, *The Tidelands Oil Controversy: A Legal and Historical Analysis* (Austin: University of Texas Press, 1953), chs. 1, 13, 15; Richard H. K. Vietor, *Energy Policy in American since 1945: A Study of Business-Government Relations* (New York: Cambridge University Press, 1984), pp. 18–19; *Congressional Quarterly Almanac 1953*, pp. 388–96, quotation at 390.

27. Tom Arrandale, *The Battle for Natural Resources* (Washington, DC: Congressional Quarterly Inc., 1983), p. 109; Warren M. Christopher, "The Outer Continental Shelf Lands Act: Key to a New Frontier," *Stanford Law Review* 6:1 (December 1953), 23–68, at 23–28; Vietor, *Energy Policy in America*, pp. 18–19; *Congressional Quarterly Almanac 1953*, pp. 397–99.

28. Ronald Stagg, *The Golden Dream: A History of the St. Lawrence Seaway* (Toronto: Dundurn Press, 2010), pp. 158–68; Donald F. Wood, "The St. Lawrence Seaway: Some Considerations of Its Impact," *Land Economics* 34:1 (February 1958), 61–73; *Congress and the Nation, 1945–1964* (Washington, DC: Congressional Quarterly Inc., 1965), pp. 955–61; Jean Edward Smith, *Eisenhower in War and Peace* (New York: Random House, 2012), p. 650.

29. Eisenhower, *White House Years: Mandate for Change*, p. 301 (first quotation); Gary W. Reichard, *The Reaffirmation of Republicanism: Eisenhower and the Eighty-Third Congress* (Knoxville: University of Tennessee Press, 1975), p. 168 (second quotation).

30. Pach and Richardson, *The Presidency of Dwight D. Eisenhower*, p. 58; Wood, "The St. Lawrence Seaway," p. 61. Eisenhower's defense argument is emphasized in Stagg, *The Golden Dream*, p. 165; Eisenhower, *White House Years: Mandate for Change*, pp. 287, 301.

31. Wood, "The St. Lawrence Seaway," p. 62.

32. Stagg, *The Golden Dream*, p. 169.

33. Baumgartner and Jones, *Agendas and Instability*, pp. 59–67.

34. Eisenhower, *White House Years: Mandate for Change*, p. 294.

35. General references: Robert J. Duffy, *Nuclear Politics in America: A History and Theory of Government Regulation* (Lawrence: University Press of Kansas, 1997), pp. 34–38; Wyatt Wells, "Public Power in the Eisenhower Administration," *Journal of Policy History* 20:2 (2008), 227–62, at 246–54; *Congress and the Nation, 1945–1964*, pp. 935–39; *Congressional Quarterly Almanac 1954*, pp. 534–48.

36. Morgan, *Eisenhower versus "the Spenders,"* p. 17.

37. The Brannan Plan, rejected by a Democratic Congress, was a public-side efficiency proposal. It aimed to serve both farmers and consumers through a design of tight

regulation. General references on the 1954 measure: Edward L. Schapsmeier and Frederick H. Schapsmeier, "Eisenhower and Agricultural Reform: Ike's Farm Policy Legacy Appraised," *American Journal of Economics and Sociology* 51:2 (April 1992), 147–59; Eisenhower, *White House Years: Mandate for Change*, pp. 287–90.

38. Schapsmeier and Schapsmeier, "Eisenhower and Agricultural Reform," p. 154.
39. Richard M. Flanagan, "The Housing Act of 1954: The Sea Change in National Urban Policy," *Urban Affairs Review* 33:2 (November 1997), 265–86, quotations at 265, 283; data at 266. See also Foard and Fefferman, "Federal Urban Renewal Legislation," pp. 96–99; *Congressional Quarterly Almanac 1954*, pp. 198–205.
40. Barry Checkoway, "Large Builders, Federal Housing Programmes, and Postwar Suburbanization," *International Journal of Urban and Regional Research* 41 (1980), 21–45, quotation at 32.
41. Dolores Hayden, *Building Suburbia: Green Fields and Urban Growth, 1820–2000* (New York: Vintage, 2003), pp. 162–64.
42. Pach and Richardson, *The Presidency of Dwight D. Eisenhower*, quotation at p. 54; Reichard, *The Reaffirmation of Republicanism*, pp. 110–13; John F. Witte, *The Politics and Development of the Federal Income Tax* (Madison: University of Wisconsin Press, 1985), pp. 144–50; Eisenhower, *White House Years: Mandate for Change*, p. 303.
43. Pusey, *Eisenhower the President*, p. 244.
44. Raymond A. Bauer, Ithiel de Sola Pool, and Lewis A. Dexter, *American Business and Public Policy: The Politics of Foreign Trade* (New York: Atherton, 1964).
45. Eisenhower, *White House Years: Mandate for Change*, pp. 208–11, 292–93, 498, quotation at 293; Dwight D. Eisenhower, *The Eisenhower Diaries* (New York: Ed. Robert H. Ferrell, W. W. Norton, 1981), pp. 228–29, 244–45 (an especially clear guide to the president's thinking); Bauer, Pool, and Dexter, *American Business and Public Policy*, pp. 29–30; Pusey, *Eisenhower the President*, pp. 245–48; *Congressional Quarterly Almanac 1955*, 289–301; Reichard, *The Reaffirmation of Republicanism*, pp. 78–84.
46. Robert Pastor, *Congress and the Politics of U.S. Foreign Economic Policy, 1929–1976* (Berkeley: University of California Press, 1980), pp. 101–04.
47. Eisenhower, *White House Years: Mandate for Change*, quotations at 389, 499.
48. General sources: Mark W. T. Harvey, *A Symbol of Wilderness: Echo Park and the American Conservation Movement* (Albuquerque: University of New Mexico Press, 1994), ch. 10 (a fine case study of the enactment process), quotation at 266; Charles W. Howe and W. Ashley Ahrens, "Water Resources of the Upper Colorado River Basin: Problems and Policy Alternatives," ch. 5 in Mohamed T. El-Ashry and Diana C. Gibbons (eds.), *Water and Arid Lands of the Western United States* (New York: Cambridge University Press, 1988), p. 180; Neal R. Peirce, *The Mountain States of America: People, Politics, and Power in the Eight Rocky Mountain States* (New York: W.W. Norton, 1972), pp. 17–18, 188, 267; Donald Worster, *Rivers of Empire: Water, Aridity and the Growth of the American West* (New York: Pantheon, 1985), pp. 273–74 on the "cash register" design; *Congressional Quarterly Almanac 1956*, pp. 408–10.
49. Peirce, *The Mountain States of America*, p. 18.
50. Eisenhower, *White House Years: Mandate for Change*, p. 548; Stephen E. Ambrose, *Eisenhower: Soldier and President* (New York: Simon and Schuster, 1990), pp. 387–88; Smith, *Eisenhower in War and Peace*, pp. 651–54.

51. Eisenhower's view cited in Mark H. Rose, *Interstate: Express Highway Politics, 1939–1989* (Knoxville: University of Tennessee Press, 1979), p. 69.
52. Eric M. Patashnik, *Putting Trust in the US Budget: Federal Trust Funds and the Politics of Commitment* (New York: Cambridge University Press, 2000), ch. 6.
53. General references: Eisenhower, *White House Years: Mandate for Change*, pp. 501–02, 547–49; Pach and Richardson, *The Presidency of Dwight D. Eisenhower*, pp. 123–24; Rose, *Interstate*, chs. 6, 7; James A. Dunn, Jr., *Miles to Go: European and American Transportation Policies* (Cambridge, MA: MIT Press, 1981), pp. 118–22; *Congressional Quarterly Almanac 1956*, pp. 398–407; Gary T. Schwartz, "Urban Freeways and the Interstate System," *Southern California Law Review* 49 (March 1976), 406–513, at 427–39.
54. Eisenhower, *White House Years: Mandate for Change*, quotations at p. 548.
55. Quoted in G.T. Schwartz, "Urban Freeways," p. 408.
56. See, for example, D. W. Meinig, *The Shaping of America: A Geographical Perspective on 500 Years of History*, vol. 4, *Global America, 1915–2000* (New Haven, CT: Yale University Press, 2004), pp. 61–69; Richard A. Schwartz, *The 1950s: An Eyewitness History* (New York: Facts on File, 2003), p. 284; Hayden, *Building Suburbia*, pp. 165–72.
57. Pastor, *Congress and the Politics of U.S. Foreign Economic Policy*, p. 103.
58. Schapsmeier and Schapsmeier, "Eisenhower and Agricultural Reform," p. 153; Charles O. Jones, "The Agriculture Committee and the Problem of Representation," ch. 8 in Robert L. Peabody and Nelson W. Polsby (eds.), *New Perspectives on the House of Representatives* (Chicago: Rand McNally, 3rd ed., 1977); *Congressional Quarterly Almanac 1958*, pp. 269–75.
59. Walter A. McDougall, *The Heavens and the Earth: A Political History of the Space Age* (New York: Basic Books, 1985), chs. 6, 7; Dwight D. Eisenhower, *The White House Years: Waging Peace, 1956–1961* (Garden City, NY: Doubleday, 1965), pp. 205–12, 257–60; Pach and Richardson, *The Presidency of Dwight D. Eisenhower*, pp. 179–80.
60. Eisenhower, *White House Years: Waging Peace*, p. 258.
61. Sundquist, *Politics and Policy*, pp. 173–80; Lawrence E. Gladieux and Thomas R. Wolanin, *Congress and the Colleges: The National Politics of Higher Education* (Lexington, MA: D.C. Heath, 1976), pp. 8–9; Eisenhower, *White House Years: Waging the Peace*, pp. 241–44; Pach and Richardson, *The Presidency of Dwight D. Eisenhower*, p. 178.
62. Paul C. Light, *The President's Agenda: Domestic Policy Choice from Kennedy to Clinton* (Baltimore, MD: Johns Hopkins University Press, 1999), pp. 70, 77; James N. Giglio, *The Presidency of John F. Kennedy* (Lawrence: University Press of Kansas, 1991), pp. 103–04; Sundquist, *Politics and Policy*, pp. 57–73, 83–85; Sorensen, *Kennedy*, p. 404; *Congressional Quarterly Almanac*, pp. 247–56. Some of the money went to urban areas, too.
63. Matusow, *Unraveling of America*, pp. 36–37; *Congressional Quarterly Almanac 1962*, pp. 546–58.
64. Matusow, *Unraveling of America*, p. 35; Weatherford and McDonnell, "Macroeconomic Policy Making," 106–07; Julian E. Zelizer, *Taxing America: Wilbur D. Mills, Congress, and the State, 1945–1975* (New York: Cambridge University Press, 1998), pp. 185–87; Witte, *Politics and Development of the Income Tax*, pp. 156–58; *Congressional Quarterly Almanac 1962*, pp. 478–509.
65. Matusow, *Unraveling of America*, p. 35.

66. Sorensen, *Kennedy*, p. 410; Pastor, *Congress and the Politics of U.S. Foreign Economic Policy*, p. 108.
67. Sorensen, *Kennedy*, pp. 410–12; Pastor, *Congress and the Politics of U.S. Foreign Economic Policy*, pp. 105–17.
68. Pastor, *Congress and the Politics of U.S. Foreign Economic Policy*, p. 190.
69. Zelizer, *Taxing America*, pp. 204–06.
70. Herbert J. Parmet, *JFK: The Presidency of John F. Kennedy* (New York: Dial Press, 1983), p. 94; Sorensen, *Kennedy*, pp. 429–30.
71. Sorensen, *Kennedy*, pp. 427–33, quotations at pp. 430, 431, 432; Matusow, *Unraveling of America*, pp. 42, 49–59; Witte, *Politics and Development of the Income Tax*, pp. 158–65.
72. Eisenhower pressed for the first and third of these, Kennedy for all three.
73. On the Nixon years, see, for example, Mayhew, *Divided We Govern*, pp. 81–91.
74. In the Kennedy case, that conflict also surfaced over regulation of pharmaceutical drugs in 1962.
75. *Congressional Quarterly Almanac 1953*, pp. 393–94; *Congressional Quarterly Almanac 1954*, pp. 540–42; *Congressional Quarterly Almanac 1962*, pp. 546–58; Reichard, *The Reaffirmation of Republicanism*, pp. 151–53, 159–60; Matusow, *Unraveling of America*, pp. 36–37; Mayhew, *Partisan Balance*, pp. 148–50.
76. See, for example, Meinig, *The Shaping of America*, pp. 61–69.
77. Eisenhower, *White House Years: Mandate for Change*, p. 388. The president credits this rise to a variety of policy moves, including bureaucratic spurs to private power development, not all encompassed in the statutes under consideration here.
78. Eisenhower, *White House Years: Mandate for Change*, p. 390.
79. Stagg, *The Golden Dream*, ch. 5.
80. David Alan Aschauer, "Is Public Expenditure Productive?" *Journal of Monetary Economics* 23 (1989), 177–200, first quoted sentence at 194; Edward M. Gramlich, "Infrastructure Investment: A Review Essay," *Journal of Economic Literature* 32:3 (September 1994), 1176–96; Catherine J. Morrison and Amy Ellen Schwartz, "State Infrastructure and Productive Performance," *American Economic Review* 86:5 (December 1996), 1095–1111; John G. Fernald, "Roads to Prosperity? Assessing the Link between Public Capital and Productivity," *American Economic Review* 89:3 (June 1999), 619–38, second quoted sentence at 620–21.
81. See, for example, Hayden, *Building Suburbia*, ch. 8.
82. Ginger Strand, *Killer on the Road: Violence and the American Interstate* (Austin: University of Texas Press, 2012).
83. Stagg, *The Golden Dream*, pp. 238–42; Neal R. Peirce and John Keefe, *The Great Lakes States of America: People, Politics, and Power in the Five Great Lakes States* (New York: W.W. Norton, 1980), pp. 25, 200–01; Joe Barrett, "Lake Invaders Face a Salty Rebuff: Salinity Test Aims to Catch Creatures Sneaking into U.S. in Ballast of Ships," *Wall Street Journal*, May 12–13, 2012, p. A4.
84. Arthur M. Schlesinger, Jr., "The Cycles of American Politics," ch. 2 in Schlesinger, *The Cycles of American History* (Boston: Houghton Mifflin, 1986); Samuel P. Huntington, *American Politics: The Promise of Disharmony* (Cambridge, MA: Harvard University Press, 1981).
85. See, for example, R. Shep Melnick, "Risky Business: Government and the Environment after Earth Day," ch. 7 in Morton Keller and Melnick, *Taking Stock:*

American Government in the Twentieth Century (New York: Cambridge University Press, 1999), pp. 156–86.

86. See Worster, *Rivers of Empire*, pp. 273–74; Harvey, *A Symbol of Wilderness*.

87. Robert S. Erikson, Michael B. MacKuen, and James A. Stimson, *The Macro Polity* (New York: Cambridge University Press, 2002), ch. 9.

88. Erikson et al., *The Micro Policy*, p. 374.

89. Yet a side feature in the Erikson et al. account is that statutes do tend to stick. On path dependence, see Paul Pierson, "Increasing Returns, Path Dependence, and the Study of Politics," *American Political Science Review* 94:2 (June 2000), 251–67.

90. On the politics of government commitment, see Patashnik, *Putting Trust in the US Budget*; Eric M. Patashnik, *Reforms at Risk: What Happens after Major Policy Changes Are Enacted* (Princeton, NJ: Princeton University Press, 2008).

91. Robert D. Leighninger, Jr., *Long-Range Public Investment: The Forgotten Legacy of the New Deal* (Columbia: University of South Carolina Press, 2007), p. 210.

92. Fred I. Greenstein, *The Hidden-Hand Presidency: Eisenhower as Leader* (New York: Basic Books, 1982). Greenstein does not dwell on Eisenhower as legislative leader.

93. Examples are Harold G. Vatter, *The U.S. Economy in the 1950's: An Economic History* (New York: W.W. Norton, 1963); John W. Sloan, *Eisenhower and the Management of Prosperity* (Lawrence: University Press of Kansas, 1991); Morgan, *Eisenhower versus "the Spenders"*; Anthony S. Campagna, *U.S. National Economic Policy, 1917–1985* (Westport, CT: Praeger, 1987), ch. 8; Collins, *More*, chs. 1, 2.

94. Relatively underinvestigated in policy studies is "the capacity of presidents to influence long-term economic developments." See Jacob S. Hacker and Paul Pierson, "Presidents and the Political Economy: The Coalitional Foundations of Presidential Power," *Presidential Studies Quarterly* 42:1 (March 2012), 101–31, quotation at 101.

95. G.T. Schwartz, "Urban Freeways," 408. This view is not universal, at least not anymore. Jacob S. Hacker, for example, points to Eisenhower's "active leadership in codifying the unique public-private structure of U.S. social policy." *The Divided Welfare State: The Battle over Public and Private Social Benefits in the United States* (New York: Cambridge University Press, 2002), p. 238. Meredith Levine discusses the ambitious infrastructure initiatives of the Eisenhower years in "Shovel Ready: The Politics of Public Works, 1800-Present," paper presented at the annual conference of the Western Political Science Association, San Francisco, April 1–3, 2010. Stephen J. Wayne reports that "the Eisenhower administration retained and even expanded the presidency's capacity to develop, coordinate, and achieve legislative policy." The source is "The Eisenhower Administration: Bridge to the Institutionalized Legislative Presidency," *Congress and the Presidency* 39:2 (2012), 199–209, quotation at 199–200.

3

Regulation, Litigation, and Reform

Sean Farhang

More than 1.6 million lawsuits enforcing federal laws were filed over the past decade, about 97 percent of which were litigated by private parties. The suits spanned the waterfront of federal regulation, covering the policy domains of antitrust, civil rights, consumer protection, environmental law, labor, and securities and exchange. Although the United States had long relied upon private litigation to enforce federal statutes, its frequency of doing so exploded in the late 1960s. From a rate of 3 per 100,000 population in 1967 – a rate that had been roughly stable for a quarter century – it climbed to 13 by 1976, to 21 by 1986, to 29 in 1996, increasing by about 1,000 percent during these three decades. Beginning around the end of 1960s, there was an utterly unmistakable explosion of private lawsuits filed to enforce federal statutes.

By the early 1980s, calls emerged in Washington for "litigation reform" in the federal system, seeking changes in federal law calculated to *reduce* incentives for lawsuits. I call this "anti-litigation reform." By the 1990s, conflict over litigation reform intensified, with Republican's predominantly arguing for anti-litigation reform and Democrats predominantly opposing them. Reduction of "frivolous" lawsuits in federal court became the central call of the anti-litigation reformers. Currently pending before Congress is the Republican-sponsored Lawsuit Abuse Reduction Act of 2011, with the goal of reducing frivolous lawsuits in federal court by increasing sanctions against those who file them. Anti-litigation reform bills have become routine in Congress, and partisan battles over the role of litigation in federal regulation have become a regular part of national regulatory politics.

Contemporary tropes of anti-litigation reform often stress overclaiming by irresponsible and gold-digging plaintiffs, represented by greedy and unethical lawyers. In contrast, this chapter argues that the origins and meaning of partisan conflicts over litigation reform in the federal system are rooted in the emergence and success of an earlier litigation reform movement, one which was part of the broader movement to reform the regulatory state in the late 1960s and early 1970s. At that time, litigation reform – though it was not called that – had the opposite ambition of today's litigation reform. Its goal was to *increase* lawsuits to compensate for perceived failures in bureaucracy, pursuing private enforcement as an alternative. This regulatory reform strategy succeeded in laying the foundation for the country's current massive reliance on private lawsuits in federal regulation. I refer to this as the "pro-litigation reform" movement.

This chapter examines struggles over litigation reform in federal regulation during roughly the two decades from passage of the Civil Rights Act of 1964 to the end of Reagan's first term. It first traces the historical and political factors that led liberal advocates of the new social regulation to grow increasing skeptical of the administrative state as an effective enforcer, and to turn instead to a strategy of creating market incentives for private lawsuits for enforcement, a model of privatization learned from the experience of civil rights. This chapter shows how the contemporary anti-litigation reform movement emerged in the early Reagan years as a challenge to the successes of the pro-litigation reform movement over the previous decade, and as one component of the administration's broader deregulatory program. Finally, it assesses why Reagan's anti-litigation reforms failed, highlighting political and institutional sources of the resilience of America's private enforcement infrastructure.

LIBERAL'S WANING FAITH IN ADMINISTRATIVE POWER IN THE LATE 1960S

During the New Deal it had been liberals who were the chief architects of the administrative state-building project, whereas its principal detractors were business interests and their allies in the Republican party. Within the sphere of regulation, liberals' state-building vision and ambition was one of regulation through expert, centralized, federal bureaucracy. According to James Q. Wilson, "The New Deal bureaucrats" piloting a centralized federal bureaucracy "were expected by liberals to be free to chart a radically new program and to be competent to direct its implementation."[1] By the late 1960s, however, there was mounting disillusionment on the left with the capacities and promise of the U.S. administrative state. As Wilson put it in 1967, "Conservatives once feared that a powerful bureaucracy would work a social revolution. The left now fears that this same bureaucracy is working a conservative reaction."[2]

The metamorphosis toward liberal disillusionment with the administrative state coincided with, and was propelled by, the proliferation starting in the mid to late 1960s in the number, membership, and activism of liberal "public interest" groups.[3] A primary focus of these groups was on regulation, mainly of business, in such fields as environmental and consumer protection, civil and worker rights, public health and safety, and other elements of the "new social regulation" of the period. The political significance of liberal public interest groups to the story of litigation reform is importantly connected to their position within the Democratic party coalition.

THE DEMOCRATIC-LIBERAL PUBLIC INTEREST COALITION

After about 1968, owing both to liberal public interest groups' increasingly assertive role in American politics, and to reforms within the Democratic party organization, such groups emerged as an important and core element of the Democratic party coalition, a position they continue to occupy to the current day.[4] David Vogel shows that within the Democratic party coalition, "During the 1970s, the public-interest movement replaced organized labor as the central countervailing force to the power and values of American business."[5] The affinity between the Democratic party and liberal public interest groups is hardly surprising. In the twentieth century, a bedrock axis distinguishing the Democratic and Republican parties is Democrats' greater support for an interventionist state in the sphere of social and economic regulation, much of which targets private business.[6] An activist state, particularly one prepared to regulate private business, is exactly what the agenda of liberal public interest groups called for, from nondiscrimination on the bases of race, gender, age, and disability to workplace and product safety to cleaner air and water to truth in lending and transparent product labeling. Between the two major political parties in the United States, the Democrats were their party.

REASONS FOR THE LIBERAL LOSS OF FAITH IN BUREAUCRACY

Capture and Timidity

What explains the liberal loss of faith in bureaucracy among public interest groups and their allies among the Democratic Party? A number of charges were leveled. Because regulatory agencies interacted with regulated industries on an ongoing basis, agencies had been "captured" by business – regulators had come to identify with regulated business, treating them as the constituency to be protected. Alongside regulated business's extensive access to and influence on bureaucracy, liberal public interest groups believed that they were, by comparison, excluded, disregarded, and ignored by administrative policymakers. Moreover, bureaucrats were by nature timid and establishment oriented, wishing to avoid controversy and steer clear of the political and economic costs associated with serious conflict with regulated business. On balance, this added up to an implementation posture hardly likely to secure the transformative goals of the liberal coalition.[7]

Democratic Legislators, Republican Presidents, and Party Polarization

As the liberal coalition's growing concern about the limits of bureaucratic regulation was gathering strength in the late 1960s, an important transformation in the alignment of American government profoundly deepened their skepticism toward the administrative state as a regulator. The new dominant governing alignment in the United States combined divided government and party polarization, primarily with the Democrats writing laws in Congress, and Republican presidents exercising important influence on the bureaucracy charged with implementing them. In the first sixty-eight years of the twentieth century, the parties divided control of the legislative and executive branches 21 percent of the time, and in the subsequent thirty-two years of it (from Nixon through George W. Bush), the figure was 81 percent. The durability of the condition of divided government that emerged in the late 1960s was exacerbated by another factor contributing to legislative-executive antagonism. Starting around the early 1970s, the growth of ideological polarization between the parties, which increased through century's end, eroded the bipartisan center in Congress and fueled the antagonisms inherent in divided government.[8]

Add to this that during the years of divided government between Nixon taking office and the end of the twentieth century, 77 percent of the time Democrats controlled one or both chambers of Congress while a Republican occupied the presidency. Congress – the legislation-writing branch of government – was predominantly controlled by the Democratic party, with its stronger propensity to undertake social and economic regulation, and with liberal public interest groups occupying an important position within the party coalition. This legislative coalition largely faced an executive branch in the hands of a Republican president, the leader of a political party more likely to resist and oppose social and economic regulation.

This new alignment in American government was unlikely to make anyone happy. Not surprisingly, periods of Democratic congresses facing Republican presidents were characterized by virtually continuous acrimonious conflict between the liberal coalition in Congress and the comparatively conservative Republican leadership of the federal bureaucracy. Liberal public interest groups and congressional Democrats regularly attacked the federal bureaucracy under Republican leadership, claiming that it was *willfully* failing to effectuate Congress's legislative will. They charged that the executive branch adopted weak, pro-business regulatory standards; devoted insufficient resources to regulatory implementation; generally assumed a posture of feeble enforcement, and at times one of abject nonenforcement. Such charges ranged across many policy domains, including civil rights, environmental, and consumer regulation.[9] The convergence of divided government, party polarization, and Democratic legislatures facing Republican presidents sent the liberal legislative coalition in search of new strategies of regulation.

PRIVATE LAWSUITS AS A REGULATORY REFORM STRATEGY

The liberal coalition pursued a number of reform strategies to address the problems underpinning its disillusionment with the administrative state, its growing anxiety about presidential ideological influence on bureaucracy, and its concern about nonenforcement of congressional mandates. One set of strategies employed sought more effective control of the bureaucracy by the liberal coalition. It advocated enlarging opportunities for effective participation in the administrative processes – particularly rulemaking – by public interest groups and their allies. It sought to force agency actions though legislative deadlines and other means when agencies failed to carry out mandatorily prescribed responsibilities. It pressed for more aggressive congressional oversight and more frequent and stringent judicial review of important agency decisions. These were all strategies of reform through enhanced influence upon and control over the bureaucracy, and they have been widely examined by scholars.[10]

An additional response, which has been less studied and is the primary focus of this chapter, was to advocate statutory rules that allowed circumventing the administrative state altogether by undertaking *direct* enforcement of legislative mandates through private lawsuits against the targets of regulation, such as discriminating employers, polluting factories, and deceptive labelers of consumer products.[11] It is important to differentiate clearly between judicial review of agency action (one of the strategies discussed in the last paragraph), and direct private enforcement lawsuits. Rather than seeking to shape and constrain the behavior of bureaucracy, the direct enforcement strategy instead privatizes the enforcement function. When Congress elects to rely upon private litigation by including a private right of action in a statute, it faces a series of additional choices of statutory design – such as who has standing to sue, how to allocate responsibility for attorney's fees, and the nature and magnitude of damages that will be available to winning plaintiffs – that together can have profound consequences for how much or little private enforcement litigation will actually be mobilized.[12] This chapter refers to this constellation of rules as a statute's "private enforcement regime."

Among incentives to encourage private enforcement of regulatory laws, statutory fee-shifting rules allowing plaintiffs to recover attorney's fees if they prevail are especially important.[13] Under the American Rule on attorney's fees, which generally controls in the absence of a statutory fee shift, each side pays their own attorney's fees regardless of who wins. In light of the high costs of federal litigation, winning plaintiffs would often suffer a financial loss under the American rule, resulting in a disincentive for enforcement. By the early 1970s, liberal regulatory reformers were urging Congress, in order to mobilize private enforcement, to include private rights of action coupled with fee-shifting provisions in the new social regulatory statutes across the fields of civil rights and environmental, consumer, labor, and public health and safety, among others.[14] Monetary damages enhancements – which allow a plaintiff to recover more than the economic injury suffered, such as double, triple, or punitive damages – can also serve incentivize enforcement.[15] This strategy was aimed to facilitate litigation by law reform organizations, and, critically, to cultivate a for-profit bar to achieve day-to-day enforcement of ordinary claims – a function vastly beyond the capacity of small nonprofit groups. The strategy did not arise from abstract reflection. Rather, it was learned from unexpected developments in the area of civil rights.

THE EMERGENCE AND SPREAD OF THE LITIGATION SOLUTION IN THE 1970S

The Civil Rights Model

Civil rights groups' embracing of private lawsuits for implementation has ironic origins in the job discrimination title of the foundational Civil Rights Act of 1964 (CRA). When that law was proposed and debated in 1963–64, liberal civil rights advocates wanted a job discrimination enforcement regime centered on New Deal-style administrative adjudicatory powers modeled on the National Labor Relations Board (NLRB), with Equal Employment Opportunity Commission (EEOC) authority to adjudicate and issue cease-and-desist orders, *with no private lawsuits*. This preference was reflected in the job discrimination bill initially introduced by liberal Democrats with support from civil rights groups. At the time, the Democratic party, although a majority in Congress, was sharply divided over civil rights, with its southern wing deeply committed to killing any job discrimination (or other civil rights) bill. In light of these insurmountable intraparty divisions, passage of the CRA of 1964 depended on conservative anti-regulation Republicans joining non-southern Democrats in support of the bill.[16]

Wielding the powers of a pivotal voting bloc, conservative Republicans stripped the EEOC of the strong administrative powers initially proposed by civil rights liberals, and provided instead for private lawsuits for enforcement. Generally opposed to bureaucratic regulation of business, conservative Republicans also feared that they would not be able to control an NLRB-style civil rights agency in the hands of their ideological adversaries in the executive branch, long dominated by Democrats, and which passed from the Kennedy to the Johnson administrations while the bill proceeded through the legislative process. At the same time, in a political environment marked by intense public demand for significant civil rights legislation, some meaningful enforcement provisions were necessary in order for the Republican proposal to be taken seriously. To conservative Republicans and their business constituents, private litigation was preferable to public bureaucracy. Thus, conservative Republican support for Title VII was conditioned on a legislative deal that traded private lawsuits for public bureaucracy. As part of the deal, liberals insisted that if private enforcement was the best they could do, a fee shift must be included, and thus Republicans incorporated one into their amendments to Title VII. Civil rights groups regarded the substitution of private lawsuits – even with fee shifting – for strong administrative powers as a bitterly disappointing evisceration of Title VII's enforcement regime.[17]

If civil rights liberals and private enforcement regimes were a forced marriage, they soon fell in love and became inseparable. Civil rights groups mobilized in the early 1970s to spread legislative fee shifting across the field of civil rights, first to school desegregation cases in the School Aid Act of 1971, then to voting rights in the Voting Rights Act Amendments of 1975, and then to all other civil rights laws that allowed private enforcement but lacked fee shifting in the Civil Rights Attorney's Fees Awards Act of 1976. Why? The two causes discussed earlier in this chapter for declining liberal faith in administrative power were critical: concerns about administrative capture and timidity, greatly exacerbated by Nixon's influence upon the federal bureaucracy. Even under the Johnson administration, civil rights liberals regarded the federal bureaucracy's enforcement of civil rights as feeble, lacking both in political will and commitment of resources. When Nixon came to power, open conflict and antagonism broke out between civil rights liberals and the administration across civil rights in employment, education, housing, and voting. Perceptions of the federal bureaucracy as lackluster were replaced by perceptions of the federal bureaucracy as purposefully obstructionist, and at times as the enemy.[18]

However, these factors explain civil rights groups turn away from bureaucracy, not their embrace of private lawsuits with fee shifting, an enforcement alternative that, when adopted in 1964, they regarded with profound disappointment. Civil rights groups' embracing of private enforcement regimes, and the widespread adoption of private enforcement regimes as a reform strategy by the liberal coalition that shaped the new social regulation, was further propelled by several other developments. First, as Shep Melnick's contribution to this volume traces in Chapter 4, the federal courts during this period took an expansive, pro-plaintiff orientation toward the CRA of 1964, making the judiciary a more hospital enforcement venue for plaintiffs than anyone expected. Second, private rights of action with fee shifting proved unexpectedly potent in cultivating a private enforcement infrastructure in the American bar. In this regard, the early 1970s was a critical period of policy learning.

Growth of the Private Enforcement Infrastructure

During the first half of the 1970s, attorney's fee awards contributed resources to existing civil rights groups that prosecuted lawsuits under the new civil rights laws, such as the NAACP Legal Defense and Education Fund (LDEF) and the Lawyers' Committee for Civil Rights Under Law, adding to their enforcement capacity.[19] By 1973, the Lawyers' Committee was devoting half of its staff to its job discrimination litigation unit, which had become nearly self-supporting through attorney's fee awards.[20] By 1975, $550,000 of the LDF's operating budget of $3 million (more than 18 percent) came from attorney's fee awards.[21] The availability of fee awards also contributed to the formation of significant new civil rights enforcement groups, with foundation seed money, on the expectation that they would be able to draw continuing operating funds from attorney's fees awards.[22]

Liberal public interest law groups fashioned on the model of these civil rights organizations grew rapidly in the late 1960s and early 1970s. A 1976 study identified seventy-two such groups in the United States, spanning the areas of civil rights and civil liberties, environmental, consumer, employment, education, health care, and housing policy. Of the seventy-two groups identified, only seven had been founded prior to 1968. When surveyed in 1975, a major share of these groups' work was litigating in the fields of the new social regulation. In the three years from 1972 to 1975, the revenue brought in by these groups in the form of attorney's fees awards from litigation grew by 239 percent. Although attorney's fees were, on average, a small fraction of these groups' revenue, for some it was a primary source of funding to sustain litigation programs.[23]

In addition to increasing enforcement resources available to civil rights groups, the private enforcement approach in parts of the CRA of 1964, and numerous civil rights laws to follow that model in the ensuing decade, fostered the growth of a private for-profit bar to litigate civil rights claims. After a slow start in the second half of the 1960s, during which time little private Title VII enforcement materialized, in the first half of the 1970s the number of job discrimination lawsuits multiplied tenfold, growing from an annual number of about 400 to 4,000, where it roughly plateaued for the balance of the decade.[24] Title VII's fee-shifting provision, according to one practitioner in the field, had "led to the development of a highly skilled group of specialist lawyers" to enforce it.[25] A 1977 report of the Ford Foundation on civil rights litigation observed that "until at least the mid-1960s the NAACP Legal Defense and Education Fund stood almost alone" as a prosecutor of civil rights suits, but by the mid-1970s "fee-generating private practice has in many areas of the South enabled an indigenous bar, engaged in litigating cases of racial discrimination, to survive."[26] An April 1976 *Washington Post* article titled "Civil Rights Turns to Gold Lode for Southern Lawyers" declared: "The lure of legal fees, paid by the loser, is fertilizing a whole new practice in civil rights disputes."[27]

As civil rights leaders pursued the spread of fee shifting and observed the remarkable mushrooming of a for-profit civil rights bar in the first half of the 1970s, they were simultaneously active and important participants in collaborative umbrella organizations that brought together groups from across the liberal public interest movement. In these networks, public interest law groups spanning the full range of the new social regulation pooled information, learning from one another's experiences. The question of how to finance public interest law, and the role of fee awards in that calculus, was a matter of extensive attention and discussion within this network in the early to mid-1970s.[28]

The Council on Public Interest Law was formed in the spring of 1974. Later succeeded by the Alliance for Justice, the Council was an association of activists in the public interest law movement, including leaders of nonprofit public interest organizations spanning civil rights, environmental, consumer, education, public health, good government, and poverty law. Its initial purpose was to develop and disseminate a strategic plan for financing public-interest legal representation – a vision for harnessing economic support for the spread and growth of public interest law, with a central focus being the enforcement of rights under the new social regulatory statutes. The Council's book-length report, titled *Balancing the Sales of Justice: Financing Public Interest Law in America*, articulated a coalition-wide, self-conscious and coordinated decision of the leaders of the liberal public interest law movement to embrace the strategy of privatizing the enforcement of social regulation.[29]

As expressed in *Balancing the Sales of Justice*, the strategy was to "bring into the marketplace" cases under the new social regulatory statutes that otherwise would not be prosecuted, making such cases "economically attractive to regular commercial lawyers" in the "commercial legal marketplace." "The passage of legislation authorizing court awards of attorneys' fees," the report advocated, "may make it possible for some matters that would now be considered public interest cases eventually to be handled on a contingent commercial basis." The report regarded the budding model of what it called "private public interest law firms," then beginning to develop under recent fee-shifting legislation, as a model to build upon and as "a significant area for growth." Such firms could be "economically viable" in the for-profit arena, could be sustained by fee awards under statutes, and could function as the backbone of the enforcement infrastructure for the new social regulation. In order to "institutionalize" this for-profit private enforcement infrastructure, the liberal public interest movement's reform strategy would need to focus on securing statutory fee-shifting provisions from Congress. The report provided a model fee-shifting statute to be pursued legislatively.[30]

Balancing the Sales of Justice was also explicit that this reform strategy was modeled on what had been learned from the success of the civil rights movement. It noted that the NAACP Legal Defense and Education Fund was a pioneer in recognizing the importance of cultivating a network of private for-profit attorneys to "convert theoretical statutory rights into practical substantive benefits," and that LDEF "tried to *institutionalize that network by obtaining legislation authorizing attorneys' fees in order to convert its work from public interest law into a marketplace endeavor in which private lawyers could routinely participate.*" By the time of the Council's strategy session in 1974, the report stated that "virtually all public interest law endeavors today follow aspects of this model in one way or another," a private enforcement model with which "the NAACP/LDEF demonstrated that it is possible for a minority not merely to challenge the constitutionality of individual statutes or policies, but also to build an agenda for change." Again and again, the report returned to the example of Title VII as a focal point, emphasizing that its fee shift created a for-profit plaintiffs' job discrimination bar and thereby demonstrated – in the face of liberals' initial skepticism – the feasibility of a private enforcement strategy that could be generalized across the waterfront of the new social regulation.[31]

Indeed, progress toward this goal was well underway by the time the Council met in 1974. A 1976 study examined private for-profit firms that devoted at least 25 percent of their practice to "non-commercial" issue areas with the goal of "law reform" – importantly including enforcement of civil rights, environmental, consumer, employment, housing, education, and health care statutes. The study identified fifty-five such firms in the United States, and of them only two had been in existence in 1966. In the eight years from 1967 to 1975, the number of such firms increased from two to fifty-five. The collection of attorney's fees from defendants was an important source of revenue to these firms.[32] In 1977, Mary Derfner, an expert on fee shifting, observed that during the first half of the 1970s, fee-shifting provisions in recent federal statutes cutting across civil rights in employment, education, and voting; environmental protection and public nuisance regulation; and consumer protection in banking and product safety had conjured into existence a for-profit bar prepared to prosecute such federal statutory claims on behalf of plaintiffs. Because of congressionally provided fee-shifting provisions, she explained, litigating such claims contributed to "a financially viable practice," and consequently "public interest laws firms burgeoned."[33]

The Success of the First Litigation Reform

The long-term success of the pro-litigation reform movement is reflected in Figure 3.1. It displays the net number of private rights of action with fee shifts and/or damages enhancements (double, triple, or punitive) added to the body of federal statutory law from 1933 to 2004, with a locally weighted least-squares curve fit through the data points. The number of these litigation incentives is "net" in that it accounts for exits from federal statutory law due to repeal, expiration by the law's own terms, or being stricken by the Supreme Court. The predicted number rose sharply from the late 1960s to the late 1970s, somewhat plateaued until the mid-1990s, and then declined after the Republican Party took control of Congress in 1995. The solid line in Figure 3.2 represents the cumulative number of private rights of action with plaintiffs' fee shifts and damages enhancements in effect annually (accounting for exits), reflecting the structural environment of private enforcement regimes in existence annually. The dashed line in Figure 3.2 is the annual rate, per 100,000 population, of private federal statutory enforcement litigation (it is only possible to distinguish privately from governmentally filed actions beginning in 1942). The strikingly close association between these two variables, and particularly the coincident sharp upward shift in both at the end of the 1960s, reinforces the plausibility of plaintiffs' fee shifts and damages enhancements as measures of the broader phenomena of private enforcement regimes, and of the efficacy of private enforcement regimes in mobilizing private litigants. It deserves emphasis that about 98 percent of these suits were prosecuted by for-profit counsel, and only 2 percent by interest groups.[34]

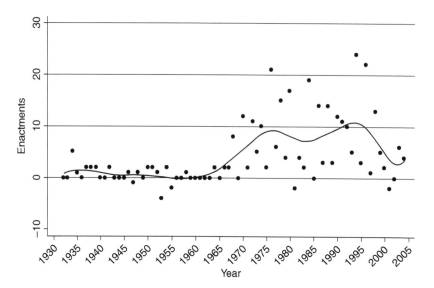

FIGURE 3.1. Enactments of Fee Shifts and Damages Enhancements

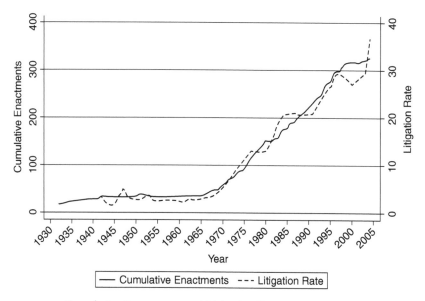

FIGURE 3.2. Cumulative Enactments and Litigation Rates

THE REAGAN YEARS

Deregulation and Administrative Power

Ronald Reagan came to power on the wave of a regulatory reform movement. It was, of course, quite different from the one that emerged in the late 1960s and early 1970s – and in some sense a reaction to it. Whereas fairness, justice, and equality were central themes of the movement behind new social regulation, in the late 1970s and early 1980s the themes were freedom, efficiency, and economic growth.[35] The reforms of the new social regulation period were driven by civil rights, environmental, consumer, labor, and other liberal public interest groups. In the late 1970s and early 1980s, it was business, trade associations, state and local officials, and newly emergent conservative public interest groups that were the primary catalysts behind the movement for reform through deregulation.[36]

Regulatory reform was high on the Reagan administration policy agenda. However, substantial continuing public support for the aspirational goals of the new social regulation, coupled with lack of cooperation from Congress, effectively ruled out the possibility of retrenching the new social regulation via legislative amendment.[37] Instead, the administration pursued an alternative strategy of deregulation, within the confines of existing statutory mandates, through a combination of withdrawal and redirection of the machinery of administrative implementation. This strategy involved appointing leadership to the new social regulatory agencies that shared the administration's deregulatory preferences, and that exercised administrative discretion to steer the bureaucracy and regulatory policy in the direction desired by the president. Under Reagan-appointed leadership, the new social regulatory agencies – in such fields as civil rights, environmental, consumer, and public health and safety – markedly reduced enforcement activity by numerous objective measures, such as the number of inspections, investigations, citations, civil penalties, administrative enforcement orders, and lawsuits prosecuted. They also embraced less interventionist regulatory standards through rulemaking, rule rescission, and other forms of regulatory policymaking. Further, the administration, acting through the Office of Management and Budget, sharply reduced agency budgets and, correspondingly, personnel.[38]

Deregulation and the Problem of Private Enforcement Infrastructures

The forgoing deregulatory strategy by the Reagan administration has been much noted and well documented by scholars. What I wish to stress here is how private lawsuits to enforce federal statutes impeded Reagan's deregulatory program. Upon assuming office, leaders of the Reagan bureaucracy well understood that private enforcement of the new social regulation had been growing steeply, and they saw it as a critical obstacle to their regulatory reform agenda.

By the mid- to late 1970s, conservative activists and leading business associations had developed considerable antipathy toward the new social regulation and its encroachment on business and governmental prerogative. Business began to claim that lawsuits under the new social regulatory statutes were having a substantial adverse impact upon business interests. Fee shifting provisions that forced business and government to pay the attorney's fees of the plaintiffs' lawyers who prosecuted invasive, disruptive, and costly lawsuits against them, were a particular target of criticism. They also believed that liberal public interest groups used litigation and courts to shape the substantive meaning of the new social regulatory statutes to their liking, thereby making regulatory policy that was injurious to the interests of business and government.[39]

Conservative activists and business associations mobilized and collaborated in forming a number of conservative public interest law groups to pursue an agenda, in part, of limiting the new social regulation.[40] Close associates of Reagan, including high-ranking members of his California gubernatorial administration that would follow him to the White House, were instrumental in founding this movement.[41] Indeed, litigation by liberal public interest groups against the Reagan gubernatorial administration, obstructing its pursuit of conservative public policies that Reagan regarded as critical, provoked members of his administration to found the first conservative public interest law group in Sacramento – the Pacific Legal Foundation – which then served as a model for many others.[42] Reagan himself was openly hostile to liberal public interest lawyers, characterizing them in the early to mid-1970s as "a bunch of ideological ambulance chasers doing their own thing at the expense of the poor who actually need help,"[43] and as "working for left-wing special interest groups at the expense of the public."[44]

Upon assuming office, the Reagan administration was acutely aware that private enforcement of federal regulatory law had surged powerfully since the late 1960s, and that the private enforcement infrastructure presented an important obstacle to its deregulatory agenda. Reagan had appointed numerous leaders and activists from the emergent conservative public interest law movement to important positions in the federal bureaucracy, ranging across counselor to the President, the White House Office of Policy Development, the Office of Management and Budget, the Equal Employment Opportunity Commission, and the Departments of Interior, Energy, and Justice.[45] The conservative public interest law movement had been born in opposition to the steep growth in litigation activity undertaken by both the for-profit and nonprofit plaintiffs bar under the new social regulatory statutes. They had watched, from Nixon's assumption of office in 1969 to Regan's in 1981, as the rate of private-enforcement lawsuits under federal statutes increased by 352 percent.[46] Now in power, they sought to retrench private enforcement. In characterizing anti-litigation reform as retrenchment, I follow Sarah Staszak.[47]

According to Michael S. Greve, a conservative legal activist and founder of the Center for Individual Rights, Reagan administration leadership saw private rights of action with attorney's fees awards as an obstacle to deregulation. Proposals to curtail fee awards under the new social regulatory statutes – along with a constellation of other efforts to reduce sources of funding for liberal public interest groups – were pursued by conservative activists as part of a strategy to "defund the left."[48] Greve explains:

When the Reagan Administration took office in 1981, one of the priorities urged upon it was to cut federal funding for liberal and leftist advocacy groups. Well known conservative activists openly advocated a strategy of "defunding the Left." This was necessary, they argued, for the success of the conservative social and deregulatory agenda. The incoming administration shared this assessment. President Reagan ... sensed that the liberal public interest movement was a primary obstacle to his campaign promises of "regulatory relief."[49]

Private enforcement litigation was a "primary obstacle" to Reagan's deregulatory agenda because his principle strategy for effectuating the agenda was to demobilize, to a significant measure, the administrative regulatory enforcement apparatus, with little prospect of actually being able to repeal or modify legislative mandates. The deregulatory reform value of withdrawing administrative enforcement is weakened if extensive private enforcement continues, and the strategy will be severely undercut if private enforcement actually expands to fill gaps left by withdrawal of administrative machinery. Important members of the Regan bureaucracy were in full agreement with Greve's characterization. Based upon archival research, Jefferson Decker finds that some were deeply concerned that the private rights of action coupled with fee shifting in the new social regulatory statutes were producing "a state-sponsored, private governing apparatus" that was *beyond the control of the elected branches.*[50]

Moreover – and this is critical – advocates of retrenching private enforcement recognized that the proliferation of fee-shifting provisions in the 1970s had produced a private enforcement infrastructure not just among liberal public interest groups, but, more significantly, among the for-profit American bar. Greve observes that when the Reagan administration sought to curtail fee awards "a sizeable portion of attorneys' fees is collected not by public interest groups but by big, for-profit law firms."[51] This became an important theme and concern among Reagan White House advocates for retrenching private enforcement, articulated repeatedly in support of an administration legislative proposal to cap fee awards (discussed below). Michael Horowitz, Reagan's general counsel of the Office of Management and Budget (OMB), played a leading role in developing the fee cap proposal. In a 1983 memo discussing the problem that the proposal sought to address, Horowitz explained: "Not only the 'public interest' movement but, *more alarmingly*, the entire legal profession is becoming increasingly dependent on fees generated by an open-ended 'private Attorney General' role that is authorized under more than 100 statutes,"[52] a large portion of which were enacted in the 1970s.

Writing to Director of OMB David Stockman, Horowitz characterized the goal of the fee-cap bill as being "designed in part to bar fee awards to entrepreneurial attorneys who now engage in contingency litigation" under federal statutes.[53] "A literal industry of public interest law firms as developed," he continued, "as a result of the legal fee awards with such groups regarding attorney's fees as a permanent financing mechanism," and one central to their commercial viability and business model.[54] When Stockman transmitted a version of the fee-cap bill in 1982 for consideration to Speaker of the House Tip O'Neill, he repeated Horowitz's lamentation that a "literal industry" had developed of plaintiffs' lawyers dependent on statutory fees awards.[55] In the same vein, a Justice Department memo to Counselor to the President Edwin Meese, reporting on the content of the fee-cap bill, stated that it was meant to address the problem of the "growing industry of attorneys capitalizing on civil fee awards."[56]

Reagan administration advocates of retrenching private enforcement were surely right, from the standpoint of a deregulatory agenda, that the statutory enforcement activity of the for-profit bar, mobilized by fee awards, was more alarming than the activity of the nonprofit bar. As noted previously, about 98 percent of the suits were prosecuted by for-profit counsel. To the extent that the "regulatory relief" sought by Reagan involved, in part, less aggressive and stringent enforcement of existing statutory mandates, and the private enforcement infrastructure posed a problem to presidential control, then the problem was emanating overwhelmingly from the for-profit bar responding to market incentives.

Attacking the Private Enforcement Infrastructure

Starting in 1981, the OMB, with Stockman as director and Horowitz as general counsel, developed a fee-cap bill which focused on suits against federal and state government defendants. They believed that the extensive fee-shifting legislation since the Civil Rights Act of 1964 was a critical part of the incentive structure generating excessive litigation, and the goal of the fee-cap proposal was to "drive a stake through that incentive structure."[57] Initially titled The Limitation of Legal Fees Awards Act of 1981, the proposed bill would amend more than 100 federal statutes allowing recovery of attorney's fees in successful suits against government, ranging across suits under consumer, civil rights, environmental, public health and safety, and freedom of information statutes, among many others. The bill went through a number of permutations from 1981 to 1984. Some core attributes of the initial version pursued of were:

- A fee cap of $53 per hour for private attorneys representing paying clients (a figure derived from the annual salaries of government lawyers, and one drastically below what courts had been awarding);
- No fee awards for public interest organizations with staff attorneys, legal services organizations receiving federal funds, or for-profit attorneys representing plaintiffs on a pro bono basis;

- The $\$53$ per hour fee award would be reduced by 25 percent of any money judgment;
- The $\$53$ per hour fee award would be reduced if it was disproportionate to the actual damages suffered by the plaintiff; and
- Fee awards would apply only with respect to issues on which the plaintiff actually prevailed, and which were necessary for resolving the dispute.[58]

Whereas this proposal's restrictions on fee awards were arguably quite extreme as applied to suits against government, the proposal is also noteworthy for the fact that it did not attempt to restrict fees in suits against the private (business) sector. It is clear that some key actors in the Reagan administration behind pushing the private enforcement issue onto the agenda wanted a more expansive retrenchment of the private enforcement infrastructure, including as applied to the private sector.[59] If the proposal had passed into law easily, it likely would have been the thin end of the retrenchment wedge. This was not to be.

How and Why Retrenchment Failed

The fee-cap bill failed. The story of its failure, traced next, teaches some important lessons about the long-run resilience of the private enforcement infrastructure. To appreciate them, it is useful first to highlight several institutional factors that make retrenchment of rights difficult. An institutionally fragmented American separation of powers system empowers many actors to block legislative reform, making legislative change difficult on contentious issues.[60] This is especially true when the legal change sought involves divesting groups of existing rights. In his work on welfare state retrenchment, Paul Pierson observes that rights-retrenching reforms confront serious political hurdles. The legal rights and interests that retrenchers seek to remove have often already given rise to "resources and incentives that influence the formation and activity of social groups ... [and] create 'spoils' that provide a strong motivation for beneficiaries to mobilize in favor of programmatic maintenance or expansion." Pierson also emphasized that the phenomenon of "negativity bias" (or an "endowment effect") leads people to be substantially more likely to mobilize to avoid the imposition of losses of existing rights and interests, as compared to securing new ones. It also leads voters to be more likely to punish politicians that have impaired their interests than to reward politicians who have benefited them, and politicians recognize this well.[61] Thus, retrenchment of rights is difficult because: (1) institutional fragmentation facilitates blocking policy reforms; (2) existing rights often contribute to group capacity to defend them; and (3) "negativity bias" enlivens group mobilization to block rights retrenchment, heightening the electoral threat to retrenching politicians. The durability of the status quo that can arise from these forces is an important part of the explanation offered by Terry Moe, in his contribution to this volume in Chapter 6, for the failure of the education reform proposals that he examines.

POLITICAL COSTS OF RETRENCHMENT

A number of high-ranking members of the Reagan administration regarded the political costs of the move to aggressively retrench private enforcement as much too high. The strongest advocates of the fee cap within the administration did not propose publicly advocating for the bill as a means of deregulation or demobilization of the private governing apparatus. Rather, they sought to publically frame it as a means of: (1) protecting scarce federal and state tax revenue from middle class lawyers; (2) compensating "private attorneys general" at the same rate as actual government lawyers rather than big law-firm lawyers; and (3) protecting state and local autonomy from overzealous private enforcement of federal mandates against states.[62] These themes linked fiscal responsibility and federalism, which were two broad aspects of the administration's core identity.

However, important administration leaders were extremely doubtful that the terms of the debate could be controlled in this way. Instead, they foresaw opponents successfully turning the battle into one over the preservation of substantive rights protected by the statutes to be amended – rights to be free of racial and gender discrimination, be shielded from predatory business practices, drink clean water and breathe clean air, an education for disabled children, and disability benefits for injured workers. That is, they knew that the administration would be attacked by liberal public interest groups and the plaintiffs' bar for seeking to take popular rights away from vulnerable groups.

Attorney General William French Smith observed that striking too severely at attorney's fees awards risked "excessive controversy." He emphasized that in the public relations battle the administration would be cast as "anti" rights. "Attorney's fee cap proposals," Smith wrote, "are thought by public interest litigating organizations to strike at a vital source of their financial support. Accordingly, these groups have characterized fee cap proposals as 'anti-civil rights' or 'anti-environmental' proposals."[63] Opponents of the proposal would be able to beat it back with "the rhetoric of rights and justice," as one supporter put it.[64] Smith also observed that the timing of the bill seemed particularly bad with an election on the horizon.[65] When the bill was sent to the president's staff to be cleared in December 1983, Counsel to the President Fred Fielding echoed Attorney General Smith's skepticism as to both the bill's political risks and its questionable timing:

The circumstances in which attorneys fees are awarded to parties prevailing against the government ... typically involved civil rights litigation, welfare entitlement suits, environmental litigation, and the like. Since the "fee cap bill" would have its greatest impact in these areas, I remain deeply concerned that it will be viewed and portrayed as yet another Administration effort to limit the delivery of legal services to minorities, the poor, and the aged. ... I am not convinced that this is the time to open another front in the ongoing battle over our record in these areas.[66]

LACK OF MODERATE REPUBLICAN SUPPORT IN CONGRESS

In light of this political calculus, it is not surprising that the fee-capping bill was ultimately unable to attract the support of moderates in Congress, even among Republicans. As the administration surveyed the bill's legislative prospects, Democratic control of the House caused many to seriously doubt that the bill could pass that chamber. But the problem was not only Democrats. Administration officials assessing the bill's prospects also recognized that it would require the support of liberal Republicans and conservative Democrats, and expressed little optimism that the bill could even pass the Republican-controlled Senate.[67] Some conservative Republicans recognized, with disappointment, that support within Congress for civil rights, environmental, and consumer groups was very broad, including many moderate Republicans, either because of their sincere preferences or because they feared being cast as an enemy of rights that enjoyed broad public support.[68] Ultimately, the views of William French Smith and Fred Fielding seemed to be shared by more liberal-leaning Republicans in Congress – even if they had any inclination to join the administration's attack on the private enforcement infrastructure, the political calculus was against it.

ONE-SIDED INTEREST GROUP MOBILIZATION

The administration appears to have significantly underestimated the degree of opposition that it would face, and overestimated the degree of support it would enjoy. Prior to announcing the bill, the administration initiated contacts with "interested groups," which it deemed to be state attorneys general, municipal law enforcement officers, mayors, business, and liberal public interest organizations. The administration, of course, naturally anticipated strong opposition from liberal public interest organizations, and also from the for-profit plaintiffs' bar, both of whom stood to lose if the fee-cap bill succeeded.[69] As discussed, the threat or reality of such opposition weakened support for the fee-cap bill within the Republican party. However, the administration anticipated support from states and business. As it turned out, both were internally divided.

With respect to state officials – attorneys general, municipal law enforcement officers, and mayors – the administration anticipated support because the bill would preserve state and city tax resources against fee awards, and reduce incentives for private federal lawsuits against cities and states.[70] However, of these groups only the National Association of State Attorneys General (NASAG) promised support; the National Institute of Municipal Law Officers (NIMLO) declined to take a public position; and United States Conference of Mayors (USCM) would at best be silent, but threatened possible public opposition. Representatives of NIMLO explained that they actually regarded fee awards as being of marginal significance relative to overall liability, and that they would take no position on the legislation. They did not explain why, even if liability was larger than fees, they would not still support capping fees, which would reduce incentives for lawsuits and liability exposure at least somewhat.[71] The position of the USCM provides possible illumination of their motivation.

A representative of the USCM explained to administration officials that most members of the Conference (which represents larger cites) "would react negatively" to the bill and would oppose it. Despite the frequency of lawsuits against cities, he explained, "the mayors themselves were more likely to be sympathetic to the interests of the plaintiffs." The representative indicated that any policy that would reduce incentives for enforcement of civil rights and environmental legislation, in particular, would be especially likely to provoke opposition given the broad popularity of such policies. The calculus by mayors was not as straightforward as simply supporting the bill because cities are the targets of lawsuits and fee awards. Rather, the calculus also included weighing the popularity of the new social regulation among the constituents of big city mayors, not to mention their potential sincere support for the laws. The USCM representative also indicated that the issue of attorneys' fees had arisen in the past and proven "so controversial that it has not been able to come to the floor of the Conference." He advised that if the Conference managed to muster any public position on the administration's fee-cap bill it would be negative. Thus, of the three state groups consulted, NASAG would support the administration, NIMLO would take no position for or against, and USCM might publicly oppose.[72]

To the administration's surprise, business was divided as well, although for different reasons. The administration anticipated that business interests would be served by reducing fee awards to plaintiffs' counsel litigating against governments under federal statutes, because such litigation includes challenges by liberal groups to administrative regulatory policymaking calculated to move regulatory law in a liberal direction. Reducing the influence of liberal public interest organizations on federal and state policymaking, the administration thought, would capture business support for the fee-cap bill. Further, as already suggested, a victory for the fee-cap bill as applied to litigation against government could be the thin end of a wedge, opening the possibility of retrenching private enforcement as applied to the private sector. After the administration gauged the preferences of business leaders, it concluded that big business could be counted upon for support. Small business, however, looked like a big problem. A strategy memo in the Office of Legal Policy suggested, with disappointment, that the bill threatened to provoke the "wrath of the small business community."[73]

The reason was that, ironically, small business had themselves developed an interest in preserving fee awards under the Equal Access to Justice Act, and that interest was threatened by the administration's bill. With Republicans and business as legislative catalysts, in 1980 Congress had enacted the Equal Access to Justice Act, which provided for attorney's fees awards for small businesses, individuals, and organizations that prevail against the federal government in administrative or judicial proceedings in which they challenge the legitimacy of federal regulatory actions. The law, passed as part of a small business assistance statute, was primarily intended to aid small businesses in challenging excessive and unreasonable regulation by the federal government, including prosecutions of small businesses accused of violating regulatory laws. In the absence of fee shifting, it was argued, small businesses often had limited capacity or incentive to resist the abuse of federal regulatory power. The fee shift would help level the playing field and curb excessive and unreasonable regulation.[74] When the Regan administration's fee-cap bill became public, small business groups made clear that they would not give up their new weapon quietly, and that any effort to take it away would be regarded as "break[ing] faith with the small-business community," as one business association leader declared in an interview published in the *Wall Street Journal*.[75]

The initial version of Reagan's fee-cap bill failed to find a congressional sponsor even within the president's own party. The administration then developed a moderated version of the bill, and in 1984 hearings were held on this bill in a Senate subcommittee chaired by Orrin Hatch (R-UT), who championed the bill as a much-needed corrective to the proliferation of statutory fee-shifting rules in the 1970s, creating "exorbitant windfalls for lawyers," leading to an "explosion of litigation" that had "clogged the courts."[76] However, despite Hatch's alignment with legal conservatives in the administration that sought to retrench the private enforcement infrastructure, he was unable to muster support in his own Republican-controlled committee, where the bill died.

LESSONS

The Reagan administration's fee-cap bill was among the most aggressive attacks on the private enforcement infrastructure in federal regulation ever undertaken. Its failure suggests three important lessons about the resilience of private enforcement. First, as a matter of political framing, it was extremely difficult for advocates of retrenching private enforcement to separate the legal structures of private enforcement (such as fee shifts) from the substantive rights to which they were attached. Their attempt to retrench enforcement provisions evoked a political response little different than if they were seeking to repeal substantive rights. This rights focus of the debate caused divisions within the Reagan White House and the Republican Party, such that the bill had only weak support in some important quarters of the administration and got no traction even in the Republican-controlled Senate. It also significantly weakened the administration's ability to command the support of groups representing state interests – interests that the administration claimed to be championing.

Second, over the course of time the interests tied to private enforcement deepened and widened, making private enforcement more difficult to uproot. The interests of liberal law reform organizations grew in retaining access to fee awards themselves, and, even more, in protecting the lifeblood (attorney's fees) of the private enforcement infrastructure that they had so assiduously cultivated.

Moreover, the private for-profit bar thereby cultivated surely sought to protect its own interests, and added heft and capacity to the coalition defending the private enforcement status quo when the anti-litigation reform movement emerged in the early Reagan years.

The interests tied to private enforcement spread even to some quarters of business, typically regarded as opponents of private enforcement. There is some irony in conservative Republicans imposing – over the objections of liberals – Title VII's private enforcement regime, which in turn became the liberal model for privatizing enforcement of the new social regulation. The irony was compounded when conservative Republicans pressed for small business to participate in the bounty of fee awards through the Equal Access to Justice Act, thereby helping to cement the whole system into place by extending its benefits into the Republican base. The EAJA was neither the first nor the last time that Republicans drew on the private enforcement model. The Republican participation in spreading private enforcement to benefit its own constituencies represented a broader trend.[77]

Third, the autopilot and durable character of the private enforcement infrastructure had real consequences for presidential power, restricting the president's ability to curtail enforcement. A deregulatory administration could not control a critical source of regulatory enforcement. To the contrary, during the period that the Reagan administration was considering strategies to reduce private enforcement of federal statutes, such enforcement actually grew by leaps and bounds. After having been roughly flat during the Carter presidency (it declined slightly), during Reagan's first term the rate of private lawsuits enforcing federal statutes *shot up by 63 percent.*[78] The significance of this growth as an obstacle to Reagan's deregulatory strategy is reinforced by considering specific policy areas within the ambit of his deregulatory agenda. The number of private statutory suits grew by 64 percent under labor statutes, 68 percent under civil rights statutes, 82 percent under environmental statutes, and 90 percent under securities and exchange statutes.[79] During the Reagan years the targets of federal regulation were more likely than ever to be hauled into court as defendants, overwhelmingly by for-profit plaintiffs' counsel.

CONCLUSION

The litigation reform strategy developed by the liberal coalition in the late 1960s and early 1970s, in the sphere of federal regulation, sought litigation to perform functions that it concluded the administrative state either could not or would not perform. The movement was largely successful, and its success had a profound and enduring influence on American government. Its model of regulatory implementation had particular appeal in the era characterized by Democratic congresses facing Republican presidents, combined with growing party polarization. This is not to say that its appeal was limited to this configuration

of partisan control of government, for its trajectory was upward nearly continuously from the late 1960s to 2004 (when my data ends).

The period examined in this chapter teaches that current debates over "litigation reform" in federal regulation should be understood largely as struggles
over the proper scope and reach of the state in the economy and society, much
like decisions about whether to create, fund, staff, and empower bureaucracy.
The liberal coalition in the late 1960s and early 1970s regarded private lawsuits
as an alternative to bureaucratic inadequacy, and this was one prong of their
broader regulatory reform agenda. Those who sought to retrench the private
enforcement infrastructure in the early 1980s did so as part of a broader deregulatory program that included diminishing the position of the federal bureaucracy in the American economy and society. They recognized that deregulation
within existing regulatory mandates would need to entail demobilization of not
just public but also private enforcement. Viewing these two reform movements
together highlights that struggles over litigation reform are struggles over
American governance.

Advocates of legislatively retrenching private enforcement in federal regulation have seldom succeeded,[80] and their successes have generally been quickly
submerged by the relentless growth of private enforcement. Indeed, calls for anti-
litigation reform have been perennial for three decades – from the Limitation
of Legal Fees Awards Act of 1981 to the Lawsuit Abuse Reduction Act of 2011.
Calls for reform become perennial when they are perennially thwarted. The
Reagan administration's fee-cap bill, which would have amended more than 100
federal statutes in one enactment, was among the most assertive moves to
legislatively retrench private enforcement ever attempted. Subsequent generations of anti-litigation reform proposals in federal regulation most often have
been narrower in scope, training their sights on particular statutes and policy
areas, as contrasted with mounting crosscutting attacks on private enforcement
in general.

The failure of the fee-cap bill contains lessons that help explain the resilience
of the American state's private enforcement infrastructure in the years since.
Retrenching rights is hard in an institutionally fragmented environment. In
public debates it is difficult to separate private enforcement regimes from underlying popular rights, which will discourage risk-averse politicians and interest
groups from supporting retrenchment. Negativity bias, or an endowment effect,
will amplify opposition and its political efficacy. As private enforcement regimes
have diffused across the American regulatory state, the interests formed around
them have become more widely spread and deeply rooted, increasing the political capacity of the coalition to defend the private enforcement infrastructure
from retrenchment.

The failure of legislative retrenchment of the private enforcement infrastructure is highlighted by the fact that even during periods of significant Republican
legislative power, although calls for retrenchment were emanating from some
quarters of the Republican Party, there was net growth in the private

enforcement infrastructure. Republican instigation of the private enforcement regimes in Title VII and the Equal Access to Justice Act were not anomalous. Indeed, while controlling the Senate and the presidency from 1981 to 1986, during which time the fee-cap proposal failed, Congress passed and the president signed, per Congress, an average of twelve new private rights of action with fee shifts and/or monetary damages enhancements (Figure 3.1). That number was down materially from the Carter years, when twenty-one per Congress were passed, but it contributed to the continuing growth of opportunities and incentives for private lawsuits enforcing federal law. This basic pattern persisted from 1987 to 2004: Democratic congresses from 1987 to 1994 passed twenty per Congress, and Republican Congresses from 1995 to 2004 – while proclaiming an anti-litigation reform agenda – passed eleven per Congress (Figure 3.1). Under Republican congresses, the rate of growth slowed, but material expansion of the private enforcement infrastructure continued ineluctably (Figure 3.2).

This chapter has focused narrowly on the two decades spanning passage of the Civil Rights Act of 1964 and the end of Reagan's first term, and on pro- and anti-litigation reform movements as they pursued legislative reform in the field of federal regulation. This narrow temporal frame and substantive focus has neglected much that is important to understanding litigation reform and efforts to retrench private enforcement. One important part of the story not examined concerns the role of the federal judiciary. Many scholars have argued that beginning in the 1980s and continuing to the present federal courts, particularly the Rehnquist court, accomplished material retrenchment of private enforcement incrementally through decisions, for example, placing limitations on attorney's fees and damages awards; enforcing contractual mandatory arbitration agreements; expansively developing the qualified immunity defense; and influencing and interpreting the federal rules of civil procedure so as to limit access to courts.[81] Sarah Staszak characterizes this body of case law as "judicial retrenchment."[82]

The "regime politics" literature teaches that federal judges are sometimes uniquely institutionally situated to achieve goals that their co-partisans in the elected branches cannot on issues that are politically conflictual both in society at large and within the party. The federal judiciary's advantage here lies in its distinct institutional properties: relative political and electoral insulation; operating under simple majority rule in a more unitary (less fragmented) institutional environment; and working on a lower visibility terrain through incremental case-by-case policy development.[83] This perspective is quite apt with respect to anti-litigation reform, where much of what conservative federal judges have accomplished was first tried and failed as Republican legislative reform, exemplified by the story of the Reagan fee-cap bill. The forces that constrain legislative retrenchment of rights have far less purchase in federal courts.

In aggregate, these decisions have surely had important effects that are obscured by looking only at net filings, adversely influencing some plaintiffs' ability to secure counsel, proceed with class litigation, prevail on the merits, or secure the relief sought. It is also possible that the net effect of such decisions limited the pace of growth of private enforcement relative to a counterfactual doctrinal terrain more favorable to private enforcement. Still, it is clear that the core aspiration of many anti-litigation reformers in the field of federal regulation has been to stop and possibly reverse the growth of private litigation in public policy implementation. Despite the anti-litigation posture of an increasingly conservative federal bench, and calls for retrenchment of private enforcement from congressional majorities from 1995 to 2005, Congress's production of opportunities and incentives for private lawsuits enforcing federal statutes, and correspondingly the rate of such lawsuits, continued to grow into the early twentieth century (Figure 3.2).

Notes

1. James Q. Wilson, "The Bureaucracy Problem," *The Public Interest* 6 (1967): 3–9, 3.
2. Ibid., at 3.
3. David Vogel, "The 'New' Social Regulation in Historical and Comparative Perspective," in *Regulation in Perspective*, ed. Thomas K. McCraw (Cambridge: Harvard University Press, 1981), 155–85, 164–75; Martin Shapiro, *Who Guards the Guardians? Judicial Control of Administration* (Athens: University of Georgia Press, 1988), 55–77.
4. Martin Shefter, *Political Parties and the State: The American Historical Experience* (Princeton: Princeton University Press, 1994), 86–94; Jules Witcover, *Party of the People: A History of the Democrats* (New York: Random House, 2003), ch. 27; Vogel, "The 'New' Social Regulation in Historical and Comparative Perspective," 164–75; David Vogel, *Fluctuating Fortunes: The Political Power of Business in America* (New York: Basic Books, 1989); Sean Farhang, *The Litigation State: Public Regulation and Private Lawsuits in the U.S.* (Princeton: Princeton University Press, 2010), 129–213.
5. Vogel, *Fluctuating Fortunes*, 293.
6. Keith T. Poole and Howard Rosenthal, *Congress: A Political-Economic History of Roll Call Voting* (New York: Oxford University Press, 1997).
7. R. Shep Melnick, "Courts and Agencies," in *Policy, Making Law: An Interbranch Perspective*, eds. Mark C. Miller and Jeb Barnes (Washington, DC: Georgetown University Press, 2004), 89–104, 93; Simon Lazarus and Joseph Onek, "The Regulators and the People," *Virginia Law Review* 57 (1971): 1069–1108; Shapiro, *Who Guards the Guardians*, 62–73; Wilson, "The Bureaucracy Problem"; Richard Stewart, "The Reformation of American Administrative Law," *Harvard Law Review* 88 (1975): 1667–1813, 1684–85, 1713–15.
8. Gary Jacobson, "Partisan Polarization in Presidential Support: The Electoral Connection," *Congress and the Presidency* 30 (2003): 1–36; Nolan McCarty, Keith T. Poole, and Howard Rosenthal, *Polarized America: The Dance of Ideology and Unequal Riches* (Cambridge, MA: MIT Press, 2006).
9. R. Shep Melnick, "From Tax and Spend to Mandate and Sue: Liberalism after the Great Society," in *The Great Society and the High Tide of Liberalism*, eds. Sidney Milkis and Jerome M. Mileur (Amherst: University of Massachusetts Press,

2005), 387–410, 398–99; Farhang, *The Litigation State*, 129–213; Farhang, "Legislative-Executive Conflict and Private Statutory Litigation in the United States: Evidence from Labor, Civil Rights, and Environmental Law," *Law and Social Inquiry* 37 (2012): 657–85; Joel D. Aberbach, *Keeping a Watchful Eye: The Politics of Congressional Oversight* (Washington, DC: Brookings Institution, 1990), 27; *Hearings on Class Action and Other Consumer Procedures Before the Subcommittee on Commerce and Finance of the House Committee on Interstate and Foreign Commerce*, 91st Cong., 2nd sess., 1970.

10. Melnick, "From Tax and Spend to Mandate and Sue," 399; Lazarus and Onek, "The Regulators and the People"; Vogel, *Fluctuating Fortunes*, ch. 5; Stewart, "The Reformation of American Administrative Law."

11. R. Shep Melnick, *Between the Lines: Interpreting Welfare Rights* (Washington, DC: Brookings Institution); Thomas F. Burke, *Lawyers, Lawsuits, and Legal Rights: The Battle Over Litigation in American Society* (Berkeley: University of California Press); Robert Kagan, *Adversarial Legalism: The American Way of Law* (Cambridge, MA: Harvard University Press, 2001); Farhang, *The Litigation State*.

12. Sean Farhang, "Congressional Mobilization of Private Litigants: Evidence from the Civil Rights Act of 1991," *Journal of Empirical Legal Studies* 6 (2009): 1–34; Farhang, *The Litigation State*.

13. Frances Kahn Zemans, "Fee Shifting and the Implementation of Public Policy," *Law and Contemporary Problems* 47 (1984): 187–210; Melnick, *Between the Lines*; Kagan, *Adversarial Legalism*; Farhang, *The Litigation State*.

14. *Hearings on Legal Fees Before the Subcommittee on Representation of Citizen Interests of the Senate Judiciary Committee*, 93rd Cong., 1st sess., 1973; Farhang, *The Litigation State*, ch. 5.

15. Farhang, *The Litigation State*, 21–31.

16. Farhang, *The Litigation State*, ch. 4; Daniel Rodriguez and Barry R. Weingast, "The Positive Political Theory of Legislative History," *University of Pennsylvania Law Review* 151 (2003): 1417–1542; Anthony S. Chen, *The Fifth Freedom: Jobs, Politics, and Civil Rights in the United States, 1941–1972* (Princeton: Princeton University Press, 2009), ch. 5.

17. Ibid.

18. Farhang, *The Litigation State*, ch. 5.

19. Armand Derfner, "Background and Origin of the Civil Rights Attorney's Fee Awards Act of 1976," *Urban Law* 37 (2005): 653–61, 656; Karen O'Connor and Lee Epstein, "Bridging the Gap between Congress and the Supreme Court: Interest Groups and the Erosion of the American Rule Governing Award of Attorney's Fees," *Western Political Quarterly* 38 (1985): 238–49, 241.

20. *Hearings on Legal Fees Before the Subcommittee on Representation of Citizen Interests of the Senate Judiciary Committee*, 93rd Cong., 1st sess., 1973 (hereinafter *1973 Hearings on Attorney's Fees*) (testimony of Armand Derfner), 1112–13.

21. O'Connor and Epstein, "Bridging the Gap," 241.

22. Robert B. McKay, *Nine for Equality under Law: Civil Rights Litigation. A Report to the Ford Foundation* (New York: Ford Foundation, 1977); O'Connor and Epstein, "Bridging the Gap," 240.

23. Handler, Ginsburg, and Snow, "The Public Interest Law Industry"; Vogel, *Fluctuating Fortunes*, 105.

24. *Federal Court Cases: Integrated Data Base, 1970–2000*, maintained by the Inter-university Consortium for Political and Social Research. The method for arriving at the estimates is explained in Farhang, *The Litigation State*, 271 n. 118.
25. *1973 Hearings on Attorney's Fees*, 1113.
26. McKay, *Nine for Equality*, 8, 13.
27. Bill Crider, "Civil Rights Turns to Gold Lode for Southern Lawyers," *Washington Post*, April 4, 1976, 59.
28. Louise Trubek, "Public Interest Law: Facing the Problem of Maturity," *University of Arkansas at Little Rock Law Review* 33 (2011): 417–33, 418–19; Council for Public Interest Law, *Balancing the Scales of Justice: Financing Public Interest Law in America* (Washington, DC: Council on Public Interest Law, 1976); Burton, *Public Interest Law.*
29. Council on Public Interest Law, *Balancing the Scales of Justice*; Trubek, "Public Interest Law," 419–23; "New Council for Public Interest Law is Formed," *American Bar Association Journal* 61 (June 1975): 769.
30. Council on Public Interest Law, *Balancing the Scales of Justice*, 9–10, 37–38, 89–90, 134–46, 318–20.
31. Ibid., 20–21, 37–38, 54, 89–90, 113–14, 140–46, 313–18 (emphasis added).
32. Handler, Ginsburg, and Snow, "The Public Interest Law Industry."
33. Derfner, "One Giant Step," 443–45.
34. For a discussion of the data underling the figures and this paragraph, see Farhang, *The Litigation State*, chs. 1 and 3.
35. Thomas O. McGarity, "Regulatory Reform in the Reagan Era," *Maryland Law Review* 45 (1986): 253–73, 253–54.
36. McGarity, "Regulatory Reform in the Reagan Era"; Decker, *Lawyers for Reagan*; O'Conner and Epstein, "Rebalancing the Scales of Justice"; Vogel, *Fluctuating Fortunes.*
37. Vogel, *Fluctuating Fortunes*, 260–65; Greve, "Why 'defunding the Left' Failed," 101–04.
38. McGarity, "Regulatory Reform in the Reagan Era"; Vogel, *Fluctuating Fortunes*, 246–51; Robert Litan and William Nordhaus, *Reforming Federal Regulation* (New Haven: Yale University Press, 1983), 119–32; Farhang, *The Litigation State*, ch. 6; Farhang, "Legislative-Executive Conflict and Private Statutory Litigation in the United States."
39. Michael S. Greve, "Why 'Defunding the Left' Failed," *Public Interest* 89 (1987): 91–106, 91; Jefferson Decker, *Lawyers for Reagan: The Conservative Litigation Movement and American Government, 1971–87*, PhD Dissertation, Columbia University, 2009, 12–149; Karen O'Conner and Lee Epstein, "Rebalancing the Scales of Justice: Assessment of Public Interest Law," *Harvard Journal of Law and Public Policy* 7 (1984): 483–505; Steven M. Teles, *The Rise of the Conservative Legal Movement: The Battle for Control of the Law* (Princeton: Princeton University Press, 2009), 60–66.
40. Ibid.
41. Decker, *Lawyers for Reagan*, 3–5; O'Conner and Epstein, "Rebalancing the Scales of Justice," 495; Teles, *The Rise of the Conservative Legal Movement*, 60–61.
42. Ronald A. Zumbrun, "Life, Liberty, and Property Rights," in *Bringing Justice to the People: The Story of the Freedom-Based Public Interest Law Movement*, ed.

Lee Edwards (Washington, DC: Heritage Books, 2004), pp. 42–43; Decker, *Lawyers for Reagan*, 3–5; Teles, *The Rise of the Conservative Legal Movement*, 62.

43. Greve, "Why 'Defunding the Left' Failed," 91; Ronald Ostrow, "Legal Services Agency Battles Reagan Attempt to Cut Off Its Funding," *Los Angeles Times*, April 12, 1981, B1.
44. Decker, *Lawyers for Reagan*, 74.
45. Decker, *Lawyers for Reagan*, 5, 160, 251.
46. See Figure 3.2.
47. Sarah Staszak, "Institutions, Rulemaking, and the Politics of Judicial Retrenchment," *Studies in American Political Development* 24 (2010): 168–89. Staszak examines retrenchment of access to courts and judicial authority, investigating a much wider range of strategies than legislative repeal, which is the focus of this chapter.
48. Michael S. Greve, "Why 'Defunding the Left' Failed," 91–106.
49. Greve, "Why 'Defunding the Left' Failed," 91.
50. Decker, *Lawyers for Reagan*, 181.
51. Greve, "Why 'Defunding the Left' Failed," 103.
52. Mike Horowitz to Dick Hauser and Bob Kabel, June 16, 1983, Reagan Library, James W. Cicconi Files, box 23, Department of Justice (folder 1) (emphasis in original).
53. Mike Horowitz to David Stockman and Edwin Harper, June 22, 1982, Reagan Library, John G. Roberts, Jr. Files, box 5, Attorney's Fees (folder 1 of 3).
54. Ibid.
55. David Stockman to Thomas P. O'Neill, July 22, 1982, Reagan Library, John G. Roberts, Jr. Files, box 5, Attorney's Fees (folder 1 of 3).
56. Joseph R. Wright, Jr. to Edwin Meese, III, July 25, 1983, Reagan Library, box 9094, Attorney Fee Reform Legislation.
57. Decker, *Lawyers for Reagan*, 186.
58. Horowitz to Stockman and Harper 7/22/1982 (attachments B and C); Robert Percival and Geoffrey Miller, "The Role of Attorney Fee Shifting in Public Interest Litigation," *Law and Contemporary Problems* 47 (1984): 233–47, 242; Fred Barbash, "... And Uncle Sam Wants to Save on His Legal Fees," *Washington Post*, February 10, 1982, A25; Mary Thornton, "Plaintiffs' Legal Fess Attacked by OMB," *Washington Post*, August 12, 1982, A21.
59. Greve, "Why 'Defunding the Left' Failed"; Decker, *Lawyers for Reagan*, 179–88.
60. E.g., Terry M. Moe, "Political Institutions: The Neglected Side of the Story," *Journal of Law, Economics, and Organization* 6 (1990): 213–53.
61. Paul Pierson, *Dismantling the Welfare State? Reagan, Thatcher, and the Politics of Retrenchment* (Cambridge: Cambridge University Press, 1994), 17–19, 39–46; William Eskridge and John Ferejohn, "Virtual Logrolling: How the Court, Congress, and the States Multiply Rights," *Southern California Law Review* 68 (1995): 1545–64, 1560.
62. Mike Horowtiz to Lee Verstandig and Rick Neal, October 19, 1983, Reagan Library, JL007 Case File 20054, Attorneys' Fees Reform Bill.
63. Decker, *Lawyers for Reagan*, 184–85.
64. Greve, "Why 'Defunding the Left' Failed," 104.
65. William French Smith to Cabinet Council on Legal Policy, June 15, 1983, Reagan Library, James W. Cicconi Files, box 23, Department of Justice (folder 1).

66. Fred F. Fielding to Richard G. Darman, December 16, 1983, Reagan Library, John G. Roberts, Jr. Files, box 31, Legal Fees Reform Act (folder 2 of 3). For additional expressions of this concern, see Fred F. Fielding to Richard Darman, September 21, 1983, Reagan Library, John G. Roberts, Jr. Files, box 31, Legal Fees Reform Act (folder 1 of 3); Edward C. Schmults to Michael Horowitz, June 1, 1983, Reagan Library, JL007 Case File 20054, Attorneys' Fees Reform Bill.

67. Edward C. Schmults to Edwin Meese III, October 31, 1983, Reagan Library, James W. Cicconi Files, box 23, Department of Justice (folder 1); Jonathan C. Rose to Edward C. Schmults, October 27, 1983, Reagan Library, James W. Cicconi Files, box 23, Department of Justice (folder 1); Decker, *Lawyers for Reagan*, 184.

68. Greve, "Why 'Defunding the Left' Failed," 101–02.

69. Rose to Schmults, October 27, 1983; Smith to Cabinet Council, June 15, 1983; Barbash, "... And Uncle Sam Wants to Save on His Legal Fees."

70. Horowtiz to Verstandig and Neal, October 19, 1983; Rose to Schmults, October 27, 1983.

71. Rose to Schmults, October 27, 1983.

72. Ibid.

73. Horowitz to Hauser and Kabel, June 16, 1983; Horowitz to Stockman and Harper, June 22, 1982; Rose to Schmults, October 27, 1983.

74. House Report No. 1418, 96th Cong., 2nd Sess., 1980, 12; Senate Report No. 253, 96th Cong., 1st Sess., 1979, 7; Susan Gluck Mezey and Susan Olson, "Fee Shifting and Public Policy: The Equal Access to Justice Act," *Judicature* 77 (1993): 13–20; Gregory C. Sisk, "The Essentials of the Equal Access to Justice Act: Court Awards of Attorney's Fees for Unreasonable Government Conduct," *Louisiana Law Review* 55 (1994): 217–360, 220–29, 280 n. 396; Ar Lewe S. Ragozin, "The Waiver of Immunity in the Equal Access to Justice Act; Clarifying Opaque Language," *Washington University Law Review* 61 (1986) 217–44, 219–21.

75. "Small-Business Groups Protest Reagan's Veto of Bill for Legal Fees," *Wall Street Journal*, November 12, 1984, 3.

76. *Hearings on the Legal Fee Equity Act (S. 2802) Before the Subcommittee on the Constitution of the Senate Judiciary Committee*, 98th Cong., 2nd sess., 1984, 1–3.

77. Farhang, *The Litigation State*, 68.

78. See Figure 3.2.

79. *Annual Report of the Administrative Office of the United States Courts*, table C-2, 1980–1984.

80. Examples of rare successes were the Portal-to-Portal Act of 1947, Securities Litigation Reform Act of 1995, and Prison Litigation Reform Act of 1996.

81. E.g., Staszak, "Institutions, Rulemaking, and the Politics of Judicial Retrenchment"; Andrew Siegel, "The Court Against the Courts: Hostility to Litigation as an Organizing Theme in the Rehnquist Court's Jurisprudence," *Texas Law Review* 84 (2006): 1097–1202; Pamela S. Karlan, "Disarming the Private Attorney General," *University of Illinois Law Review* 1 (2003): 183–209; Erwin Chemerinsky, "Closing the Courthouse Door to Civil Rights Litigants," *University of Pennsylvania Journal of Constitutional Law* 5 (2003): 537–57.

82. Staszak, "Institutions, Rulemaking, and the Politics of Judicial Retrenchment."

83. Keith Whittington, *Political Foundations of Judicial Supremacy* (Princeton, NJ: Princeton University Press, 2007); Howard Gillman, "How Political Parties Use the Courts to Advance Their Agendas," *American Political Science Review*

96 (2002): 511–24; Kevin J. McMahon, "Constitutional Vision and Supreme Court Decisions: Reconsidering Roosevelt on Race," *Studies in American Political Development*, 14 (2000): 20–50; Mark Graber, "The Nonmajoritarian Difficulty: Legislative Deference to the Judiciary," *Studies in American Political Development* 7 (1993): 35–73; Mitchell Pickerill and Cornell Clayton, "The Rehnquist Court and the Political Dynamics of Federalism," *Perspectives on Politics* 2 (2004): 233–48.

4

Courts and Agencies in the American Civil Rights State

R. Shep Melnick

Major policy change almost always has multiple causes and generates a variety of far-reaching consequences, some intended, many not. This was certainly true of the civil rights revolution of the 1960s that culminated in passage of two of the most important laws in American history, the Civil Rights Act of 1964 (CRA) and the Voting Rights Act (VRA) of 1965. The resulting destruction of the racial caste system in the South not only profoundly affected the position of African Americans within American society, but created a new party system in which the solid Democratic South became solidly Republican. Prohibitions against racial discrimination were quickly extended to ban discrimination based on gender, language, disability, and age. The civil rights revolution changed our understanding of federalism, the proper role of the courts, the powers of Congress, and the authority of administrative agencies. In short, this was a profound constitutional moment that rivaled that of the New Deal.

In this chapter I cannot hope to describe the events that precipitated the civil rights revolution or evaluate the extent to which these laws have reduced racial discrimination and inequality. For the latter I would direct the reader to succinct essays by Orlando Patterson and Jennifer Hochschild.[1] As for the former, I will simply say that the traditional view – namely, that civil rights protests stretching from the 1955–56 Montgomery bus boycott to the 1963 March on Washington briefly made civil rights the most salient political issue in the nation, forcing citizens and politicians to choose between fidelity to the Constitution and the American creed on the one hand and more decades of hypocrisy and unrest on the other – remains more convincing than the various revisionisms that have accumulated over the years. I do not mean to suggest that other factors (such as the growing political power of African Americans in northern cities or the legislative skill of Lyndon Johnson or the fact that decades of international conflict with Nazi racism and Soviet totalitarianism shone a spotlight on our failure to abide by our own principles) were not important. No change as significant as this one can be attributed to a single cause. But in the end it was the nobility of the protestors and their cause and the hideousness of the southern response to them that forced Americans outside the South to decide whose side they were on.

The question I will address here is this: After the Civil Rights Act and the Voting Rights Act were passed and public attention wandered, why did the federal government's efforts to attack racial discrimination and inequality become increasingly aggressive? To put the matter another way, why did the Second Reconstruction not go the way of the first? There are, after all, a number of reasons to have expected that federal enforcement of these laws would be weak-kneed and short lived. Consider the following:

1. After 1965, the salience of civil rights issues plummeted. We know that in many areas of regulation this produces a notable decline in the zeal of regulators. To make matters worse, the urban unrest of the second half of the decade contributed to racial backlash exploited by a number of politicians, most notably George Wallace and Richard Nixon.

2. Most of the enforcement mechanisms in the 1964 act were weak to begin with, largely as a result of the legislative compromises required to garner enough Republican support to overcome the Dixiecrat filibuster in the Senate. In its early years the Equal Employment Opportunity Commission (EEOC) was repeatedly described (by its friends, no less) as a "poor enfeebled thing."[2] The Office for Civil Rights (OCR) within the Department of Health, Education, and Welfare was not only seriously understaffed, but run, according to the seasoned administrative veteran Wilbur Cohen, by young lawyers with "no political knowledge" and "no real administrative ability," "just a bunch of amateurs with real good ideas and very socially minded, wandering around in the desert of Sinai."[3] Neither agency had credible sanctions to impose against employers or subnational governments that violated the new laws.

3. School desegregation remained largely in the hands of federal courts, which had produced virtually no desegregation in the Deep South in the decade following *Brown v. Board of Education.*

4. Opposition to school desegregation and the enfranchisement of black voters remained strong in the South, and southern officials had proven adept at finding ways to circumvent previous civil rights laws.

5. Although there was little chance that the Supreme Court would gut civil rights laws as they had done a century before, some features of the 1964 and 1965 acts – especially the preclearance provisions of the VRA – pushed the limits of what even the Warren court would allow. Both Congress and the Supreme Court emphasized that some parts of the VRA could be justified only as *temporary* measures to deal with *extraordinary* circumstances. That is why key provisions of the act were set to expire after five years. At the time, few expected these temporary provisions to remain in effect until 2031, the date they are currently set to expire.

6. All the new laws prohibited racial "discrimination," but none explained with any precision what that pivotal term means or how it can be proven. These laws did specify what the term does *not* mean: efforts to achieve racial balance, whether in schools or in the workforce. With a directness that often frustrated civil rights administrators, these laws adopted a "color-blind" understanding of civil rights that required a finding of intentional discrimination. Devising a way to give the laws teeth without too obviously demanding some form of racial balance has been a challenge for all civil rights agencies for decades.

7. Above all, we should not forget the monumental nature of the task at hand, changing the behavior of thousands upon thousands of school districts, employers, voting officials, labor unions, banks, realtors, policemen, and ordinary citizens. Not only was this among the most extensive regulatory efforts ever undertaken by the national government, but it challenged deeply rooted customs and mores. In most instances the federal government could not count on the states to carry out these policies, as it had so often done in other contexts. Here the states were the heart of the problem, not a potential administrative ally.

In retrospect, enforcement of two controversial parts of the civil rights legislation of the mid-1960s proved to be relatively easy. The public accommodations section of the 1964 act – at the time its most contentious title – encountered little resistance. It freed commercial establishments from state laws demanding segregation. In most instances violations would have been highly visible. Once Ollie's Barbecue and the Heart of Atlanta Motel were ordered to shape up, resistance collapsed. Second, the prohibition of literacy tests in the seven states of the Deep South had remarkably swift and dramatic consequences for voter registration. Not only was the prohibition clear – thou shall not employ literacy tests – but states were prohibited from engaging in end-runs without first getting approval from federal officials. Clarity and prohibitory language – these were crucial.

One should add that the very passage of the 1964 and 1965 legislations contributed to an underlying cultural shift. Racial discrimination, segregation, and exclusion would no longer be considered acceptable behavior. Racial prejudice did not end – indeed, it may be impossible ever to banish it from the face of the earth – but increasingly it was something that could not be announced or defended in broad daylight. This is hard to quantify. But its importance is even harder to deny.

Other parts of the project announced in the years between 1964 and 1968 proved much harder to achieve. Desegregating southern schools required a monumental effort; the debate over the meaning of desegregation in the North was long and angry. Although the racial achievement gap narrowed significantly in the decade and a half after the civil rights revolution, it remained stubbornly resistant to change thereafter. Guaranteeing "equal employment opportunity" proved even more difficult, especially as good-paying blue-collar jobs began to disappear. Years of "fair housing" regulation did depressingly little to change housing patterns. Housing segregation in turn produced single-race public schools in most large cities. These problems are well known. But it cannot be said that the federal government did not take aggressive action to address them.

THE STRENGTH OF A MISUNDERSTOOD STATE

The assumption that the American state is small and weak compared with those of Western Europe is deeply ingrained in contemporary scholarship. But a number of recent comparative studies have emphasized that when it comes to civil rights, the usual transatlantic pattern has been reversed: American government has been more energetic and more efficacious than its European counterparts. In his examination of race policy in the United States, Britain, and France, Robert Lieberman points out that "the 'weak' American state ... not only produced more active and extensive enforcement of antidiscrimination law; it also managed to challenge the color-blind presumptions of its own law and to forge an extensive network of race-conscious policies and practices that have proven strikingly resilient in the face of political and legal challenges."[4] Abigail Saguy's 2003 book on sexual harassment shows both that American law deals much more harshly with sexual harassment than French law, and that much of the credit for this goes to federal judges. The United States, in effect, has developed a federal common law of sexual harassment despite the fact that Congress has never squarely addressed the issue.[5] Erik Bleich has shown how heavily – and consciously – Britain borrowed from the United States when it sought to strengthen its civil rights laws in the 1970s.[6] Sociologists who study employment discrimination policy have struggled to explain the "paradox" of a weak state producing aggressive regulation.[7]

These comparative studies of civil rights policy are part of a growing recognition that we have seriously underestimated the size and strength of the American state because we have failed to appreciate how it differs from the more centralized and unitary states of Western Europe. For example, Christopher Howard has shown that when one takes into account the many indirect ways in which American government distributes income supports – such as tax credits and loans – the United States sits close to the middle of advanced industrial democracies in terms of percentage of gross domestic product devoted to social provision.[8] Susanne Mettler has described our "submerged state" as a "conglomeration" of federal policies "that incentivize and subsidize activities engaged in by private actors" rather than acting more directly and visibly to achieve public goals.[9] Other policy studies have shown that especially during the 1970s and 1980s, environmental protection in the United States was more stringent than in Europe.[10] Historians have demonstrated that the American "state" was never quite the 100-pound weakling we have imagined.[11]

As both John Skrentny and Paul Frymer have noted in important review essays, a major reason historians, political scientists, and sociologists consistently underestimate the strength of the American state is that they overlook the many ways in which courts can contribute to the power of the central government.[12] By equating state with "centralized bureaucracy," the conventional scholarly wisdom dismiss courts either as irrelevant or as obstacles to the creation of administrative capacity. Their images of courts comes from the *Lochner* era and the New Deal, when it was certainly reasonable to believe that strengthening the administrative capacity of both the federal government and the states required curbing the courts. Both before and after the New Deal, however, "judicial authority has been absolutely essential to the power and reach of the modern regulatory state."[13] Starting in the 1960s, Frymer emphasizes, the federal judiciary "became one of the leading engines of the regulatory state."[14]

The most comprehensive explanation of how courts and litigation have strengthened the American state can be found in Robert Kagan's writing on "adversarial legalism." Adversarial legalism combines an expansion of the responsibilities of the central government with a decentralized, party-driven form of decision making. This odd combination arises from a "fundamental tension" between a political culture "that expects and demands comprehensive governmental protection from serious harm, injustice, and environmental dangers – and hence a powerful, activist government" and "a set of governmental structures that reflects mistrust of concentrated power and hence that limits and fragments political and government authority."[15] Adversarial legalism has become our homegrown alternative to bureaucratic centralization and thus an essential element of the contemporary American state.

FROM "ENLIGHTENED ADMINISTRATION"
TO ADVERSARIAL LEGALISM: CIVIL RIGHTS
AS CRITICAL JUNCTURE AND MODEL FOR EMULATION

As Jeffery Jenkins and Sidney Milkis have shown in Chapter 1 of this book, the conceit that "the day of enlightened administration has come" underlay both the constitutional revolution of the 1930s and the design of most New Deal programs.[16] Three decades later, however, those who considered themselves progressives were growing wary of administrative centralization – especially when Republicans held the White House – and searched for new methods for achieving their traditional goals. Nowhere was the shift from the New Deal commitment to administrative expertise to the fragmented, volatile, and rights-based modes of adversarial legalism clearer or more important than in civil rights regulation. Not only was civil rights the first major policy area in which this change became apparent, but civil rights became the model for a wide variety of policy initiatives. Republicans and Democrats, Congress and the White House all found it convenient to employ this court-based form of policymaking rather than one that created new bureaucracies or required more government spending. The complex nature of the resulting regulatory system – especially the fact that it was hard to see and understand – turned out to be one of its greatest political advantages.

To understand this profound shift in state-building strategies, it is useful to look at the assumptions of civil rights advocates both inside and outside of government on the eve of the 1964–65 civil rights revolution. They were painfully aware of the fact that years of school desegregation litigation by the NAACP had produced virtually no real desegregation in the Deep South, and that the Department of Justice had depressingly little to show for its efforts to use litigation to end the disenfranchisement of African-American voters. Nearly everyone agreed with Judge John Minor Wisdom's assessment in a 1965 school case: "The courts acting alone have failed."[17] The greatest civil rights victory of the pre-1964 era was the desegregation of the military, and this was the result of a presidential order rather than court action. The lesson seemed clear: significant change requires replacing litigation with administration.

The New Deal commitment to "enlightened administration" was particularly evident in the legislative proposals of the Kennedy and Johnson Administrations in the mid-1960s. Consider the following examples:

- To combat discrimination by private employers they proposed creating an Equal Employment Opportunity Commission (EEOC) with powers similar to those of the National Labor Relations Board (NLRB). The EEOC would have authority to investigate complaints, promulgate legally binding rules, and above all issue enforcement orders on hiring practices, reinstatement, and back-pay. The administration's version of the bill made no provision for private enforcement suits. As Sean Farhang has noted, this "administratively-centered enforcement framework" reflected the enforcement preferences of Democratic civil rights advocates in Congress and leading civil rights groups, including the NAACP and the Leadership Conference on Civil Rights. In fact, civil rights leaders "had consistently advocated this administrative enforcement frame-work, with no private right to litigate, in job discrimination bills since 1944, and ... it was the dominant model at the state level."[18]
- What eventually became Title VI of the Civil Rights Act required all federal agencies to deny federal funding to recipients who engage in racial discrimination. This applied above all to state and local governments, including public schools. Since such discrimination was already unconstitutional, Title VI's significance lay in the fact that it added a swift administrative remedy for unconstitutional action, and gave federal agencies authority to write rules defining what constitutes discriminatory behavior. In his explanation of the initial version of Title VI, President Kennedy stated, "Indirect discrimination, through the use of Federal funds, is just as invidious" as direct discrimination "and it should not be necessary to resort to the court to prevent each individual violation."[19]

- The "preclearance" provision of the 1965 Voting Rights Act took the unprecedented step of requiring "covered" states – that is, those states in the Deep South that had engaged in egregious discrimination against black voters – to receive prior approval before making any changes in their elections laws. States could seek approval either from the Department of Justice (DOJ) or from federal courts in the District of Columbia (not the more sympathetic local federal judges). Everyone expected that the DOJ would be the primary forum for resolving these issues, as the delay associated with the judicial process would in this instance work against the states, which would crave quick approval of their laws and specific guidance on what sort of changes would be needed to pass federal muster.[20]
- In 1967 the Johnson administration endorsed fair housing legislation based on a bill previously introduced by Rep. John Conyers and backed by the Leadership Conference on Civil Rights. That legislation "would create a potentially powerful new watchdog agency called the Federal Fair Housing Board ... patterned after the NLRB, and similarly armed with cease-and-desist authority."[21]

This administrative strategy quickly disintegrated. The most obvious problem was Republican opposition to the creation of any agency that resembled the hated NLRB. Republicans on the House Judiciary Committee warned in their 1964 minority report that it would be "a major mistake to model legislation in the field on the National Labor Relations Board, which has one of the sorriest records of all the Federal agencies for political involvement."[22] The GOP's staunch opposition to granting administrative agencies cease-and-desist power, Hugh Davis Graham notes, "reflected the great battle over administrative reform of the 1940s, in which a coalition of Republicans and southern Democrats attacked the regulatory abuses they associated with the New Deal."[23] As Sean Farhang has shown, the House first "judicialized the enforcement forum" for Title VII and the Senate then "privatized the prosecutorial function."[24] As a result, the EEOC came into this world without the power to resolve disputes or even to initiate judicial proceedings – thus earning its reputation as "a poor enfeebled thing."

The funding cutoff, originally viewed as a powerful sanction in the hands of the new offices for civil rights in Health Education and Welfare (HEW) and other federal departments, proved significantly less potent than civil rights advocates had hoped. Administrators quickly discovered that termination of funding for state and local governments is too blunt and extreme a sanction to be politically palatable or administratively attractive in ordinary times. In a report critical of federal agencies' lax enforcement of Title VI, the United States Commission on Civil Rights identified a central dilemma facing these funding agencies: "Although funding termination may serve as an effective deterring to recipients, it may leave the victim of discrimination without a remedy. Funding termination may eliminate the benefits sought by the victim."[25] Just as importantly, funding cutoffs threatens to damage relations between the federal agency and those state and local officials with whom they worked on a regular basis – not to mention antagonizing members of Congress upon whom administrators rely for appropriations.

Statistics provided by Beryl Radin vividly demonstrate the weakness of the funding cutoff. Between 1964 and 1970, the period in which OCR was most aggressive and successful in attacking southern school segregation, it initiated administrative proceedings against 600 of the more than 4,000 school districts in the South. Federal funding was "terminated in 200; in all but four of these 200 districts, federal aid was subsequently restored, often without a change in local procedures."[26] Not only was the termination process procedurally cumbersome and politically hazardous, but some of the most recalcitrant rural districts were willing to forgo federal funds rather than desegregate.[27] At that point, litigation was the only option. As Congress replaced small categorical grants with much larger block grants in the 1970s, termination of funding became all the more awkward. The history of Title IX of the 1972 Education Amendments, perhaps the most popular and successful of Title VI's many "clones," provides additional evidence: the federal Department of Education has *never* terminated funds to enforce Title IX. As we will see, what gave teeth to Title VI and Title IX was the willingness of the federal courts to enforce them by issuing injunctions in suits brought by private parties.

This is not to say that administrative agencies such as the EEOC, Civil Rights Division in the Department of Justice, or various offices for civil rights were unimportant. In fact, since the mid-1960s they have steadily gained new authority and responsibilities. But their power comes above all from the symbiotic relationships they have developed with federal courts. To understand this central feature of both civil rights regulation and adversarial legalism, it will be useful to take a closer look at both Title VII and Title VI.

TITLE VII: TO ENFORCE IS TO INTERPRET

Sean Farhang's chapter in this volume and his important book *The Litigation State* not only trace the way in which enforcement of Title VII was judicialized and privatized, but, even more importantly, why civil rights advocates who had originally regarded this shift "as a bitterly disappointing evisceration of Title VII's enforcement regime" had within a few short years fallen "in love" with it.[28] A big part of the explanation is the remarkable success of court suits brought by the NAACP Legal Defense and Education Fund, which gave high priority to Title VII cases in the late 1960s. Its chief litigator, Jack Greenberg, was not exaggerating when he bragged,

Our Title VII operation was a major triumph in making legal doctrine and achieving social gain – blacks, other minorities, and women won a dramatic increase in the number of jobs available to them and in the higher pay they received in those jobs. In terms of the impact of the change wrought, it was almost on par with the campaign that won *Brown*.[29]

Civil rights groups' faith in the courts was revived, and with the election of Richard Nixon their trust in the EEOC plummeted. In 1969 Greenberg told the Senate Judiciary committee that "the entire history of the development of civil rights law is that private suits have led the way and government enforcement has followed." He added, "With private enforcement we were the captains of our own ship. We took initiatives that more cautious government agencies wouldn't."[30]

In 1972 Congress gave the EEOC power to file employment discrimination suits, but not to issue cease-and-desist orders. Republicans later offered to strengthen the EEOC even further in exchange for limits on private litigation. But civil rights leaders were no longer interested. The institutional issues that had seemed so important to New Dealers of the old school now seemed insignificant. By the early 1970s, Hugh Davis Graham noted, it was clear that both sides in the 1964 debate had been "betting on the wrong horse."[31]

Saying that court cases initiated by civil rights organizations promoted aggressive enforcement of Title VII does not do justice to the enormous changes in public policy wrought by the employment discrimination litigation of the 1970s. One cannot hope to understand the significance of judicial enforcement of Title VII without acknowledging that the federal courts essentially *rewrote* key sections of Title VII, turning a weak law focusing primarily on *intentional* discrimination into a bold mandate to compensate for past discrimination and prohibit employment practices that have a "disparate impact" on racial minorities and women.

When the Senate accepted the "Dirksen-Mansfield substitute" in order to assure passage of the 1964 Act, civil rights advocates were despondent not just over the weakness of the EEOC, but also about the numerous substantive constraints the revised language placed on policymakers. One section of the law explicitly permits employers to use "professionally developed ability tests" as long as they are not "designed and intended or used to discriminate because of race, color, religion, sex, or national origin." Another, added to appease labor unions, protects any "bona fide seniority or merit system." This meant that the significant advantages conferred upon white male employees by previous discriminatory actions could not be taken away, even if this "inevitably had the consequence of impeding the progress of minority employees and women into jobs from which they had previously been excluded."[32] Protecting seniority systems, one district court judge wrote in a frequently cited opinion, threatened "to freeze an entire generation of Negroes into discriminatory patterns that existed before the act."[33]

Even more important were Title VII's explicit endorsement of an "intent" standard and its concomitant rejection of any demands for racial balance in the workplace. The law provides that a court can impose sanctions on an employer only if it "finds that the respondent has *intentionally* engaged in or is *intentionally* engaging in an unlawful employment practice."[34] Anticipating the coming fight over affirmative action, §703(j) announced,

Nothing contained in this title shall be interpreted to require an employer ... to grant preferential treatment to any individual or to any group because of the race, color, religion, sex, or national origin of such individuals or groups on account of an imbalance which may exist with respect to the total number or percentage of persons of any race, color, religion, sex, or national origin employed.

The bill's Senate floor leaders emphasized over and over again that Title VII prohibited only intentional discrimination, not failure to create a racially balanced workforce. In Hubert Humphrey's words,

There is nothing in it that will give any power to the Commission or to any court to require hiring, firing, or promotion of employees in order to meet a racial "quota" or to achieve a certain racial balance. That bugaboo has been brought up a dozen times; but it is nonexistent. In fact, the very opposite is true. . . . Title VII is designed to encourage hiring on the basis of ability and qualifications, not race or religion.[35]

The "Clark-Case memorandum" – a statement by Title VII's floor leaders designed to serve as a de facto committee report – did not mince words: "Any deliberate attempt to maintain a racial balance, whatever such a balance may be, would involve a violation of title VII because maintaining such a balance would require an employer to hire or refuse to hire on the basis of race."[36] The act's chief sponsors' eagerness to demonstrate that Title VII would not institute racial or gender quotas was not just a prudent legislative strategy since "the traditional liberalism shared by most of the civil rights establishment was philosophically offended by the notion of racial preference."[37] As President Kennedy put it a few months before his death, "I think it would be a mistake to begin to assign quotas on the basis of religion, or race, or color, or nationality. I think we'd get into a good deal of trouble."[38]

Although EEOC staff members and civil rights advocates had initially shared this focus on eliminating intentional discrimination rather than mandating racial balance, they soon came to believe that a law limited to attacking overt, intentional discrimination and committed to protecting existing seniority and merit hiring systems would do little to change long-term employment patterns and practices. Alfred Blumrosen, the consultant who spearheaded the EEOC's subsequent policy shift, insisted that adhering to the restrictions embedded in Title VII "would have plunged Title VII investigations into an endless effort to identify an 'evil motive'" and prevented it from "changing industrial relations systems."[39] As violence and unrest spread through the urban North, civil rights groups attacked the EEOC for shuffling paper while the cities burned. The EEOC, John Skrentny notes, "had a limited audience for its performance, and that audience was already booing loudly."[40] It became obsessed with "finding something that *works*, that gets *results*, even if that included race consciousness."[41] According to Hugh Davis Graham, by 1967 the EEOC's commissioners and staff were determined "to mount a 'wholesale' attack on institutionalized racism," ready "to build a body of case law that would justify its focus on effects and its disregard of intent," and "prepared to defy Title VII restrictions." They well understood that this would constitute a major departure from the wording and intent of the 1964 law: "Commission lawyers acknowledged that such a course would set it at odds with the compromise language that was the key to Title VII's passage."[42]

The big story of the first fifteen years of Title VII litigation was how willing the federal courts were to carry out the legislative revisions the EEOC had expected would need to come from Congress. Critics of these decisions have explained in detail how federal judges tortured the wording of the law, most notably in the Supreme Court's 1979 decision in *Steelworker v. Weber*.[43] Even the courts' defenders concede that judges played fast and loose with the statutory language. Paul Frymer, for example, writes that "courts significantly rewrote aspects of the law ... and, in the process, got rid of very carefully placed loopholes that unions and other civil rights opponents had demanded in order to pass the act, turning it from one that emphasize color-blindness to one that underscored affirmative action."[44] Some of this de facto revision of the statute was achieved in Supreme Court decisions.[45] Nearly as significant were lower court decisions such as *Quarles v. Phillip Morris*,[46] *Contractors Association v. Secretary of Labor Association*,[47] and a series of Fifth Circuit decisions on seniority systems.[48]

The Supreme Court's 1971 decision in *Griggs* was particularly important in establishing a disparate impact alternative to the Act's explicit but inherently hard-to-prove "disparate treatment" test. Chief Justice Burger's opinion held that "Under the Act, practices, procedures, or tests neutral on their face, *and even neutral in terms of intent*, cannot be maintained if they operate to 'freeze' the status quo of prior discriminatory employment practices." Under *Griggs*, once the plaintiff shows that a hiring, firing, or promotion practice will have a disparate impact on racial minorities (or women), the burden shifts to the employer to prove that the practice is "related to job performance" and justified by "business necessity."[49] The Court later added a third stage: if the employer offers a convincing business necessity argument, the plaintiff then has an opportunity to show that this is merely a pretext for discrimination. None of these tests or requirements were mentioned in the original version of Title VII.

It is possible, of course, that if the EEOC had been given as much power as Democrats had originally hoped, it would have done much the same as the courts. After all, the courts often followed agency guidelines and advice. It is hard to believe, however, that such action by the EEOC would not have generated serious political opposition. Republicans would have said, "We told you so," and launched an attack on the "runaway bureaucracy." This almost certainly would have led Republican Presidents Nixon and Ford to appoint commissioners less committed to amending the statute through administrative action. Labor unions, too, were highly dissatisfied with the new enforcement policies, adding significantly to the political pressure for greater restraint. Although Blumrosen's claim of imminent agency "capture" by "the interests it set out to regulate" understates the extent to which the EEOC continued to push for aggressive action, the EEOC was certainly more susceptible to pressure from Congress and the president than were federal courts.

Not only were the federal courts more insulated from political pressure, but unlike the EEOC they engaged in statutory revision in a slow, incremental, even stealthy fashion. As a result, it took years for the judicially revised Title VII to emerge. Meanwhile, employers had time to adapt to the new regime. Even more importantly, the Congress that had enacted the original Title VII no longer existed by the time the courts had handed down their major interpretations of the statute. The power of southern Democrats plummeted in the 1970s, as did the number of Republicans in the House and Senate, especially after 1974. By 1975, liberal Democrats dominated the party leadership as well as key positions on the Judiciary Committees, which would be the first stop for any legislative effort to overturn judicial interpretations of the Civil Rights Act. One could say that the courts proved particularly adept at the art of political "salami slicing," that is, piling one incremental change upon another until one has achieved a major policy shift. By the time the Supreme Court, lower courts, and EEOC had assembled the Title VII "sandwich," Congress had changed sufficiently to enjoy the meal. Or at least this was true of the leaders of the key committees, who stood ready to block any legislative amendment of these judicial revisions.

John Skrentny points out that the judiciary was also skillful at *legitimating* this "new model of discrimination." A key part of the judicial art, he argues, is "asserting that what is new (the controversial case at hand) is *not* new."[50] The novelty of the policy established in the pivotal case of *Griggs v. Duke Power* was disguised not only by the Court's rhetorical effort to tie disparate impact analysis to the ultimate purposes of Title VII, but also by the fact that it was written by Chief Justice Burger, a Nixon appointee, for a unanimous Court. For all these reasons, the division of labor established by Title VII proved to be a particularly good mechanism for slowly redesigning the government's attack on employment discrimination without revising the underlying statute.

Ironically, although Congress has repeatedly demonstrated its support both for a disparate impact definition of discrimination and for court-centered private enforcement, by the late 1980s the Supreme Court has become a major *critic* of the regulatory regime created in the 1970s. The Rehnquist court made it more difficult for plaintiffs to get into court, increased the burden of proof on those claiming to have been the victim of discrimination, provided additional defenses to employers, reduced the availability of attorneys fees, limited damages, and generally made it harder for plaintiffs to pursue disparate impact cases. A series of decisions announced by the Court in June 1989 produced a firestorm of criticism from civil rights organizations, Democrats in Congress, and the now-substantial employment discrimination bar. When Congress passed legislation overturning a number of these decisions in 1990, President Bush wielded his veto, denouncing it as a "quota bill." Congress responded by passing the Civil Rights Act of 1991, which overturned even more Court decisions and significantly expanded the damages available to plaintiffs in employment discrimination cases. This time President Bush signed the legislation, which contained enough ambiguities to allow both sides to declare victory. The 1991 Act made it easier than ever for plaintiffs to prevail in employment discrimination cases and – even more importantly – significantly increased the value of winning. After that, as Sean Farhang shows in Chapter 3 in this volume, the number of Title VII cases filed in federal court quickly shot up once again.

No one would ever suggest that the resulting regulatory process is either pretty or efficient. Consider the following description provided by a leading legal expert on Title VII:

Title VII establishes an enforcement scheme that is . . . inherently more complicated than any simple mechanism for purely administrative or judicial enforcement. . . . As result, the legal doctrine governing these issues has become ever more complex, making litigation of employment discrimination cases highly technical and specialized. The doctrinal complexity, moreover, does not point in a single direction, but serves a variety of different purposes, some favorable to plaintiffs, others to defendants. . . . considered together, these policies yield a complex system of enforcement that threatens to side-track employment discrimination cases into a multitude of collateral procedural issues.[51]

Uncertainty, procedural complexity, redundancy, lack of finality, high transaction costs, blurring of lines of responsibility and accountability – these are the central features of adversarial legalism described by Robert Kagan.

The result, however, is *not* weak government regulation. Facing the prospect of paying very large damage awards if they lose in court, employers inevitably look for ways to avoid the financial risks (and bad publicity) of litigation. And the EEOC has been eager to offer them a "safe harbor" from the uncertainties of adversarial legalism. Since 1979 the EEOC has maintained that employers can protect themselves from disparate-impact suits by adopting "voluntary" affirmative action plans consistent with its Uniform Guidelines on Employee Selection Procedures and Guidelines on Affirmative Action.[52] The major effect of the 1991 Civil Rights Act was to increase employers' incentives to sail into this safe harbor. With employers facing greater potential losses and a heavier burden of proof, Rutherglen notes, "affirmative action becomes less and less a voluntary option and more and more a mandatory requirement. It becomes the only realistic way to avoid liability under the theory of disparate impact."[53] This is why many business leaders oppose "reverse discrimination" attacks on affirmative action: victory in these cases would have left them perched precariously between the Scylla of disparate-impact lawsuits and the Charybdis of reverse discrimination challenges, depriving them of any safe harbor in a sea of legal uncertainty. Whatever the flaws of the adversarial legalism, it does not produce a less-powerful central government.

AN "INSPIRED MODEL" FOR ATTACKING THE "OFTEN INTRACTABLE PROBLEM" OF DISCRIMINATION: THE TRANSFORMATION OF TITLE VI

Title VI of the 1964 Civil Rights Act established the principle that "no person in the United States shall be excluded from participation in, be denied the benefits of, or be subject to discrimination under any program or activity receiving Federal financial assistance." It directed federal agencies to issue "rules, regulations, or orders of general applicability" to carry out this provision, and to terminate funding for any "particular program" that failed to comply. Although Titles VI and VII both target racial discrimination (Title VI, unlike Title VII, makes no mention of gender), in several ways they are mirror images of one another. The original version of Title VII applied only to private employers, not public officials. Title VI, in contrast, applies primarily to state and local governments. Title VII was extremely controversial in 1963–64, the focus of the most important bargaining over the legislation. But "almost no attention was paid to Title VI," which Hugh Davis Graham describes as "the sleeper that would become by far the most powerful weapon of them all."[54]

Most importantly, although the Dirksen-Mansfield substitute made private judicial enforcement central to implementation of Title VII, Title VI was consistently presented and defended as a mechanism for replacing costly, time-consuming constitutional litigation with decisive administrative action. President Kennedy, as noted previously, shared this view.[55] Moreover, the Congress that had focused so intently on the enforcement role of the courts under Title VII said nothing about the role of the courts in implementing Title VI. There is no mention of private enforcement suits either in the statute itself or in its legislative history. This was not an oversight. Because it was already unconstitutional either for state and local governments to discriminate on the basis of race or for the federal government to support such activity, suits by aggrieved private individuals were already available – just too cumbersome to be effective. While Title VII made illegal private activities that had previously been legal under federal law, Title VI applied new administrative sanctions against those who violated preexisting *constitutional* norms.

One consequence of that Congress made little effort to explain what would constitute a violation of Title VI. Another was that administration and Department of Justice officials promised members of Congress that HEW would consider any school district subject to a judicial desegregation order in compliance with Title VI, even if that order was not consistent with appellate precedent and even if there were doubts about whether the school district had obeyed that court order.[56] The ambiguous nature of Title VI's substantive requirements – part statutory, part constitutional – at first slowed down southern school desegregation, but it later provided an opportunity for courts and agencies to play a game of policy leapfrog, with each building on the initiatives of the other.[57]

Congressional debate on Title VI focused exclusively on the extent of the powers granted to federal agencies. The House and Senate imposed several constraints on their authority: rules issued under Title VI must be approved by the president himself; federal agencies must give Congress thirty days advance warning of funding terminations; state and local governments are entitled to public hearings prior to termination of funds and judicial review after the fact; and such terminations apply only to the particular program found guilty of discrimination, not to the entire institution receiving funding. Having delegated substantial power to federal administrators, members of Congress wanted to make sure they did not wield it precipitously, arbitrarily, or without giving Congress a heads-up. Congress later prohibited agencies from using "deferrals" to evade these restrictions.

We know from detailed accounts of school desegregation that administrative action under Title VI initially proved a potent weapon for change.[58] Desegregation guidelines issued by HEW in 1965 and 1966 were a crucial component of the "reconstruction of southern education" accomplished at long last in the late 1960s and early 1970s. The threat of fiscal sanctions was made particularly compelling by the new pot of money Congress made available to southern school systems when it passed the landmark Elementary and Secondary Education Act of 1965. But it still took a subtle combination of judicial and administrative action to desegregate southern schools. According to Gary Orfield, who has provided one of the best descriptions of OCR's early years, "The policy shift announced by the Office of Civil Rights was possible only because of a series of helpful court decisions."[59]

The breakthrough on school desegregation came in 1966–67, when judges on the Fifth Circuit incorporated key elements of HEW's guidelines into their rulings in Fourteenth Amendment cases. In a particularly important opinion, *United States v. Jefferson County Board of Education*, Judge John Minor Wisdom acknowledged that Title VI "was necessary to rescue school desegregation from the bog on which it had been trapped for years." HEW's guidelines "offer, for the first time, the prospect that the transition from a de jure segregated dual system to a unitary integrated system may be carried out effectively, promptly, and in an orderly manner."[60] If administrative guidelines provided courts with the "judicially manageable standards" essential for desegregating schools, the courts offered HEW's Office for Civil Rights crucial political support and credible sanctions. As Stephen Halpern explains in his detailed analysis of this court-agency partnership,

HEW officials realized that federal courts were a good ally, and the agency had few allies in beginning the politically touchy task of enforcing Title VI. ... Time after time, the Fifth Circuit intervened ... to give HEW's school desegregation efforts "a boost." Moreover, in meetings with angry southern educators HEW officials could claim that their hands were tied – that court decisions and hence, indirectly, the Constitution itself, required HEW to be as insistent as it was.[61]

According to Halpern, the southern desegregation effort revealed "the synergistic power of the bench and bureaucracy working together": "federal judges lauded HEW's 'expertise' in writing the Guidelines, and HEW officials, in turn, extolled and relied on the 'objective' policies of the courts." Ironically, as Halpern notes, "The enforcement of a law intended as a substitute for litigation became heavily dependent on and linked to the standards advanced in litigation."[62]

It did not take long for administrators to realize that termination of funding for state and local governments is not politically palatable or administratively attractive in ordinary times. By the late 1960s, HEW's Office for Civil Rights was relying almost entirely on federal courts to enforce the regulations it had issued under Title VI. Judges in school desegregation cases were developing structural injunctions to create detailed, demanding regulatory regimes tailored to the specific circumstances of each school district. These injunctions could be modified on a regular basis. Many remained in effect for decades. Public officials who violated these injunctions could be found in contempt of court, a powerful weapon for compelling compliance. In the five years after *Jefferson County* the Fifth Circuit also adopted novel procedural rules that sharply limited the authority of obstructionist district court judges, significantly reduced the cost of mounting desegregation litigation, and in effect turned appellate review into a form of administrative oversight. Frank Read, who has provided us with a detailed account of these innovations by the Fifth Circuit, notes that these appellate procedures produced a "quantum leap in school desegregation activities." Between December of 1969 and September of 1970, the newly created standing panels of the Fifth Circuit issued 166 "opinion orders" on desegregation.[63] With school districts throughout the South facing the near certainty of specific judicial desegregation orders, funding sanctions faded into irrelevancy.

What courts – especially those in the Fifth Circuit – needed from administrators were guidelines to make their newly acquired tasks judicially manageable. If agency rules had merely tracked previous court rulings defining racial discrimination under the Fourteenth Amendment, they would have been of little help and little policy significance. But agency rules under Title VI went far beyond what the courts had deemed constitutionally required. In order to provide specific guidance to recipients of federal funding, agency rules often created a presumption in favor of racial proportionality. OCR's 1966 desegregation guidelines, the most important set of rules ever issued by that organization, set specific targets for the percentage of black students enrolled in formerly white schools. The Fifth Circuit's embrace of these guidelines not only broke the logjam on school desegregation, but constituted a major step in the redefinition of desegregation. Although the 1964 act specifically stated that desegregation shall not mean the assigning of children to particular schools in order to achieve racial balance, OCR took the first step in that direction and the courts, claiming to defer to agency expertise, took many more. Together they established the expectation that all school districts that had previously engaged in segregation must reconstitute their schools so that none of them are "racially identifiable" – which in effect meant that the racial composition of each school should reflect the racial composition of the district as a whole.[64]

This redefinition of desegregation coupled with the enhanced enforcement capacity of the federal courts not only produced the "reconstruction of southern education," but also raised the enormously controversial issue of busing, first in the South, then in northern and western cities. Both Congress and the White House prohibited OCR from participating in busing cases. This did not mean that OCR merely walked away with its tail between its legs. Instead, it looked for new ways to promote equal educational opportunity using the institutional arrangements now at its disposal. With the blessing of the Nixon White House it undertook a major investigation of racial discrimination within New York City schools and promoted bilingual education for Latino students.[65]

Bilingual education provides a good example of the emerging division of labor between federal courts and federal agencies. In 1970, the Office for Civil Rights in HEW issued new rules on "school districts with more than 5% national origin minority group children." The regulations announced that "when the inability to speak and understand the English language excludes national origin minority group children from effective participation in the educational program offered by a school district, the district must take affirmative steps to rectify the language deficiency in order to open its instructional program to those students."[66] The original rules were not very specific about the content of those affirmative steps. But before long it had issued detailed guidelines for bilingual education. HEW Secretary Elliot Richardson told a Senate committee that OCR would require schools with a significant number of non–English-speaking students to engage in

"total institutional reposturing (including culturally sensitive teachers, instructional materials, and educational approaches) in order to incorporate, affirmatively recognize, and value the cultural environment of ethnic minority children so that the development of positive self-concept can be accelerated".[67]

Failure to follow these guidelines would constitute discrimination on the basis of "national origin" and thus called for termination of federal funding to the school district.

The impetus for these regulations came not from newly formed Hispanic groups but from idealistic young lawyers in the Office of Civil Rights. They received unexpected political support from the White House, which was courting Hispanic voters in anticipation of the 1972 election. But OCR had neither the capacity nor the political will to translate these demanding guidelines into enforcement action. By 1974 it had reviewed only 4 percent of the covered school districts. It found more than half of these districts out of compliance with its regulations. Some of them agreed to remedial plans, but others refused to negotiate at all. Only once did the Office of Civil Rights take even the first step toward termination of federal funds. It was easy for school districts to see that OCR was not willing to use its limited political capital to enforce its demanding regulations.[68]

Once again it was the federal judiciary that came to the rescue of the OCR. In 1974 the Supreme Court heard a Title VI bilingual education class action suit filed by legal assistance lawyers representing Chinese American parents in San Francisco. In its brief opinion in *Lau v. Nichols*,[69] the Court avoided the question of whether the Fourteenth Amendment required school districts to provide education in students' native language by finding that the school was bound by HEW's Title VI regulations. Those regulations, the Court concluded in summary fashion, were well within the power granted to HEW by Title VI. The court implied – but did not specifically state – that the regulations could be enforced by the federal courts. The next year HEW issued more specific bilingual education guidelines, known appropriately as the "*Lau* Remedies". Federal district courts in New York and New Mexico ordered school districts with large numbers of Hispanic students to comply with them.[70]

In school desegregation cases federal judges had required school districts to comply with HEW's guidelines in order to remedy *constitutional* violations. But no one claimed that failure to provide bilingual education constituted a violation of the Constitution. *Lau v. Nichols* thus marked a subtle yet important shift that few appreciated at the time: the federal courts were now willing to entertain private suits to enforce administrative regulations issued under Title VI, even those without any clear connection to the Fourteenth Amendment. This transformed a mechanism designed to create an administrative alternative to constitutional litigation into one that combined broad rulemaking authority for federal agencies with judicial enforcement through private suits.

It is easy to argue that Title VI was intended to give agencies authority to issue "prophylactic" regulations that extend beyond the basic requirements of the Constitution. At the same time, as we have seen, many restrictions were placed on the agency's power to enforce these rules. And everyone knew that termination of funding was a highly visible action that most agencies would take only in unusual circumstances.

The addition of judicial enforcement for private rights of action significantly altered this political equation. Now agencies could write broad Title VI regulations and allow others to take the political heat for enforcing them, something civil rights organizations and federal judges were more than happy to do. Even more importantly, federal judges could enforced these rules not by ordering the termination of funding – by far the most obvious remedy for the violation of Title VI – but by issuing injunctions requiring recipients to alter their practices in specific ways to comply with agency rules. After all, private parties did not go to court asking for termination of funding for the programs in which they participated; they wanted state and local officials to use federal money in different ways. Remarkably, for years the Supreme Court heard many cases under Title VI and its various "clones" (especially Title IX of the 1972 Education Amendments and §504 of the 1974 Rehabilitation Act) without directly addressing the underlying questions of who could file suit and what kind of relief could be ordered by the courts. The lower courts understandably took the Supreme Court's silence as a green light to entertain private rights of action and to issue injunctions requiring compliance with agency rules.

In the 1970s private rights of action under Title VI and Title IX were usually brought by civil rights organizations. Not only were these cases too expensive for most private individuals to pursue, but prospective injunctive relief promised few benefits for those initially aggrieved. In the 1980s, however, the Supreme Court authorized federal judges to award *monetary damages* to plaintiffs in Title VI and Title IX cases. The Court first permitted the award of back pay in a splintered, garbled decision on racial discrimination in the employment practices of the New York City Police Department.[71] A decade later the Court announced that federal courts can require public schools to pay damages to students who have been subjected to sexual harassment by teachers.[72] Soon thereafter it ruled that a student could sue a school district for monetary damages when it fails to take adequate steps to prevent sexual harassment by a fellow student.[73] In each case the Court placed substantial weight on sexual harassment guidelines issued by the Department of Education's Office of Civil Rights, which, it argued, had afforded schools clear notice of what was expected of recipients who received federal funding.

The combination of congressionally authorized attorney's fees and judicially authorized monetary damages significantly increased incentives for private parties to file suits under Titles VI and IX. Eventually a private bar developed to litigate these cases. This had the effect not just of increasing the number of cases filed, but of augmenting the political support for this enforcement mechanism. A better example of path dependency in action would be hard to find.

In 2001 Justice Stevens compose the following ode to the "integrated remedial scheme" that the courts, Congress, and agencies had developed under Title VI:

This legislative design reflects a reasonable – indeed inspired – model for attacking the often-intractable problem of racial and ethnic discrimination. On its own terms the statute supports an action challenging policies of federal grantees that explicitly or unambiguously violate antidiscrimination norms (such as policies that on their face limit benefits or services to certain races). With regard to more subtle forms of discrimination (such as schemes that limit benefits or services on ostensibly race-neutral grounds but have the predictable and perhaps intended consequence of materially benefiting some races at the expense of others), the statute does not establish a static approach but instead empowers the relevant agencies to evaluate social circumstances to determine whether there is a need for stronger measures. Such an approach builds into the law flexibility, an ability to make nuanced assessments of complex social realities, and an admirable willingness to credit the possibility of progress.[74]

In the case then before the Court, the state of Alabama had refused to comply with Department of Justice rules requiring drivers' tests to be conducted in Spanish as well as English. The plaintiffs claimed that Alabama's English-only rule would have a disproportionate impact on those born outside the United States, and therefore violated Title VI. For Justice Stevens this rule reflected "the considered judgment of the relevant agencies that discrimination on the basis of race, ethnicity, and national origin by federal contractees are significant social problems that might be remedied, or least ameliorated, by the application of a broad prophylactic rule." Because the issue in this case, *Alexander v. Sandoval*, was virtually identical to the one decided by the Court a quarter-century before in *Lau v. Nichols*, Stevens consider it an easy one to resolve.

Surprisingly, Stevens lost. As he bitterly and accurately complained, "In a decision unfounded in our precedent and hostile to decades of settled expectations, a majority of this Court carves out an important exception to the right of private action long recognized under Title VI." The Court's majority held that although private parties could sue to enforce the explicit statutory mandate contained in the first section of Title VI, they could not sue to enforce agency *regulations* issued under its second section. Because the Court had repeatedly deferred to federal agencies' interpretation of Title VI in previous cases, this was an odd ruling, to say the least.

Alexander v. Sandoval was in large part a reflection of the Rehnquist court's hostility to affirmative action and to "effects" tests in discrimination cases. The Court's five-member majority in essence said, "Since we interpret Title VI to outlaw only *intentional* discrimination, we will not allow agencies to impose a broader definition through the rulemaking process." But *Sandoval* also indicated that some members of the court – perhaps a majority, but a fleeting one at best – entertain serious doubts about the entire array of institutional arrangements that have grown up around Titles VI and IX. Under *Sandoval*, it would seem, when agencies seek to go beyond the Court's interpretation of Title VI and the Fourteenth Amendment, they are on their own in the enforcement process. They must invoke the awkward funding termination process rather than rely on court-based enforcement by private parties.

Yet it is much too early to write the obituary for Steven's inspired model for attacking discrimination. In a 2005 "retaliation" case brought under Title IX, a closely divided Court seemed to retreat from *Sandoval's* narrow interpretation of the judicially enforceable rights contained in crosscutting federal mandates.[75] In early 2012 the Supreme Court issued a much anticipated decision on private rights of action to enforce federal reimbursement rules for Medicaid. Although the precedents here seemed unusually clear – just a year before the Court had held that the statute did not contemplate such suits – a five-member majority waffled, leaving the door ajar to private lawsuits.[76] That decision was announced just five months before the Court's much-hyped Obamacare decision, *National Federation of Independent Businesses (NFIB) v. Sebelius*. In *NFIB* seven justices took the unprecedented step of holding that new conditions imposed on state Medicaid programs – conditions that were accompanied by an especially generous federal grant – could not be enforced through the threat of termination of funding for previously created Medicaid programs. Telling states that they must expand their Medicaid programs or risk losing billions of dollars of current federal aid, the Court argued, "serves no purpose other than to force unwilling States to sign up for the dramatic expansion in health care coverage effected by the Act."[77] This is "a gun to the head" of the states and "economic dragooning that leaves the States with no real option but to acquiesce." The apparent holding of the Court – that new conditions cannot be enforced through termination of "old" money – not only will be extremely difficult to implement, but seems to imply that any revision of Title VI and its clones will not apply to previously existing programs. It is hard to imagine the justices following the logic of this part of the opinion, at least when civil rights statutes are involved. This area of the law, to put it bluntly, remains a convoluted mess, with the Supreme Court issuing solemn pronouncements about the importance of protecting the "dignity" of the "sovereign" states but often drawing back when it comes to actually restricting enforcement of federal civil rights mandates.

Just as importantly, it has not been unusual for Congress to respond to restrictive court rulings by passing legislation to explicitly authorize private damage suits to enforce agency rules. As Thomas Burke has shown, Congress and state legislatures are often reliable supporters of adversarial legalism.[78] Consequently, it is more useful to examine the reasons behind the growth of this enforcement regime than to speculate about the likelihood of its demise.

The institutional arrangements that gradually evolved under Titles VI and IX were the product of two convictions. The first is that for every federal right there should be an effective federal remedy, created, if necessary, by the courts. As the Supreme Court stated in an earlier "implied private right of action" case, *J.I. Case v. Borak*, "it is the duty of the courts to be alert to provide such remedies as are necessary to make effective the congressional purpose."[79] The second is that neither the tools wielded by civil rights agencies under these statutes nor those employed by the courts – most notably, structural injunctions and §1983 suits – were adequate for uprooting subtle yet invidious forms of discrimination. Implicit in the Court's marrying of private damage suits with administrative regulation is recognition that neither federal agencies nor the federal judiciary can go it alone in creating an effective regulatory regime.

CONCLUSION

The most important moral of the Title VI and VII stories is that adversarial legalism can promote aggressive federal regulation of the private sector and subnational governments. A symbiotic relationship between federal courts and federal agencies has been central to the development of the American civil rights state. They have developed a subtle yet effective division of labor: administrators can focus on writing rules and guidelines, which more politically insulated judges can then enforce. Freed from the politically onerous job of taking enforcement actions against well-connected businesses and state and local officials, civil rights agencies were emboldened to promulgate aggressive regulations they could never hope to carry out on their own. These administrative rules supplied judges with the judicially manageable standards they so often have had difficulty devising on their own. Courts' ability to issue injunctions, award monetary damages, and provide attorney's fees not only put real teeth into the enforcement process, but provided strong incentives for private litigants to monitor the behavior of employers and recipients of federal funding. The growth of the civil rights bar, in turn, provided crucial political support for these institutional arrangements when they were threatened by adverse Supreme Court decisions.

In the early 1970s, just as these new patterns were emerging under civil rights statutes, innovative judges on the D.C. Circuit were marking the arrival of what Judge David Bazelon famously called "a new era in the long and fruitful collaboration of administrative agencies and reviewing courts."[80] According to his colleague Judge Harold Leventhal, courts and agencies "are in a kind of partnership for the purpose of effectuating the legislative mandate."[81] "Our duty," Judge Skelly Wright of the same court announced, "is to see that the legislative purposes hearalded in the halls of Congress, are not lost in the vast halls of the federal bureaucracy."[82] These quotations capture the sense that judges had come to view their job not as constraining administrators, but as collaborating with them to produce more effective – and often more ambitious – government programs. As the history of Title VII so vividly illustrates, sometimes vindicating broad "legislative purposes" meant ensuring that inconvenient statutory provisions *are* in fact "lost in the vast halls of the federal bureaucracy." Such a purposive, non-textualist approach to statutory interpretation, Justice Stevens has told us, "builds into the law flexibility, an ability to make nuanced assessments of complex social realities, and an admirable willingness to credit the possibility of progress."

These new institutional arrangements were not carefully planned, but slowly evolved through accidents, miscalculations, experimentation, opportunistic lawyering, and assorted other forms of "muddling through." In the long run these arrangements survived and prospered because they fit so well with key features of the new political environment. Years of divided government eroded Democrats' and civil rights leaders' faith in the executive branch and in New Deal institutional norms. Growing public suspicion of "big government" – and especially centralized bureaucracy – led advocates to search for ways to attack various forms of discrimination without seeming to expand the power of federal bureaucrats. Within a decade of passage of the civil rights laws of the 1960s, it was clear that the days of enlightened administration had come and gone. The era of it adversarial legalism was upon us.

The Rehnquist court's decisions in *Sandoval*, in the Title VII cases overturned by the Civil Rights Act of 1991, and in a large number of cases limiting the jurisdiction of the federal courts indicate that since the late 1980s the Supreme Court has had second thoughts about the wisdom of the policies and institutional arrangements described above. One cannot hope to understand the divisions within the Rehnquist and Roberts Courts without appreciating the extent to which the justices disagree profoundly on whether the civil rights state created through adversarial legalism constitutes an "inspired model" for attacking discrimination or a judicially abetted perversion of federalism and separation of powers.[83]

Once created, however, institutions are hard to displace. Despite repeated warnings about imminent retrenchment, the civil rights policies and institutions established in the 1960s and 1970s have proved remarkably resilient. Legal protections first provided to African Americans on the basis of the extraordinary and unique injury done to them have now been extended to a variety of additional groups, some of them defined in rather ambiguous terms. Much of this regulatory regime remains, to use Suzanne Mettler's term, submerged. But it is not weak or ineffective, and it will not soon fade away.

Notes

1. Orlando Patterson, "The Paradox of Integration," in *The Ordeal of Integration: Progress and Resentment in America's "Racial" Crisis* (New York: Basic Books, 1997); and Jennifer Hochschild, "You Win Some, You Lose Some: Explaining the Pattern of Success and Failure in the Second Reconstruction," in Morton Keller and R. Shep Melnick, eds. *Taking Stock: American Government in the Twentieth Century* (Cambridge: Woodrow Wilson Center Press and Cambridge University Press, 1999).
2. The phrase initially appeared in Michael Sovern, *Legal Restraints on Racial Discrimination in Employment* (New York: Twentieth Century Fund, 1966), p. 205.
3. Quoted in Gareth Davies, *See Government Grow* (Lawrence, KS: University Press of Kansas, 2007), pp. 112–13.
4. Robert Lieberman, "Weak State, Strong Policy: Paradoxes of Race Policy in the United States, Great Britain, and France," *Studies in American Political Development* 16 (2002): 139. Also see Robert Lieberman's *Shaping Race Policy: The United States in Comparative Perspective* (Princeton, NJ: Princeton University Press, 2005).
5. Abigail Saguy, *"What is Sexual Harassment?" From Capital Hill to the Sorbonne* (Berkeley: University of California Press, 2003). Also see Steven Teles, "Positive Action or Affirmative Action? The Persistence of Britain's Antidiscrimination Regime," and Erik Bleich, "The French Model: Color-Blind Integration," both in John Skrentny, ed., *The Color Lines: Affirmative Action, Immigration, and Civil Rights Options for America* (Chicago: University of Chicago Press, 2001): 241–69 (Teles), 270–96 (Bleich).
6. Erik Bleich, *Race Politics in Britain and France: Ideas and Policymaking since the 1960s* (New York: Cambridge University Press, 2003), ch. 4.
7. Frank Dobbin and John R. Sutton, "The Strength of a Weak State: The Rights Revolution and the Rise of Human Resources Management Divisions," *American Journal of Sociology* 104 (1998): 441–76; Frank Dobbin, *Inventing Equal Opportunity* (Princeton, NJ: Princeton University Press, 2009). The first chapter of Dobbin's book is titled "Regulating Discrimination: The Paradox of a Weak State." For another example, see Pedriana and Stryker, "The Strength of a Weak Agency: Enforcement of Title VII of the 1964 Civil Rights Act and the Expansion of State Capacity, 1965–71," *American Journal of Sociology* 110 (2004): 709–760.

8. Howard, *The Welfare State Nobody Knows* (Princeton, NJ: Princeton University Press, 2007).

9. Mettler, "Reconstituting the Submerged State: The Challenges of Social Policy Reform in the Obama Era," *Perspectives on Politics* 8 (2010): 803–24; also see Adam Sheingate, "Why Can't Americans See the State," *The Forum* 7 (2009).

10. See, for example, David Vogel, *National Styles of Regulation: Environmental Policy in Great Britain and the United States* (Ithaca, NY: Cornell, 1986).

11. William Novak, "The Myth of the 'Weak' American State," *American Historical Review* 113 (2008): 752–772; and *The People's Welfare: Law and Regulation in Nineteenth-Century America* (Chapel Hill, NC: University of North Carolina Press, 1996); Brian Balogh, *A Government Out of Sight: The Mystery of National Authority in Nineteenth-Century America* (Cambridge: Cambridge University Press, 2009).

12. Paul Frymer, "Law and American Political Development," *Law and Social Inquiry* 33 (2008): 789–803; Skrentny, "Law and the American State," *Annual Review of Sociology* 32 (2006): 213–244.

13. Frymer, "Law and American Political Development," p. 789.

14. Frymer, *Black and Blue: African Americans, the Labor Movement, and the Decline of the Democratic Party* (Princeton, NJ: Princeton University Press, 2008), p. 16.

15. Robert Kagan, *Adversarial Legalism: The American Way of Law* (Cambridge, MA: Harvard University Press, 2001), p. 15.

16. Jeffery A. Jenkins and Sidney M. Milkis, "Introduction: The Rise of a Policy State?" in this volume.

17. *U.S. v. Jefferson County Board of Education I*, 372 F. 2d 859 (1966).

18. Sean Farhang, *The Litigation State: Public Regulation and Private Lawsuits in the U.S.* (Princeton, NJ: Princeton University Press, 2010), pp. 99.

19. H.R. Document #124, 88th Cong., 1st Sess. (1963), p. 12.

20. Abigail Thernstrom, *Voting Rights and Wrongs: The Elusive Quest for Racially Fair Elections* (Washington, DC: AEI, 2009); and Maurice Cunningham, *Maximization, Whatever the Cost: Race, Redistricting, and the Department of Justice* (New York: Praeger, 2001).

21. Graham, *The Civil Rights Era: Origins and Development of National Policy* (Oxford, 1990), p. 261. A year later this strong-agency approach was jettisoned in order to attract the support of Senator Dirksen and other Republicans. The details are laid out in Graham, ch. 10.

22. House Report #570, p. 19, quoted in Farhang, *Litigation State*, p. 101.

23. Graham, *Civil Rights Era*, p. 130.

24. Farhang, *Litigation State*, p. 106.

25. "Federal Title VI Enforcement to Ensure Nondiscrimination in Federally Assisted Programs," Report of the U.S. Commission on Civil Rights, June, 1996, p. 40.

26. Beryl Radin, *Implementation, Change, and the Federal Bureaucracy* (New York: Teachers College Press, 1977), p. 14.

27. Stephen Halpern, *On the Limits of the Law: The Ironic Legacy of Title VI of the Civil Rights Act* (Baltimore: Johns Hopkins University Press, 1995), pp. 51–52; Gary Orfield, *The Reconstruction of Southern Education: The Schools and the 1964 Civil Rights Act* (New York: Wiley-Interscience, 1969), pp. 241–43.

28. Farhang, "Regulation, Litigation, and Reform," in this volume.

29. Greenberg, *Crusaders in the Courts: Legal Battles of the Civil Rights Movement*, Anniversary Edition (New York: Twelve Tables Press, 2004), p. 443.
30. Quoted in Farhang, *Litigation State*, p. 145.
31. Graham, *Civil Rights Era*, pp. 430–31.
32. George Rutherglen, *Employment Discrimination Law: Visions of Equality in Theory and Doctrine*, second edition (St. Paul, MN: Foundation Press, 2007), p. 152.
33. *Quarles v. Phillip Morris*, 279 F. Supp. 505 (E.D.Va., 1968), at 516.
34. 7036(g), emphasis added.
35. 110 Congressional Record 6549 (1964).
36. Quoted in Graham, *Civil Rights Era*, pp. 150–51.
37. Graham, *Civil Rights Era*, p. 120.
38. Quoted in Graham, *Civil Rights Era*, p. 106.
39. Alfred W. Blumrosen, *Modern Law: The Law Transmission System and Equal Employment Opportunity* (Madison: University of Wisconsin Press, 1993), p. 75.
40. John David Skrentny, *Ironies of Affirmative Action: Politics, Culture, and Justice in America* (Chicago: University of Chicago Press, 1996), p. 127.
41. Ibid., p. 115, emphasis in the original.
42. Graham, *Civil Rights Era*, p. 250.
43. See, for example, Justice Rehnquist's dissent in *Weber*, Justice Scalia's dissent in *Johnson v. Transportation Agency* 480 U.S. 616 (1987); Nelson Lund, "The Law of Affirmative Action In and After the Civil Rights Act of 1991: Congress Invites Judicial Reform," *George Mason Law Review* 6 (1997): 87, and Herman Belz, *Equality Transformed: A Quarter-Century of Affirmative Action* (Piscataway, NJ: Transaction Publishing, 1991).
44. *Black and Blue: African Americans, the Labor Movement, and the Decline of the Democratic Party* (Princeton, NJ: Princeton University Press, 2008), p. 87.
45. In addition to *Weber* these included *Griggs v. Duke Power* 401 U.S. 424 (1971), *Albemarle Paper Co. v. Moody*, 422 U.S. 405 (1975), and *Franks v. Bowman Transportation Co.*, 424 U.S. 747 (1976).
46. 279 F. Supp. 505 (E.D. Va., 1968).
47. 442 F.2d 159 (3rd Cir., 1971).
48. These decisions are described in Blumrosen, *Modern Law*, pp. 95–96.
49. *Griggs v. Duke Power* 401 U.S. 424 (1971) Emphasis added.
50. *The Ironies of Affirmative Action*, pp. 159–60.
51. Rutherglen, *Employment Discrimination Law*, pp. 157–59.
52. Blumrosen, *Modern Law*, pp. 237–46.
53. *Employment Discrimination Law*, p. 90.
54. *Civil Rights Era*, p. 83.
55. H.R. Document #124, 88th Cong., 1st Sess. (1963), p. 12.
56. Orfield, *The Reconstruction of Southern Education*, pp. 72–75; Beryl Radin, *Implementation, Change and the Federal Bureaucracy* (New York: Teachers' College Press, 1978), pp. 106–07; Allan Wolk, *The Presidency and Black Civil Rights: Eisenhower to Nixon* (Hackensack, NJ: Fairleigh Dickinson University Press, 1971), p. 126.
57. I have developed this theme in excessive length in "The Crucible of Desegregation: 'Unitary' Schools in a Divided Court," Paper Prepared for delivery at the Annual Meeting of the American Political Science Association, Seattle, Washington Sept. 1–4, 2011.

58. Halpern, *On the Limits of the Law*; Orfield, *The Reconstruction of Southern Education*; Hugh Davis Graham, "Since 1964: The Paradox of American Civil Right Regulation," in Melnick and Keller, eds., *Taking Stock*; Radin, *Implementation, Change and the Federal Bureaucracy*.

59. Orfield, *Reconstruction*, p. 340.

60. Quoted in Halpern, *On the Limits of the Law*, p. 61.

61. Ibid., p. 73.

62. Ibid., pp. 73, 67, and 76.

63. Frank Read, "Judicial Evolution of the Law of School Integration since *Brown v. Board*," *Law and Contemporary Problems* 39 (1975): 32. For an extended examination of the innovations and internal politics of the Fifth Circuit during the 1960s, see Frank Read and Lucy McGough, *Let Them Be Judged: The Judicial Integration of the Deep* South (Lanham, MD: Scarecrow Press, 1978).

64. See *Green v. County School Board*, 391 U.S. 430 (1968) and *Swann v. Charlotte-Mecklenburg Board of Education*, 402 U.S. 1 (1971). I describe the roles played by OCR, the Fifth Circuit, and the Supreme Court in moving toward a policy of desegregation "by the numbers" in "The Crucible of Desegregation," op. cit., n. 58.

65. For an extended examination of the former, see Michael Rebell and Arthur Block, *Equality and Education: Federal Civil Rights Enforcement in the New York City School System* (Princeton, NJ: Princeton University Press, 1985). On the latter, see Gareth Davies, *See Government Grow*, ch. 6 and John Skrentny, *The Minority Rights Revolution* (Cambridge, MA: Harvard University Press, 2002), ch. 7.

66. Quoted in Davies, *See Government Grow*, p. 151.

67. Quoted in Davies, *See Government Grow*, p. 153.

68. Davies, pp. 147–57.

69. *Lau v. Nichols* 414 U.S. 563 (1974).

70. Davies, *See Government Grow*, pp. 160–61.

71. *Guardians Association of NYC Police Dept. v. Civil Service Commission* 463 U.S. 582 (1983).

72. *Franklin v. Gwinnett County Public Schools* 503 U.S. 60 (1992); and *Gebster v. Lago Vista Independent School District* 524 U.S. 274 (1998).

73. *Davis v. Monroe County Board of Education* 526 U.S. (1999).

74. *Alexander v. Sandoval*, 532 U.S. 275 (2001).

75. *Jackson v. Birmingham Boar of Education*, 544 U.S. 167 (2005).

76. *Douglas v. Independent Living Center of Southern California*, 565 U.S. – (2012); and *Astra USA v. Santa Clara County*, 563 U.S. – (2011).

77. 567 U.S. – (2012).

78. Burke, *Lawyers, Lawsuits, and Legal Rights: The Battle over Litigation in American Society* (Berkeley: University of California Press, 2002), esp. chs. 2 and 5.

79. 377 U.S. 426 (1964), at 433.

80. *EDF v. Ruckelshaus*, 439 F.2d 589 (D.C. Cir., 1971) at 597.

81. *Portland Cement Assoc. v. Ruckelshaus*, 486 F. 2d 375 (D.C. Cir., 1973), at 394.

82. *Calvert Cliffs Coordinating Committee v. AEC*, 449 F. 2d 1109 (D.C. Cir., 1971), at 1111.

83. For examples, see Andrew Siegel, "The Court Against the Courts: Hostility to Litigation as an Organizing Theme in the Rehnquist Court's Jurisprudence," *Texas Law Review* 84 (2006): 1097; and Melnick, "Deregulating the States: The Political Jurisprudence of the Rehnquist Court," in Tom Ginsburg and Robert Kagan, eds., *Institutions and Public Law: Comparative Approaches* (New York: Peter Lang, 2005).

5

The Politics of Labor Policy Reform

Dorian T. Warren

For more than sixty years, since Congress passed the Taft-Hartley Act in 1947 over President Truman's veto, organized labor has sought major labor law reform to shift the industrial playing field on which unions and employers play. In five attempts over six decades, the American labor movement has failed every time to achieve reform of national labor policy, including most recently in the first two years of the Obama Administration.[2] In addition to failing to win new legislative enactments, organized labor has also failed to prevent policy drift in labor law to respond to significant changes in the American economy and increasingly hostile employer behavior toward unions over the last half of the twentieth century.[3] Indeed, in recent years there have been strong attacks on staple union rights such as collective bargaining, most notably in Michigan – the home of the once-powerful United Auto Workers – which became the twenty-fourth state to enacted a "right to work" law in March 2013.

This failure of the American labor movement over six decades – at moments of both organizational strength and weakness – to enact its most important legislative priority and respond to shifting environmental conditions raises a puzzle. Why and how has organized labor, the largest and strongest mass-membership interest group in American politics, failed repeatedly over sixty years to win labor policy reform through the political system? And how is it that the Democratic Party has failed to deliver reform for its core constituency of the twentieth century, especially at moments of party control over Congress and the White House? These two questions are even more puzzling considering the unique position of the labor movement within the Democratic Party in the United States, especially considering the absence of a labor party.[4] One cannot understand the politics of the Democratic Party without understanding the central role of organized labor. Indeed, since the 1930s New Deal era, organized labor has been the most powerful core constituency of the national Democratic

Party by several measures, including campaign contributions, grassroots mobilization efforts of the party's key voters, lobbying, and setting the party's legislative agenda.[5] The 1932 critical election sparked a political realignment that permanently incorporated the labor movement as a core constituency of the twentieth century Democratic Party, so much so that J. David Greenstone proclaimed organized labor as the "national electoral organization of the national Democratic Party."[6] And after eight years of Republican rule of the executive branch at the beginning of the twenty-first century, the labor movement spent more money than ever to get a Democrat successfully elected to the White House in 2008.[7]

In this chapter, I analyze organized labor's attempts at labor law reform since the 1940s. To account for failure, I argue that several long-term institutional and political obstacles present throughout twentieth century American politics including the geographical concentration of labor and conservative coalition in Congress, combined with antimajoritarian features of the American state, have been and continue to be insurmountable for the labor movement. However, in lieu of the continuing and unsurprising failure of labor law reform, prolabor Democratic presidents do offer inducements and advance some labor policy reforms through administrative politics – appointments and rulemaking – with the potential to strengthen unions politically. Yet these minor reforms and redirection of labor policy have not been enough to change organized labor's overall postwar trajectory, with short- and long-term political implications for labor, the Democratic Party, and American politics.

AMERICAN INEQUALITY AND THE CRISIS
OF ORGANIZED LABOR

Why are attempts at labor policy reform important for the American labor movement and American politics? The severe decline in union membership over the latter half of the twentieth century and the related rise in economic inequality are two reasons why labor law reform is and has been the most important national legislative priority for organized labor, especially over the last twenty years. With membership numbers peaking in the mid-1950s when roughly one in three American workers was a member of a labor union, unions have lost millions of members in the subsequent decades with ramifications for both the labor movement and patterns of inequality in the United States. Today, only one in ten American workers are members of a union, the lowest level in more than seventy years, with union density now at just 11.9 percent overall and 6.9 percent in the private sector, historic lows not seen since the previous Gilded Age.[8] And in 2009, unionized workers in the *public sector* became the majority of all union workers for the first time in American history. This shift became consequential in 2010–2011 as public sector employees in several states, most notably Wisconsin, lost significant rights to organize and engage in collective bargaining, a development taken up in more detail later. This steep decline of union membership rates over the postwar period resulted in a subsequent decline in organized labor's economic bargaining power vis-à-vis employers, and a potential decline in political bargaining power vis-à-vis elected officials.

The decline in labor's stature even weakened its influence within the Democratic Party. So much was dramatically revealed during the 1960s. As Nelson Lichtenstein has argued, Lyndon Johnson and the architects of the Great Society showed indifference to workplace reform: "During the very same years in which the social imagination of American reformers took wing, labor's historic agenda – for a democratic workplace, an organizational breakthrough into the new white collar occupations, and a progressive reform of the labor law – sank from sight in all but the most radical circles." Sixties activists, Lichtenstein reveals, tended to view labor unions as a privileged interest group that obstructed liberating reform.[9] By the 1980s, "New" Democrats – seeking to withstand the Reagan "Revolution" – argued that unions served as a drag on the party's ability to come to terms with developments such as globalization and deindustrialization. Bill Clinton's administration pushed the North American Free Trade Agreement through Congress, even though most labor unions strongly opposed it.

The long-term loss of union members and labor's declining economic and political power raise the question of the future survival of the labor movement. Without some kind of national labor policy reform and a modernization of labor law that adapts to the new economic and political context and decades of policy drift, private-sector unionization and the overall power of labor will continue to decline. Labor decline is even more likely with the subtraction of rights and added constraints on unions in the public sector more recently. The decline in union membership numbers and bargaining power has implications for both the labor market and political outcomes. Deunionization since the 1970s explains at least a third of the rise in wage inequality among men and a fifth of the rise in wage inequality among women.[10] In addition, many unions argue that labor law reform that encourages union organization would be a significant, if indirect, policy solution to the problem of growing economic inequality and the catastrophe of the Great Recession.[11] Insofar as unions rectify the inequality in bargaining power between workers and employers, one of the original aims of the 1935 Wagner Act,[12] higher union density decreases wage inequality in the American labor market while increasing purchasing power of consumers.[13] Yet, relative to other advanced industrialized democracies, organized labor is weakest in the United States, partly explaining the cross-national variation in labor market outcomes and government redistribution.[14] The organizational structure of American labor is less encompassing, less centralized, and less powerful absent the institutional conditions for strong unions and an effective labor party.[15] This matters for issues of economic inequality; in industrial and post-industrial democracies, labor unions are often the necessary and decisive actors in efforts to reduce pretax and transfer inequality in the labor market as well as inequality through government redistribution.[16]

The steep loss of union members over the last four decades is also consequential for political outcomes. Rising economic inequality has been coupled with political inequality in American politics, affecting the political voice of middle- and working-class citizens, government responsiveness, and public policy outcomes.[17] Organized labor has often served as a countervailing force against economic power in American politics, giving voice to less-powerful constituents in the political system.[18] Yet with the stark decline in union economic and political power, "big business" and the affluent have regained power vis-à-vis "little labor" and the economically disadvantaged in the contemporary politics of "organizational combat."[19] Across political issues, the labor movement, in spite of its declining stature, is still the strongest organizational force in the Democratic Party, and unions still wield power through electoral campaigns as well as lobbying and pressure in the national political system.[20] As Larry Jacobs and Desmond King argue, analysts must take into account the central fact of imbalances in *organized forces* that pressure Congress and the White House on a range of issues.[21] Absent a strong countervailing political constituency such as organized labor, well-organized and more powerful stakeholders such as business, industry groups, and the wealthy are able to exert undue influence in American democracy.[22] Measured by both members and money, the labor movement is the most powerful and resourceful political constituency on the political left in American politics. This is increasingly true relative to the decline in mass membership organizations over the last half-century.[23] Thus, the political implications of union decline are clear: if the labor movement does not stop the continued haemorrhaging of union members and spark a widespread renewal, it loses its ability to deliver votes and resources for the Democratic Party in future elections and affect policy outcomes in national politics.

THE POLITICS OF UNION DECLINE AND LABOR POLICY

The organizational strength and power of the American labor movement is political, not economic, and labor policy is decisive in shaping its trajectory. Labor policy is a broad and expansive area comprising regulation of the American workplace as well as the promotion of international labor standards, often through trade policy. At the federal level, labor and employment policies are monitored and enforced by a plethora of agencies such as the National Labor Relations Board, National Mediation Board, Equal Employment Opportunity Commission, Departments of Commerce and State, and Department of Labor (which includes the Occupational Safety and Health Administration). These agencies are sometimes mutually reinforcing, yet often come into conflict.[24] Workplace regulation encompasses more than 150 laws focused on setting workplace standards and protections for *individual* workers such as minimum wage, antidiscrimination, and health and safety standards. Labor and employment policy also includes enabling laws that govern labor relations for *collectives* of workers via union organization and representation, as well as class-action lawsuits in the judicial system. Several aspects of trade policy also fall under labor policy, with implications for labor standards around the world.

The economic and political strength of organized labor is strongly shaped by the state and its role in structuring labor market institutions and the rules of the game for labor-business interactions.[25] Political conflicts around labor policy within the American political economy are often characterized by organized capital and business interests attempting to shape markets to their benefit by lobbying for favorable rules and subsidies, whereas labor, on the other hand, often responds to the vicissitudes of market outcomes in capitalist democracies by pushing for what T.H. Marshall called "social citizenship": social protections for workers and the disadvantaged, whether through social welfare legislation, favorable rules for organizing and collective bargaining, or other mechanisms advancing economic rights.[26] Yet these political contests do not occur in a vacuum; the political construction of racial and economic orders directly shapes social groups' rights and the political opportunities they have to organize and mobilize.[27] As sociologist Fred Block writes:

Labor markets, in short, are politically structured institutions in which the relative power of the participants is shaped by legal institutions that grant or deny certain baskets of rights to employers and employees. And this, in turn, generates an ongoing process of political contestation to shape and reshape these ground rules to improve the relative position of the different actors.[28]

This central insight describes the always-contentious politics of labor law and policy in the United States, from slave codes in the eighteenth century, anti-conspiracy legal reforms in the nineteenth, the Wagner Act and Taft-Hartley in the twentieth, to EFCA[29] in the twenty-first century.[30] Labor law strongly shapes the development of labor movements as economic and political actors,[31] but in racially specific ways in the case of the United States.[32] Thus, the politics of labor policy in democracies means that both organized labor and organized capital always attempt to shape this legal framework – the rules of governing the industrial playing field – to their respective advantage. But whether political elites offer inducements or constraints to labor is a function of the power of organized labor and its opponent, organized capital, at any given historical moment and under specific political conditions.[33]

With a brief and temporary exception during World War I, the American labor movement did not gain explicit and positive rights to form and act on behalf of workers until the 1930s. And from the moment the union-enabling 1935 National Labor Relations Act (NLRA) was ruled constitutional two years after its passage,[34] the inducements labor won for the right to organize, right to collective bargaining, and right to strike have each been under attack and successfully curtailed by organized capital and its political allies. After recovering their temporarily displaced structural and instrumental power caused by the Great Depression,[35] employers fought for and won several significant victories from the 1940s and throughout the latter half of the twentieth century, from legislative reforms encoding their backlash to New Deal labor reforms that constrained the power of workers (1947 Taft-Hartley and 1959 Landrum-Griffin bills) to successful attempts to block prolabor labor law reforms meant to address policy drift in the 1960s, 1970s, 1990s, and 2000s.[36]

Now over seventy-five years old, the Wagner Act is a relic of the industrial economic and political New Deal orders under which it was enacted.[37] Scholars have described its "ossification" and inability to address the major challenges facing workers under a new economic regime with new norms and practices.[38] Job instability and insecurity caused by increased global competition for goods and services, contingent and part-time work, short-term contracts and employment attachments, and volatile and frequent shifts in consumer demand requiring flexible management practices characterize the dominant features of the contemporary postindustrial, service-based digital workplace.[39] But while these economic factors might account for many of the challenges facing organized labor and describe its decline,[40] political explanations far better explain the plight of the labor movement.[41]

Taking advantage of such ossification of the Wagner Act over the last decades of the twentieth century, employers have become much more aggressive at violating workers' rights to organize under a much less protective labor law regime that, contrary to the intent of the NLRA, now provides perverse incentives for employers to break the law.[42] Although American employers have always been "exceptionally" hostile to workers and broader issues of workplace democracy,[43] since the 1970s firms have increased their "union avoidance" practices, particularly illegal ones, with drastic consequences for labor. Economists Richard Freeman and James Medoff first described this shift its effects in their classic 1984 book, *What Do Unions Do?*[44] In 1984, they estimated 25 percent to 50 percent of the decline in union density was due to increased management opposition, as opposed to deindustrialization for workers' preferences. By 1994, the Clinton-appointed Dunlop Commission confirmed the increase in employer opposition and illegal conduct during union organizing drives.[45] The Commission found that "in the early 1950s, approximately 600 workers were reinstated each year because of a discriminatory discharge during a certification campaign. By the late 1980s, this number was near 2,000 a year."[46] From the mid-1950s to 1990s, the Commission concluded "the probability that a worker will be discharged or otherwise unfairly discriminated against for exercising legal rights under the NLRA has increased over time."[47] A more recent study with data through 2003 finds that when workers attempt to unionize through NLRB elections, 57 percent of employers threaten to close the worksite, 47 percent threaten to cut wages and benefits, and most egregious, employers illegally fire pro-union workers in 34 percent of union election campaigns.[48] Even when workers are able to overcome intense employer hostility and vote successfully for union representation, a year after the election more than half (52 percent) are still without a collective bargaining agreement due to employer resistance to bargaining in good faith.[49]

What explains this increased and effective employer hostility to unions in the contemporary postindustrial economic era? The identification of the plausible factors to answer this question determines the range of labor policy responses and illuminates the core assumptions behind key provisions of labor law reforms since the 1970s, including the most recent, the Employee Free Choice Act. Scholars have advanced four explanations, each unsatisfactory alone: exceptionality of American employers; breaking of the postwar social contract; weak administrative state capacity; and regulatory capture by big business. The first explanation for the increased and effective hostility of employers is that management in the United States is exceptionally hostile toward workers exercising collective action via unionization. But this is not new. Historically, American employers have always been exceptionally antagonistic toward organized workers, often with the state on their side.[50] What the framing of employer hostility to unions in most accounts today imply (as do the data) is that there was an immediate postwar détente between labor and management, where employers implicitly agreed to a labor-management "accord." It is the breaking of this postwar social contract that scholars offer as the second explanation for employer behavior today.[51] Yet, as Nelson Lichtenstein argues, maybe there was never such a postwar labor-management accord.[52] Instead, after their short-lived victory winning the 1935 Wagner Act permitting them the rights to exist and engage in collective bargaining, unions simply got beat back by employers, as symbolized by the passage of Taft-Hartley at the height of union power.[53]

Although they advance this argument to explain the financial collapse and economic crisis of 2008 leading to our current Great Recession, the third and fourth explanations for increased employer opposition to unions both reflect "a political crisis of the American state," to borrow from Jacobs and King.[54] It is true that the federal government did itself become more hostile to organized labor, as infamously symbolized by former Screen Actors Guild President Ronald Reagan's firing of the Professional Air Traffic Controllers Organization (TCO) workers in 1981. But the larger and longer-standing issue of the American state is its comparatively weak administrative capacity.[55] From its inception, the National Labor Relations Board (NLRB) lacked the adequate enforcement power to monitor and enforce labor law effectively.[56] This might not have been as problematic in the early years when employers were still on the defensive and in some ways did adhere to certain norms as the social contract proponents might argue.[57] But beginning in the immediate postwar period and accelerating in the 1970s and 1980s, NLRB remedies for employer violations of the law have been ineffectual at best, and provide perverse incentives for employers to break the law at worst.[58] Indeed, as early as the 1950s, unions were noting the rise of employer violations of labor law. Several labor officials testified about willful employer violations and the lack of strong enough penalties to discourage such behavior at a House subcommittee on the NLRB (known as the Pucinski Committee) in 1961.[59]

Weak administrative capacity is related to the fourth explanation: regulatory capture. Even if the NLRB had the capacity to monitor and enforce labor law effectively, it would still be prone to regulatory capture by business interests, as we have seen during periods of conservative governance.[60] Initiated by the sharp change in enforcement of the Eisenhower-appointed NLRB, the Labor Board has been a fundamentally partisan agency, swinging back and forth between prolabor and antilabor rulings depending on the party controlling the presidency.[61]

Taken together, all four of these explanations for effective management opposition under the ossified late twentieth century labor law regime capture partial empirical truths. Each factor alone, but especially their interaction with each other, creates enormous historical, institutional, and policy constraints on the ability of the labor movement to halt the decline in unionization and rebuild itself as a real countervailing power to business and corporate interests. It is in this context of increasing hostility to workers' rights and unionization efforts that labor organizations have advocated for labor law reform since the 1970s to fix what they consider a broken system. The hope for such reforms has been that they would reverse labor's organizational fortunes by changing the rules to make it easier to overcome management opposition in organizing drives to recruit new workers and increase the penalties on employers for violating the law.

THE UNSURPRISING FAILURE: LABOR LAW REFORM IN HISTORICAL PERSPECTIVE

As Table 5.1 reveals, for more than sixty years, organized labor has attempted to reform labor laws that circumscribe and limit its strategies, tactics, and power. Labor advocates have attempted major labor policy reforms throughout American political history, with successes coming at rare and exceptional moments.[62] Employer hostility to organized labor, with the national legal

TABLE 5.1. *Labor Law Reform, 1950–2010*

Year: Administration	Reform	House	Senate	Reason
1949–1950: Truman	Repeal Taft-Hartley	Fail	Fail	Conservative Coalition deny repeal
1965–1966: Johnson	Repeal Taft-Hartley	Pass	Fail	Senate filibuster
1977–1978: Carter	Labor Law Reform Act	Pass	Fail	Senate filibuster
1993–1994: Clinton	Striker Replacement	Pass	Fail	Senate filibuster
2009–2010: Obama	Employee Free Choice Act	————	Fail	Senate filibuster

regime on its side, has been the more normal and routine state of affairs.[63] Yet the story of labor law reform failure has deep historical roots and familiar political dynamics.

The business countermovement to retract the Wagner Act, labor's "Magna Carta," began in 1939, when the powerful anti-New Dealer, anti-Communist and anti-labor Representative Howard Smith (D-VA), a leader of the conservative coalition of southern Democrats and Republicans, led a congressional investigation of the National Labor Relations Board.[64] Several of the resulting recommendations from the Smith Committee in 1940 found their way into Representative Fred Hartley's House bill in 1947, which became law after a Republican-led Congress overrode President Truman's veto of Taft-Hartley.[65] The passage of Taft-Hartley, enacted by the political alignment of the "conservative coalition" of southern Democrats with a majority of Republicans, many of whom had voted previously for the Wagner Act,[66] contained several provisions weakening the rules of the game for organized labor. Even the NLRB, the administrative agency responsible for enforcing labor law, took an unusually active role in opposing its passage.[67]

In 1947, exactly a decade after the Wagner Act was ruled constitutional by the Supreme Court, business interests were finally able to accomplish their decade-long campaign to roll back the rights of workers and the national government's explicit encouragement of collective bargaining. Discontent with an inflationary economy and strike waves in 1945 and 1946 propelled Republicans to gain control of Congress for the first time since 1928 in the midterm elections. Both chambers quickly went to work on legislation aimed at reversing much of the Wagner Act passed in 1935, the top domestic policy issue of the 80th Congress. Arguably the most important element of Taft-Hartley was Section 14(b), giving states the right to pass "right-to-work" laws that forbade "closed" and "union" shops.[68] *Closed shops*, workplaces where one is required to become a union member before becoming employed, and *union shops*, where one is required to pay union dues whether or not they support the union, are two institutional mechanisms on which unions rely to overcome the "free-rider" problem.[69] This provision, along with the other aspects of the law, including anti-Communist affidavits for union leaders and a ban on secondary boycotts, would have far-reaching implications for the development of the American labor movement. The new legal framework under Taft-Hartley would ensure that organized labor would remain geographically, economically, and politically contained in a minority of states in the North and far West for the rest of the twentieth century.

Thus was born the first effort to reform labor law. President Truman ran and was reelected on a platform of repealing Taft-Hartley in 1948. Organized labor was as confident then as it would be sixty years later; William Green, president of the American Federation of Labor, proclaimed a few weeks after election day that Taft-Hartley would be "past history" by March 1, 1949.[70] In the Truman administration from 1949 to 1950, labor failed to muster the necessary votes in both the House and Senate. In every attempt at labor law reform since – in the Johnson, Carter, Clinton, and Obama administrations – the political alignment of the conservative coalition (of southern and moderate Democrats with a majority of Republicans), and the supermajoritarian Senate have been the primary stumbling block for labor, despite unions garnering majority support for reform efforts in both chambers. Ironically, it was the Senate that previously served as the stumbling block for employers to reform labor law to their liking from 1935 until Taft-Hartley in 1947.

In the Johnson administration, labor had more access to the White House than it had since the Roosevelt administration, playing a coordinating role on many of Johnson's most ambitious social policy successes including civil rights and broad social welfare policies such as Medicare and War on Poverty programs.[71] But, as noted, labor reform took a back seat to civil rights and other social welfare programs. After acquiescing to Johnson's demand to get his Great Society programs passed before labor law reform, the White House finally gave the green light in mid-1965. Labor law reform – to repeal Taft-Hartley – did pass the House in the summer by a vote of 221-203 over the opposition of the conservative coalition; southern Democrats, in contrast to their northern and western counterparts, voted overwhelmingly along with a majority of Republicans against the reform bill.[72] Johnson overcame filibusters in the fight for civil rights reform; however, in late 1965, when labor law reform arrived in the Senate, a first cloture vote failed to reach a supermajority of two-thirds needed to invoke cloture. Again in 1966, the bill would suffer the fate of a successful filibuster even though labor did reach a majority for cloture. Political scientist Taylor Dark foreshadows the first two years of the Obama administration and labor in describing unions and the Johnson administration: "Ultimately, the grand sweep of liberal accomplishment during the Johnson presidency would bypass a long-standing goal of the labor movement [to win labor law reform via repeal of Taft-Hartley]."[73]

With the election of Jimmy Carter in 1976 and strong Democratic majorities in the House and Senate in the immediate post-Watergate era, organized labor again saw a short political opportunity to achieve labor law reform. After first losing a more narrow "common situs" labor law reform bill in the House aimed at reversing a 1951 Supreme Court ruling limiting the ability and effectiveness of picketing and strikes, unions regrouped and proposed a broader reform bill. The Labor Law Reform Bill of 1978 dropped labor's previous goal of repealing Taft-Hartley that it had pursued since the Truman Administration in favor of a bill that included several provisions aimed at addressing several of the causes of union decline as the labor movement then perceived it. The bill included: faster elections (to be held within thirty days of requesting one with the requisite number of membership cards from workers in a bargaining unit); stronger remedy power for the board including increased penalties for employer violations of the law; expansion of the NLRB from five to seven members to expedite case handling to deal with delays; denial of federal contracts to employers who violated labor laws; back pay for workers in cases where the company refused to negotiate a first contract with a union after a successful certification election; and equal access to company property for unions during election campaigns.[74] Although this labor reform bill passed the House in late 1977 by a wide margin, it stalled in the Senate during 1978 despite majority support, when Senator Orrin Hatch (R-UT) successfully led a nineteen-day filibuster, defeating six attempted cloture votes that brought passage to within two votes.[75] Again, the regionally based conservative coalition of southern Democrats and a majority of Republicans were able to use the supermajority rules in the Senate to block labor law reform over a majority in favor as well as lobbying by President Carter.

The next opportunity for labor law reform was the 1992 election of Bill Clinton, the first Democrat to occupy the White House since Carter. With control of Congress, labor pushed a reform bill focused on ending the practice of the permanent replacement of strikers (as opposed to the second broader reform bill that was defeated under Carter). This proposed reform would help restore the greatly weakened strike tool for labor by banning the use of permanent replacement workers during economic strikes. Although the striker replacement bill won majority support in the House during the summer of 1993, it stalled and was ultimately defeated by filibuster over in the Senate. In the meantime, in an effort to assuage labor leaders who strongly opposed his trade policy, President Clinton appointed the Dunlop Commission to study the problems with labor law and make recommendations for legislative remedies. Unfortunately, although the Commission described in detail the ineffectiveness of the national labor regime in protecting workers' rights and encouraging collective bargaining (as reported earlier), because of the unforeseen Republican takeover of Congress in the fall of 1994, "the work of the Commission was dead on arrival," in the words of Wilma Liebman, Obama's choice to chair the NLRB who stepped down in 2011.[76]

CLOSE, BUT NO CIGAR: THE FAILURE OF EFCA

The 2008 election of Barack Obama with Democratic congressional majorities opened the door for labor law reform for the first time since 1992. First introduced in 2003 and reintroduced in the 111th Congress in early March 2009 by Senator Tom Harkin (D-IA) and Representative George Miller (D-CA), the Employee Free Choice Act (EFCA), the labor movement's number one legislative priority, is the most significant labor law reform legislation in decades. EFCA is seen by many as the twenty-first century version of the Wagner Act, which could alter the rules of the game for organizing workers into unions.[77] Based on the core assumptions of the problems leading to increased and effective management opposition to unionization described previously, the EFCA would amend the National Labor Relations Act in three ways. First, it would allow union certification by the NLRB on the basis of a majority of signed authorization cards by employees in a bargaining unit. Often called "card-check" or "majority sign-up," this mechanism for union recognition would be in addition to the traditional NLRB-sponsored secret-ballot elections, which most unions view as favoring employers. Second, the act would mandate first-contract mediation and arbitration through the Federal Mediation and Conciliation Service if a union and employer are unable to reach agreement on a contract within ninety days. This provision is meant to address the failure of almost half of newly unionized firms to reach a first contract a year after certification.[78] Third, the act would increase penalties for employer violations of workers' rights under the NLRA. These would include treble back pay for workers illegally fired during an organizing or first-contract campaign, and for the first time, civil penalties against employers of up to $20,000 per violation of the law.[79]

EFCA seemed to have momentum toward passage at various moments during the first two years of the Obama administration. At the start of the Obama administration in January 2009, there was no foreseeable path to sixty votes in the Senate, with Senator Tom Harkin (D-IA) proclaiming, "We're waiting for Mr. Franken to arrive. There's no doubt that has a bearing on it."[80] But once Pennsylvania Senator Arlen Specter switched parties and Al Franken (D-MN) was finally seated after sustained business opposition delayed his arrival for months, efforts around the bill began to heat up. A path to the sixty votes needed to overcome southern and conservative Democratic opposition and a threatened Republican filibuster in the Senate seemed possible. At one point during the summer of 2009, Senator Harkin, chair of the Senate Labor Committee and the chief sponsor in that chamber, claimed he would force a vote on the bill before the August recess, only to later backtrack: "I was wrong," he said in one interview. "I think we're 80 [percent] to 90 percent there."[81] But in September, hopes were again revived that labor law reform had enough votes to pass when Senator Specter (D-PA) announced to delegates at the AFL-CIO convention that a compromise deal had been reached on EFCA that he thought would "bring 60 votes for cloture," allowing passage "before the year is up."[82] The compromise would drop the card-check provision from the bill, replacing it with measures for quick or "snap" NLRB elections, meant to speed up the process to rectify the issue of often illegal employer opposition during lengthy election campaigns. Although many union leaders privately agreed with Senator Specter's assessment of the possibility of a compromise garnering the requisite supermajority in the Senate, very few said so publicly (confidential interviews). In fact, there was no compromise according to top labor leaders; the AFL-CIO is "still on card check" proclaimed the newly elected head of the labor federation, Richard Trumka, in response.[83]

Labor's strategy to advance EFCA was two-fold: first, following the patience it displayed during the Johnson presidency, to work with the Obama administration's policy priorities of the economic stimulus and health and financial reform to secure quick victories while waiting for the "right time" for the president to push labor law reform.[84] The second element of the strategy was to reach the magic and necessary number of sixty pro-reform senators by continuing to apply grassroots pressure for EFCA on targeted Democratic moderates in sixteen states through letters, telephone calls, and civil demonstrations.[85] For example, in July of 2009, the AFL-CIO coordinated a rally of about 1,500 union activists and their allies at Senator Blanche Lincoln's Arkansas office to pressure her into supporting EFCA.[86]

But the short window of opportunity to pass labor law reform in late 2009 would come to an abrupt and surprising end at around the one-year mark of the Obama administration. With an already very narrow path to sixty votes in the supermajoritarian Senate, a nail in the coffin for EFCA was the surprise election in January 2010 of Republican candidate Scott Brown to Edward Kennedy's old senate seat in Massachusetts, ending Democrats' short-lived sixty-vote majority in the chamber. When asked about the prospects for labor law reform in response, Senator Harkin replied, "Well, it's, it's, it's there. But it doesn't look too good. I'm not going to give up on it. I'll never give up on it."[87] Even Karen Ackerman, the AFL-CIO's political director, admitted that "there has not yet been laid out a clear strategy of how to win on the Employee Free Choice Act."[88] Proclaiming EFCA "dead" as a result a month later, a prominent liberal journalist declared that "for American labor, year one of Barack Obama's presidency has been close to an unmitigated disaster."[89]

By early spring, the Obama administration sought to reassure unions that labor issues were still vitally important. Meeting with the AFL-CIO Executive Council in March 2010, Vice President Joe Biden assuaged angry labor leaders, telling them that the administration had not given up on labor's priorities.[90] Just a couple of weeks later after a year-long battle with strong union support, President Obama signed health reform into law, renewing labor's hopes that such a huge victory would change the tenor of American politics and shift focus to EFCA, a second stimulus, and financial reform legislation.[91] Said one labor leader, "We expected the Administration and Congress to pursue these other issues that had been on hold during the fight over health care. At that point, jobs and the economy, and a second stimulus to deal with unemployment and economic misery was a priority. And of course EFCA."[92] By late spring, as the president was still publicly supporting EFCA by proclaiming his administration was doing all it could "to make sure that people just get the fair chance to organize," the AFL-CIO was still trying to mobilize around labor law reform by "continuing to move the campaign on the field," according to one labor official.[93] Yet organized labor was at a loss strategically as to how to score a victory. Fred Azcarate, an AFL-CIO official, hinted at defeat when he said that the labor federation was "investigating other ways to get it done. We are exploring lots of options [for passage] ... this Congress or next."[94]

By early summer of 2010, Senator Harkin admitted what many knew but were reluctant to admit publicly: EFCA was dead.[95] Admitting he did not have the votes to get to the supermajority sixty needed to invoke cloture, Harkin told a group of management attorneys that he was "within one vote, but something happened in Massachusetts."[96] By July, even AFL-CIO President Trumka acknowledged the death of EFCA in this Congress, yet still held out hope, telling a reporter, "We're looking for methods to pass it."[97] Senator Harkin, trying to keep the labor law reform flame alive, claimed EFCA could still potentially be passed during the lame duck session after the November midterm elections. "To those who think it's dead, I say think again.... A lot can happen before Election Day, or maybe in lame duck too."[98] In August, Barack Obama again sought to reassure organized labor when speaking to the AFL-CIO Executive Council for his first time ever as president (on the day of his forty-ninth birthday). Recommitting to fighting for and signing labor law reform, the president acknowledged that getting EFCA "through a Senate is going to be tough. It's always been tough, it will continue to be tough, but we'll keep on pushing."[99]

Despite its death in the Senate, EFCA went further than expected according to some in the labor movement.[100] "The theory we had in 2005 that building our capacity in individual unions, rallying to elect a president in 2008, and then passing" labor law reform was a "totally thoughtful strategic plan that we got really far down the line," according to Andy Stern, the former president of the politically powerful Service Employees International Union (SEIU) and the most frequent visitor to the Obama White House during the first year of the administration.[101] At least publicly, Stern did not doubt the strategy labor took: "We did a good job of setting up EFCA that would have allowed that energy to be channeled in a new context that had a lot of possibility. I think we made the right decision, allocated the resources, chose the strategy, and tried to change the environment."[102] External factors such as the protracted struggle over health care reform – another one of labor's top legislative priorities – and the loss of sixty votes in the Senate with the election of Scott Brown (R-MA) in January of 2010 were his attributed sources of failure.[103]

But privately, others in the labor movement were more critical of labor's strategy.[104] One official at a national union explained "the labor movement never really had a realistic nor coordinated strategy for getting to 60 independent of the President. It's not clear we ever really had Lincoln (D-AR) or Nelson (D-NE). And none of us could foresee, even though we should have, the backlash to the President's agenda, especially health care reform."[105] Another top official at another union described how acquiescing to the administration's policy priorities and sequencing was possibly a mistake: "We should have gone along when it made sense, like on health care, but really pushed hard early on to force EFCA on the agenda ... especially during those first 100 days."[106] Given the ambivalent support of Democratic administrations for labor reform since the 1960s, it remains to be seen whether the Obama White House would have given unions the priority it accorded to health care legislation.

LABOR'S HISTORIC FOE: THE FILIBUSTER

What explains organized labor's continued failure to win labor policy reforms over six decades? Is it organizational strength and power, public opinion, Congressional alliances, strategic mistakes, or institutional variables? Several institutional and political obstacles including the supermajoritarian rules of the Senate, the role of interest groups, especially the Chamber of Commerce's intense opposition, Democrats' sometimes tepid support for labor reform, and organized labor's strategic choices explain labor law reform failure over the last sixty years. One factor is uniquely important in defeating labor law reform over time: the filibuster. Every serious reform effort since 1950 has been defeated by the use of the filibuster in the Senate, which requires a supermajority of sixty senators to invoke cloture.[107] There are few issues that arouse such persistent obstruction throughout the last sixty years of American politics as labor law reform. Why? Obviously, as discussed earlier, the stakes are high for shaping the rules of the game for labor-business interaction. But over the last decade, the number of filibusters has increased dramatically, with the 111th Congress setting the all-time record for cloture motions with 137.[108] This is even more remarkable considering the change in Senate rule 22 in 1975, lowering the threshold for the number of senators required to overcome a filibuster. A quick summary of successful filibusters over labor law reform illuminates its importance:

- In fall of 1965 and again in 1966, Senate Minority Leader Everett Dirksen (R-IL) led successful filibusters against labor law reform.[109]
- After fighting for two decades for filibuster reform, the labor movement rejoiced with the change in Senate Rule 22 in 1975, reducing of the necessary number of votes for invoking cloture from two-thirds (sixty-seven) to three-fifths (sixty).
- Yet in 1978, organized labor was stymied again by a Senate filibuster despite the change that lowered the supermajority requirement for cloture, when they came within two votes of defeating and winning on a labor law reform package that substantively is very similar to the current EFCA.
- In 1993, feeling hopeful from the Democratic presidential and congressional victories, organized labor pushed labor law reform in the form of a striker replacement bill. After passing the House, it was defeated by a Republican filibuster in 1994, led again by Senator Orrin Hatch (R-UT) and joined by Bob Dole (R-KS) and Don Nickles (R-OK).[110]
- In 2007, the Employee Free Choice Act passed the House, but stalled in the Senate. Its fate in 2009, when hopes were high, was similar: no action in the Senate due to a threatened filibuster and not enough votes to invoke cloture (the House decided this time around to wait until the Senate voted successfully to pass the bill before taking action).

Senator Tom Harkin explained in plain language why the more recent EFCA failed as a result of the inability to reach a supermajority in the Senate: "What happened? We had an election in Massachusetts. We lost our 60th vote," he said to a union audience in May of 2010.[111] As it had before in response to its failure to overcome filibusters of labor law reform in the 1950s and 1960s, the AFL-CIO again recently advocated for yet another change in Senate Rule 22 to "end legislative gridlock."[112] One national union, the Communication Workers of America, went further than the vague AFL-CIO language by passing a resolution at their convention demanding that the "filibuster must be eliminated and the use of holds to deny the appointment of qualified individuals must come to an end."[113] By the beginning of the 112th Congress in January 2011, these efforts by the AFL-CIO and Communications Workers of America (along with the Sierra Club and fifty other liberal national organizations) had coalesced into an official coalition advocating for filibuster reform called Fix the Senate Now.[114]

PUBLIC OPINION, UNION DENSITY, AND DIVIDED LABOR MOVEMENT?

Low union density, public opinion, and a divided labor movement are three popular explanations offered repeatedly for organized labor's inability to achieve labor law reform since the 1950s. Although each determinant of the fate of reform is important in its own right, these factors are often advanced in lieu of the more durable and longer-term obstacles such as the geographical concentration of labor, the conservative coalition in Congress, and the antimajoritarian features of the American state. The decline in union membership numbers, the argument goes, has resulted in a decline in labor political power.[115] Where unions are strongest in numbers, particularly in the Northeast and Midwest, the bluer the state. There is an obvious correlation between levels of union density and whether a state tends to vote Democratic or Republican. Thus, many labor activists and scholars argue that as unions have lost members and overall density since their peak in 1955, so, too, have they lost political power and the ability to win labor law reform. As one labor leader told me, "Until we have higher union density, we won't have the political power we need to win EFCA."[116]

This explanation makes sense, and is even a seductive mantra for those hoping to build a stronger labor movement. But on closer inspection, it is not as convincing as other factors for explaining the failure of labor law reform. For instance, the logic of higher union density as the necessary condition for labor law reform does not explain the failures of reform efforts under Presidents Truman, Johnson, and Carter (compared to Clinton and Obama). Under Johnson, union density was double what it is currently, with strong Democratic majorities in Congress. This argument also cannot explain how labor reforms unfavorable to labor were successful over labor opposition at the moments of highest union density in American history: most notably, Taft-Hartley in 1947 (31.9 percent union density) and Landrum-Griffin in 1959 (union density of 28.9 percent).[117] Indeed, union density was low at the moment of the passage of the Wagner Act itself seventy-five years ago at only 13.3 percent, statistically insignificant from the union density rate of 12.7 percent in 2009.

A second popular explanation offered for labor's failing fortunes is public opinion. Unions have fallen out of favor with the public and therefore cannot muster enough public support to convince Congress to pass labor law reform. Recognizing the role of public opinion on labor's influence, one union leader explained: "We have to make a better argument to the American people why they should care about reforming our labor laws ... we're losing the framing battle to the Chamber."[118] It is true that on many issues, politicians tend to follow public opinion over time,[119] and attempts by business to tar unions in the public's mind have long been an explicit strategy in their efforts to win employer-friendly labor reforms.[120] And recent evidence suggests business is winning; Americans' current attitudes about unions, in particular, do not bode well for significant support for labor policy reform. For the first time since Gallup first took a poll asking Americans their opinions about organized labor in 1936 (the year after the NLRA was passed), a majority did *not* approve of unions in the first year of the Obama administration. In 2009, only 48 percent of Americans approved of labor unions, down from 59 percent in 2008, 72 percent when the poll was first conducted in 1936, and the high of 75 percent registered in 1953 and 1957.[121] And public approval of unions has declined overall since the first poll in 1936, supporting the thesis of a relationship between public opinion and labor law reform. In addition, public sector unions have declined in the public's eyes, with many Americans even becoming resentful at the perceived luxurious health and pension benefits many government employees are much more likely to have relative to their private sector counterparts. Add the fiscal crises of most state and local governments to this mix, brought on by the economic downturn and partly due to pension obligations, and public sector union members, now the majority of all unionized workers, begin to look like the much reviled "labor insiders" in Western European countries.[122] Indeed, in the wake of the November 2010 elections, newly elected governors and state legislators have proclaimed their goals of demanding wage and benefit cuts from state and local government employees to address budget deficits. This targeting of public sector union contracts is a bipartisan affair, as both Republican and Democratic governors have taken nearly identical – and popular – policy stances.[123]

Yet, it is important to note that public opinion of the labor movement is far from determinative of labor's political fate; approval of unions was much higher during periods of labor law reforms unions opposed: 64 percent of the public approved of unions in 1947 when Taft-Hartley passed, whereas 68 percent and 73 percent approved of unions in January and August of 1959, respectively, the year Landrum-Griffin passed. What is important in the relationship between public opinion and efforts at labor law reform is the timing of the public's souring on unions. For instance, during the Johnson-era reform effort, a two-week strike of transportation workers in New York City in January 1966 provoked a backlash in public approval of unions and especially public sector workers.[124] Similarly, during the Carter-era reform effort, a 110-day strike by United Mine Workers members from late 1977 to 1978 also irritated the broader public about the pending labor law reform, providing political material for the National Association of Manufacturers and the Business Roundtable to lobby moderate congressional leaders to vote against the bill.[125]

A third and final often-advanced explanation for the failure of labor law reform is internal divisions within the labor movement. These internal divisions, it is argued, prevent a unified and coordinated strategy to garner all of the resources of the labor movement to advance a unified approach to winning reform. A divided labor movement has in fact proved ruinous in previous labor law reform efforts. During the 1949–1950 reform effort under Truman, the American Federation of Labor explicitly refused to coordinate with the Congress of Industrial Organizations the legislative campaign to repeal Taft-Hartley.[126] The AFL-CIO Executive Council was divided on its approach to reform during the Johnson administration, and there was broad "institutional disarray" in the House of Labor during the Carter Administration.[127] The most recent division, during the Clinton administration, was what John Logan calls "traditionalists," who advocated for a limited reform in the guise of the striker replacement bill, versus "modernizers," who wanted a much broader package of reform, similar in content to EFCA.[128]

Some labor movement officials attributed the failure of labor law reform in 2009–2010 to the divisions in the contemporary labor movement between the two rival federations, the AFL-CIO and Change to Win.[129] In particular, several national officials pointed to the highly contentious internal fight within SEIU over the national union's controversial trusteeship of its West Coast organization of health care workers, the internal fight and divorce within UNITE-HERE, and the interunion squabble between SEIU and UNITE-HERE. Although it is true that many resources used to wage these internal battles might have been allocated toward a political strategy for advancing EFCA in Congress (via grassroots lobbying in targeted states and districts, or public opinion, etc.), it is unlikely that a unified labor movement could have overcome the deeper and longer-term structural obstacles, including the use of the filibuster and the Chamber of Commerce's lobbying effort to defeat reform.

CONCLUSION

At the end of the final book in his trilogy on twentieth-century labor policy, historian James Gross describes the lukewarm relationship between the presidency and workers' rights in this way:

In the White House, no matter who the occupant, courageous leadership has been lacking. No president has been willing to risk pursuing a clear statement of the rights of workers or delineating statutory solutions to serious labor relations problems. Instead, administrations have done the minimum necessary to respond, or at least appear to be responding, to political pressure, to gain political backing, or to reward business or organized labor for its support in election campaigns. They then go through the motions of seeking reform while manipulating the situation for maximum political gain.[130]

This historic pattern was on display yet again as President Obama addressed the AFL-CIO Executive Council, outlining his accomplishments but recommitting to labor's most important legislative priority:

We passed the Fair Pay Act to help put a stop to pay discrimination. We've reversed the executive orders of the last administration that were designed to undermine organized labor. I've appointed folks who actually are fulfilling their responsibilities to make sure our workplaces our safe, whether in a mine or in an office, a factory or anyplace else. And we are going to keep on fighting to pass the Employee Free Choice Act.[131]

These executive actions are vitally important, if small, victories for the labor movement.[132] Indeed, in an attempt to educate its leaders and members in the lead-up to the midterm elections in November 2010, the AFL-CIO highlighted the important accomplishments of labor reforms through administrative politics, in addition to the significant legislative victories it supported such as health care reform, financial reregulation and the stimulus package.[133]

But suppose EFCA had passed successfully; although maybe necessary, it is doubtful it would be sufficient to spark a wholesale revitalization of the labor movement. Even the Chair of the NLRB is not sanguine on this particular labor law reform, arguing that "EFCA does not represent comprehensive labor-law reform. What is represents, rather, is the prospect of an end to the ossification of our law."[134] Yet labor has always known that changing the law, by itself, is a necessary but not sufficient condition toward revitalizing the union movement. As one leader put it:

To change the plight of workers in this country, we can't just rely on the law. Unions themselves must change. Unions have to commit to organizing on a massive scale in spite of the law. We have to change the internal organizational cultures of unions to get them to support organizing. That way, we'll make gains while waiting for the law to come back on our side, but we'll also be ready to organize once it does.[135]

Notes

1. Much of the material for this chapter on the recent labor policy reforms over 2009–2010 draws on Dorian Warren, "The Unsurprising Failure of Labor Law Reform and the Turn to Administrative Action," in Theda Skocpol and Lawrence Jacobs, eds. *Reaching for a New Deal: Ambitious Governance, Economic Meltdown, and Polarized Politics in Obama's First Two Years.* New York, Russell Sage, 2011, 191–229.
2. Warren, "The Unsurprising Failure of Labor Law Reform and the Turn to Administrative Action."
3. Jacob S. Hacker. 2004. "Privatizing Risk without Privatizing the Welfare State: The Hidden Politics of Social Policy Retrenchment in the United States." *American Political Science Review*, vol. 98, no. 2, 243–260; Jacob S. Hacker and Paul Pierson. 2002. "Business Power and Social Policy: Employers and the Formation of the American Welfare State." *Politics and Society.* 30(2): 277–326; Kate Bronfenbrenner. 1994. "Employer Behavior in Certification Elections and First-Contract Campaigns: Implications for Labor Law Reform," in S. Friedman, R. Hurd, R. Oswald, and

R. Seeber, eds., *Restoring the Promise of American Labor Law* (Ithaca: Cornell University Press), pp. 75–89; Kate Bronfenbrenner. 2009. "No Holds Barred: The Intensification of Employer Opposition to Union Organizing." *EPI Briefing Paper* #235, Washington, DC: Economic Policy Institute; Michael Goldfield, *The Decline of Organized Labor in the United States* (Chicago: University of Chicago Press, 1987); Paul C. Weiler, *Governing the Workplace* (Cambridge, MA: Harvard University Press, 1990).

4. Seymour Martin Lipset and Gary Marks. 2000. *It Didn't Happen Here: Why No Socialism Failed in the United States* (New York: Norton).

5. J. David Greenstone. 1969. *Labor in American Politics* (New York: Alfred A. Knopf); Taylor Dark. 1999. *The Unions and the Democrats: An Enduring Alliance* (Ithaca: Cornell University Press); Marie Gottschalk, 2000. *The Shadow Welfare State: Labor, Business, and the Politics of Health Care* (Ithaca: Cornell University Press); Peter L. Francia. 2006. *The Future of Organized Labor in American Politics* (New York: Columbia University Press).

6. Greenstone, 1969, xiii.

7. According to opensecrets.org, the "labor sector" spent more than $150 million during the 2008 election cycle, although business spending was more than double that amount. Lindsay Renick Mayer. 2009. "Labor and Business Spend Big on Looming Unionization Issue." Retrieved from http://www.opensecrets.org/news/2009/02/labor-and-business-spend-big-o.html. Another source puts the number at $250 million labor spent. Alec MacGillis. August 29, 2008. "Labor Leaders Stress Unions' Importance for Obama." *Washington Post.* Retrieved from http://www.washingtonpost.com/wp-dyn/content/article/2008/08/28/AR2008082804003.html.

8. Union density in 2010 was 11.9 percent compared to 10.5 percent in 1929. Union density reached a postwar high in 1955 at 31.8 percent. Bureau of Labor Statistics. 2010. Current Population Survey, News Release. Union Members in 2009. Washington, DC: U.S. Department of Labor. Retrieved from http://www.bls.gov/news.release/pdf/union2.pdf, accessed on April 5, 2010; Steven Greenhouse. 2011. "Labor Board Adopts Rules to Speed Unionization Votes," *New York Times*, December 21, B5.

9. Nelson Lichtenstein, "Pluralism, Postwar Intellectuals, and the Demise of the Union Idea," in Sidney M. Milkis and Jerome M. Mileur, eds. *The Great Society and the High Tide of Liberalism*. Amherst: University of Massachusetts Press, 2005, 83; Daniel J. Galvin, "Resilience in the Rust Belt: Michigan Democrats and the UAW," prepared for presentation at the Annual Meeting of the American Political Science Association, August 31–September 1, 2013, Chicago, Illinois. Galvin shows that labor became so closely joined to the Democratic Party in Michigan that it supported the party's adaptation to changes in the political economy, even if such flexibility hurt the union's short-term interests.

10. Bruce Western and Jake Rosenfeld. 2010. "Unions, Norms, and the Rise in American Wage Inequality." Unpublished manuscript.

11. AFL-CIO. 2009. "AFL-CIO Legislative Guide 2009." On file with author.

12. The National Labor Relations Act is also often referred to as the Wagner Act, after its champion and chief sponsor, Senator Robert Wagner (D-NY).

13. Richard B. Freeman. 2007. *America Works: Critical Thoughts on the Exceptional U.S. Labor Market* (New York: Russell Sage Foundation); Western and Rosenfeld, "Unions, Norms, and the Rise in American Wage Inequality."

14. David Bradley, David and Evelyne Huber, Stephanie Moller, Francois Nielsen, and John D. Stephens. 2003. "Distribution and Redistribution in Postindustrial Societies." *World Politics.* 55 (2): 193–228.
15. Margaret Levi. 2003. "Organizing Power: The Prospects for an American Labor Movement." *Perspectives on Politics.* 1: 45–68; Kathleen Thelen. 2001. "Varieties of Labor Politics in the Developed Democracies," in Peter A. Hall and David Soskice, eds. *Varieties of Capitalism: The Institutional Foundations of Comparative Advantage.* New York: Oxford University Press, 71–103; Michael Wallerstein and Bruce Western. 2000. "Unions in Decline? What Has Changed and Why." *Annual Review of Political Science.* vol. 3: 355–377.
16. Bradley, et al., "Distribution and Redistribution in Post Industrial Societies"; Gosta Esping-Anderson. 1990. *The Three Worlds of Welfare Capitalism* (Princeton: Princeton University Press); Walter Korpi. 1983. *The Democratic Class Struggle* (London: Routledge); Michael Wallerstein, 1989. "Union Organization in Advanced Industrial Democracies." *American Political Science Review.* 83 (2): 481–501; Bruce Western. 1997. *Between Class and Market* (Princeton: Princeton University Press).
17. Lawrence R. Jacobs and Theda Skocpol. 2005. *Inequality and American Democracy: What We Know and What We Need to Learn* (New York: Russell Sage Foundation); Larry M. Bartels. 2008. *Unequal Democracy: The Political Economy of the New Gilded Age* (New York and Princeton: Russell Sage Foundation and Princeton University Press); Kay Lehman Schlozman and Tracy Burch, "Political Voice in an Age of Inequality," in Robert Faulkner and Susan Shell, eds. In *America at Risk: The Great Dangers* (Ann Arbor: University of Michigan Press, 2009), 140–173.
18. Steven J. Rosenstone and John Mark Hansen. 1993. *Mobilization, Participation and Democracy in America* (New York: MacMillan); Margaret Levi. 2003. "Organizing Power: The Prospects for An American Labor Movement." *Perspectives on Politics.* 1: 45–68; Jeffrey A. Winters and Benjamin I. Page. 2009. "Oligarchy in the United States?" *Perspective on Politics* 7 (4): 731–751.
19. Jacob S. Hacker and Paul Pierson. 2010. "Winner-Take-All Politics: Public Policy, Political Organization, and the Precipitous Rise of Top Incomes in the United States." *Politics & Society.* 38 (2): 152–204.
20. Francia, 2006; Hacker and Pierson, 2010.
21. Jacob S. Hacker. 2004. "Privatizing Risk without Privatizing the Welfare State: The Hidden Politics of Social Policy Retrenchment in the United States." *American Political Science Review.* vol. 98, no. 2, 243–260; Larry R. Jacobs and Demond King. 2010. "Varieties of Obamaism: Structure, Agency and the Obama Presidency," *Perspectives on Politics,* 8 (3): 793–802.
22. Charles Lindblom. 1977. *Politics and Markets: The World's Political Economic Systems* (New York: Basic Books); Bartels, 2008; Winters and Page, 2009; Hacker and Pierson, 2010.
23. Theda Skocpol. 2003. *Diminished Democracy* (Norman, OK: University of Oklahoma Press).
24. Paul Frymer. 2008. *Black and Blue: African Americans, the Labor Movement, and the Decline of the Democratic Party* (Princeton: Princeton University Press).
25. Victoria C. Hattam. 1993. *Labor Visions and State Power: The Origins of Business Unionism in the United States* (Princeton: Princeton University Press); David Brian Robertson. 2000. *Capital, Labor & State: The Battle for American Labor*

Markets from the Civil War to the New Deal (Lanham, MD: Rowman & Littlefield); Mancur Olson, *The Logic of Collective Action: Public Goods and the Theory of Groups* (Cambridge, MA: Harvard University Press, 1965).

26. Karl Polanyi. 2001. *The Great Transformation: The Political and Economic Origins of Our Time* (Boston: Beacon); T. H. Marshall. 1950. *Citizenship and Social Class and Other Essays* (Cambridge: Cambridge University Press); Lindblom, 1977; Fred Block. 2003. "Karl Polanyi and the Writing of The Great Transformation." *Theory and Society.* 32 (3): 275–306; Beverly J. Silver, *Forces of Labor, Workers' Movements and Globalization Since 1870* (New York: Cambridge University Press, 2003); Hacker and Pierson, 2002, 2010.

27. Desmond King and Rogers M. Smith. 2005. "Racial Orders in American Political Development." *American Political Science Review.* 99 (1): 75–92; Dorian T. Warren, "The American Labor Movement in the Age of Obama: The Challenges and Opportunities of a Racialized Political Economy." *Perspectives on Politics.* 8 (3): 2010, 847–860.

28. Block, 2003, 6.

29. EFCA is the Employee Free Choice Act, organized labor's labor reform legislation drafted in the mid 2000s.

30. William E. Forbath. 1991. *Law and the Shaping of the American Labor Movement* (Cambridge, MA: Harvard University Press); Karen Orren. 1991. *Belated Feudalism: Labor, the Law, and Liberal Development in the United States* (Cambridge: Cambridge University Press); Melvyn Dubofsky. 1994. *The State and Labor in Modern America* (Chapel Hill, NC: University of North Carolina Press); Hattam, 1993; John Godard. 2009. "The Exceptional Decline of the American Labor Movement." *Industrial and Labor Review.* 63 (1): 82–108.

31. Ruth Berins Collier and David Collier. 1979. "Inducements versus Constraints: Disaggregating 'Corporatism'". *American Political Science Review.* 73 (4): 967–986.

32. Herbert Hill. 1985. *Black Labor and the American Legal System: Race, Work and the Law* (Madison: University of Wisconsin Press); Frymer, 2008.

33. Sean Farhang and Ira Katznelson. 2005. "The Southern Imposition: Congress and Labor in the New Deal and Fair Deal." *Studies in American Political Development.* 19 (Spring): 1–30; Collier and Collier, 1979; Hacker and Pierson, 2002.

34. *NLRB v. Jones & Laughlin Steel Corp,* 301 U.S. 1 (1937).

35. Hacker and Pierson, 2002.

36. Taylor Dark. 1999. *The Unions and the Democrats: An Enduring Alliance* (Ithaca: Cornell University Press); Farhang and Katznelson, 2005; Warren, 2011.

37. David Plotke. 1996. *Building A Democratic Political Order: Reshaping American Liberalism in the 1930s and 1940s* (New York: Cambridge University Press).

38. Cynthia L. Estlund. 2002. "The Ossification of American Labor Law." *Columbia Law Review.* 102.

39. Katherine V. W. Stone. 2004. *From Widgets to Digits: Employment Regulation for a Changing Workplace* (Cambridge: Cambridge University Press).

40. David Clawson and Mary Ann Clawson. 1999. "What Has Happened to the Labor Movement." *Annual Review of Sociology.* 25 (January): 95–119.

41. Hattam,1993; Hacker and Pierson, 2010.

42. Weiler, 1990; Bronfenbrenner, 2009.

43. Sanford M. Jacoby. 1997. *Modern Manners: Welfare Capitalism since the New Deal* (Princeton: Princeton University Press).

44. Freeman strongly defends this argument twenty years later in a reassessment of the 1984 book. Freeman, 2007.
45. U.S. Department of Labor and U.S. Department of Commerce. 1994. "The Commission on the Future of Worker-Management Relations." Retrieved from http://digitalcommons.ilr.cornell.edu/dunlop/.
46. U.S. Dunlop Commission, 1994.
47. Ibid.
48. Bronfenbrenner, 2009.
49. Ibid.
50. Hattam, 1993; Jacoby, 1997.
51. Steve Fraser and Gary Gerstle. 1989. *The Rise and Fall of the New Deal Order, 1930–1980* (Princeton: Princeton University Press); Rick Fantasia and Kim Voss. 2004. *Hard Work: Remaking the American Labor Movement* (Berkeley: University of California Press); Frances Fox Piven and Richard A. Cloward. 1997. *The Breaking of the American Social Contract* (New York: New Press); Clawson and Clawson, 1999.
52. Nelson Lichtenstein. 2002. *State of the Union: A Century of American Labor* (Princeton, New Jersey: Princeton University Press).
53. Farhang and Katznelson, 2005.
54. Jacobs and King, 2009, 3.
55. Jacobs and King, 2009.
56. Compare the remedies available to the NLRB versus its just-as-weak sister workplace agency, the Equal Employment Opportunity Commission (EEOC). At least the EEOC has the ability to impose punitive damages on employers for violating employment law (Frymer, 2008). See also: James A. Gross. 1985. "Conflicting Statutory Purposes: Another Look at Fifty Years of NLRB Law Making." *Industrial and Labor Relations Review*. vol. 39, no. 1. October.
57. See also Western and Rosenfield, 2009, for a recent iteration of the norms/social contract argument.
58. Paul C. Weiler. 1990. *Governing the Workplace: The Future of Labor and Employment Law* (Cambridge, MA: Harvard University Press).
59. James. A. Gross. 1995. *Broken Promise: The Subversion of U.S. Labor Relations Policy, 1947–1994* (Philadelphia: Temple University Press), 153–156.
60. Gross, 1995.
61. Ibid.
62. Theda Skocpol and Kenneth Finegold. 1982. "State Capacity and Economic Intervention in the New Deal," *Political Science Quarterly* 97 (2): 255–278; Michael Goldfield. 1989. "Worker Insurgency, Radical Organization, and New Deal Labor Legislation." *American Political Science Review*. 83 (4): 1257–1282; Jacob S. Hacker and Paul Pierson. 2002. "Business Power and Social Policy: Employers and the Formation of the American Welfare State." *Politics and Society*. 38 (2): 277–326.
63. Orren, 1991; Victoria C. Hattam. 1993. *Labor Visions and State Power: The Origins of Business Unionism in the United States* (Princeton: Princeton University Press); Jacoby, 1997.
64. Smith, also a staunch segregationist, would later become Chair of the House Rules Committee, where he often successfully stymied civil rights legislation in the 1950s and 1960s. James A. Gross. 1981. *The Reshaping of the National Labor Relations Board: National Labor Policy in Transition, 1937–1947* (Albany: State University of New York Press); Gross, 1985.

126   *Warren*

65. Gross, 1985.
66. Farhang and Katznelson, 2005.
67. Gross, 1995, 15–25.
68. There were of course several other provisions of Taft-Hartley aimed at undercutting the power of unions.
69. Mancur Olson. 1965. *The Logic of Collective Action* (Cambridge, MA: Harvard University Press).
70. Louis Stark. November 4, 1948. "Labor Chiefs Hail Vote as 'Mandate.'" *New York Times*; Louis Stark. November 15, 1948. "Quick Return to Wagner Act Pressed on Congress by AFL." *New York Times*.
71. David J. Greenstone. 1969. *Labor in American Politics* (New York: Alfred A. Knopf); Alan Draper. 1994. *Conflict of Interests: Organized Labor and the Civil Rights Movement in the South, 1954–1968* (Ithaca: Cornell University Press); Taylor Dark. 1999. *The Unions and the Democrats: An Enduring Alliance* (Ithaca: Cornell University Press).
72. Dark, 1999.
73. Dark, 1999, 59.
74. Gross, 1995, 236–241; Dark, 1999.
75. Gross, 1995, 239.
76. William B. Liebman. February 17, 2010. "The Revival of American Labor Law." Comments prepared for Access to Justice Lecture Series, Washington University Law School. On file with author.
77. Although many scholars say EFCA has not going nearly far enough.
78. Kate Bronfenbrenner. 1994. "Employer Behavior in Certification Elections and First-Contract Campaigns: Implications for Labor Law Reform," in S. Friedman, R. Hurd, R. Oswald, and R. Seeber, eds. *Restoring the Promise of American Labor Law*. Ithaca: Cornell University Press, pp. 75–89; Kate Bronfenbrenner. 2009. "No Holds Barred: The Intensification of Employer Opposition to Union Organizing." *EPI Briefing Paper # 235*, Washington, DC: Economic Policy Institute; John-Paul Ferguson. 2009. "The Eyes of the Needles: A Sequential Model of Union Organizing Drives, 1999–2004." *Industrial & Labor Relations Review*. vol. 62, no. 1. 3–21.
79. Unlike most employment regulations such as the 1964 Civil Rights Act, labor law has not allowed civil penalties for violators of the law, creating perverse incentives for employers to violate the law in union organizing or contract campaigns. According to recent research (Bronfenbrenner, 2009), employers fire workers engaged in union activity in 34 percent of NLRB election campaigns.
80. Derrick Cain. March 12, 2009. "EFCA Introduced in Both House, Senate; Senate to Take Up Bill after Easter Recess." *Labor Relations Week*. 23 LRW 385; Derrick Cain. May 6, 2009. "AFL-CIO Continues EFCA Pursuit Despite Lack of Votes in Senate." *Labor Relations Week*. 24 LRW 729.
81. Bureau of National Affairs. July 30, 2009. "EFCA Vote Slips Until After August Recess, 'May Be Longer Than That,' Harkin Says." *Labor Relations Week*. 23 LRW 1212.
82. Michelle Amber. September 17, 2009. "Specter Says Compromise Reached on EFCA, but AFL-CIO Says No Deal Yet." *Labor Relations Week*. 23 LRW 1478.
83. Ibid.; confidential interview.
84. Confidential interviews. For more on labor's role in the health care battle, including pushing for a "public option" while protecting their members' existing health insurance plans, see Lawrence R. Jacobs and Theda Skocpol. 2010. *Health Care Reform*

and American Politics: What Everyone Needs to Know (New York: Oxford University Press).

85. Confidential interviews; Cain, 2009.
86. Confidential interview. A year later, the AFL-CIO funded a primary challenger to Senator Lincoln to the tune of $10 million, only to lose.
87. Jeanne Cummings. January 26, 2010. "Labor Helps Kill Its Own Top Priority." *Politico.* Retrieved from http://dyn.politico.com/printstory.cfm?uuid=6CD9C06C-18FE-70B2-A8F39148A7BC8614.
88. Cummings, 2010.
89. Harold Meyerson. February 10, 2010. "Under Obama, Labor Should Have Made More Progress." *Washington Post.* Retrieved from http://www.washingtonpost.com/wp-dyn/content/article/2010/02/09/AR2010020902465.html.
90. Michelle Amber. March 4, 2010. "Biden Tells Labor Chiefs that Administration Is Not Abandoning Their Priorities Like EFCA." *Labor Relations Week.* 24 LRW 334; confidential interviews.
91. Confidential interviews.
92. Confidential interview.
93. Derrick Cain. May 6, 2009. "AFL-CIO Continues EFCA Pursuit Despite Lack of Votes in Senate." *Labor Relations Week.* 24 LRW 729.
94. Ibid.
95. Confidential interviews.
96. Derrick Cain. May 20, 2010. "Harkin Says He Does Not Have Enough Votes to Approve EFCA." *Labor Relations Week.* 24 LRW 820.
97. Michael Rose. July 1, 2010. "Trumka Says AFL-CIO's Focus on Economy Sets His Administration Apart from Others." *Labor Relations Week.* 24 LRW 1092.
98. Derrick Cain. May 20, 2010. "Harkin Says He Does Not Have Enough Votes to Approve EFCA."
99. Barack Obama. August 4, 2010. "Remarks by the President to the AFL-CIO Executive Council." Retrieved from http://www.whitehouse.gov/the-press-office/remarks-president-afl-cio-executive-council.
100. Having passed EFCA by a strong majority in the previous Congress, the House always had a majority of votes to pass the bill, but decided to wait for the super-majority Senate to pass it first this time around.
101. Michelle Amber. September 17, 2009. "Specter Says Compromise Reached on EFCA, But AFL-CIO Says No Deal Yet." *Labor Relations Week.* 23 LRW 1478.
102. Ibid.
103. Ibid.
104. Confidential interviews.
105. Confidential interview.
106. Confidential interview.
107. Before a change in Rule 22 in 1975, the required number to invoke cloture was two-thirds, or sixty-seven.
108. United States Senate. 2010. "Cloture Motions-111th Congress." Retrieved from https://www.senate.gov/pagelayout/reference/cloture_motions/111.htm.
109. Dark, 1999, 47–75.
110. John Logan. 2007. "The Clinton Administration and Labor Law: Was Comprehensive Reform Ever a Realistic Possibility?" *Journal of Labor Research.* 28: 609–628.

111. Bureau of National Affairs. July 8, 2010. "NAM Report Outlines Proposals on Growth, Opposes Labor Law Changes." *Labor Relations Week*. 24 LRW 1138.

112. AFL-CIO. July 2010. "Obama Administration Accomplishments." On file with author.

113. Michelle Amber. August 6, 2010. "AFL-CIO Joins One Nation, Calls on Senate to Change Rules to End Legislative Gridlock." *Daily Labor Report*. 151 DLR B-2.

114. The coalition's Web site is http://fixthesenatenow.org/, accessed on January 3, 2011.

115. Confidential interviews.

116. Confidential interview.

117. Leo Troy, *Trade Union Membership, 1897–1962* (New York: National Bureau of Economic Research, 1965).

118. Confidential interview.

119. Benjamin I. Page and Robert Y. Shapiro. 1992. *The Rational Public: Fifty Years of Trends in Americans' Policy Preferences* (Chicago: University of Chicago Press).

120. Gross, 1995.

121. Fifty-two percent of Americans approved of labor unions in the most recent Gallup poll in August, 2010. "U.S. Approval of Labor Unions Remains Near Record Low." August 12, 2010. Retrieved from http://www.gallup.com/poll/142007/americans-approval-labor-unions-remains-near-record-low.aspx.

122. Teachers' unions are also driving this increasingly negative image of the labor movement, as both Republican and Democratic Parties, including President Obama, have targeted education unions as the chief obstacles to public school reform.

123. Martin Z. Braun and Holly Rosenkrantz. 2011. "Public-Worker Unions Confront U.S. Governors Over Benefits in Role Switch." *Bloomberg News*. Retrieved from http://www.bloomberg.com/news/2011-01-20/public-worker-unions-battle-governors-on-benefits-in-role-shift.html, accessed on January 20, 2011.

124. Dark, 1999, 60.

125. Ibid.

126. Gross, 1995, 42–57.

127. Dark, 1999, 113.

128. Logan, 2007.

129. Confidential interviews; Tom Hamburger. May 19, 2009. "Labor Unions Find Themselves Card-Checked." *L.A. Times*. Retrieved from http://articles.latimes.com/2009/may/19/nation/na-unions19.

130. Gross, 1995, 276.

131. Remarks by the President to the AFL-CIO Executive Council, August 4, 2010, Retrieved from http://www.whitehouse.qov/the-press-office/remarks-president-afl-cio-executive-council.

132. Confidential interviews.

133. AFL-CIO. July 2010. "Obama Administration Accomplishments." On file with author.

134. Wilma B. Liebman. February 17, 2010. "The Revival of American Labor Law." Comments prepared for Access to Justice Lecture Series, Washington University Law School. On file with author.

135. Confidential interview.

6

Teachers Unions and American Education Reform: The Power of Vested Interests

Terry M. Moe

Shortly after taking office as President Barack Obama's secretary of education, Arne Duncan was blunt in assessing the nation's public schools. "It's obvious the system's broken," he said. "Let's admit it's broken, let's admit it's dysfunctional, and let's do something dramatically different, and let's do it now. But don't just tinker about the edges. Don't just play with it. Let's fix the thing".[1]

Such calls for major change in American education are hardly unusual. The consensus among policymakers – Democrat and Republican, liberal and conservative – is that the public schools are not providing the nation's children with the quality education so necessary for a modern, competitive world.

This consensus has been the norm, however, for over a quarter century. *A Nation at Risk* warned in 1983 of a "rising tide of mediocrity" in America's schools, convincing policymakers of the imperative for action – and the result, in the decades since, has been a whirlwind of reform bringing change upon change to the laws, programs, structures, and curricula of public education, as well as countless billions of extra dollars.[2]

All this activity might seem to be the sign of a well-functioning democracy, one that recognizes social problems and dedicates itself to solving them. But pull away the curtain and the picture is not nearly so pretty. The reforms of the last few decades, despite all the fanfare, have been incremental and weak in practice. The nation is constantly busy with education reforms not because it is responsibly addressing social problems, but because it never actually solves them and they never go away. The modern history of American education reform is a history of dashed hopes – and continuing demands, such as those of Arne Duncan, for *more* reforms that will finally bring real improvements. This is what keeps the never-ending "education reform era" alive and kicking: not democracy, not responsibility, but failure.[3]

Why has the reform era been such a disappointment? Why has a nation so publicly dedicated to dramatic improvement continually pulled up short, embracing weak reforms unsuited to the challenge and refusing to take bold action?

This chapter is an effort to provide some answers. The temptation is to revel in complexity – by exploring, for example, the dynamics of historical processes, a multitude of groups and players, and the intersections of events, forces, and institutions. All of these, of course, are relevant. But the fact is, in American education – and most areas of public policy, for that matter – there are simple fundamentals at work that go a long way toward explaining the obstacles to productive change. The first of these is the power of vested interests. The second is checks and balances. The combination is a formula for inertia, stagnation, and the inability of policymakers to bring about major changes in the governmental status quo, even when the system's performance is dreadful and the need for change dire.

In the American public school system, the vested interests are the teachers unions: the National Education Association (NEA), American Federation of Teachers (AFT), and their state and local affiliates – which represent the system's key employees and are by far the most powerful groups in the politics of education. Their power is magnified, moreover, because – like vested interests in other realms of policy – they operate within a larger policy process that is filled with checks and balances, which create veto points that make it difficult for reformers to get major new legislation passed and correspondingly easy for opponents to block.

The teachers unions have been masters of the politics of blocking for the past quarter century. Major reform is threatening to their vested interests in the existing system, and they have used their formidable power – leveraged by checks and balances – to repel and weaken the efforts of reformers to bring real change. This is the basic story of the modern reform era. The rest is detail.[4]

Fortunately, for reasons I will explain, abnormal developments are under-way, and the prospects for change are much brighter in the decades ahead. But by then the nation – and generations of children – will have paid a terrible price.

THE RISE OF UNION POWER

The public school system emerged in roughly its present form about 100 years ago, and for most of its history was a union-free zone. Many teachers belonged to the NEA, which, even in the early 1900s, was the vanguard of the education establishment. But the NEA was a professional association controlled by admin-istrators, and it was opposed to unions.[5]

All this changed during the 1960s and 1970s, when most of the states (outside the South) adopted public-sector labor laws. These new legal frameworks fueled dramatic increases in public-sector union membership and collective bargaining. They also triggered a transformation of the NEA, which, in competing with the AFT to represent the nation's teachers, turned itself into a union – and soon grew to be the biggest union *of any type* in the country.[6] The portion of teachers covered by collective bargaining soared from nearly zero in 1960 to 65 percent in 1978, and the system then settled into a new steady state. Bargaining coverage has remained virtually unchanged among teachers ever since. Membership levels have consistently been much higher, at about 79 percent, and stable.[7]

By the early 1980s, the teachers unions reigned supreme as the most powerful force in American education: with millions of members, armies of political activists, enormous wealth for campaign contributions and lobbying, and more. The rise of union power transformed the world of American public education, creating what amounted to a new education system, one that has been in equilibrium now for roughly thirty years – and protected from change by the very union power that created it.

Along with this transformation came a great historical irony. The most influential report in the annals of American education, *A Nation at Risk*, burst onto the political scene at precisely the same time that the teachers unions were consolidating their power. From the very beginning of the modern reform era, then, the proponents of change were butting their heads against a wall of union power. They would continue to do exactly that, with little success, for the next quarter century.

COLLECTIVE BARGAINING AND INEFFECTIVE ORGANIZATION

Teachers unions have exercised their power over American education in two ways: from the top down through politics and from the bottom up through collective bargaining. My focus in this chapter is largely on politics, yet it is impossible to understand the problems of the current system without also paying attention to collective bargaining.

In the politics of education, the great power wielders are the NEA, the AFT, and their state affiliates. But teachers join *local* unions, and it is the locals that attract the members, money, and activists that are the ingredients of union power. Their ability to attract these resources is aided immensely by collective bargaining, for this is what teachers care most about as union members and, thanks to state labor laws, it is what ties them securely to their unions. Were it not for collective bargaining and its protected legal status, the NEA, the AFT, and their state affiliates would not be nearly as *politically* powerful as they are – and as able to stand in the way of education reform.[8]

Collective bargaining is also profoundly important for another reason: it has allowed the unions to impose – and then protect – ineffective forms of organization on the schools, thus exacerbating the very problems the reform movement has been trying to correct. That the unions have been creators and defenders of ineffective organization is to be expected. It grows inevitably out of their own interests, which are simply *not the same* as the interests of children. Like all unions, they seek to increase wages and benefits, protect jobs, expand teacher rights in the workplace, and restrict managerial discretion. In collective bargaining, they do these things by winning restrictive contract rules that specify how districts must operate, spend their money, allocate their resources – notably, teachers – and in general, how they must *organize* the schools to educate children. Once these rules are in place, moreover, district leaders that later try to change them in the interests of more effective organization will find that the unions are in a position to block – just as they are in the political system. For in a world of collective bargaining, the core features of the organization of schools cannot be changed without their consent.

As collective bargaining has played out over several decades and many thousands of school districts, therefore, the teachers unions have heavily shaped the organization of America's schools. Here are a few examples of contract provisions that are quite common.[9]

(1) *Salary rules* that pay teachers on a formal schedule based on seniority and formal credits – thus ensuring that good and bad teachers are paid the same and that salary cannot be used as an incentive for productive behavior.

(2) *Transfer rules* that give senior teachers their choice of available jobs – thus making it impossible for districts to place teachers where they can do the greatest good for children.

(3) *Layoff rules* that require staffing reductions in reverse order of seniority – ensuring that excellent young teachers will automatically be let go, whereas low-performing teachers with lots of seniority will automatically be kept on.

(4) *Evaluation rules* that set out onerous procedures to be followed – monitoring, reporting, mentoring, and so forth – if a teacher is rated as unsatisfactory, thus giving principals strong incentives to rate all teachers as satisfactory, however awful their performance. The best evidence is that 99 percent of the nation's teachers get satisfactory ratings.[10]

(5) *Dismissal rules* that, together with evaluation rules and state tenure laws, spell out additional onerous procedures to be followed if a teacher is to be dismissed – thus making it virtually impossible to dismiss anyone. Studies suggest that it takes roughly two years and more than $200,000 just to dismiss one poorly performing teacher – and that it almost never happens.[11]

These and countless other rules are designed to promote the job-related interests of teachers, not to create good schools. Indeed, from the standpoint of effective organization, they are simply perverse. Yet this is how America's schools are actually organized. There is a disconnect between what the public schools are supposed to do and how they are organized to do it – and this disconnect is a built-in feature of the modern American school system, a reflection of its underlying structure of power.

Why have the districts, in their negotiations with the unions, "agreed" to ineffective organization? In part it is because the unions can unleash sanctions if dissatisfied, and no district wants a fight or (much worse) a strike. Another reason is that most work rules do not cost the districts anything in direct outlays. And another is that, as monopolies with a lock on kids and money, the districts have had little incentive historically to insist on effective organization.

Finally, there is a political reason whose importance is hard to exaggerate. School board members are elected, and the teachers unions are typically the most powerful forces in those elections. As a result, many board members are union allies, others are reliably sympathetic to collective bargaining, and the rest have reason to fear that, if they cross the unions, their jobs are at stake. District management, then, is not independent of the unions. The unions help *select* management, and it tends to be biased in their favor.[12]

Over the last decade, districts have had their spines stiffened a bit. Accountability has put them under pressure to raise achievement, charter schools have proliferated (in some cities) to offer families exit options, and both have strengthened district incentives to resist debilitating union rules. The financial crisis that began in 2008, moreover, has forced districts to be more confrontational with their unions over money and organization.

Yet the districts remain weak.[13] Where districts have been willing to fight for effective organization, it has almost always occurred in cities where mayors have taken control of the schools. Mayoral control is fairly rare, but where it has occurred it is potential trouble for unions. Mayors have more diverse constituencies than school board members do; they have more resources for wielding power; and they are more accountable for results. An "education mayor" can be a force for reform in a way that schools boards rarely are.[14]

It is no accident that the highest profile cases of districts fighting hard for effective organization have come in the mayor-controlled systems of New York City and Washington, DC. In both, the mayors were committed to major reform, and they appointed school chancellors – Joel Klein in New York City, Michelle Rhee in DC – who were willing to launch all-out assaults on restrictive work rules in the face of fierce union resistance. And they won important victories – especially far-reaching in Rhee's case – on seniority, performance pay, and teacher evaluations.[15]

These victories were remarkable, however, precisely because they were so unusual. They also took many years of agonizing struggle, were enormously expensive, and the districts were still left a long way from effective organization. The Rhee and Klein experiences testify to how difficult it is, even when all the ducks are in a row, to make even *partial* progress toward effective organization.

Their victories, moreover, are inherently vulnerable. For reformist mayors ultimately leave office. In Washington, DC, Mayor Adrian Fenty lost his 2010 reelection bid, Michelle Rhee quickly resigned, and the schools were soon in the hands of Vincent Gray, the union-supported candidate. In New York City, Joel Klein stepped down in 2010 after eight years of constant battles, and Mayor Michael Bloomberg was replaced as mayor in 2014 by Bill de Blasio: a union ally and opponent of charter schools and accountability – which means that virtually everything that Bloomberg struggled for 12 years to achieve is at risk of being weakened or dismantled."

New York City and Washington, DC, are best-case scenarios. There are a few other districts where unusual changes are underway as well – for example, in Hillsborough County (FL), Memphis, and Pittsburgh, where heaps of money from the Gates Foundation have induced the unions to "collaborate" in teacher-evaluation reforms, and in New Haven where a thin contract has been adopted.[16] But it is important not to interpret these signs of progress as monumental transformations. Yes, reformers are inching ahead here and there (as I will discuss). But the big picture is that the unions remain hugely powerful, and through collective bargaining they impose ineffective organization on the schools.

The unions are not the sole causes of ineffective organization, of course. The districts have done their share of damage too, particularly in the decades before accountability and charter schools gave them stronger incentives to boost student achievement. And state and national governments have added to the problem, imposing an avalanche of programs and rules that are often designed (via politics) with little attention to effective organization.[17]

Even so, the teachers unions stand out because the restrictions they impose bear directly on the role of *teachers*, and quality teaching is the single most significant determinant of student learning. Precisely because the unions are in the business of representing teachers, collective bargaining shapes the organization of schooling to its very core, and it ensures that this core is ill-suited to effective performance.[18]

This is the reality of American education at the local level. It is a reality of ineffective organization created and protected by power.

THE POLITICS OF BLOCKING

By law and tradition, the public schools are governed mainly by the states. The enduring American myth is one of local control, and from the late 1800s until the mid-1900s the states largely chose to run their schools that way. But in the years since, mainly in response to court requirements for funding equalization and accountability pressures to improve the schools, they have reasserted their authority. The overarching reality is that the school districts are state creations, and all of their essential features – their boundaries, organizations, funding, programs, involvement in collective bargaining – are subject to state authority. Any group that hopes to wield power over the public schools, therefore, needs to wield power in state politics. This is where the real action is.[19]

The national government has also gotten more involved since mid-century. Its main vehicle has been the 1965 Elementary and Secondary Education Act (ESEA), which authorizes a variety of programs – particularly for disadvantaged children – and funnels billions of dollars through the states to the districts. In 2002, the feds moved aggressively into the reform era with No Child Left Behind (NCLB), a groundbreaking revision of ESEA that sought to create a nationwide system of school accountability (with much state discretion). Still, the states continue to reign as the key authorities in public education.

For the teachers unions, politics can be enormously advantageous – and enormously threatening. Governments (especially state governments) are in a position to adopt virtually any work rules, education programs, or funding arrangements they want for the public schools, and the decisions automatically apply to all districts and schools in their jurisdictions. When the unions wield decisive power, all these wonders can be theirs. But reformers can do the same: by pushing for accountability, school choice, pay for performance, and other reforms the unions find threatening – and turning them into law. Either way, the stakes are huge. So for the unions, getting involved in politics (especially state politics) is essential, and they have invested heavily in political organization.

For well over a quarter-century, the NEA and AFT have been the most powerful groups in the politics of education.[20] No other groups have even been in the same ballpark. Since the unions were first established, they have had millions of members (today, more than 4 million). They have had astounding sums of money coming in regularly (mainly from dues) for campaign contributions and lobbying. They have had well-educated activists manning the electoral trenches – ringing doorbells, making phone calls. They have been able to orchestrate well-financed media campaigns on any topic or candidate. And their organizations have blanketed the nation, allowing them to coordinate all these resources toward their political ends.

Most aspects of the union power formula are difficult to quantify. But good information is available on their campaign contributions, and the evidence vividly shows that they are money machines of the first order: ranking among the very top contributors – compared to other interest groups *of all types* – at the national level, and in virtually all of the states. They dwarf other education groups. In ballot-measure campaigns, moreover, they are consistently the top contributors on their side of the issue, even on matters of taxing and spending that have nothing directly to do with education.[21]

Superior power does not mean that the teachers unions always get the policies they want. The American system of checks and balances makes that impossible, because its multiple veto points ensure that shepherding new laws through the political process is extremely difficult. Victories must be won at every step along the way to overcome all the hurdles. The flip side is that *blocking* new laws is much easier, for opponents need succeed at just *one* veto point to win. The American system is designed, then, to make defending the status quo far easier than taking positive action. And this is how the teachers unions have used their political power in shaping the nation's schools: not by imposing the policies they want, but by blocking or weakening those they do not want – and thus preventing true reform.[22]

Throughout, they have relied on their alliance with the Democratic Party. Democratic candidates receive almost all of the unions' campaign contributions, their in-the-trenches manpower, and their public-relations machinery: resources that are enormously valuable. In return, the unions can usually count on the Democrats to go to bat for them in the policy process: by insisting on bigger budgets, higher salaries, job protections, and other union-favored objectives – and most important, by standing in the way of major reform. The teachers unions have been the raw power behind the politics of blocking. The Democrats have done the blocking.[23]

MAINSTREAM REFORMS

In the wake of *A Nation at Risk*, the key drivers of reform during the 1980s were business groups and state governors. Deeply concerned about a faltering economy and growing international competition, business groups saw mediocre schools as a big part of the problem. They demanded action and found allies in the nation's governors, who became the political leaders of the reform movement.

Early on, the ideas that gained traction were decidedly incremental: spending more money, raising teacher salaries, adopting more rigorous curricula, training teachers better, and other mainstream reforms that fit comfortably within the existing system – and posed little or no threat to the unions. Indeed, the unions saw the new environment as a golden opportunity to push for spending and salary objectives that they had long yearned for anyway.[24]

These reforms did nothing to change the system itself: its structure, its incentives. National spending, for example, shot up by 74 percent between the 1982–83 and 1989–90 school years, providing schools with 35 percent more money per student in real dollars.[25] Yet the money would be spent by the same districts that had spent money so unproductively in the past, and their incentives were as weak as ever. Teacher salaries were raised substantially across the board, increasing 52 percent during this same period, for a gain of 17 percent in real dollars.[26] Yet good and bad teachers were still paid the same, and no one was being held accountable for student learning.

This was a tumultuous time, and much bolder ideas – for school choice, pay for performance, and more – were finding their way into policy debates. But precisely because these reforms were threatening to the traditional structure of jobs, the unions were staunchly opposed and used their power (with the help of allies) to derail them. The level of reform activity triggered by *A Nation at Risk* was unprecedented. But it was an inside-the-box affair, stifled by the politics of blocking.[27]

As the 1980s came to an end, these early efforts had clearly failed, and increasingly the talk among reformers turned to fundamental change.[28] Support surged for two major movements that soon amassed political power of their own: the choice movement and the accountability movement. Even so, states continued to invest heavily in mainstream reforms. Indeed, the reforms they pursued during the 1990s and most of the 2000s were mostly the *same* kinds of reforms they pursued during the 1980s – more spending, stricter requirements, more training – all with great fanfare, as though this time their recycled efforts would pay off.[29]

A number of "new" mainstream reforms gained support along the way. Of these the most popular was class size reduction, heavily promoted by President Clinton via his effort to fund 100,000 new teachers for the public schools. It was also aggressively pursued in a number of states, notably in California, which was the pioneer in 1996, and in Florida, where a 2002 ballot initiative required drastic reductions in class size. Needless to say, the teachers unions were strongly supportive, for teachers like the reduced workload, and it can only be implemented by hiring lots more of them, which increases union membership and power. But like the other mainstream reforms, class size reduction has proved a disappointment. It leaves teacher quality and incentives the same, and there is no evidence that it brings notable improvements in student learning beyond the first few years of school. Worse, it is among the most expensive of all possible reforms and cannot be justified in terms of bang for the buck.[30]

What is the problem here? Why, over the last quarter-century, have the states invested so heavily in reforms that offer so little promise? The answer is that, in addition to having a superficial appeal that makes them an easy sell, these reforms are not threatening to the teachers unions (or their usual allies such as the school districts and education schools) – and the unions do not use their power to block. The political gates are swung open, and governments are allowed to take action in ways that fit comfortably with the status quo.

From the standpoint of politics and power, then, mainstream reforms are all pluses and no minuses. The only downside is that they do not work.[31]

School Accountability

The ideas behind accountability have obvious merit. If the school system is to promote academic excellence, it must have clear standards defining what students need to know. It must test students to measure how well the standards are being met. And it must hold educators accountable for results – and give them incentives to do their best – by attaching consequences to outcomes. Writ large, these are simply the principles of effective management that business leaders live by every day: setting goals, measuring performance, attaching consequences, creating incentives.

As the 1980s drew to a disappointing close, accountability offered a path to fundamental change. And because it was essentially a demand for effective management that business leaders, governors, and the public could readily understand, it attracted broad support. The teachers unions, however, saw it very differently. Historically, teachers had been granted autonomy behind classroom doors, and their pay and jobs had been secure regardless of how much their students learned. Why would they want to have new requirements thrust upon them, their performance seriously evaluated, real consequences attached to their performance, and their jobs made less secure? These were radical departures from a performance-is-irrelevant past, and the unions were opposed.[32]

They were not alone. They had allies among (some) district superintendents, who saw it as a threat to their traditional autonomy; among (some) civil rights groups, concerned that testing could lead to high failure rates for minority kids; among certain experts, who claimed that tests are flawed and culturally biased;

and among certain Republican policymakers, who wanted to protect local control.

Yet this was not much of a coalition, especially as time went on. Many superintendents came to *support* accountability, because it gave them leverage for improving their schools. Key groups speaking for disadvantaged kids – Education Trust, for example – emerged as strong supporters of accountability. As opinion surveys consistently showed, most parents and citizens supported accountability, as well. Most experts believed that test scores could be put to valid, reliable use. And many Republicans – although resistant to *national* accountability efforts during the 1990s – have come to believe that, at least at the state level, educators need to be held accountable.[33]

In addition, the various members of the anti-accountability coalition have long been grossly unequal in terms of numbers, organization, money, and political clout. Except when it comes to national versus state accountability (which mobilizes Republican policymakers), the teachers unions really *are* the coalition. Without them, the whole thing would collapse in a heap, and the opposition to accountability (at the state level) would lack sufficient power to stand in the way of true reform. The anti-accountability movement is driven by union power.[34]

From the beginning, the unions could have drawn a line in the sand. Yet because this reform was so broadly popular, they opted for a more sophisticated course of action: to "support" accountability, participate in its design, and water it down. This was their approach throughout the 1990s, when many states actually adopted some form of accountability. And it continued during the 2000s in the wake of NCLB.

A key part of the union strategy has been the embrace of stronger curriculum standards – which, in themselves, are not threatening to teachers. It is the testing and the consequences for poor performance that the unions have sought to weaken and render ineffectual.

The science of testing is the most sophisticated component of the academic field of education. The unions' concern is that tests provide concrete evidence on the performance of teachers, not just of students. If tests show that kids are not learning, the publicity will inevitably bring public complaints, pressures to improve, and consequences. A rigorous testing system, moreover, would quickly reveal that some teachers are much better than others and that some are very bad. Indeed, that is precisely what the research literature *does* reveal.[35] Were such information routinely available, there would be objective grounds for removing bad teachers from classrooms. There would be objective grounds for giving better teachers higher pay. Accountability would begin to have real teeth.

The unions, accordingly, have long acted to prevent test scores from being put to serious use in evaluating teacher performance.[36] In New York City, for example, Joel Klein sought to improve teacher quality by bringing student scores to bear – along with much other relevant information – in evaluating new teachers for tenure. The United Federation of Teachers reacted by playing its trump card: getting legislative allies to enact a new law prohibiting any district in the state from using test scores in tenure evaluations. The information was available, but the unions had made it illegal to take the information into account.[37]

The New York case highlights the information challenge that unions are up against nationwide. The rise of information technology has dramatically enhanced the ability of state governments to collect data on students, schools, teachers, finances, and other aspects of the education system; to store this information in "data warehouses"; and to employ it in better organizing their schools. Nothing could be more basic to school improvement than good information. Yet the unions see good information as a threat – because it gives states and districts the capacity to link the evaluation, pay, and job security of teachers to student performance.[38]

In legislatures around the country – Texas, Colorado, California, and elsewhere – they have fought these data battles over and over again. They have pressured policymakers not to authorize teacher identifiers that can be linked to student identifiers in state data systems. And if they have lost on that score, they have pushed for laws that (as in New York) simply prohibit the linked data from being used in the evaluation or compensation of teachers. For many years, they were quite successful. Until Race to the Top intervened in 2009–10, only eighteen states had data systems that were even capable of connecting teacher data to student data.[39]

The unions' ultimate goal is not to fight test scores. What they aim for is a system that has *no negative consequences* – so that no one loses a job, no one's pay suffers, and no schools are shut down or reconstituted due to poor performance. Unions attack test scores to try to ensure that there is no evidentiary basis for such negative consequences. But it is the negative consequences that are truly threatening, not the test scores.

The unions have been extraordinarily successful over the last two decades at blocking negative consequences. Even the most straightforward reforms have almost always gone nowhere. It would have been a simple matter, for example, for states to relax or eliminate their tenure laws in order to make it easier – in conjunction with new data – to remove low-performing teachers from the classroom. But this obvious reform was rarely even considered, and virtually nothing was changed. An exception occurred in Georgia, when Democratic Governor Roy Barnes eliminated tenure for incoming teachers in 2000. But he was the exception that proved the rule: the state teachers union targeted him in the 2002 elections – and was widely credited with his defeat.[40]

The story is not much different for performance-based evaluations, performance-based pay, the reconstitution of failing schools, and other reforms that would put teeth into accountability (although there are very recent signs of change, discussed shortly). For the greater part of twenty years, as accountability systems were being adopted in state after state – and then nationally via NCLB – the specific reforms that promised to make accountability real were not adopted.

The politics of blocking was almost universally successful at ensuring that the states would have accountability systems that were literally *not designed to hold anyone accountable.*

The unions' blocking power is not uniform across the states. They tend to be weaker in the South, for instance, and that is why some of the pioneering efforts in accountability have come from states such as Texas, North Carolina, and Kentucky. Their influence also tends to be weaker at the national level than at the state level, because national politicians have larger, more diverse constituencies and the unions have much more interest-group competition.

It was due to this relative disadvantage at the national level, plus the fact that the political stars happened to line up just right for reformers – with Republican President George W. Bush leading the way, with key Democrats on board (in part, out of concern that Republicans might become the "education party"), and with key groups representing the disadvantaged on board as well – that the teachers unions lost control of the politics of NCLB. With the enactment of this legislation, the unions suffered their biggest defeat in the entire reform era.[41]

By comparison to other reforms enacted throughout this period, NCLB deserves to be regarded as a major policy change. It was a watershed event, initiating a radical shift in the federal government's role in public education that, for years to come, set states and districts scrambling to meet its requirements and put a national spotlight on performance. Yet despite its stunning break from the past, there is much less here than meets they eye.

NCLB was weak from the outset. As it was being designed, the unions and their allies scored important victories in watering the act down. Most important, they were able to ensure that it was *almost devoid of enforceable consequences* when schools and teachers failed to do their jobs.[42] They were also able to weaken it through politics – pivoting from their loss in Congress to a years-long, nation-wide campaign to undermine the act's implementation. Soon after NCLB was adopted, the NEA went to court to try to have it declared illegal and thus to block it after the fact. Both unions, meantime, launched public relations campaigns that loudly criticized accountability – claiming that students were over-tested, teachers were teaching to the test, and so on – to convince Americans that NCLB was fatally flawed.[43] And both put heavy pressure on their Democratic allies in hopes that, when the bill came up for reauthorization (originally scheduled for 2007), it could be permanently defeated or at least substantially weakened.

As of late 2014, NCLB *still* has not been reauthorized. And with the post-2010 rise of the Tea Party and a renewed Republican embrace of local control, which have (unintentionally) aided the unions' cause, it is clear that NCLB is in its death throes. If it is ever resurrected at all, it will be unrecognizable, putting almost total discretion back in the hands of the same state and local governments that had long refused to pursue serious accountability on their own: precisely what NCLB had reacted against and was trying to avoid.

This, then, is what "major change" has amounted to in American education. Yes, NCLB was a disruptive and surprising break from the past. But it was substantively weak at its core. It was hobbled – and ultimately eviscerated – by relentless political opposition from defenders of the traditional system. And it is *has not endured.*

As of today, more than a decade after NCLB was passed, the nation has fifty-one different accountability systems – one for each state and the District of Columbia – that conform to national requirements but have their own standards, their own tests, and their own sets of (supposed) consequences.[44] To call them accountability systems, however, is more symbolic than a description of what they actually do. Although Race to the Top and other recent developments may be generating positive movement, as I will discuss, the reality on the ground is that true accountability has remained elusive. Among other things,

– Tenure is virtually ironclad, and mediocre teachers stay in the classroom year after year even if their children learn absolutely nothing.
– Data on student performance are regularly collected but still play little or no role in measuring the performance of most teachers, virtually all of whom continue to get satisfactory evaluations.
– Teacher pay continues to follow the traditional salary schedule and is rarely linked to how much students learn.
– Schools rarely suffer any sanctions (such as reconstitution) for failing to teach their children.

School Choice

School choice, like accountability, has obvious advantages. Most important, when parents have the right to choose, they can leave bad schools: an empowerment that is especially valuable to poor and minority children, who are often trapped in the nation's worst schools.

Choice also shapes incentives. The public schools have traditionally had their kids and money guaranteed, regardless of how well they perform – but with choice the guarantees evaporate. If schools do not do their jobs well, they stand to lose children and resources. There are *consequences* for ineffective behavior, giving schools stronger incentives to perform and innovate.[45]

Choice was first proposed in the 1950s by economist Milton Friedman (1955), who advocated vouchers and envisioned a free market in education. Yet the modern choice movement, which picked up steam around 1990 (when accountability did), is not about free markets. Proponents recognize that choice can generate challenges – of equal access, parent information, transportation, accountability, and more – and that government needs to play a key role in designing appropriate rules.[46]

To the teachers unions, choice is deeply threatening. When families are given new options, the regular public schools lose children and money – and jobs. Indeed, were choice widely adopted, it could well trigger a devastating plunge in union membership, resources, and power. So the unions do *not* want families to have alternatives to the schools where their members teach. This is true even if the families are desperately poor and the kids are trapped in chronically bad schools.

The teachers unions are the nation's leading opponents of choice, but they do have allies. The NAACP has long seen choice as a veiled opportunity for whites to flee blacks; it is also concerned about job protection, because urban school systems are a prime source of minority jobs. The American Civil Liberties Union (ACLU) and the People for the American Way see vouchers for private schools (many of them religious) as a breach in the "wall of separation" between church and state. Liberals tend to be supportive of government, suspicious of markets, and worried that the poor cannot make good choices for themselves. And Democratic officials – who do the actual blocking – tend to be liberal in beliefs and electorally dependent on the unions.[47]

The choice movement has long been more anemic than its opponents. Unlike the accountability movement, moreover, it has never benefited from broad business support. A few well-heeled individuals (such as the late John Walton) have been major contributors, but most business leaders have seen education reform as a *management* problem (and thus an accountability problem), because management is what they do for a living. Throughout the 1980s, as a result, the choice movement was fueled by conservative activists, churches, private schools, parent groups, and the like: an enthusiastic lot, but hardly the kind of power base necessary to take on the unions. To have any hope, the movement needed to broaden its constituency.[48]

It did that by taking a left-hand turn from its libertarian roots. The signal event came in 1990, when frustrated parents in inner city Milwaukee rose up to demand vouchers as a means of escaping their abysmal public schools. With pivotal support from Wisconsin's Republican governor, Tommy Thompson, they won a surprising victory over strident union opposition. It was just a pilot limited to 1,000 disadvantaged kids. But the nation got its first voucher program.[49]

Since 1990, choice advocates have focused on poor and minority families in urban areas. The modern arguments for vouchers have less to do with free markets than with social equity, and opinion polls have consistently shown that its greatest supporters are poor and minority parents.[50]

Energized by this focus on the disadvantaged, voucher supporters have managed to eke out victories here and there despite all-out union opposition. The Milwaukee program has been vastly expanded, and there are now a number of other voucher programs as well – almost all of them small, some just recently adopted – for low-income children: in Cleveland and other parts of Ohio, Washington, DC, Louisiana, Indiana, and Racine (WI). There are also voucher programs for special needs children in Florida, Ohio, Utah, Georgia, Oklahoma, and Louisiana. And there are voucher-like programs that, through tax credits and nonprofit foundations, provide scholarships for low-income children (Florida, Arizona, Indiana, Iowa, Pennsylvania, and Rhode Island), for special needs kids (Arizona, North Carolina), and children generally (Arizona, Georgia, Louisiana, Illinois, Iowa, Minnesota).[51]

Yet the battles never really end, because the unions want all voucher and tax-credit programs eliminated. When Utah's legislature passed a voucher bill in 2007, the unions overturned it by putting it on the ballot and spending heavily to defeat it.[52] They attacked the Milwaukee and Cleveland programs for years in the courts – leading to the landmark *Zelman* decision in 2002, which ruled, in a union loss, that including religious schools in a voucher program is constitutional.[53] They got the courts to invalidate the Colorado voucher program and one of the three Florida voucher programs, and to create uncertainty for others as well, such as the Arizona program for special needs kids.[54] When the Democrats gained control of Congress and the presidency in 2008, they took swift action to kill the Washington, DC, voucher program for disadvantaged kids – which supporters were able to reinstate at least temporarily in 2011 as part of a high-stakes budget deal.[55] And these are just the highlights.

The voucher programs left standing (for now) are impressive victories given the opposition. Even so, they are hardly transformative. Of roughly 50 million public school students in this country, only about 210,000 children are receiving vouchers or tax-credit scholarships. This is a drop in the bucket. And most enrollments are due to just a few (relatively) large programs: the Milwaukee voucher program (24,915), the Florida McKay scholarship program for special education kids (27,040), the Arizona tax credit program (23,959), the Florida tax credit program (59,674), and the Pennsylvania tax credit program (59,218).[56] Outside the larger programs, vouchers today provide little choice, little competition for public schools, and few new incentives. The bottom line is that the teachers unions have been extremely successful at preventing vouchers (or tax credits) from altering the educational status quo.[57]

The idea of vouchers is an old one. The other seminal idea for expanding choice came along much later – again, around 1990. This was the idea of charter schools: public schools of choice that would operate independent of district control and most state regulations. For many policymakers, especially the more liberal and Democratic, charters offered a politically attractive middle ground. With charters they could support *public sector* choice for disadvantaged (and other) families – thus responding to demands for new options – yet they could also appease the unions by opposing vouchers and burdening charters with myriad restrictions. The unions, for their part, preferred charters to vouchers, because charters were potentially easier to control through politics. But the threat was much the same: charters allow kids to leave the regular public schools, taking money and jobs with them – and the unions did not want to see charters truly expand and take root.

Still, charters changed the political equation and gave choice a wider opening. And the 1990s became America's charter decade. In 1991, Minnesota adopted the first charter law (authorizing just eight schools statewide), followed by California in 1992 (with a ceiling of just 100 charters in a state with some 7,000 regular public schools). And by 2003, forty states (including Washington, DC) had adopted charter legislation.[58]

As the dominoes were falling, charters became the most widely accepted approach to school choice. They grew increasingly popular with parents and students, especially in urban areas with underperforming public schools. They spawned some stunningly effective schools for disadvantaged kids – most famously, the KIPP schools (which now number 162 nationwide). They gained considerable positive attention in the media and were featured in widely seen films (such as *Waiting for Superman*). They attracted support from prominent Democrats – including, during the 1990s, President Bill Clinton and Vice President Al Gore. And in recent years, President Barack Obama and his secretary of education, Arne Duncan, have been more than vocal, making charter reform a key part of their Race to the Top.

These are important developments. Yet throughout this time, the teachers unions fought to keep charters weak, and they continued to work through their Democratic allies, who talked a better game of charter support than they actually played. The result was legislation often high on symbolism and weak on substance. Among the usual restrictions: stiflingly low ceilings on the number of charters allowed statewide, lower per-pupil funding than the regular public schools (by an average of 23 percent), districts as the sole chartering authorities (because they have incentives to refuse), no charter access to district buildings, and no seed money to fund initial organization. The result is that almost all charter systems have been designed, quite purposely, to provide families with very little choice and the public schools with very little competition.[59]

Once these programs are in place, moreover, the unions try to weaken them further. One line of attack is through public relations: they regularly generate claims, reports, and studies attacking charter performance and aiming to shrink their popularity.[60] Another line of attack is through the courts, where the unions have taken action – in New York, New Jersey, Minnesota, Ohio, and elsewhere – to argue that charter schools violate state constitutions and that charter legislation should be annulled.[61]

In certain cities, the situation has gotten away from them and charters have made impressive gains. In New Orleans, where the school system was destroyed by Katrina in 2005 and reformers gained the upper hand, charters enroll more than 90 percent of students. This is obviously an unusual situation. The charter "market share" is also quite high, however, in Washington, DC (47 percent), Detroit (45 percent), Kansas City (36 percent), Dayton (31 percent), Gary (36 percent), St. Louis (24 percent), and a number of other urban districts, where they are clearly offering families many new choices and creating meaningful competition for the regular public schools.[62]

Reformers have been far less successful in the rest of the country. Eight states do not even have charter laws. And in those that do, there are very few charter schools and only small percentages of kids attend them. Here are some "charter states" and their enrollments: Connecticut (1.5 percent), Iowa (0.2 percent), Kansas (1.4 percent), Maine (0.3 percent), Virginia (0.2 percent), Illinois (3.1 percent), Oklahoma (1.3 percent), and Tennessee (2.6 percent). Nationwide, after twenty years of reformist effort, there are only 6,000 charter schools in a population of more than 95,000 and they enroll only 5 percent of the nation's public school children.[63]

Tiny enrollments are no indication of the underlying demand. Most charters have long waiting lists of children eager to get in. In Harlem, for instance, charter schools are enormously popular, enrolling nearly 25 percent of local public school kids; but many more are clamoring to get in and cannot, because there are not nearly enough charters to take them. In the spring of 2010, some 14,000 Harlem children submitted applications for just 2,700 open slots, and more than 11,000 were turned away.[64] Nationwide, about 920,000 children are on wait lists, hoping to get into schools that do not have room to take them.[65] The demand for charters far outstrips the supply.

With 42 states having adopted charter laws, it is natural to think that charters must be making great progress almost everywhere, but this is far from the truth. Most charter laws are filled with restrictions designed to limit the spread of charters and keep enrollments down. And that is what they do. The real winner here is not the charter movement or the countless families that seek new alternatives for their kids. The real winner is the politics of blocking.

THE FUTURE

As long as the teachers unions remain powerful, America's schools cannot be organized in the best interests of children. At the local level, the unions use their power in collective bargaining to impose – and then protect – special-interest work rules that make no sense from the standpoint of effective schooling. In the policymaking process, where higher-level policies are battled out, they use their power to block or weaken reforms that threaten their interests, making it impossible for governments to correct for the system's pathologies and create organizations that are built for top-flight performance.

Is there any hope, going forward, that the problem of union power can somehow be overcome? Under normal conditions, the answer would be no. The teachers unions have been enormously powerful for decades; they are powerful now; and aided by the checks and balances built into the political system, they are in a position to *use* that power to block any attempts to take their power away. This is the Catch-22 of power: you cannot take away the power of powerful groups, because they will use their power to stop you.

Yet these are not normal times. American education stands at a critical juncture – and due to an unusual confluence of events, the stars are lining up in a unique configuration that augers well for major change.[66]

Endogenous Change

Two separate dynamics are at work. The first is arising endogenously *within* the education system and its politics. The teachers unions are on the defensive like never before: blamed for obstructing reform, defending bad teachers, under-mining effective organization. Reformers are gaining political strength.

Why is this happening? Partly, the unions have been caught in a perfect storm. With the onset of the Great Recession, the states have been in financial crisis. And Republicans, propelled by Tea Partiers and huge gains in the 2010 elections, have used the crisis as a vehicle for trying to limit the collective bargaining rights of public workers, including teachers, thus threatening the fundamentals of union power. In several states – Wisconsin, Ohio, Indiana, Tennessee, Idaho, Florida – new Republican legislation dramatically limited the scope of collective bargaining and (depending on the state) the ability of public unions to collect fees and dues and attract members. The unions and their Democratic allies launched massive counterattacks – street demonstrations, recall elections, court cases, and more. But except in Ohio and Idaho, where the reforms were overturned through union-inspired ballot measures, the Republican victories still stand at this writing.[67]

It is tempting to think that the antiunion forces now have the upper hand. Yet the unions remain enormously powerful, and the perfect storm will pass. Yes, it has wreaked havoc, but only in a few Republican-controlled states. This is not a uniform, national phenomenon. And even in these few states, the financial crisis will soon fade, the Democrats will eventually gain power, and the unions will find opportunities for reversing their losses (although checks and balances will now work against them, with Republicans in a position to block).

Another political development is much more widespread and fundamental – and much more damaging, long-term, to the teachers unions. This one is taking place among Democrats. With many urban schools abysmally bad and staying that way, accountability putting the spotlight on poor performance, and school choice offering attractive opportunities for escape that the unions system-atically snuff out, advocates for the disadvantaged are fed up. More than ever before, they are demanding major reform, and they are overtly critical of the unions for obstructing it. Moderate and liberal opinion leaders – writing in *Time, Newsweek*, and other respected outlets – regularly excoriate the unions for putting job interests ahead of children. A new group (formed in 2007), the Democrats for Education Reform, has attracted a bevy of high-profile Democrats eager to distance their party from the teachers unions, and it is taking serious action – in elections, legislatures, the media – to make it happen.[68]

Energizing this new movement is a growing network of activists, many of them (it appears) moderates and liberals, who are increasingly occupying influ-ential positions within the education and political systems – and are openly critical of the unions for blocking reform. The most vibrant source of this activism is Teach for America, whose alumni – including Michelle Rhee – have immersed themselves by the thousands in the cause of reform.[69] Working side by side with these activists are well-heeled philanthropic foundations – Gates, Broad, Walton – that have poured big money into reforms (such as performance-based evaluations and pay) the unions have long opposed and the new activists very much favor.[70]

This ferment has not come close to converting most mainstream Democratic officeholders, who remain union allies. Yet during the 2008 presidential primaries, there was one Democratic candidate who did *not* toe the union line; and that candidate, Barack Obama, managed to win the nomination and become president. In office, he and his secretary of education, Arne Duncan, cast their lot mainly with the new reformers – producing (among other things) the 2009–10 Race to the Top, in which states competed for shares of $4.35 billion by embracing, or saying they would later embrace, system-challenging reforms: in promoting performance-based evaluations and pay, charter schools, state data systems, and more. Whether the results have real substance remains to be seen. But the sheer level of reformist activity during the Race to the Top was striking, and many states have continued to enact changes in the years since.

This is particularly true with regard to performance-based evaluations, which have become the centerpiece of the nation's reform agenda. As of 2014, forty-one states have enacted laws requiring that teachers be evaluated with some reference to objective measures of student achievement, and thirty-five of these require that student achievement be a significant, or the most significant, factor.[71] On paper, of course, these are significant breaks from the past. But they have yet to be translated into action, and the devil is in the details – which will be worked out over a period of years, usually through "collaboration" with unions intent on minimizing the role of test scores, ensuring job security, and using their power in both politics and collective bargaining to water the new policies down considerably.[72]

As this snapshot can only suggest, a lot has been happening recently in the politics of American education. Over the last decade or so, the tide has begun to move against the teachers unions. As far as politics goes, this is the big educational story of our era. It is not, first and foremost, a story about the Republican victories in Wisconsin and a few other states. It is largely a story about the unions' eroding base of support base among Democrats. Without this support base, they lose. Everywhere.

Yet the erosion will only go so far. The reason is that, by their words and deeds, even these reformist Democrats – from Obama and Duncan on down – have made it clear that they believe in unions and collective bargaining, and they have no intention of taking action to limit collective bargaining or weaken the power of the unions. They are serious about improving the nation's schools. But they intend to do it collaboratively, and thus within an education system filled with powerful unions that must somehow be accommodated and made "part of the solution." This intention is reinforced by a brute political fact: the power of the Democratic Party itself is highly dependent on the power of the unions, and thus on the continuation of collective bargaining.[73]

The political dynamic we are now witnessing in American education, then – an endogenous development that has emerged within the system itself – is not equipped to bring about major change. It is exciting. It is unprecedented. It propels the education system in the right direction. But it is inherently limited, because it does very little to *reduce the power* of the teachers unions – and they will continue to use their power to prevent the schools from being effectively organized.

Something more is needed. Something that *does* reduce union power.

Exogenous Change

That something is the worldwide revolution in information technology – an exogenous development, originating entirely *outside* the education system and its politics, that is among the most profoundly influential forces ever to sweep the planet. Clearly, it is fast transforming the fundamentals of human society. And with its rooting in information and knowledge, there can be no doubt that it will ultimately transform the way students learn, teachers teach, and schools are organized. It is the future of American education – indeed, of world education.

Even today, with education technology in its early stages, online curricula can be customized to the learning styles and life situations of individual students: giving them instant feedback on how well they are doing, providing them with remedial work when they need it, allowing them to move at their own pace, and giving them access – wherever they live, whatever their race or background – to a vast range of courses their own schools do not offer, and ultimately to the best the world can provide. By strategically substituting technology (which is cheap) for labor (which is expensive), moreover, schools can be far more cost-effective than they are now, and thus provide far more education per dollar – which is crucial as we enter an era of tight budgets.[74]

Because technology stands to have enormous impacts on jobs and money, the teachers unions find it threatening. And throughout the 2000s, they have used their political power – in state legislatures, in the courts – to try to block its advance. But education technology is not a reform. It is not a new law. Reforms and laws are small things by comparison, and they can be blocked. Education technology is a tsunami that is only now beginning to swell, and it will hit the American public school system with full force over the next decade and those to follow. Long term, the teachers unions can't stop it. It is much bigger and more powerful than they are.[75]

The advance of technology will then have dire consequences for established power. There will be a growing substitution of technology for labor, and thus a steep decline in the number of teachers (and union members) per student; a dispersion of the teaching labor force, which will no longer be so geographically concentrated in districts (because online teachers can be anywhere); and a proliferation of new online providers and choice options, attracting away students, money, and jobs. All of these developments will dramatically undermine the membership and financial resources of the teachers unions, and thus their political power. Increasingly, they will be *unable to block*, and the political gates will swing open. The era of a union-protected status quo will come to an end. A new era – and a new education system – will begin.[76]

CONCLUSION

I did not write this chapter to gaze into the future and solve the problem of union power in American education. I wrote it to describe and document the problem as it has emerged and taken hold since the 1960s, and to try to understand it. As it happens, there are solid grounds for believing that there *is* a solution, at least over the long haul. But it is only a solution because of an accident of history: the revolution in information technology. This is a monster development, entirely beyond the realm of normal reform activity, which is being thrust upon the education system from the outside.

It is quite likely that, were it not for this bombshell from without, there would be no solution. Especially within a government of checks and balances, power is its own protection. Under normal conditions, the Catch-22 of union power guarantees the stability of the existing education system, along with the stability of union power itself. And normal conditions have prevailed, tenaciously and despite all the hullabaloo about reform, for well over a quarter-century.

Much has happened during this time. But if we step back from it all, what do we see? We see a nation whose leaders have fully agreed that improving the public schools is absolutely critical to the well-being of the country, and who have invested heavily to bring that improvement about. We also see an education system that has been protected from change by vested interests – in the form of the teachers unions – with a deep stake in preserving the status quo, however inadequate its performance.

Their power has had enormous consequences. In collective bargaining, they have imposed bizarre forms of organization on the public schools that no one would favor if they were simply concerned with what works best for children. The schools are organized mainly to benefit the adults who work there. In the political process, the unions block or weaken reforms they find threatening, however helpful those reforms might be for schools and kids. This is obviously true for major and eminently sensible reforms, such as accountability and choice. It is also true for very simple, easy-to-accomplish reforms, such as getting bad teachers out of the classroom.

Fortunately, we are not in normal times anymore. The winds of change are blowing. Technology aside, the ferment within the Democratic Party and the growing network of moderate and liberal activists have given reformers considerably more clout in the policy process. These are exciting developments, and they may well grow in strength and intensity. But they still leave the teachers unions with enormous power. Indeed, these new-wave reformers actually have no intention of undermining the unions' power base – and without a big boost from technology, they are unlikely to bring about anything like transformative change. They are capable of bringing about more performance-based evaluations, more data, and thus of winning small victories for sanity that are beneficial and much needed. But small victories are still small. And they need to be recognized for what they are.

Technology, by contrast, has the unyielding force to deliver a true break-through. It will probably happen slowly, however, over a long period of time. And it may take decades – which is little comfort to the children of today, who deserve much more than they are getting.

Children should always come first. Yet in America's system of public educa-tion, governed as it is by power and special interests, they simply do not. And in the near term, they will not. As things now stand, the United States has an education system that is not organized to be effective for children, cannot be productively reformed in their best interests, and is powerfully protected to ensure that the interests of adults prevail. This is our reality.

Notes

1. Cruz, Gilbert. 2009. "Can Arne Duncan (and $5 Billion) Fix America's Schools?" *Time*, September 14.
2. President's Commission on Excellence in Education. 1983. *A Nation at Risk: The Imperative for Educational Reform*. Washington, DC: U.S. Department of Education; Toch, Thomas. 1991. *In the Name of Excellence*. New York: Oxford University Press; Hess, Frederick. 2004. *Common Sense School Reform*. New York: Palgrave Macmillan.
3. For copious evidence on the failures of the American reform era, see: Moe, Terry M. 2011. *Special Interest*. Washington, DC: Brookings Institution Press; Hanushek, Eric A. 2003. "The Failure of Input-Based Schooling." *Economic Journal*, 113, 64–98; and Hanushek, Eric A., and, Alfred A. Lindseth. 2009. *Schoolhouses, Courthouses, and Statehouses: Solving the Funding-Achievement Puzzle in America's Public Schools*. Princeton: Princeton University Press.
4. For a much more extensive treatment and documentation of this argument, see: Moe (2011). For a more expansive theoretical treatment of vested interests that applies to institutions generally, including public schools, see: Moe, Terry M. 2015. "Vested Interests and Political Institutions." *Political Science Quarterly*, forthcoming as this writing. See also: Moe, Terry M. 2012. "Teachers Unions and American Education Reform: The Politics of Blocking." *The Forum*, vol.10, no. 1, Article 4, which is a longer version of the current chapter, and contains many details and references that could not be included here due to space limitations.
5. Murphy, Marjorie. 1990. *Blackboard Unions*. Ithaca, NY: Cornell University Press.
6. Freeman, Richard B. March 1986. "Unionism Comes to the Public Sector." *Journal of Economic Literature*. XXIV, 41–86; West, A. M. 1980. *The National Education Association: The Power Base for Education*. New York: Free Press.
7. These figures are taken from the National Center for Education Statistics' Schools and Staffing Surveys of 2003–04 and 2007–08 and averaged to give more reliable numbers. See Moe (2011) for details by state. Recent labor reforms in Wisconsin, Tennessee, and a few other states may lower the national figures slightly (depending on which reforms prove enduring), as could the Great Recession that began in 2008 and resulted in teacher layoffs.
8. For extensive survey-based evidence on the key role of collective bargaining and union locals to the organizational (and political) success of the unions, see chapter 3 of Moe (2011).
9. For a more extensive discussion of these and other contract rules, as well as their implications for effective organization, see chapter 6 of Moe (2011).

10. Weisberg, D., Sexton, S., Mulhern, J., and Keeling, D. 2009. "The Widget Effect: Our National Failure to Acknowledge and Act on Differences in Teacher Effectiveness." Brooklyn, NY: The New Teacher Project. Retrieved from http://widgeteffect.org/down-loads/TheWidgetEffect.pdf.

11. See, e.g., the path-breaking detailed research of journalist Scott Reeder, which covers an eighteen-year period in the state of Illinois. Available on his Web site at www.thehiddencostsoftenure.com.

12. See Moe, 2011. See also: Moe, Terry M. Spring 2006. "Political Control and the Power of the Agent." *Journal of Law, Economics, and Organization*, 22, 1–29; and Moe, Terry M. 2005. "Teachers Unions and School Board Elections." In William G. Howell, ed., *Beseiged: School Boards and the Future of Education Politics*. Washington, DC: Brookings Institution Press, pp. 254–287.

13. On why districts are weak and have recently had greater incentive to fight back, see Moe (2011), chapters 4 and 7.

14. Viteritti, Joseph. 2009. Editor. *When Mayors Take Charge: School Governance in the City*. Washington, DC: Brookings Institution Press; Henig, Jeffrey R. and Wilbur C. Rich (2004). Editors. *Mayors in the Middle: Politics, Race, and Mayoral Control of Urban Schools*. Princeton: Princeton University Press; and Wong, Kenneth K., Francis X. Shen, Dorothea Anagnostopoulos, and Stacey Rutledge. 2007. *The Education Mayor: Improving America's Schools*. Washington, DC: Georgetown University Press.

15. For detailed accounts of the labor clashes in both these city school districts, see Moe (2011), chapter 7.

16. United Press International. November 19, 2009. "Gates Foundation Program Aimed at Schools." Retrieved from www.upi.com/Top_News/US/2009/11/18/Gates-Foundation-program-aimed-at-schools/UPI-46821258569176/; Anderson, Nick. July 12, 2010. "Gates Foundation Playing Pivotal Role in Changes for Education System." *Washington Post*; and Carroll, Thomas W. October 21, 2009. "New Haven's Teacher Contract a Model? Not So Fast." *Huffington Post*. Retrieved from www.huffingtonpost.com/thomas-w-carroll/new-havens-teacher-contra_b_328950.html.

17. Chubb, John E., and Terry M. Moe. 1990. *Politics, Markets, and America's Schools*. Washington, DC: Brookings Institution Press.

18. For studies of the impact of unions and labor contracts on student achievement, see especially: Hoxby, Caroline M. (1996). "How Teachers Unions Affect Education Production." *Quarterly Journal of Economics*. 111 no. 3, 671–718; and Moe, Terry M. January 2009. "Collective Bargaining and the Performance of the Public Schools." *American Journal of Political Science*. 53, 156–174. For a review of the larger research literature, see Moe (2011), chapter 6.

19. Kirst, Michael, and Frederick M. Wirt. 2009. *The Political Dynamics of American Education*, 4th ed. Richmond, CA: McCutchan.

20. Although policymakers and opinion leaders are increasingly recognizing as much, academic scholarship (aside from my own) does not emphasize this theme at all. Researchers have barely studied the politics of education over the decades, much less the political role of teachers unions. There do exist two small literatures on education politics, but neither sheds much light on its structure of power. One literature centers on NCLB, whose national-level politics are simply not representative of the broader – mainly state and local – politics that shape American education generally. These studies portray the politics of reform as a fractious brand of pluralist politics filled with large numbers of diverse, competing groups; they pay little attention to the

teachers unions; and they provide little insight into the structure of power that protects the status quo and ensures that events like NCLB almost never happen. See, e.g.: McGuinn, Patrick. 2006. *No Child Left Behind and the Transformation of Federal Education Policy*. Lawrence, KS: University of Kansas Press; Rhodes, Jesse H. 2012. *An Education in Politics: The Origin and Evolution of No Child Left Behind*. Ithaca, NY: Cornell University Press; Manna, Paul. 2006. *School's In: Federalism and the National Education Agenda*. Washington, DC: Georgetown University Press; Anderson, Lee W. 2007. *Congress and the Classroom: From the Cold War to "No Child Left Behind."* University Park, PA: Penn State University Press; Kaestle, Carl F., Alyssa E. Lodewick, and Jeffrey R. Henig. 2007. Editors. *To Educate a Nation: Federal and National Strategies of School Reform*. Lawrence, KS: University of Kansas Press; Debray, Elizabeth, and Carl Kaestle. 2006. *Politics, Ideology, and Education: Federal Policy during the Clinton and Bush Administrations*. New York: Teachers College Press; and McAndrews, Lawrence. 2008. *The Era of Education: The Presidents and the Schools, 1965–2001*. Champagne-Urbana, IL: University of Illinois Press. The second body of literature focuses on urban education reform, with special attention to race. Its focus is on "civic capacity" – on whether mayors, stakeholders, and civic groups can concert their education reform efforts for the greater good – and it does little to explore the role of unions or to lay bare the structure of power that invariably resists and derails major change. See, e.g.: Stone, Clarence N., Jeffrey R. Henig, and Carol Pierannunzi. 2001. *Building Civic Capacity*. Lawrence, KS: University Press of Kansas; Henig, Jeffrey R., Richard C. Hula, Marion Orr, and Desiree S. Pedescleaux. 1999. *The Color of School Reform*. Princeton: Princeton University Press; and Henig, Jeffrey R., and Wilbur C. Rich. 2004. Editors. *Mayors in the Middle: Politics, Race, and Mayoral Control of Urban Schools*. Princeton: Princeton University Press. The exception is Wilbur Rich, whose work highlights the role of the "public school cartel" in powerfully resisting change. See Rich, Wilbur. 1996. *Black Mayors and School Politics*. New York: Garland Publishing.

21. For data on contributions, see Moe (2011), chapter 9. See also the Center for Responsive Politics at www.opensecrets.org for national spending figures, and the National Institute on Money in State Politics at www.followthemoney.org for state spending figures.

22. These features of American government are well known. For a theoretical treatment of how veto points and veto politics shape the making and blocking of public policy, see Tsebelis, George. 2002. *Veto Players: How Political Institutions Work*. Princeton: Princeton University Press. On the power of interest groups and their capacity for preventing change, see e.g.: Pierson, Paul. July 1993. "When Effect Becomes Cause." *World Politics*. 45, 595–628; Pierson, Paul. 2004. *Politics in Time*. Princeton: Princeton University Press; Schattschneider, E. E. 1960. *The Semi-Sovereign People: A Realist's View of Democracy in America*. New York: Holt, Rinehart, and Winston; and Lowi, Theodore. 1969. *The End of Liberalism: Ideology, Policy, and the Crisis of Public Authority*. New York: Norton.

23. See Moe (2011), chapters 9 and 10.

24. Toch, Thomas. 1991. *In the Name of Excellence*. New York: Oxford University Press; Currence, Cindy. May 15, 1985. "Teachers' Unions Bringing Reform Issues to Bargaining Table." *Education Week*.

25. National Center for Education Statistics, 2009. *Digest of Education Statistics, 2008*. Washington, DC: NCES.

26. National Center for Education Statistics. 1995. *Digest of Education Statistics, 1995.* Washington, DC: NCES.
27. Toch, 1991.
28. O'Day, Jennifer A., and Marshall S. Smith. 1993. "Systemic School Reform and Educational Opportunity." In Susan Fuhrman, ed., *Designing Coherent Education Policy: Improving the System.* San Francisco: Jossey-Bass, 250–312; Toch, 1991.
29. Hess, Frederick. 2010. *The Same Thing Over and Over Again.* Cambridge, MA: Harvard University Press; Tyack, David, and Larry Cuban. 1997. *Tinkering toward Utopia.* Cambridge, MA: Harvard University Press.
30. Hanushek, Eric A. 2002. "Evidence, Politics, and the Class Size Debate." In Lawrence Mishel and Richard Rothstein, eds., *The Class Size Debate.* Washington, DC: Economic Policy Institute.
31. Hanushek, Eric A. 2003. "The Failure of Input-Based Schooling." *Economic Journal*, 113, 64–98.
32. For a perspective on how the early politics of accountability unfolded across states, see Izumi, Lance T., and Williamson M. Evers. 2002. "State Accountability Systems." In Williamson M. Evers and Herbert J. Walberg, eds., *School Accountability.* Stanford: Hoover Institution Press, pp. 105–153.
33. Most accounts of the politics of education put too much emphasis on Republican resistance to accountability. This is because the focus of these studies is on NCLB and its attempt to nationalize accountability, rather than on accountability more generally and its state-level politics. See my earlier note on the NCLB literature.
34. On the unions' centrality, see, e.g., Williams, 2006.
35. Hanushek, Eric A. and Steven Rivkin (2006). "Teacher Quality." In Eric A. Hanushek and Finis Welch, eds., *Handbook of the Economics of Education.* Amsterdam: Elsevier, 1051–78.
36. Recently, under intense pressure – and sometimes in response to big money (as in the Hillsborough County, Memphis, and Pittsburgh cases I discussed earlier) – the unions have indicated a willingness to consider at least some role for test scores in the evaluation of teachers. But these are strategic concessions, and not an indication that the unions are truly embracing this line of reform. Their underlying opposition remains the same, as do their interests – and as time goes on, they can be expected to try to minimize the role that test scores are allowed to play. See Moe (2011), especially chapters 8 and 10.
37. Medina, Jennifer. March 18, 2008. "Bill Would Bar Linking Class Test Scores to Tenure." *New York Times.*
38. Moe, Terry M., and John E. Chubb. 2009. *Liberating Learning.* San Francisco: Jossey-Bass.
39. Data Quality Campaign. 2007 NCEA State P–12 Data Collection Survey Results: State of the Nation. Retrieved from www.dataqualitycampaign.org/survey_results/state_of_nation.cfm.
40. Salzer, James. June 20, 2010. "Teacher Vote at Center of Race." *Atlanta Journal-Constitution.*
41. For studies of NCLB, its history, its politics, and its aftermath, see McGuinn, 2006; Rhodes, 2012; Manna, 2006; Anderson, 2007; Kaestle and Lodewick, 2007; Debray and Kaestle, 2006; McAndrews, 2008.

42. Williams, Joe. 2007. "District Accountability: More Bark Than Bite?" In Frederick M. Hess and Chester E. Finn, Jr., eds., *No Remedy Left Behind: Lessons from a Half-Decade of NCLB*. Washington, DC: AEI Press, pp. 290–308.

43. Honawar, Vaishali. July 12, 2006. "NEA Opens Campaign to Rewrite Federal Education Law." *Education Week*; Honawar, Vaishali. July 8, 2008. "New Aft Leader Vows to Bring Down NCLB Law." *Education Week*; Klein, Alyson, and David J. Hoff. September 19, 2007. "Unions Assail Teacher Ideas in NCLB Draft." *Education Week*.

44. The details of state accountability systems can be found on the Web site of the Council of Chief State School Officers at www.ccsso.org and the Web site of the Education Commission of the States at www.ecs.org. Note that, as of late 2014, forty-five states have signed on to Common Core Standards and, if all goes as planned – a big if – will adopt this set of common academic standards for English and Math in 2014–15. See, e.g., the Common Core Web site at www.corestandards.org/.

45. See, for example, Chubb and Moe, 1990; Moe, Terry. 2008. "Beyond the Free Market: The Structure of School Choice," *Brigham Young University Law Review* no. 2: 557–592; and Coulson, Andrew J. 1999. *Market Education*. New Brunswick, NJ: Transaction Publishers."

46. Moe, 2008.

47. Moe, Terry M. 2001. *Schools, Vouchers, and the American Public*. Washington, DC: Brookings Institution Press; Morken, Hubert, and Jo Renee Formicola. 1999. *The Politics of School Choice*. London: Rowman and Littlefield; Hill, Paul T., and Aschley E. Jochim. 2009. "Political Perspectives on School Choice." In Mark Berends, Matthew G. Springer, Dale Ballou, and Herbert J. Walberg, eds., *Handbook of Research on School Choice*. New York: Routledge, 3–18.

48. Moe, 2001; Henig, 1995; Finn, Chester E. 2008. *Troublemaker: A Personal History of School Reform since Sputnik*. Princeton: Princeton University Press; and Cookson, Peter. 1995. *School Choice*. New Haven: Yale University Press.

49. Witte, John F. 2000. *The Market Approach to Education*. Princeton: Princeton University Press.

50. Moe, 2001; Howell, William G., Paul E. Peterson, and Martin R. West. Fall 2009. The 2009 Education Next-PEPG Survey of Public Opinion. *Education Next*.

51. For an overview of voucher plans across the nation, see Friedman Foundation. 2014. *The ABC's of School Choice, 2014 Edition*, at www.friedmanfoundation.org. See also the Web site of the American Federation for Children at www.federationforchildren.com/existing-programs.

52. McNeil, Michele. November 7, 2007. "Utah Vouchers Rejected in Overwhelming Vote." *Education Week*. For a discussion of the political logic of ballot measure campaigns, where "when in doubt, vote no" is the norm among voters and anti-voucher money has been very effective at making voters worry that vouchers may hurt the public schools, see Moe, *Schools, Vouchers, and the American Public*. This explains why vouchers would be defeated even in a conservative state such as Utah.

53. Stout, David. June 27, 2002. "Public Money Can Pay Religious-School Tuition, Court Rules." *New York Times*.

54. Hurst, Marianne D. June 9, 2004. "Colo. Supreme Court Strikes Down Voucher Law." *Education Week*; Richard, Alan, January 11, 2006. "Fla. Court: Vouchers Unconstitutional." *Education Week*; Kossan, Pat. May 16. 2008, "Ariz. School Voucher Programs Ruled Unconstitutional." *Arizona Republic*.

55. *Washington Post*. April 11, 2009. Editorial. "Presumed Dead: Politics Is Driving the Destruction of the District's School Voucher Program"; Pershing, Ben. April 9, 2011. "Budget Deal Includes D.C. Abortion Rider, Money for School Vouchers." *Washington Post*.

56. These are the most recently available figures as of 2014. See Friedman Foundation, 2014.

57. There is a research literature on the impact of vouchers on student achievement, but I do not explore it here because my focus is on the politics of blocking – and union opposition has nothing to do with what the research does or does not show. On the research, see: Howell, William G., and Paul E. Peterson. 2002. *The Education Gap: Vouchers and Urban Schools*. Washington, DC: Brookings Institution Press; Wolf, Patrick J. April 2008. "School Voucher Programs: What the Research Says about Parental School Choice." *Brigham Young University Law Review*. 2, 415–46; and Figlio, David. 2009. "Voucher Outcomes." In Mark Berends, Matthew G. Springer, Dale Ballou, and Herbert J. Walberg, eds., *Handbook of Research on School Choice*. New York: Routledge, 321–37.

58. Finn, Chester E., Bruno V. Manno, and Gregg Vanourek. 2001. *Charter Schools in Action*. Princeton: Princeton University Press; Mintrom, Michael. 2000. *Policy Entrepreneurs and School Choice*. Washington, DC: Georgetown University Press; Morken, Hubert, and Jo Renee Formicola. 1999. *The Politics of School Choice*. London: Rowman and Littlefield.

59. Hill, Paul T. 2006. Editor. *Charter Schools against the Odds*. Stanford: Hoover Institution Press; Center for Education Reform. 2012. *Charter School Laws across the States 2012*. Retrieved from http://www.edreform.com/2012/04/02/2012-char ter-laws/.

60. As with vouchers, the unions are opposed to charters for reasons unrelated to their impacts on student achievement, and I will not be reviewing that research here. But see Center for Research on Education Outcomes. 2009. "Multiple Choice: Charter School Performance in 16 States." Available on the center's Web site at http://credo. stanford.edu/reports/MULTIPLE_CHOICE_CREDO.pdf; Hoxby, Caroline M., Sonali Murarka, and Jenny Kang. September 2009. "How New York City's Charter Schools Affect Achievement." Second report in series. Cambridge, MA: New York City Charter Schools Evaluation Project; and Teasley, Betty. 2009. "Charter School Outcomes." In Mark Berends, Matthew G. Springer, Dale Ballou, and Herbert J. Walberg, eds., *Handbook of Research on School Choice*. New York: Routledge, 209–26.

61. See, for example, Ohlemacher, Stephen. June 10, 2004. "Ohio Educators File Federal Lawsuit; Teachers Union Deems Charters Illegal." *Cleveland Plain Dealer*.

62. The figures are for 2012–13 and taken from the "dashboard" data compiled by the National Alliance for Public Charter Schools. Retrieved from http://dashboard. publiccharters.org/dashboard/home.

63. Ibid.

64. Brill, Steven. May 17, 2010. "Teachers Unions' Last Stand." *New York Times Sunday Magazine*.

65. As of 2012–13. Figure is from the "dashboard" data compiled by the National Alliance for Public Charter Schools. Retrieved from http://dashboard.publicchar ters.org/dashboard/home.

66. On critical junctures and how they figure into analyses of institutional change, see, e.g., Pierson, Paul, and Theda Skocpol. 2002. "Historical Institutionalism in Contemporary Political Science." In Ira Katznelson and Helen V. Milner, eds., *Political Science: The State of the Discipline.* New York: W.W. Norton, 693–721; Pierson, Paul. 2004. *Politics in Time.* Princeton: Princeton University Press; and Collins, Ruth Berins, and David Collier. 1991. *Shaping the Political Arena: Critical Junctures, the Labor Movement, and Regime Dynamics in Latin America.* Princeton: Princeton University Press.

67. See, for example, Greenhouse, Steven. March 31, 2011. "Ohio's Anti-Union Law Is Tougher than Wisconsin's." *New York Times*; Locker, Richard. May 20, 2011. "Tennessee Legislature Ok's Ban of Teacher Bargaining." *The Commercial Appeal*, Memphis, TN; and Epstein, Jennifer. March 8, 2011. "Idaho Ok's Bill Limiting Bargaining." *Politico.*

68. Brill, 2011.

69. Brill, 2011; Graves, Lucia. October 17, 2008. "The Evolution of Teach for America." *U.S. News and World Report.*

70. Anderson, Nick. July 12, 2010. "Gates Foundation Playing Pivotal Role in Changes for Education System." *Washington Post*; Colvin, Richard Lee. Fall 2005. "The New Philanthropists." *Education Next*, 34–41.

71. National Council on Teacher Quality (2014). *State of the States 2014: Teacher Effectiveness Policies.* Washington, DC: National Council on Teacher Quality.

72. Moe, 2011.

73. For a detailed discussion of this widespread belief in "reform unionism" – what it is, why it exists, and why it is based on a fundamental misunderstanding of union behavior and what is possible – see Moe (2011), chapter 8 (also chapter 10).

74. Christensen, Clayton, Curtis W. Johnson, and Michael B. Horn. 2008. *Disrupting Class: How Disruptive Innovation Will Change the Way the World Learns.* New York: McGraw-Hill; Moe and Chubb, 2009; and Peterson, Paul E. 2010. *Saving Our Schools.* Cambridge, MA: Harvard Education Press.

75. For detailed information on how this is happening – through the advance of fully online charter schools, blended learning charters, state-led virtual schools, district online programs, and more – see, e.g., Watson, John, et al., 2013. "Keeping Pace with K-12 Online and Blended Learning: An Annual Review of Policy and Practice." Evergreen Education Group. http://kpk12.com/cms/wp-content/uploads/EEG_KP2013-lr.pdf

76. Moe and Chubb, 2009; Moe, 2011.

7

Progressive Federalism and the Contested Implementation of Obama's Health Reform

Lawrence R. Jacobs and Theda Skocpol

At a celebratory ceremony held in the East Room of the White House on March 23, 2010, President Barack Obama signed into law the Patient Protection and Affordable Care Act of 2010 – potentially a landmark in U.S. social provision comparable to the Social Security Act, Civil Rights Act, and enactment of Medicare and Medicaid.[1] "Potentially a landmark" was, however, the right way to think of the reform when first signed into law. This comprehensive measure promised to regulate private health insurance and extend affordable coverage to more than 30 million Americans, mostly people with low or lower-middle incomes. But these reforms would not be fully implemented until 2014–2019, and the law had to run perilous legal and partisan gauntlets first. The presidential signing ceremony came at the end of fifteen contentious months of partisan and interest group maneuvering in Congress, and launched the fledgling law into new rounds of legal challenges, plus efforts by conservative Republicans to win sufficient leverage in the November 2012 elections to repeal or eviscerate health reform before its major provisions went into full effect.

To the surprise of some, the Affordable Care Act survived the early death threats. The Supreme Court upheld its core provisions on June 28, 2012, and President Barack Obama was reelected on November 6, 2012, reinstalled in Washington, DC, along with a strong majority of Democratic Senators. Although Republicans determined to frustrate the implementation of Affordable Care at every turn remain in charge of the House of Representatives, the legal framework and much of the programmed funding for comprehensive health reform are here to stay.[2] Led by the capable and savvy Secretary Kathleen Sebelius, Obama's Department of Health and Human Services (DHHS) continues to work out regulatory details in negotiations with major interest groups, while much of the administrative and political drama shifts to the fifty U.S. states, which will have a lot to say about the implementation and success of reforms in coming years.

Often decried by opponents as a "federal government takeover" of American health care, Affordable Care is far from that – not only because it preserves and regulates private health insurance for most employed Americans, but also because state-level authorities have crucial decisions to make and roles to play in shaping the specifics of reform. Much of the expansion of health insurance coverage under Affordable Care is slated to occur through enlargements of eligibility for insurance through existing public programs, Medicaid and Children's Health Insurance, jointly managed and funded by state and national authorities. In addition, under the terms Congress hammered out in the final legislative maneuvers over Affordable Care, the states are central to setting up and running the health insurance exchanges that will allow individuals and businesses to purchase private health insurance plans, often with the aid of new federal subsidies and tax credits.

A federal division of labor between national and state authorities is at the heart of this new plan for health reform – and of course there is nothing unusual about federal divisions of labor in American social welfare and social insurance programs. Quite the opposite. Only rarely in the history of U.S. social provision has a landmark law called for purely national implementation. The foundation of the modern U.S. welfare state, the Social Security Act of 1935, initiated a new national old-age insurance program that now bears the label Social Security. But that same charter law also included an unemployment insurance program that required all states to create jobless benefits yet left them free to decide levels of benefits and taxes on businesses to fund the benefits. And the Social Security Act also established federal subsidies for state-run welfare programs for poor mothers, impoverished older people, and the blind, yet left state and local authorities with enormous discretion – over benefit levels, eligibility, and indeed whether to offer a particular program at all.

Looking back at the post-1935 evolution of the major components of the Social Security Act, both America's liberals and most scholars who analyze the U.S. variant of the welfare state have concluded that, although nationally administered programs tend to become more generous and inclusive over time, programs where states are pivotal become penurious and more restrictive in the help they provide to needy populations. Social Security's nationally run retirement and disability benefits have obviously grown into a relatively generous and very popular entitlement, and have evolved to include impoverished racial minorities and do more to fight poverty than any other U.S. social program.[3] In contrast, despite federal efforts to use enhanced subsidies to encourage states to be more generous and uniform, welfare programs have remained very uneven in coverage and often leave large sectors of state populations in desperate poverty, and unemployment insurance, too, also eroded over the decades. Only a few states, mostly in the North, collect sufficient taxes to replace wages for most unemployed workers, whereas the vast majority of states have competed to lower business taxes in a "race to the bottom" that leaves them unable to include all wage earners in coverage or offer jobless benefits sufficient to maintain much aggregate consumer demand in sharp economic downturns.[4]

In short, in U.S. social insurance and welfare programs where governmental responsibility is divided and shared within U.S. federalism, national government efforts to limit races to the bottom have had only limited success. Regional differences in industrial structure, labor markets, politics, and race relations have left benefits and coverage for welfare and unemployment insurance very uneven and often inadequate to meet the needs of the poor and racial minorities. The same story also played in the federal arrangements for Medicaid benefits for the indigent after 1965, with southern states in particular opting for less-generous provisions than in other regions.

Given these evolutions in earlier social spending programs, it is not surprising that, originally, Obama administration officials and many congressional Democrats hoped to include a purely national health insurance exchange in the Affordable Care Act, bypassing the states in this component of reform. When we interviewed White House officials in late 2009, they dreamt of taking clear national control of the exchange, planning the rules to be followed by all insurers offering plans on the exchange, and getting the word out to all American citizens about reform's new benefits and procedures for them. And many congressional Democrats shared these hopes. Indeed, the House Democratic version of the final legislation included a national health insurance exchange.

But a critical minority of Senate Democrats always insisted on state-level exchanges, and in final legislative compromises and maneuvers a fully national exchange was blocked in the Senate and an innovative kind of federalist compromise emerged instead. "Progressive federalism" is our label for this compromise, because it calls for state-level authorities to have the first crack at planning and running health insurance exchanges, but should any states refuse to proceed, the national DHHS is legally empowered to step in and set up an exchange for the residents of that state. The national government, in short, does not preempt the states, but it does have the authority to serve their citizens should state authorities choose not to act or fail utterly in their attempts. This plan is far from a single national health insurance exchange; but it also prevents an all-out "race to the bottom" and ensures a considerable measure of uni-formity in basic regulations and subsidies across all fifty states.[5]

As Affordable Care is implemented, state variations will remain and continue to reflect distinct business conditions, political proclivities, and administrative capacities. Although the original Affordable Care legislation built on Medicaid was one route for extending health insurance coverage by using federal money and regulations to enable and require all fifty states to expand coverage to many more low-income people, the Supreme Court decision in June 2012 enlarged state authority to leave gaps and variations in insurance coverage in place in one vital respect. The majority of the justices ruled that states can turn down Affordable Care's federally subsidized expansions of Medicaid without any risk of losing existing federal subsidies for their current Medicaid programs, no matter how many low-income residents a state currently leaves out. It has not been easy for states to turn down the new Affordable Care subsidies for

Medicaid expansions, because states that turn those down leave their hospitals and businesses and local communities to pay the cost of care for people who would otherwise be insured (entirely at federal expense until 2017 and mostly at federal expense after that). A substantial number of Republican-run states, especially in the South, have refused the Medicaid expansions – although a steady trickle are taking second looks and, like Michigan, decide to accept the expansion after the fiscal impact of refusing so much federal money becomes clear. An even larger number of states run by Republicans are not taking steps to plan and set up health insurance exchanges in 2014. For the exchanges, however, pure refusal cannot block their establishment, because the law includes the federal backstop we have described. The DHHS is providing an online exchange mechanism for people in such states to comparison shop for regulated insurance plans and learn what subsidies they are eligible to receive. This federal backup does not prevent states from deciding later to take responsibility for their own exchanges, and that may well happen once it becomes clear even to the firmest opponents that Affordable Care is here to stay.

Federalism in the implementation of Affordable Care allows room for various choices and outcomes, including in the norms and functioning of the health insurance exchanges, because states that choose to set up their own have room to maneuver over insurance rules and the kinds of plans offered to residents. Whereas states such as Utah have reserved a major role for private insurers within public rules, the wide latitude for state experimentation also enables liberal states to experiment with cooperatives or public insurance options on their exchanges, and also allows Vermont to move toward the sort of "single payer" unified public health insurance system long favored by American progressives. In short, the shapers of Affordable Care have launched a new pathway in social policy development within America's constitutional federal system – a pathway that might generate creative room for constructive state experimentation and interstate competition and emulation, without setting off races to the bottom.

The balance of this chapter looks more closely at how the distinctive form of federalism in Affordable Care took shape in the legislative process during 2009 and 2010, and then probes what might happen with this variant of federalism as health reform moves forward. What were various groups involved in the legislative maneuvers, including reformers, trying to accomplish? And how did the final compromises take shape? What is likely to happen in coming years? We have already indicated that progressive federalism is likely to compress interstate differences and prevent an outright race to the bottom. But our analysis toward the conclusion of this chapter will also acknowledge that federalist dynamics in the further implementation of Affordable Care will continue to play out in a highly partisan-polarized political context.

Outright opponents of Affordable Care have lost the battle to have it entirely repealed or thrown out by Congress in 2013, or declared unconstitutional by the Supreme Court. But the fiercest opponents are not retiring from the field of battle – and the November 2012 elections have left state governance in a remarkable partisan-polarized form, because all but a half dozen states have governorships and legislatures entirely in either Republican or Democratic hands. Republicans in the United States right now are mostly antigovernment ultraconservatives who do not accept "ObamaCare," even now, and many of them are determined to use the state-level discretion built into the Affordable Care Act to refuse cooperation with its implementation and leave Republicans free to decry the entire law as glitches in implementation occur.

NATIONAL AND STATE AUTHORITY IN AFFORDABLE CARE

In the fifteen months of political battles over health reform before its passage in March 2010, key actors in the drama acted out the usual scripts. Congressional progressives and members of the Black Caucus tried to nationalize provisions. They wanted standardized benefits, a national-level exchange to apply uniform rules to private insurance plans, and consistent eligibility for subsidies. Liberal lawmakers did *not* want a strong state-level role in fashioning Medicaid expansions under Affordable Care or setting up the rules for private insurers to offer plans on health insurance exchanges, because they feared that southern and some western states would try to minimize benefits for lower-income families, many of them black or brown, while catering to business preferences to offer minimalist benefits and still collect federal subsidies. Reformers took it as an article of faith that the states that had lagged on social policy would continue to refuse to act, drag their feet, or create ever-lower standards of social provision served.

At the same time, Republicans who uniformly opposed reform in any form publicly fashioned themselves as defenders against a "Washington take-over." More consequential were the views of moderate and conservative Democrats such as Nebraska Senator Ben Nelson who firmly resisted national administration and insisted on a strong role for states and their insurance commissioners – a source of often nonpartisan technical capacity in many states. Some of these Democrats harbored genuine commitment to state administration (Nelson was impressed by state insurance commissioners based on his own service as one); others worried about the political fallout from GOP warnings of a Washington takeover – a fear that would gain traction with the arrival of the Tea Party and the "shellacking" of Democrats – as President Obama put it – in the 2010 midterm elections.

In the end, Affordable Care struck a compromise that reshuffled the division of labor between Washington, DC, and the fifty states in the making of social welfare policy. The health reform law could not pass through Congress without accepting a strong state-level role in setting up insurance exchanges that would attract the votes of Nelson and other moderate and conservative Democrats. In addition to winning broad discretion for establishing the new insurance exchanges, states also became star players in the implementation of Affordable Care because Medicaid programs, which are run by the states and paid for with a mixture of state and federal funds, were used to expand coverage for many low-income and poor Americans. The Supreme Court's ruling in June 2012 affirmed the constitutionality of health reform while also expanding the state's discretion on whether to pursue Medicaid expansion; the Court ruled that the federal government could only withhold new funding (rather than all Medicaid support) from states that refused to act.

On the other hand, state inaction or inadequate performance triggers federal government intervention to achieve national standards for private insurance market operations and benefit packages. Washington also wields "carrots" in the form of billions of dollars in planning grants and subsidies as well as sticks in the form of a national insurance exchange for residents of states that did not act. State business interests are especially leery of the national default because they anticipate exercising more influence on state legislators, executive branch officials, and civil servants than on their national counterparts. Governors (including Republicans) were also alert to the opportunities created by new federal funding and authority and the pressure from state health care providers, insurers, consumers, and others.[6] The result is that even the most Tea Party-oriented GOPers in the states face pressures to move forward with Affordable Care implementation rather than open the door to the feds taking over.

Why Reformers Insisted on National Limits on the States

As they designed Affordable Care in 2009–2010, liberals were well aware of the history of state resistance to generous social welfare and took for granted that efforts to widen state discretion would produce uneven and stunted health reform. Indeed, some proponents of comprehensive health reform suspected that the push for federalism was a backdoor strategy for crippling reform. In this worrisome scenario, even if a law passed, southern and western states would jealously guard state and local autonomy and well-organized businesses and their allies could be counted on to capitalize on the tradition of "state's rights" to block social policies that benefited middle- and lower-income people. Reformers confronted a daunting question: How could they retain the votes of Nelson and other centrist Democrats who insisted on significant state discretion and still foster progressive policy development?

Reformers recast the federalism of social policy to counteract two persistent conservative dynamics and foster progressive reform. First, reformers tried to reposition federal measures not as hostile threats to states but as enlargements of state authority above a national floor. Second, they distributed national resources to state-based employers, insurers, and provider groups, in the hope that new beneficiaries of federal resources would disrupt conservative coalitions and attract support from stakeholders as well as middle- and lower-income citizens. We clarify how reformers defined each threat in turn.

Growing bodies of research on policy development in the United States show that new federal initiatives not only supply benefits or services but also create or recast structures of governance – the "political ground of practices, rules, leaders and ideas" that constitute political authority in a particular place in time.[7] Paul Pierson specifically spotlights the institutional effects of federalism: "Social policy debates in federal systems are frequently as much or more about the locus of policy control as about policy content."[8] Historically, as we have seen, federalism as a system of governance in the United States has retarded social policy by generating institutional incentives for state and local government officials to equate their mission and responsibilities with decentralized power and authority. Controlling policy protects and extends the institutional positions of state-level authorities by producing tax revenue and other resources to sustain their positions and garnering credit for themselves in the form of votes and additional forms of support.

U.S. federalism invites state officials to adopt zero-sum calculations that lead them to equate their interests not only with fending off what they perceive as threats from Washington but also with winning the competition against other states by producing the greatest value for businesses and citizens.[9] In particular, low-wage, low-benefit states are motivated to protect their competitive advantage by resisting national social policies that set uniform floors and blocking any efforts to establish generous benefits that may serve as a magnet for residents of other states. This dynamic of competitive federalism is exemplified in the United States by the enduring resistance and opposition by southern congressional Democrats and Republicans to generous social benefits, even though their region would gain disproportionately from such benefits if funded from national resources. The zero-sum competition of states against each other and perceived threats from Washington is wired into U.S. politics. The constitutional system anchored representation in territory – Congress is elected from geographic areas and territory trumped population in the granting of two senators to each state. The localism invited by this national system of representation implants itself on most fiscal policy, producing leverage for state and district interests.

Inherited trends in U.S. federalism collided with the making of the Affordable Care Act in the decisive legislative moment in fall 2009 when Congress started to take votes that counted. Democratic Majority Leader Harry Reid decided to include a national public option in the Senate bill and the White House threw its support behind the play for a national reform approach. But Nelson and other moderate or conservative Senate Democrats pushed back against the national public opinion in favor of a "state-based approach." For those counting votes, Nelson reminded them that "I'm not being shy about making that point."[10] In short, as Affordable Care bills moved through Congress, health reformers worried about two different ways in which federalist dynamics could undercut reform. Health reform might be legislated to defer to state control in ways that would allow conservative interests to undercut regulations and benefits, or they could insist on a purely national design for reforms, only to see legislation defeated in Congress by representatives anxious to retain state-level leverage.

Stakeholder interests were also implicated in the fights about federalism. Research on comparative social policy finds that federal systems "change the power, preferences, and strategies of social groups."[11] In the United States, federalism breeds diffuse interests and a playing field that favors those with the resources and motivations to organize to advance themselves at the national, state, and local levels. This has been a death potion for bringing to life social policies that would widely distribute benefits. It is a well-known fact of U.S. politics that the broad public of consumers and middle- and lower-income people are not well organized, especially in comparison with encompassing organizations abroad and business and professional associations.

By contrast, federalism's dispersion of power particularly motivates and advantages groups representing business and the affluent that possess the resources to press their specific and concentrated interests at multiple decision points around the country.[12] Their ability to launch federated strategies multiplies their opportunities to press their interests – fights that are lost in Washington can be refought in states where the scrutiny and opposition may be less potent among unformed and underfunded groups representing consumers, the economically vulnerable, and minorities. In addition, although national policy sets the rules of the road throughout the country, state decision making equips well-established groups with an "exit option": the competition among states for business, capital, and the affluent creates incentives for them to exit higher benefit, higher tax regions for less onerous areas.[13] In short, superior organizational resources and an advantaged decision-making context has persistently blocked or retarded the distributional consequences of national social policy in the South and other regions lacking robust representation of labor, consumer groups, and minorities.

The general uneven pattern of state social policy development is evident in health policy. When Medicaid was enacted in 1965 as the primary government program to cover the indigent, reformers deferred to the states to determine eligibility and other key administrative decisions. The result has been wide variations across states. The quality and timing of medical care received through Medicaid is uneven and has been described as "welfare medicine." These disparities are compounded by variations in state health insurance coverage: many states in the South used their control over eligibility to limit coverage, with some as low as a quarter or less of the federal poverty level; other states (particularly in the Northeast and Northwest) used their discretion to widen eligibility well above the poverty line and include adults who did not have children.[14] These divergent patterns of health policy reinforced political coalitions; whereas business and the affluent continued to effectively resist programs expansion in the South, states that developed generous Medicaid policies strengthened the coalitions among advocates of the poor and local government as well as hospitals, physicians, and nursing home operators.

REFORMERS OPT FOR PROGRESSIVE FEDERALISM

Sobered by the pattern of uneven and exclusionary social policies that deferred to states, the progressive designers of Affordable Care insisted on pairing politically necessary deference to states with new national government responsibilities and resources that were expected to undercut established political coalitions and foster new identities and organizations in support of state implementation of Affordable Care. Reformers used four strategies to reconfigure the rules of the game and norms of state governance and recalibrate the expectations and identities of constituencies and organized groups. We take up each strategy in turn.

"Buying" States

In the heat of the legislative battle in December 2009, the conservative Heritage Foundation accused Affordable Care proponents of trying to "buy state silence" by offering "enhanced matching rates to lower state liabilities." Reformers, said Heritage, were trying to lure states into accepting reform even though it runs against traditions and would reduce them to being "merely an agent of the federal government." Heritage analysts tried to claim that promised new national funding would be inadequate and would "impose new costs on states."[15] More rigorous analysis casts doubt on Heritage's calculations and suggests that states get a "good deal."[16] But Heritage's basic charge did correctly identify a key component of the reform strategy to entice state participation: attractive financing.

Governors (including Democrats and sympathetic Republicans) warned the Obama White House and members of Congress in 2009 that the Great Recession made it impossible for the states to "pick up the tab [immediately because they] can't meet their [current] payroll, are cutting services and laying off employees."[17] The White House and legislators expressed – as one White House official put it – "concer[n] about what's going to happen to the states" and were, as Senator Max Baucus, chairman of the Senate Finance Committee, reported, in "close contact with a number of governors ... to ensure health care is more affordable for families, businesses – and state budgets."[18]

Lawmakers moved to make health reform a "good deal" to states in four ways. First, they shielded states from paying any additional cost as the Great Recession continued to ravage state budgets: Washington agreed to pay 100 percent of the cost for expanding Medicaid for three years (2014 through 2016). The state's share for Medicaid would grow slowly (1.25 percent) and over a long period that stretched to 2020. Second, the Affordable Care Act granted states a more generous match for the program's expansion – health reform would match 96 percent of costs on average as compared to 57 percent under the existing Medicaid program. Third, lawmakers extended tens of billions to states to help them plan and establish health insurance exchanges, supply subsidies for the near poor (individuals with incomes between 138 percent and 400 percent of the federal poverty level), and enlarge community health clinics for the poor. Fourth, Affordable Care's range of efforts to widen access were expected to lower expenditures that typically landed on the state's budgets such as hospital care that goes unpaid by patients lacking health insurance.[19]

Fifth and lastly, lawmakers, in effect, offered a bonus to states that were most resistant to implementing Affordable Care. States in the South and West with the highest unemployment rates and less generous Medicaid programs were slated to receive disproportionately larger shares of federal funding. Ironically, state congressional delegations representing regions where Democrats dominated favored social policy reforms that would most benefit regions primarily represented by Republicans who uniformly opposed Affordable Care. This odd juxtaposition of geography and politics fits a persistent historic pattern: "Southern politicians have opposed – while northern interests have supported – reforms that would have paid disproportionate benefits in the South from taxes raised largely in the rest of the country."[20] This disproportionate national support to the South represents a form of compensation for reducing the region's competitive strength as a low-wage, low-benefit, and low-tax market for labor and businesses.

The use of national levers to prod states to expand Medicaid contrasts with a more general conservative pattern since the late 1960s of using block grants and greater state independence to sideline social policy. In energy, transportation, and aid to the poor, this so-called new federalism has often entailed leaving matters to the states. In contrast, the steady expansion of Medicaid had taught reformers by 2009 of the liberalizing effects of attractive financing and national mandates. They knew the impact of the requirement of the Supplementary Security Income program in 1972 that all states widen eligibility to the aged, blind, and disabled. In addition, reformers in 2009 were well aware of the powerful effects of the quiet and subtle liberalizing of Medicaid's funding formula for states during the Reagan and Bush presidencies in the 1980s – expanded eligibility to 5 million children and half a million pregnant women and children. They had witnessed Medicaid's development into the financier of last resort among those lacking the resources for long-term care (consuming about a third of its budget) and for Medicare's Part B premiums for physician and outpatient services.[21] A new program – State Children's Health Insurance Program – was started in the 1990s to cover children in families with income well beyond the poor relief system, marking Medicaid's "most significant programmatic shift away from welfare medicine."[22] By Obama's inauguration in January 2009, reformers had witnessed the liberalizing effects of steady institutional expansion of state funding and legal authority: Begun as a backstop to the poor that was targeted to supply "welfare medicine," tweaks in funding formulas and legal requirements transformed Medicaid to extend wider and more even access across the country for both the poor and millions of previously middle-class Americans including many seniors who required long-term care.

Institutional Grafting

Another strategy pursued by reformers was to anchor Affordable Care's most significant expansions of insurance coverage in Medicaid, an existing program that was familiar to states and already administered by them. Lawmakers aimed to undermine the expected conservatism of some states by capitalizing on Medicaid's well-developed administrative structures and support among recipients and medical providers, especially hospitals. This strategic decision is consistent with a growing body of research demonstrating that diverse social programs from Social Security and GI programs to assistance for the poor generate reinforcing and supportive identities, resources, and motivations; ACA's designers attempted to graft onto Medicaid's developmental path.[23]

Following the enactment of Affordable Care in 2010, the Obama administration began vigorous rounds of negotiations and rule writing to implement the law. Not surprisingly, the polarization in Washington seeped into states and party control of state government often impacted whether states implemented the law. The most dramatic pattern was delay and defiance in states controlled by Republican governors and legislatures. Although the partisan cast to implementation is not surprising, it is not the entire story – states with Republican governors took active steps to plan for implementation and took steps to put Affordable Care into operation.[24] What explains this unusual departure from rigid partisan politics?

Policy legacies and, in particular, the development of Medicaid and other programs to expand access have moderated the effects of party control and particularly Republican control. In particular, ACA moved closer to a reality in states that had both established a familiar administrative framework and constructed supportive coalitions of the poor and local government as well as hospitals, physicians, and nursing home operators.

Maine and Michigan illustrate a pattern. The 2010 elections put Republicans in control of both lawmaking branches, and yet, each has taken steps toward implementing Affordable Care. In both states, Medicaid's aggressive development carved well-established policy paths for expanding access that erected administrative capacities for social welfare services and spurred the organization of beneficiaries and supportive groups of consumers, medical providers, and insurers.

The moderating effects of established policy paths on party control fit a pattern that has been observed in other state health policies. For instance, Colleen Grogan and Eric Patashnik report, "There is only a weak [and statistically insignificant] relationship between state efforts to implement SCHIP expansions and political factors. States led by Republican Governors and/or controlled by Republican state legislatures appear to be just as likely as their Democratic counterparts to take steps to expand Medicaid and SCHIP enrollment".[25]

The development of Medicaid policy created foundations for health exchanges and benefit expansion under Affordable Care. DC lawmakers targeted the exchange and its subsidies on the near poor – a constituency that many Medicaid programs are familiar with covering. And they encouraged states to integrate Medicaid into the construction of their new insurance exchanges. In particular, reformers required both a "seamless" coordination of Medicaid with the new exchanges and the merging of "welfare medicine" for the poor and mainstream medicine geared to Middle America.[26] Rooting Affordable Care in the practices, group preferences, and institutional actors already involved in Medicaid amounted to an attempt to fulfill this program's potential to "serve as a stepping stone to a more universal system that incorporates large numbers of working and middle class Americans."[27]

Leveraging State Administrative Capacity

Another strategic move by Affordable Care's designers was to base reform on sturdy administrative foundations already found in many state-level insurance offices. Research demonstrates that competent administration generates political dynamics favorable to policy expansion by both boosting the confidence of authoritative policymakers and their allies and equipping government with the tools to design, adopt, and implement effective programs.[28]

To make Affordable Care work, reformers knew that the states would need to exercise significant administrative capacity to regulate medical care and health insurance, and they wanted to build on earlier capacities where they existed. The McCarran-Ferguson Act of 1945 and, more recently, the Financial Modernization Act of 1999 (or Gramm-Leach-Bliley) authorizes states to regulate insurance businesses where federal law is absent. The result is that states have assumed primary responsibility for overseeing health insurers; much of this responsibility has been wielded by publicly obscure, but, in some states, administratively significant insurance commissioners who are elected in eleven states and appointed by the governor in the remaining states.

The offices of state insurance commissioners have developed into sites of expertise and, in certain states, sophisticated regulation. They generate significant revenue for states – more than $10 billion from insurance operations in 2000.[29] Overall, they employ 12,500 regular personnel, with a number possessing technical skills as actuaries. A review of insurance commissioners described them as generally "com[ing] to the job with a mindset that is more technocratic than political" – a key resource for reform implementation and why lawmakers elevated their responsibilities.[30]

One of the primary functions of state insurance commissioners is to regulate and license health insurers – positioning them within the states as an institutionally crucial player in the operation of health insurance. Private insurers are required in forty states to submit information about their premium rates and relevant documentation; some states mandate insurers to cover certain medical services and submit requests to increase premiums before they can implement them with the possibility of having rate-hike requests rejected.[31] State governments alone or in collaboration with insurance commissioners also police against fraudulent billing from medical providers as well as expanding access by forming insurance pools for high-risk individuals and providing subsidies to lower-income residents to purchase insurance.

Administrative competence and the associated confidence in the capacity of state insurers appear to be influencing how governors in particular are approaching Affordable Care. Studies by the U.S Government Accounting Office and the Kaiser Family Foundation stress the significance of each state's "motivation, resources, and staff capacity" to account for its actual oversight and regulation of insurers. Another study stresses "adequate capacity in the states" as a necessary condition for states to conduct effective reviews of insurer rates.[32]

Designers of the Affordable Care Act took steps to capitalize on existing state administrative capacity. In the first place, they empowered state insurance commissioners with specific and important responsibilities that leveraged their "non-political" reputation and administrative capacity for actuarial science, insurance market reform, and other core functions.[33] This nonpolitical approach is particularly prevalent among insurance commissioners who are appointed (as they are in thirty-nine states) rather than running for election.

Many states rely on insurance commissions to take responsibility for new responsibilities assigned to them by Affordable Care. For insurers of small businesses and individuals and some carriers for large employers, the law expects states to establish financial standards, review premium rates and publicly disclose unreasonable hikes, and protect consumers against insurer efforts to avoid risks and review consumer complaints. They are also trusted with the more complicated aspects of establishing the new insurance exchanges and facilitating insurance markets; this may involve making adjustments for adverse selection, certifying qualified plans, distributing subsidies, and designing the information technology necessary to accomplish many of these responsibilities. Conducting these and other functions requires a high level of functional specialization possessed by the better-equipped state insurance commissioners and departments of insurance.[34]

Reformers also latched onto an existing federated structure of administrative experts – the National Association of Insurance Commissioners or NAIC – that eschewed politics (including knee-jerk partisan opposition to reform) in favor of a narrow technical approach of collaboratively working across state lines to identify best practices. Affordable Care designated NAIC to advise DHHS and its Center for Consumer Information and Insurance Oversight to specify standards for the operation of the new insurance exchanges, criteria for health plans to be designated as "qualified" to be listed on the exchanges, parameters for risk adjustment, and other key operational details. One of NAIC's most important set of recommendations developed hotly contested regulations that required insurers to devote at least eighty percent of premiums for medical care and improving health (what is known as medical loss ratio). Commenting on the potency of NAIC's technical prowess in the face of intense lobbying by insurers and other special interests as well as political resistance, an observer of NAIC marveled at its success in demonstrating "openness, integrity, and dignity" in making recommendations to DHSS and "mov[ing] this forward for the benefit of our consumers."[35] Indicative of this pattern, the Republican insurance commissioner from the all-red state of Kansas rejected dire warnings from insurers and, instead, stressed NAIC's technical and nonpolitical approach: "The [insurers'] sky is falling argument is just not accurate. ... [W]e will adjust and make recommendations to modify [policy] if we see a need."[36] Similarly, the insurance commissioner in Georgia rebuked Tea Party efforts to block implementation of the insurance exchange as tantamount to an "ostrich sticking its head in the sand and saying it's not a problem. But it is a problem. We need to be prepared to implement a state solution."[37]

In addition to tying Affordable Care to the stable administrative platforms existing within states, reformers made heavy investments in enhancing state capacity to implement reform. In particular, lawmakers authorized the DHHS to award a variety of financial awards to states to strengthen or build new administrative capacity to regulate insurers and operate core components of the law – especially its new insurance exchange. About a year after Affordable Care was signed into law, the U.S. Government Accounting Office (2011) found that forty-one states were enhancing their capacity to oversee insurance premiums by reviewing the operations of insurers, seeking new legislative authority, and strengthening their administrative competence – hiring staff, contracting with outside actuaries, and upgrading information technology to collect and analyze the data submitted by the plans.

During 2011 and 2012, officials and reformers moving forward with Affordable Care invited and equipped states to plan implementation of their parts of the law – especially the insurance exchanges – while standing ready to eventually step in if national fallbacks were necessary. Republican-run states were thrust into a no-win situation – enact a reform that their fiercest partisans disliked, or abdicate to Washington. As they waited for the 2012 elections, this Hobson's choice prompted many Republican governors to denounce ObamaCare publicly but also foster quiet preparations to implement reform, warning against "one size fits all" if their state was not prepared to offer its own variants. Supporters of health reform could use hopes for state autonomy to urge every state, even Republican-led ones, to plan for implementation in 2014 or a staged process that initially included a "partnership" with Washington and then transitioned later to a state exchange.

Even so, partisan standoffs and foot dragging leading into November 2012 left nearly two-thirds of states unable or unwilling to declare their intent to establish insurance exchanges and expand Medicaid. After the 2012 elections, the Obama administration took both a hard line and a flexible line in continuing attempts to make federalist dynamics support rather than undercut the implementation of health reform. On the hard-line side of the ledger: Although Republican governors pushed to be allowed to take full federal subsidies for only partial implementation of the expanded eligibility for Medicaid legislated in Affordable Care, the Obama administration said no to this effort to institute a new race to the bottom led by conservative states unwilling to give generous help to low-income people.[38] On December 10, 2012, Secretary Sebelius told GOP governors that they would have to implement the full expansions of Medicaid to 133 percent of the poverty line if they wanted federal subsidies beyond those they have for their pre–Affordable Care Medicaid programs.[39] Meanwhile, on the flexible side of the ledger, Secretary Sebelius has pushed back deadlines and signaled considerable policy discretion for state authorities who choose to set up health exchanges.[40] Obama administration officials believe that inducing states to participate in building the insurance exchanges and accepting the new Medicaid benefits is the surest path toward sustaining health reform.

THE PATHS AHEAD

As it moves forward, however fitfully, the Affordable Care Act is not only remaking large parts of the U.S. system of health care financing and delivery, it is also furthering a new form of federalism in U.S. social policy. Once lawmakers were compelled to incorporate substantial state discretion, reformers designed Affordable Care both to weaken the conservative coalitions that had long used state discretion and variations to limit social provision, and to set up a new set of federal rules of the game that they hoped would foster interests, group identities, and organizational leverage that would favor full implementation of Affordable Care and limit opposition forces. A crucial aspect of the reformers' strategy was to capitalize on state fears of federal control by redefining health policy from a zero-sum battle to a positive-sum dynamic that would reward states that accepted the new law with important responsibilities and expanded resources. Another part of the strategy is to channel benefits to organized groups that align themselves with reform implementation, and refocus crucial stakeholders such as insurers, employers, and hospitals and other medical-care providers on the payoffs from reforms in which states participate actively and cooperatively.

If developments unfold over time as reformers hope, the Affordable Care Act's distinctive form of federal division of labor will rewrite the longstanding story of U.S. federalism as a barrier to redistributive policies and the establishment of national standards for decent social provision and market regulations. Economic and social differences across the United States ensure that policy variations will persist, as they do in Britain's National Health Service and national health insurance systems around the globe. Nonetheless, if progressive federalism works as designed, differences across the states in access to health insurance and regulatory protections against insurance abuses will likely narrow over time. New national standards for transparency, eligibility for subsidized coverage, and regulated business practices may encourage states to experiment with races to the top, rather than the bottom. And states that do better at combining quality care with affordable coverage may create policy models that other states will want to emulate or adapt some years from now.

That is one way to think about where federalism in Affordable Care may lead – toward a new, relatively uniform and inclusive yet flexible system of health insurance for the United States, even if not a purely national system. But we would be remiss if we did not acknowledge that the various levels of state discretion built into the compromised Affordable Care legislation – discretion further enhanced by the Supreme Court's decision to strengthen the hands of states in refusing Medicaid expansions – is sustaining profound unevenness in U.S. health insurance coverage and excluding for some time large numbers of poor Americans, particularly minorities in the South. Continued gaps and downward pressures on benefits will remain not just because of the way Affordable Care is written or adjudicated on paper, but because no one can presume cooperation or good will in carrying through this landmark reform, at least not any time soon. U.S. politics is extraordinarily polarized by ideology – and the two parties and their core supporters, both voters and interest groups, continue to take opposite stands at the level of their overall reactions to the Affordable Care Act. State-level discretion has become one more source of leverage in partisan battles.

When Americans are asked about the core provisions of Affordable Care (the new rules for insurance companies; the subsidies to make coverage more affordable; and the health exchanges as virtual marketplaces) most state their approval to pollsters by big margins, including across partisan lines.[41] But when people are asked about the law overall and the vague and ominous sounding "individual mandate," their general reactions remain polarized and divided, reinforcing partisan elites in their continued opposite stances toward the survival of reform. What is more, many citizens do not understand exactly what reforms Affordable Care includes, or know what it might mean for their families, businesses, and state or region when fully implemented from 2014 onward. This situation means that how smoothly Affordable Care is implemented in each state and region matters for the ultimate political judgments Americans will one day render about the reform.

The breakdowns and glitches in the start-up of the insurance exchanges beginning in 2013 were, in important respects, planned by conservatives and Republicans opposed to Affordable Care. Opponents have tried to sabotage implementation in order to undermine public acceptance of the Affordable Care reforms. At the national level in the fall of 2013, they launched a scorched-earth strategy of shutting down the government and refusing to raise the debt ceiling in a last-ditch attempt to stop Affordable Care. Federalism has also given plenty of leverage to die-hard opponents, who repeatedly press Republican governors and state legislators to obstruct or delay implementation. Unremitting pressures from Tea Party activists and moneyed interests help explain why an unexpectedly large number of states have refused to expand Medicaid or help run the exchanges. In a *Wall Street Journal* op-ed entitled "Why ObamaCare Is Still No Sure Thing" published shortly after Obama won reelection in November 2012, two conservative pundits called upon Republican state officials to "repeal" Affordable Care by refusing to accept Medicaid expansions or cooperate in setting up the exchanges.[42] Their scheme closely foreshadows what actually happened in the early phases of implementation, leaving the federal government overwhelmed with efforts to get reforms up and running in dozens of noncompliant states. Republicans in Congress also refused the extra funding the federal authorities needed to meet the larger-than-expected challenges. All this was intended to make the 2014 launch of Affordable Care appear botched in the eyes of many citizens and businesses, allowing Republicans to make calls for repeal in the 2014 and 2016 elections. In the oppositional game plan, in short, the state leverage built into Affordable Care was used as a tool of long-term ideological warfare and obstruction, undermining full and efficient implementation.

Because of Affordable Care's preemptive provisions, the national government has stepped in to provide workable, if overtaxed, exchanges – and these federally run exchanges will persist and develop at least through Obama's second term, and perhaps continuously after 2016, as well, if another Democratic president is elected and various states still refuse to participate in running their exchanges. In many states, authorities are offering a degree of cooperation even in the early stages, and more will move toward cooperation as the years go by. A likely scenario will be quiet cooperation at the level of officials in charge of health insurance programs in the resisting states, even if GOP governors and legislators continue to lead loud public choruses of criticism. GOP governors who look in the mirror and see themselves as potential presidential or vice presidential nominees – who thus would have to win support from conservative activists in primaries – will have the greatest incentives to continue public chest thumping against ObamaCare, at least through 2016. But governors also have to deal with social and economic realities in their states and many face voters in 2014 who may wonder about lost opportunities seized in neighboring states. The sweet spot for many such cross-pressured GOP governors may be to let subordinate officials quietly cooperate with the feds.

The extraordinary conservative onslaught on Affordable Care has imposed significant costs on the Republican Party "brand" and officials, however. The budget and debt ceiling showdowns in October 2013 propelled congressional Republican disapproval ratings to new highs and appeared to dim the party's once-promising prospects for winning a majority in the U.S. Senate in 2014. In addition to the self-inflicted wounds, the conservative's scorched-earth strategy in Congress boosted public interest in signing up for the insurance exchanges and, ironically, distracted from the Obama administration's failures in making the federal ObamaCare Web site work smoothly from the start. After the shutdown and fall 2013 debt ceiling debacle ended, Republicans belatedly turned to highlighting all the glitches and breakdowns in early implementation that their own efforts had helped create. But as long as Barack Obama (or any Democrat) remains in the White House, it is highly implausible that any outcries from the GOP will stop the steady march toward adjustments and full implementation.

In the final reckoning, interstate competition and emulation will remain forces generally favorable to spreading acceptance of both the Medicaid expansions and state participation in the exchanges. Medicaid is, after all, a matter of money to pay for care that cannot be avoided. Very sick people and people in serious accidents do not go without any care. They arrive at hospital emergency rooms, and the cost of their last-minute care is passed on to hospitals, doctors, charities, local governments, and businesses. Those interests are pressing all states to accept the new Medicaid funds included in Affordable Care, and the pressures they place on recalcitrant GOP governors and legislators will grow as health providers in other states get federal funds to expand care and protect providers' bottom lines. Where the new exchanges are concerned, cooperative states fashioned their own versions for 2014, while recalcitrant states watched the federal authorities set up bare-bones and relatively standardized exchanges. For the exchanges as for the Medicaid expansions, stakeholders ranging from insurance companies to employers to consumer advocates will soon want further adjustments to fit local conditions and interests. States with their own exchanges or exchanges built in partnership with the federal government will be able to let local interests play a continuing role in working out problems and making adjustments; and states that accept Medicaid expansions will buoy the bottom lines of their hospitals and businesses. But the states that loudly refuse cooperation will have to tell their stakeholder groups to go to Washington, DC, for adjustments. Republican officials will claim that problems are flaws in ObamaCare and call for repeal, but this approach will not prove sustainable – especially not as voters and powerful business stakeholders in the recalcitrant states watch businesses in the cooperative states make full use of the state levers and discretion allowed by the Affordable Care Act and federal DHHS. Pressure on Republicans to retake the reins is likely to grow. Certainly, such pressures will swell if the states that want Affordable Care to succeed expand coverage and limit price increases and fiscal deficits as they set up their exchanges and use the new federal monies to help their citizens, businesses, and health care providers.

Over time, Affordable Care will move forward unevenly yet inexorably across all of the states, and both administrative glitches and political battles will gradually recede from the realm of loud political grandstanding to the murmuring of jostling interest groups. National ideological battles and partisan finger-pointing will not disappear, but for everyday Americans and most businesses such antics will fade in importance with every passing year. When health reform returns to the top of the national agenda, the development of Affordable Care will ensure a quite different debate and set of options for debate by presidential contenders, governors, and legislators in Washington, DC, and state capitols. Some states may design models that defer to markets (such as the premium assistance model of using Medicaid funding to pay for private insurance). There may also be half a dozen or more quite viable state-level versions of the federal-state partnership built into Affordable Care, with impressive track records of access and cost control to examine. Ironically, if dozens of Republican-led states cede extra authority to the national government from 2013 to 2016, such an abdication of their own potential leverage may speed the emergence of the very sorts of national models reformers originally wanted to see built into Affordable Care.

Historical institutional perspectives in political science suggest that the implementation of Affordable Care will create entrenched practices and precedents. Changes will continue later, but they will build upon and react against the formative steps. Both state and national authorities are already fully involved in setting the grooves and models for Affordable Care implementation; and the possibilities for using state-level obstruction are fewer than reform's strongest opponents imagine.[43] Affordable Care's innovative form of federalism creates both resiliency and flexibility, much more than it offers levers for sustained total obstruction. Following the Supreme Court's decision and the reelection of President Obama, health reform has moved into what Max Weber once called the "slow boring of hard boards" – the standing up of new rules and procedures, emergence of new identities and interests, and shift of political calculations toward investment in the new program.

To secure the necessary votes to pass Affordable Care back in 2010, reformers reluctantly accepted state discretion and, in exchange, got extensive new carrots for state cooperation plus critical national fallback options. By now, the ongoing implementation of Affordable Care holds the promise of establishing a new upward-trending path in U.S. social policy development that supplements and eventually replaces race-to-the-bottom federalist dynamics that historically stunted and undercut nationally effective social provision. The routes forward will not be singular, nor will they be free of setbacks and fierce political controversies in the states and at the national level. But truly national health reform is on its way for the United States of America, and the day will come when health care reformers will look back with satisfaction on the achievements set in motion by the messy compromises forged during Obama's historic first term in the White House.

Notes

1. Jacobs, Lawrence and Theda Skocpol. 2012. *Health Care Reform and American Politics.* New York: Oxford University Press.

2. Jacobs, Lawrence and Joel Ario. December 2012. "Postelection, The Affordable Care Act Leaves the Intensive Care Unit for Good." *Health Affairs.* 31: 2603–2608.

3. Lieberman, Robert C. 2001. *Shifting the Color Line: Race and the American Welfare State.* Cambridge, MA: Harvard University Press.

4. Hertel-Fernandez, Alexander. February 2012. "Why U.S. Unemployment Insurance Is in Financial Trouble." *Basic Facts* brief, Scholars Strategy Network.

5. Affordable Care's combination of state discretion and national government fallback is unique in social policy but does have conceptual precedents in the domains of regulation. David Beam classifies this form of federalism as "partial preemption" because the states are required to establish regulations or the federal government will intervene. Beam illustrates this model by describing the Clean Air Act where states are required to establish State Implementation Plans to meet national air quality standards; the backstop to state intransigence is the national government's imposition of a Federal Implementation Plan. Shep Melnick demonstrates, however, that the federal government has failed to perform its backstop function in regulating air quality and transportation because it lacks the expertise or the political will. Of course, time will tell whether and how the federal government performs the backup function spelled out in the Affordable Care Act. Beam, David. 1984. Chapter 1 in *Regulatory Federalism: Policy, Process, Impact and Reform. A Commission Report* sponsored by the Advisory Commission on Intergovernmental Relations; Melnick, Shep. 1983. Regulation and the Courts: The Case of the Clean Air Act. Washington, DC: Brookings Institution Press.

6. Ario and Jacobs, 2012.

7. Orren, Karen and Stephen Skowronek. 2004. *The Search for American Political Development.* Cambridge: Cambridge University Press, 20; Skocpol, Theda. 1992. *Protecting Soldiers and Mothers: The Politics of Social Provision in the United States, 1870s-1920s.* Cambridge: Harvard University; Mettler, Suzanne and Joe Soss. 2004. "The Consequences of Public Policy for Democratic Citizenship: Bridging Policy Studies and Mass Politics." *Perspectives on Politics.* 2 (March): 55–73.

8. Pierson, Paul. October 1995. "Fragmented Welfare States: Federal Institutions and the Development of Social Policy." *Governance.* 8: 449–478, 455.

9. Tiebout, Charles. 1956. "A Pure Theory of Local Expenditures." *Journal of Political Economy.* 64: 416–424; Breton, Albert. 1987. "Towards a Theory of Competitive Federalism." *European Journal of Political Economy.* 3: 263–329; Kenyon, Daphne and John Kincaid (eds.). 1991. *Competition among States and Local Governments: Efficiency and Equity in American Federalism.* Washington, DC: Urban Institute.

10. Brown, Carrie. October 22, 2009. "Nelson: Reid, WH 'Leaning Toward' Public Option." *Politico.* Retrieved from http://www.politico.com/livepulse/1009/Nelson_Reid_WH_leaning_towards_public_option_.html?showall.

11. Pierson, 1995, 472.

12. Chandler, William M. and Herman Bakvis. 1989. "Federalism and the Strong-State/Weak-State Conundrum: Canadian Economic Policymaking in Comparative Perspective." *Publius.* 19(1): 59–78.

13. Tiebout, 1956; Breton, 1987; Kenyon and Kincaid, 1991; Robertson, David Brian. 1989. "The Bias of American Federalism." *Journal of Policy History.* 1: 262–291.

14. Grogan, Colleen and Eric Patashnik. October 2003. "Between Welfare Medicine and Mainstream Entitlement: Medicaid at the Political Crossroads." *Journal of Health Politics, Policy, and Law.* 28: 821–858.

15. Smith, Dennis and Edmund Haislmaier. December 1, 2009. "Medicaid Meltdown: Dropping Medicaid Could Save States $1 Trillion." Heritage Foundation. Retrieved from http://www.heritage.org/research/reports/2009/11/medicaid-meltdown-dropping-medicaid-could-save-states-1-trillion.

16. Angeles, January. June 18, 2010. "Health Reform Is a Good Deal for States." Center for Budget and Policy Priorities. Retrieved from http://www.cbpp.org/cms/index.cfm?fa=view&id=3171; Holahan, John and Irene Headen. May 2010. "Medicaid Coverage and Spending in Health Reform: National and State-by-State Results for Adults at or Below 133% FPL." Kaiser Commission on Medicaid and the Uninsured.

17. Pear, Robert and David Herszenhorn. August 6, 2009. "Senators Hear Concerns over Costs of Health Proposal." *New York Times*. Retrieved from http://www.nytimes.com/2009/08/07/health/policy/07health.html?ref=todayspaper&_r=0.

18. Senator Max Baucus quoted in Krauss, Clifford. August 7, 2009. "Governors Fear Added Costs in Health Care Overhaul." *New York Times*. http://www.nytimes.com/2009/08/07/business/07medicaid.html; Nancy-Ann DeParle quoted in Young, Jeffrey. August 6, 2009. *The Hill*.

19. Holahan, 2010; Angeles, 2010.

20. Pierson, 1995, 467–469.

21. Rosenbaum, Sara. 1993. "Medicaid Expansions and Access to Health Care" in *Medicaid Financing Crisis* ed. by Diane Rowland, Judith Feder, and Alina Salganicoff. Washington, DC: AAAS Press, 45–82.

22. Grogan and Patashnik, 2003, 853.

23. Orren and Skowronek, 2004, 20; Skocpol, 1992; Mettler and Soss, 2004; Pierson, 1995.

24. Jacobs, Lawrence and Theda Skocpol. "Progressive Federalism: The Implementation of Health Care Reform." Prepared for the American Political Science Association Meeting, August 3–September 2, 2012, New Orleans, Louisiana.

25. Grogan and Patashnik, 2003, 849–850.

26. Jacobs and Skocpol, *Health Care Reform and American Politics*, 2012.

27. Grogan and Patashnik, 2003, 853; Brown, Lawrence and Michael Sparer. January 2003. "Poor Program's Progress: The Unanticipated Politics of Medicaid Policy." *Health Affairs*. 22: 31–44.

28. Skocpol, 1992; Pierson, Paul. June 2000. "Increasing Returns, Path Dependence, and the Study of Politics." *American Political Science Review*. 94: 251–267; Skocpol, Theda and John Ikenberry. 1983. "The Political Formation of the American Welfare State in Historical and Comparative Context." *Comparative Social Research*. 6: 87–148.

29. U.S. Government Accounting Office. 2011. *Private Health Insurance: State Oversight of Premium Rates*. (GAO-11-701). Washington: Government Printing Office; National Association of Insurance Commissioners. "State Insurance Regulation: History, Purpose and Structure." Retrieved from www.naic.org/documents/consumer_state_reg_brief.pdf, accessed on August 10, 2012.

30. Jacobson, Louis. April 12, 2011. "Insurance Commissioners Prepare for Health Care Policy Conflicts." *Governing*. Retrieved from http://www.governing.com/blogs/politics/Insurance-Commissioners-Prepare-for-Health-Care-Policy-Conflicts.html.

31. Linehan, Kathryn. September 28, 2011. "Individual and Small-Group Market Health Insurance Rate Review and Disclosure: State and Federal Roles after Affordable Care." National Health Policy Forum, Georgetown University. Issue Brief No. 844.

32. U.S Government Accounting Office. 2011; Corlette, Sabrina and Janet Landy. December 2010. "Rate Review: Spotlight on State Efforts to Making Health

Insurance More Affordable." Kaiser Family Foundation. Retrieved from www.kff. org/healthreform/8122.cfm; Linehan, 2011, 11.

33. Jacobson, 2011.
34. Linehan, 2011.
35. Tim Jost quoted in Kliff, Sarah and Jennifer Haberkorn. October 21, 2011. "State Health Officials Approve Key Reform Plan." *Politico*. Retrieved from http://www.politico.com/news/stories/1010/43956.html.
36. Sandy Praeger quoted in Kliff and Haberkorn, 2011.
37. Kliff, Sarah. March 30, 2011. "Tea Party Notches Health Reform Wins." *Politico*. Retrieved from http://www.politico.com/news/stories/0311/52231.html.
38. Aizenman, N. C. December 8, 2012. "GOP Governors Seek Leeway on Medicaid Expansion." *Washington Post*.
39. Radnovsky, Louise. December 11, 2012. "Feds Nix Partial Medicaid Expansion." *Wall Street Journal*. A6.
40. Kliff, Sarah. November 15, 2012. "States Get More Time to Decide Whether to Build Health Exchanges." *Washington Post*; Louise Radnovsky. November 21, 2012. "States Get a Say in Health Law." *Wall Street Journal*. A4.
41. Jacobs, Lawrence and Suzanne Mettler. 2011. "Why Public Opinion Changes: The Implications for Health and Health Policy." *Journal of Health Policy, Politics and Law*; Kaiser Family Foundation. 2012, 917–933. "Kaiser Tracking Poll." Retrieved from http://www.kff.org/kaiserpolls.
42. Capretta, James C. and Yuval Levin. November 19, 2012. "Why ObamaCare Is Still No Sure Thing." *Wall Street Journal*. A19.
43. Jacobs and Ario, 2012.

8

Federalism and the Politics of Immigration Reform

Carol M. Swain and Virginia M. Yetter

> The National Government has significant power to regulate immigration. With power comes responsibility, and the sound exercise of national power over immigration depends on the Nation's meeting its responsibility to base its laws on a political will informed by searching, thoughtful, rational civic discourse. Arizona may have understandable frustrations with the problems caused by illegal immigration while that process continues, but the State may not pursue policies that undermine federal law.
>
> – Justice Stevens (Majority)[1]

INTRODUCTION

What happens when the national government fails to do its job? In *Arizona v. United States*, the U.S. Supreme Court upheld the federal government's ability to prevent a state from enacting certain types of immigration laws and regulations perceived by the state as necessary to fill a void in federal enforcement. Nevertheless, the Court allowed the state to continue background checks on people detained for other purposes. Immigration would seemingly work best if different levels of government agreed to coordinate their efforts and share enforcement power. Shared and overlapping powers between the federal government and the individual states lies at the heart of constitutional federalism. It is how our political system was meant to work. Malcolm Feeley and Ed Rubin describe federalism as a means of governance "that grants partial autonomy to geographically defined subdivisions of the polity." Accordingly, they explain that a "political entity that is governed by a single central government making all significant decisions cannot be described as federal without abandoning the ordinary meaning of the term.[2] Under a federal arrangement, subunits can have considerable authority in certain spheres that overlap with the jurisdictional areas of the central government. Federalism was designed to operate as an important check against the centralized powers of the national government.

The foundation for federalism is found in eight constitutional amendments and in Articles I and VI. Article I, Section 8 lists the enumerated powers of the federal government and contains the "necessary and proper clause," which gives Congress the authority to pass laws that are necessary for it to carry out its enumerated powers. Article VI's Supremacy Clause makes clear that federal laws trump state laws whenever conflicts occur. The 10th Amendment forms the basis for an expansive view of the rights of states to look after the common welfare of their inhabitants. It states that "the powers not delegated to the United States by the Constitution, nor prohibited by it to the States, are reserved to the States respectively, or to the people." In many areas, the state and federal government share concurrent powers. Areas of shared and overlapping power include education, healthcare, and immigration as well as traditional areas such as taxing, borrowing, and spending money; enacting general legislation; and regulating election times and places. In recent years, state activism on immigration reform appears to be pervasive and growing. Nevertheless, it remains a policy area where state governments have lost and continue to lose considerable power to the federal government.

Changes in the percentage of foreign-born and undocumented persons in the United States have no doubt encouraged state and local governments to wade into the controversial waters of immigration reform. With few exceptions, these bills have met with considerable resistance from those who believe that states have overstepped their bounds. In December 2011, the National Conference of State Legislatures reported that state legislators "introduced 1,607 bills and resolutions relating to immigrants and refugees in all 50 states and Puerto Rico." These numbers represented an increase over 2010, when 46 states considered more than 1,400 immigration bills and resolutions. However, most of these bills were not enacted. Eleven percent fewer bills were passed in 2011. Forty-two states and Puerto Rico enacted 197 new laws and resolutions totaling 306. Fifteen bills that were passed by state legislatures died at the hands of governors who vetoed the bills.[3]

The concept of immigration federalism was birthed during the late 1990s, when legal scholars observed the increasing tendency of state and local governments to pass laws and ordinances pertaining to immigration. Clare Huntington argues that by 2008, state activism had become "a central political issue of our times."[4] Much of the discussion surrounding immigration federalism has focused on the constitutionality of state intervention in an area many legal experts say is reserved for the federal government. Other scholars have grudgingly acknowledged a role for state governments even while expressing deeply held fears that state and local governments cannot be trusted to protect the civil rights and civil liberties of racial and ethnic minorities.[5] Although examples of nonfederal involvement in immigration abound, such involvement leaves some legal scholars questioning whether this allocation of authority is justified by our constitutional tradition and the cases surrounding it.[6]

Bosniak argues that there are two distinct questions about immigrants that guide how they should be treated in the regulatory system. There are questions about admission, deportation, and political asylum that clearly fall into the purview of the federal government, and there are other issues that concern how people are treated once they are here.[7] Access to legal rights, criminal procedures, education, health care, and welfare benefits fall into the category of alienage law. Alienage law "is a composite of rules and standards set by state and federal law across a wide variety of regulatory domains" where aliens are only one of many potential groups affected by the law.[8]

Bosniak points out that courts have traditionally drawn a sharp distinction between permissible areas of regulation based on the content of suggested policies. If legislation governs removal or admission of immigrants, referred to as "pure" immigration, the federal government controls; if the legislation governs rights and obligations of noncitizens while in the country, states may jointly govern.[9]

Due to the profound impact of immigration on state and local governmental budgets, these entities often act out of desperation in response to the failure of the federal government to act. Although the federal government has been the dominant force in immigration for more than 100 years, the recent increase in state and local involvement in immigration issues offers a real hope for policy change and innovation.

This chapter provides a historical background of immigration policy that shows federal dominance over the last century. The rise in immigration federalism became particularly pronounced in the late 1990s and the 2000s. We concur with scholars who argue that the Constitution does not forbid state involvement in immigration reform.[10] We believe that state invention can be a positive force for change because it offers new possibilities for innovative policy solutions. In fact, state action can become the needed boost that Congress needs to stop kicking the can down the road and begin to exercise its power under the Supremacy Clause to reform the policy.

If states overstep their bounds, the national government can preempt by statute and by the Supremacy Clause. As recently as 2012, the Court reaffirmed the position of federal dominance in its ruling in *Arizona v. United States*.[11] The Court concluded that the federal government's broad power over immigration and alien status rests, in part, on its constitutional power to "establish an uniform Rule of Naturalization," and on Article I, Section 8, Clause 4's acknowledgement of the federal government's inherent sovereign power to control and conduct foreign relations.[12]

HISTORICAL BACKGROUND

For more than 100 years our nation has struggled with its immigration policy. The struggle is evidenced in the public backlash against the Irish in the 1840s, and the Chinese in the 1880s. Early concerns about the foreign-born population, particularly the Irish Catholics, led to the birth of the Know Nothing Movement, composed of white Protestant nativists alarmed by the rapidly growing Irish Catholic population.[13] Roger Daniels argues that restrictionist immigration policies were birthed in 1882 with the Chinese Exclusion Act[14] and that it extended through congressional adoption of a literacy test in 1917.[15] These efforts helped determine who could legally enter the United States and on what terms; therefore, touching at the core of what shapes and defines an American identity.[16]

At the beginning of the twentieth century, immigrants primarily traveled from Europe; by the end of the century, immigrants were predominantly from Asia and Latin America. Although immigrants in the first half of the twentieth century were motivated by the prospect of employment, immigrants today are often drawn to immigrate in order to be reunited with family and enjoy political freedom.[17] Yet despite the significant shift in the nature of immigration over the years, many of the issues of the past remain constant. Influxes of new immigrants create concern about job competition and the direct and indirect impact on low-wage, low-skill Americans, particularly African Americans, legal Hispanics, and poor whites. In addition, new concerns about the rising cost of entitlement programs and additional burdens unskilled immigrants can place on the strained budgets of local governments can come into play. Public debate about the impact on the nation is tempered by the frequency in which allegations of nativism and racism are hurled against organizations that have argued against unrestricted immigration.

Despite reforms toward the end of the twentieth century, immigration remains one of the most divisive political issues today. No major reform has been enacted into federal law since 1986, and policy preferences have found expression through state action. Although the politics of immigration policy were once dominated by labor unions and policy groups, states have proved essential parties to success in the twenty-first century. The challenges created by expanding legal immigration and the out-of-control growth of illegal immigration demand new solutions to perennial problems.

Immigration and Nationality Act of 1965 (The Hart-Cellar Act)

The 1960s was an era of massive social and political change that resulted in the passage of four major civil rights acts: The Civil Rights Act of 1964, which outlawed discrimination in public accommodations; the Voting Rights Act of 1965; and the Open Housing Act of 1968, which prohibited discrimination in the rental and sale of houses.[18] Alongside these domestic changes, Congress passed the Hart-Cellar Act, which eliminated racist national-origin quotas that had existed since the 1920s; instituted a family reunification policy that established priority for close relatives of naturalized citizens; and established an immigration policy that favored highly skilled professionals, scientists, and artists along with unskilled laborers for jobs in fields experiencing a labor shortage.

A general assumption surrounding the creation of the Hart-Cellar Act was that the volume and nature of immigration would not change with the elimination of nation-based quotas. However, the Hart-Cellar Act had the unintended consequence of radically changing the racial and ethnic complexion of America. The two most noteworthy changes from the act were a significant expansion in legal immigration from Asia and increased movement of undocumented workers across the U.S.-Mexico border. Although the majority of immigrants previous to passage of the law were European, the secondary emphasis on skilled workers allowed for an influx of Asian immigrants. Visas for Asian professionals quickly overwhelmed the quota allotted for skilled workers. As these professionals immigrated, they soon brought their families from abroad.

The Act placed quotas on the Western Hemisphere for the first time, leading to the second unexpected effect of increased border crossings between Mexico and the United States. In a piece of legislation that lifted so many barriers to immigration, this restrictive provision is often overlooked. Previous to 1965, Canada and Mexico had enjoyed unlimited visas as neighboring economies. Following passage of the law, economic crisis gripped Latin America, increasing immigrant flow into the United States. The growing Mexican-American population led to expanding influence for ethnic rights groups, which would play an important role in the immigration reform of the coming decades.

Prior to passage of the law, politicians argued any change in the ethnic makeup of immigration was unlikely. The act permitted immigrants to bring in not only spouses and children, but parents and siblings, as well. It was thought that prioritization of family unification ensured the dominance of immigration from Europe. However, the impact of the law quickly disproved these theories: of the ten countries that predominantly sent immigrants in 1965, only two (Germany and Italy) were among the nations the State Department predicted would send the most immigrants in 1969.[19] By the 1980s, immigrants from Asia and Latin America constituted the majority of immigration, which continues to be true today.[20]

Despite the unintentional expansion of immigration following the passage of the Act, the law remained difficult to challenge, resulting in relatively stable immigration policy for the next twenty years. The strength of the law lay in the role of bipartisanship in passing it, the impact of family-based immigration on the electorate, and the reduction of labor contentions for a short space of time. Despite the unexpected impact of the law that rapidly changed the racial and ethnic composition of the nation, politicians were unable to challenge the legislation without being misunderstood as racially-motivated.[21] With a growing immigrant population, attempts to overturn the family unification goal that brought in low-skilled workers in favor of a more skill-based system grew even more difficult.

The Immigration and Reform Act of 1986 (IRCA)

John Skrentny has described IRCA and the bargaining process behind the final passage of the legislation as "one of the great policy failures of American history."[22] IRCA contained a legalization component that offered a form of amnesty to millions of undocumented persons who were offered a pathway to citizenship, and the legislation contained enforcement provisions designed to secure the borders while making it more difficult for undocumented persons to enter and remain in the United States. According to Skrentny, "IRCA's failure to seal the border taught restrictionists not to make any more grand bargains," and it has led to the inability of groups to work together to solve common concerns.[23] IRCA has left behind a legacy of distrust that has contributed to the inability of Congress to make needed reforms.

A crisis was the backdrop for IRCA. By the early 1980s, America faced new immigration challenges that included the presence of large numbers of undocumented workers. The debate over how to address undocumented workers was not salient during the 1960s, but by the mid-1980s it had become an issue too significant to ignore. Labor unions, civil rights groups, employers, and ethnic groups staked out sides on the issue. By the mid-1970s, three major Hispanic groups opened offices in DC, initiating a new era of political activism.[24] Gradually, with a growing legal and illegal population of Hispanic immigrants, the Hispanic policy groups became major actors in policy reform. They eventually cut deals and joined forces with the Congressional Black Caucus and the Leadership Conference for Civil Rights to advance an agenda that gutted employer sanctions and other reforms that might have decreased illegal migration while protecting the jobs of America's most vulnerable populations.[25]

As was true in previous decades, labor unions maintained their concerns about job competition and downward pressure on wages resulting from the oversupply of low-wage undocumented workers. But the importance of labor unions was waning, and immigrants were essential to reviving the weakening institutions. Labor groups eventually began to pressure Congress to address the deluge of illegal workers entering the country, while the National Association for the Advancement of Colored People (NAACP) continued to point out that illegal aliens were depriving lower-income citizens of jobs for which they qualified.[26] Focusing on the need for employer sanctions, the AFL-CIO and groups such as the NAACP, United States Conference for Catholic Bishops, and League of United Latin American Citizens demanded penalties for employers who contributed to the problem by encouraging illegal migration.

In response to the interest groups, agricultural lobbyists rallied to prevent the imposition of civil fines on employers who demonstrated a "pattern or practice" of hiring undocumented aliens. In response, Congress created the H-2 program, which allowed agricultural and nonagricultural employers to hire contract workers from foreign countries under certain conditions. Claiming this program was too expensive and insufficient to meet their needs, the Western growers began a debate that would lead into the reforms years later.

By the early 1980s, Congress attempted to address both legal and illegal immigration in a single legislative effort. In their initial attempt to deal with both issues through one piece of legislation, various senators suggested caps on legal immigration, leading to a strong push back from the Reagan administration. President Reagan had praised America as a "shining city upon a hill," welcoming immigrants to a land of opportunity and freedom. Interpreting any caps on legal immigration as an affront to this ideal, the administration was able to lobby for separation of these portions of the legislation to be dealt with in the future. Thus, the legislative effort was split, with illegal immigration to be dealt with first.

The Immigration Reform and Control Act of 1986 was the first stage of the legislation, addressing the rising tide of illegal immigrants in an attempt to close the "back door" to illegal immigration in order to "keep the front door open."[27] Voicing concerns about the possibility of racial profiling and discrimination by employers, Hispanic groups successfully fought against more severe employer sanctions. By the time the employer sanctions were enacted into law, they had been debated for a full fifteen years.[28] But despite the initial alliance between Hispanic groups and western growers to prevent harsh employer sanctions, the debate began to shift to the topic of an agricultural worker program. Once it was determined employers would have an "affirmative defense," releasing the employers from the obligation to check the authenticity of documents provided to them, western growers shifted their focus to establishing alternative sources of foreign labor. Hispanic policy groups also saw the opportunity for advancing immigrant interests in the offer of amnesty, eventually accepting the trade-off of employer sanctions for the prospect of citizenship. Over time the two most controversial and noteworthy elements of the bill were the issue of amnesty and a future guest-worker program, both of which were divided along ideological lines.

There were no hearings on the bill; instead, representatives of Western growers, labor unions, and Hispanic interest groups engaged in several rounds of political trading, leading to the compromises of the final legislation. The primary accomplishments of the law were sanctions on employers who knowingly hired illegal immigrants, grants of amnesty for immigrants who had resided in the United States since January 1, 1982, and a path to citizenship for those who had worked as seasonal laborers for a certain amount of time. Many considered the sanctions against employers to be the centerpiece of the law, although the sanctions would prove insufficient to address the uncontrollable flow of illegal immigration. The legislation criminalized the act of knowingly hiring an undocumented immigrant, although it did not require employers to question the authenticity of documents presented to them. The act also established a probationary guest-worker program, which granted "earned-stay" rights to special agricultural workers, labeled SAWs. After working for at least ninety days within the agricultural sector, SAWs were able to pursue employment in other industries and eventually gain citizenship. Ultimately, 1.3 million agricultural workers would take advantage of this provision.[29]

The Immigration and Reform Act of 1990 and the George H.W. Bush Administration

After the passage of the IRCA, Congress turned its attention to legislation dealing with legal immigration. In the few years between the legislative enactments, the economy had significantly improved, changing the context of reform. Several studies indicated a skill gap in the workforce, suggesting the possibility of a shortage of skilled labor.[30] In response, the Select Commission on U.S. Immigration and Refugee Policy called for increased admissions of highly trained immigrants that could contribute to American industry, simultaneously arguing for preservation of existing family-unification goals. Several high-technology companies in computer and electronic industries, including Microsoft, also joined forces to push for improved access for trained professionals from foreign countries. Republicans were largely in favor of the suggested increase in professional visas, but they opposed the demands of ethnic groups to increase the number of family visas. Democrats, particularly from the Northeast, acted in support of the ethnic groups, lobbying for an increase in visas for family purposes.

More expansive reform would ultimately be determined by the ability to build powerful coalitions among pro-immigration groups. Like the Reagan administration, the George H.W. Bush administration was generally supportive of liberal legal immigration, and their influence won over a large block of Republicans to vote in favor of the legislation. But the most noteworthy coalitions were the business groups and ethnic policy groups, referred to as the "family coalition." As discussed previously, the business groups were driven by a desire to bring in more skilled professionals and improve the ability to recruit temporary employees. Although there was no explicit agreement between the business groups and the family coalition, there was a tacit acknowledgement that they would act in support of each other, and not oppose each other's demands.[31] Another particularly important coalition was between the ethnic groups in favor of family reunification policies and the older immigrant groups who favored a special type of visa for nations in the minority of immigration. As many of the original immigrants to America no longer had living relatives in their native countries, they were unable to benefit from family-reunification policies, and they demanded an additional "diversity" visa that would permit increased immigration from these nations. Although the two groups arguably had competing interests, their cooperation ensured success for both goals.

Lastly, although forming no new coalitions, labor unions continued to play a powerful role in negotiations over reform. Labor argued aggressively for protection of jobs for native workers, attempting to limit visas for temporary professionals at 65,000 and suggesting a head tax on employers who hired foreign workers, higher standards of proof that business had attempted to recruit American workers, and a requirement that any hiring be linked to state and federal certification of a labor shortage. Eventually the suggested head tax would be eliminated, but the cap on admission of temporary foreign workers was retained as a concession to organized labor.

Largely based on bipartisan support, the Immigration Act passed in 1990. The most significant accomplishments of the final legislation included an increase in the total number of legal immigrants allowed into the United States each year, and the creation of diversity visas for countries from which immigration had been low. Eventually, the diversity program would be awarded 55,000 visas a year, and the legislation would increase the visas for non-immediate relatives by 300,000, including siblings.[32]

Despite attempts to limit family-unification policies, the act preserved the visas allotted prior to the legislation. The act also removed homosexuality and AIDS as grounds for exclusion from immigration and provided for exceptions to the English testing process required under the Naturalization Act of 1906. The enactment of this legislation increased annual immigration to the United States by 500,000 additional immigrants.[33]

In an attempt to tighten policy on illegal immigration, the act also significantly strengthened the power and resources of the U.S. Border Patrol. This legislation would eventually lead to the "prevention through deterrence" policy of the Immigration and Naturalization Service (INS) in the early 1990s. In one of the earliest examples of the lessons to be learned from immigration federalism, this particular federal strategy mimicked an attempt by the Texas government to address illegal entry in Operation Blockade. Immigrants who had previously entered through El Paso, the targeted city, were forced into more rural areas as a result of the operation. The Border Patrol adopted the plan on a national level in 1994. With the increased resources granted from the 1990 legislation, the Border Patrol began Operation Gatekeeper near San Diego, using high-intensity floodlights to deter illegal entry. Similar to Operation Blockade, Operation Gatekeeper pushed immigrants into more rural areas, although it is arguable they did little to deter overall migration.

The buildup of resources on the border continued in the Illegal Immigration Reform and Immigrant Responsibility Act of 1996, discussed shortly. Once more, legislation focused on increasing physical obstacles to illegal entry, along with increased Border Patrol agents and the technology available to them. By 2002, the total INS budget was thirteen times its 1986 level, the Border Patrol budget was ten times its former level, with three times as many officers, and eight times as many hours patrolling the border.[34] Formal deportation also grew rapidly, increasing nearly tenfold from 1986 to 2002. Douglas Massey[35] argues that instead of deterring illegal immigration, these policies eventually led to an increased retention of illegal immigrants, as the costs and dangers of making a border crossing rose. Due to increased border security, many immigrants were hesitant to return once they had entered the country, a "perverse consequence" of heavy border enforcement.[36] Thus, the illusion of a "controlled border," begun in the 1990 legislation, may have only exacerbated illegal entry and the greater illegal immigrant population on the whole.[37]

Immigrant Responsibility Act of 1996 and the Clinton Era

By the early 1990s, American opinion had turned against illegal immigration. Several highly publicized attempts of illegal migration, including multiple boats from China filled with immigrants attempting to land illegally, renewed attention to the ongoing problem of improper border crossings.[38] There was a sense that the policies of the 1986 legislation had failed. There was no reliable system in place to determine the authenticity of laborer's documents, and an underground industry for false identification was thriving. During this period states began to demonstrate both their frustration with federal attempts to address the issue of immigration, and their ability to sway national politics through their own legislation. Most notably, in California citizens enacted Proposition 187 and elected a Republican governor who ran on the platform of fighting against illegal immigration. Proposition 187 was an initiative to deny public services to illegal immigrants in California. The measure passed by 59 percent of the vote in 1994, expressing the deep and desperate frustration of the people of California.[39] As one of the more populous states in the union, California drew attention to the growing problem of illegal border crossings, and the failed attempt by the federal government to restrict the number of illegal migrants entering the county each year. Alongside the events in California, Republicans gained control of both houses of Congress for the first time in forty years. Part of that victory was a Contract with America, a list of promises and goals to be achieved with a conservative majority. Among other goals, an attempt to address illegal immigration was originally listed in the contract with the people.[40]

In response to the Republican congressional victories and the backlash displayed in California, Senator Alan Simpson and Texas Representative Lamar Smith introduced bills calling for restrictions to be placed on legal immigration alongside limitations on illegal immigration. Although initially it appeared the country was eager for the suggested measures, there were several political hints that the severe legislation would not have a smooth journey. Eventually, due to divisions within the party, immigration was struck from the list of goals within the Contract with America.

Once more, Hispanic and Asian groups relied on a left-right coalition to manipulate the legislation in favor of their policy goals. High technology companies, including the National Association of Manufacturers, Intel, and Microsoft, also rose up against the bill, staging several high profile "fly-ins" to the capital to argue against any limits on legal immigration.[41] The Business Coalition explained that international operations made employment of immigrants vital to the future success of their companies.

The bill was initially introduced as a reform of both legal and illegal immigration. Pro-immigration interest groups recognized the current hostility toward illegal immigration, and knew that if the two issues were joined, there was a great risk that legal immigration would be blamed for the problems of illegal immigration. Pro-growth libertarians and economic conservatives were soon persuaded by the family coalition that legal immigration must be protected, and they also joined the struggle against a bill attempting to address all types of immigration. As there was significantly less momentum attached to the issue of legal immigration, these interest groups were able to stall this portion of the legislation. A series of "dear colleague letters" went out in support of splitting the bill, tying legal immigration to free trade and free markets. Conservatives explained that they would be willing to address legal immigration at a later time, but it was necessary to separate the issues in order to address them effectively. Eventually, with the approval of the Clinton administration, support for splitting the bill was widespread, and the cuts to legal immigration were deferred for another legislative session.

Despite their importance in previous immigration reform, labor unions had a significantly diminished voice in the 1996 legislation. Without a Democratic majority, it was difficult for labor unions to gain a seat at the table. Even so, Senator Edward Kennedy lobbied aggressively on their behalf, arguing for protections to be added to the bill in favor of American workers. But with a weak political position, the unions were ultimately cut out of any significant discussions, and even the reforms added by Senator Kennedy were largely eliminated by the time the bill was passed.

Once the bill was split, the final legislation was focused on increased protection of the border, and greater responsibility for incoming immigrants and their family sponsors. A significant factor in the call for reform was a belief that the employer sanctions put in place by the 1986 legislation had failed. With no reliable method of determining the authenticity of documentation, employers could easily claim an affirmative defense against the sanction's force. Originally, it was suggested that a phone verification system should be put in place to provide certification of documents. Although a pilot version of this phone verification system was put into place, the focus of reform shifted away from a correction of the sanctions to stricter control over the border. One thousand U.S. Border police were added, alongside more severe consequences for those entering the country illegally. The proposed legislation barred admission for three years for aliens unlawfully present in the United States for 180 days, and barred admission or any legal status for ten years if an illegal immigrant was present in the country for more than a year. The legislation changed laws for excluding and removing aliens, limiting the judicial review of INS decisions.

The suggested reforms also placed greater responsibility on family sponsors to prevent increased dependence of new immigrants on public services. Financial responsibility rules limited admission of immigrants that were likely to be reliant on the welfare system by requiring sponsors of relatives to prove the requested immigrant had an income 25 percent above the poverty line. Once an immigrant had entered the United States, their family sponsor was required to sign a legally binding affidavit of support, and the sponsor's income was included with the alien's income for any qualification for public support. Under the welfare reforms of 1996, states were also delegated the authority to determine immigrant eligibility for federal benefits. Some scholars argue this authorization of state-level discretion put an end to the era of federal exclusivity that had dominated the twentieth century, inviting states into the debate on the legal status of immigrants.[42] Peter Spiro argues that the provision ensured that the alien's status would no longer be fixed in Washington, but also in the states.

In the final stages of passage, a controversial amendment arose that threatened to destroy the legislation. The Gallegy Amendment, an early attempt to increase the role of immigration federalism, granted power to states to deny public schooling to children present in the country illegally. Opponents of the bill argued that keeping immigrant children out of school would increase crime and victimize children who had no part in the illegality of their entry. Although conservative Democrats from the South favored the amendment, President Clinton came out strongly against it and threatened to veto the entire bill if the amendment was included. In the midst of the presidential election, the Republican candidate for president, Robert Dole, lobbied aggressively for inclusion of the amendment, believing this would force President Clinton to either veto the bill, losing votes in California, or backtrack on his promise, losing legitimacy with the electorate. But despite the pressure from Republican leaders, Republican representatives saw the risk that the bill would fail, and stood firm on excluding the Gallegy Amendment in the final legislation.

The Bush Era and the Attacks on September 11, 2001

At the commencement of the George W. Bush presidency, there was hope that more comprehensive reform would be possible. President Bush invited Mexican President Vincente Fox as the first foreign dignitary under the new administration, signaling the importance of the relationship between the two countries. As the two national leaders debated the terms of a trade agreement, pro-immigration groups remained hopeful that immigration reform within the United States would follow. On September 11, 2001, American policy goals experienced a severe and unexpected shift. An opening of American borders was taken off the table, and policies focused on tightening the border and determining who was in the United States illegally. The Department of Homeland Security was created, absorbing various units of the INS. U.S. visas dropped precipitously and perception of illegal immigration, and even legal immigration, began to grow unfavorable.

Just two years later, immigration would become increasingly politicized. After the auspicious climate for immigration reform had faded away with the attacks on September 11, 2201, the momentum for a new guest-worker program with Mexico and a possible grant of amnesty had been replaced with increased attention on border control and security. Out of frustration over delayed reforms and unfulfilled promises of possible amnesty, more than 800 people departed from nine major cities, traveling by bus to Washington, DC.[43] In an attempt to mimic the black Freedom Rides of the 1960s, the protestors hoped to use the journey to recast amnesty and further immigration policy liberalization as the great civil rights struggle of our time, and presenting secure borders and effective immigration law enforcement as the new Jim Crow.[44] The protestors lobbied for the legalization of more than 10 million immigrants, and an increase in opportunities for immigrants to bring family members into the country. But rather than raising awareness of their cause, these protestors highlighted the growing size of the illegal immigrant population.[45] American citizens who had stayed out of the debate previously could no longer avoid the vivid images of immigrants boldly waving flags of their own country, fearlessly declaring their undocumented status.

In response, the general public demanded greater enforcement of existing laws, leading to the Real ID Act of 2005. The Real ID Act focused primarily on security and authentication standards for state driver's licenses and identification cards, along with various immigration issues including terrorism concerns. The act created restrictions on political asylum, increased enforcement mechanisms, restricted some due process rights, and imposed federal restrictions on state driver's licenses for immigrants, making it more difficult for illegal immigrants to procure and use certain types of documents for official purposes.

On May 1, 2006, protestors once more thrust immigration issues into the public view. Mass protests had begun in the spring of 2006, with breathtakingly large turnouts in April and May. The organized rallies had continued the politicization of immigrants begun with the Freedom Rides, inadvertently raising the national consciousness about illegal immigration and the financial burdens it imposed. On May 1st, immigrants coordinated an economic protest labeled A Day without Immigrants. The nationwide protest was an effort to display the necessity of immigrants to the U.S. economy, further bolstering calls for reform and amnesty. Despite the participation of more than fifty cities, from Las Vegas to Miami, the impact of the boycott was minimal. But the political significance of the protests was lasting and widespread. The sea of Mexican and Latin American flags, the language of a "stolen land" and "reconquista," and the sight of thousands of illegal immigrants demanding citizenship shook American conceptions regarding immigration. The image presented by the protests stood in direct contradiction to earlier portraits of illegal immigrants as frightened or docile people, cowering behind locked doors, never knowing if the next knock would bring deportation. Citizens became concerned, rather than empathetic.[46]

Largely in reaction to the protests, the House and the Senate passed two vastly different immigration bills. In December 2005, the House of Representatives passed a restrictionist immigration bill (H.R. 4437) that many people saw as punitive, although it seemed to be in harmony with public wishes.[47] The bill would have criminalized being in the country illegally, required the deportation of illegal aliens, and imposed new penalties on employers and service providers who offered assistance to illegals. It provided no provisions for guest workers, nor did it offer a pathway to citizenship. In reaction to a public outcry, a few months later, the Senate passed a friendlier bill (S. 2611) that offered a tiered path to citizenship, a guest-worker program, and a provision for bringing more legal immigrants into the country. It also included a controversial provision that would require private and public employers to pay the prevailing wage to guest workers on all construction projects. The proposed bills died in the conference committee where members of both houses tried to reconcile differences to create a single bill to be voted up or down. Thus, the federal government failed in its last major attempt to reform immigration.

Perhaps, in reaction to federal failure the states increased their activism in the area of immigration reform. By July 2006, thirty states had passed fifty-seven laws that dealt with some aspect of immigration reform. Although a few of these laws expanded benefits for noncitizens, the vast majority made it more difficult for illegal immigrants to receive government benefits such as unemployment, driver's licenses, employment in government-funded projects, and gun permits.[48] Aggressive actions by state and local governments are likely to continue until Congress offers some real leadership on the issue.

The Obama Era

Despite the intensity of the debate, Congress has been unable to reach consensus on the issue of immigration, with most changes in the last decade coming from the state level or through administrative channels. Even so, legislation to address immigration has been the subject of virulent debate within the legislative branch, spilling over into state legislatures. One of the most salient pieces of legislation has been the DREAM Act, a suggested program for development, relief, and education of alien minors that lingered in Congress for years. In June 2012, it was partially implemented by a presidential directive of the Department of Homeland Security that temporarily ended the deportation of thousands of illegal aliens who met certain criteria.[49]

The DREAM Act has been debated for more than ten years as a solution to the plight of hundreds of thousands of young illegal aliens brought to the country by their parents. Originally introduced in 2001, the initial version of the legislation was placed alongside various other immigration-related bills that eventually failed. Politicians expressed concern that the bill could encourage chain migration, aggravating rather than solving the issue of illegal immigration. Other politicians agreed with the principals of the bill, but refused to act on the legislation unless it was a part of a more comprehensive immigration reform. Others recognized the importance of the measure, but found it to be distracting in light of more pressing issues.

The act was reformulated to address these concerns, resulting in what remains the most current version of the legislation (S.3992). The DREAM Act would allow illegal alien students to gain "conditional nonimmigrant status" if they have had "good moral character" since entry into the United States, as determined by the Department of Homeland Security; have graduated from a U.S. high school, have a GED or otherwise have gained admittance to an institution of higher education; arrived in the United States before the age of sixteen, prior to enactment of the bill; and have lived in the country continuously for at least five years. If an applicant meets these qualifications, they may be granted temporary residence once they have completed two years of armed service, acquired a degree from an institution of higher learning, or completed two years and are in good standing in a program for a bachelor's degree or higher. Previous to completion of two years of any of these activities, partic-ipants in the program would only qualify for nonimmigrant status. The age cap previously placed at thirty-five was lowered to thirty in recent changes to the bill. The legislation also bars any immigrant who has committed marriage or voter fraud, committed a felony or three misdemeanors, abused student visa provi-sions, engaged in persecution, poses a public health risk, or is likely to become a public charge. Applicants must also agree to pay taxes; demonstrate an ability to read, write, and speak English; and have an understanding of the fundamentals of the history, principles, and form of government of the United States typically required for naturalization. The bill specifically states that the measure will not force states to charge in-state tuition rates to illegal immigrants, although they would be permitted to do so if they choose to.

Despite significant changes to the proposed act, some citizens disagree with the fundamental assumptions of the legislation, and the undesirable effects they believe it will create. Opponents also claim that the act provides an unjustified reward for illegal immigration, because not everyone benefits from the proposed legislation. Although the act is still pending, the presidential directive gives temporary status to as many as 800,000 formerly undocumented persons who can now work openly with government-issued identifications. The presidential directive was a controversial sidestepping of congressional intent. Not surpris-ingly, the presidential directive came during an election year in which many Hispanics had voiced disappointment with the president's failure to keep his promises about reforming immigration.

The Dream Act ignited state action focused on addressing the plight of young people in the affected categories. Several states have acted on the model provided by the federal bill, demonstrating the ability of states to test policies the nation is not yet prepared for. California recently enacted a state version of the DREAM Act, granting access to state-funded financial aid for illegal immigrants who meet GPA requirements, graduate from a California high school, and enter the U.S. before age sixteen (A.B. 131). In August of 2011, Illinois followed suit, also providing privately funded scholarships for legal and illegal immigrant children (S.B. 2185).

Although little has been accomplished in terms of bringing about expansive immigration reform through the legislative process, the Obama administration has communicated a broad policy to reduce deportation of certain groups of immigrants. In June 2011, the administration quietly announced new rules in a memo from top officials at the U.S. Immigration and Customs enforcement agency.[50] Many have labeled the memo as an attempt to pass the DREAM Act through an executive order, as the memo highlights the use of "prosecutorial discretion," encouraging officers to limit enforcement of immigration laws if illegal immigrants are enrolled in an education center or their relatives have volunteered for the U.S. military.

The overall Obama record on immigration enforcement is mixed. Although the administration boasts of having had an unusually high record of deportations (close to 1 million to Bush's 1.57 million in two years), most of its deportations have been of criminal aliens. A much more lenient policy of catch and release for noncriminal aliens seems to have been the norm. Representative Lamar Smith (R-TX), chairman of the House Judiciary Committee, has questioned the administration's record of enforcement. Smith has accused the administration of inflating its numbers.[51] According to Smith, the numbers are misleading because they "include voluntary removals in the deportation statistics." Voluntary removals are not deportations because the "illegal immigrant is not then subject to penalties for returning to the United States ... a single illegal immigrant can show up at the border and be voluntarily returned numerous times in one year – and counted each time as a removal."[52]

THE RETURN OF IMMIGRATION FEDERALISM

States have always been active in immigration regulation, occasionally enforcing sanctions against employers, and regulating immigrant access to public services. But the trend in state and local immigration legislation in the twenty-first century has been dramatic.[53] The noticeable rise of state action on immigration issues can be explained by several factors. First, since 1990 the nation has been in the midst of a demographic reordering, as the majority of immigrants now come from Asia and Latin America rather than the traditional Europe.[54] By 2006, approximately 11.5 million immigrants were also unauthorized.[55] The year 2011 brought dismally low rates of unemployment, but immigration was at the highest rate ever recorded.[56] Due to changes in border control, immigrants have been dispersed deeply and broadly across the nation, bypassing traditional urban centers. These changing immigration patterns have brought noncitizens into new regions of the country that feel the need to generate a policy response. Effective integration of new citizens has required states to adopt positions, often in tension with federal immigration policy. The city of Hazelton, PA, developed laws stricter than federal regulation, enforcing sanctions against landlords in addition to employers; whereas cities such as New Haven, CT, provided ID cards and other benefits to undocumented immigrants the federal government does not yet recognize.[57] State and local government responses to immigration are also motivated by a sense that the cost of unauthorized immigration falls unevenly across the levels of government, with some states going so far as to sue the federal government for reimbursement.[58] Lastly, since the terrorist attacks of

September 11, 2011, the federal government has come to rely on law enforcement assistance from the states, which have willingly accepted the authority granted by federal agencies.

State and local governments have had growing incentive to become involved in immigration policy as they respond to the necessity of local enforcement, the lack of federal enforcement, and the need to integrate new immigrants into their societies. Clare Huntington[59] recognizes three primary areas of growing state and local involvement in immigration policy flowing from these motivations: acceptance of delegated authority from the federal government to local governments, state enforcement of existing federal law without a delegation of authority, and laws generated by the states regarding noncitizens. The federal government began to delegate authority to state and local law enforcement with congressional enactment of the Immigration Reform and Immigrant Responsibility Act of 1996, which added Section 287(g) to the Immigration and Nationality Act. Section 287(g) authorized the federal government (most recently, the secretary of Homeland Security) to enter into agreements with state and local governments to enforce federal immigration law. This delegated authority entailed broad responsibilities, including the power to arrest and detain noncitizens for immigration violations, investigation of immigration violations, and collection of evidence in preparation for immigration cases brought before an immigration judge. Several states and localities entered into such agreements, accepting oversight by federal immigration officials. The second clear delegation over immigration authority came from the Personal Responsibility and Work Opportunity Reconciliation Act, which granted states the ability to determine immigrant eligibility for federal benefits programs. Although it was expected most states would use this authority to enforce stricter limits on access to benefits, states were commonly more generous than the federal government had been.[60] Although a few states took advantage of these opportunities in the 1990s, twenty-three states have signed the mutual agreement provided under 287(g) in the last ten years.[61]

The next category of growing state action is enforcement of existing federal laws that the federal government either enforces ineffectively or not at all. In a controversial opinion by the Office of Legal Counsel, the Justice Department found that states and localities possess inherent authority to enforce both the criminal and civil provisions of the INA in 2002.[62] Although this formal opinion provides more limited authority than that granted under section 287(g), there is an indication that assistance of local and state agents in arresting noncitizens and delivering them to federal officials will be accepted in certain instances. With rising populations of undocumented immigrants, states are showing an increasing willingness to enforce existing federal law to protect the interests of their citizens.

The final category of state action is legislation that affects noncitizens either indirectly or directly. These laws range from granting in-state tuition to immigrants to forbidding businesses from employing undocumented workers.

Although critics of the rise of immigration federalism fear increased discrimination against immigrants, many state laws benefit noncitizens, including unauthorized migrants, through provision of health care, identification cards, access to higher public education, and limits on racial profiling of employers.[63] Other states have acted in response to the federal government's failure to curb unauthorized migration, with Arizona enacting one of the more far-reaching laws in the nation to date.

CONSTITUTIONAL AUTHORITY OVER IMMIGRATION

Proponents and opponents of immigration federalism often share one basic assumption: immigration is the exclusive responsibility of the federal government. Those who oppose recent state action reason that states are legislating on a matter forbidden to them, which must be stopped. Proponents of state action argue that states are forced to act because the federal government has failed to do so. But neither side recognizes the powerful marriage of innovation and authority the federal-state-local dynamic offers in solving the issues of immigration. In order for such an arrangement to succeed, courts must abandon the political rhetoric and legal doctrine of federal exclusivity that has blocked and limited the potential for state solutions. Although immigration has been viewed as an area of exclusive federal authority, this is only an accurate description of the current legislative landscape. There is no constitutional mandate for federal exclusivity over immigration law, and the states' access to such authority is far more legitimate than the debate suggests.

There are three ways to perceive federal authority over immigration: structural, with no appropriate role for state or local governments; dormant, requiring the federal government to activate underlying state authority; and statutory, where state and federal governments have initial authority to regulate, but the federal government may exclude state action through preemption. Dormant preemption requires explicit delegation, which does not apply in the case of immigration. Typically, structural preemption also requires a clear textual basis in the Constitution, as seen with copyright and bankruptcy law, although some scholars have argued that structural preemption is implied when dual regulation on an issue would be undesirable.[64]

Structural preemption is one of the more common classifications of immigration authority, as many perceive a need for a uniform standard for exit and entry into the country. But the Constitution refers only to the need for a uniform rule of naturalization, not sole authority over immigration by the federal government. Rather than rely on an explicit textual mandate, proponents for the structural view of immigration insist that the issue is comparable to treatment of foreign affairs, and must be exclusively controlled by the federal government to preserve sovereignty and uniformity. But the classification of immigration as a purely national issue has grown increasingly outdated, and all that remains is a formal doctrine without strong constitutional justifications. Several countries with powerful central governments now allow subnational regions to control their immigration policy.[65] With the rise of non-state actors, other nations are less likely to interpret the actions of a state as indicative of broader national policy. Foreign affairs are only tangentially related to the issue of immigration, and an attempt to join the two overlooks the nuances of immigration policy. Although the federal government largely dominated immigration policy throughout the twentieth century, this was a consequence of the need for a more uniform standard, not recognition of exclusive federal authority.

If authority over immigration is viewed under statutory preemption, states would share regulatory authority, but the national government would maintain the ability to preempt through federal statute according to the Supremacy Clause. This enables the federal government to maintain a consistent federal policy while allowing for state innovation within its primary goals.[66] Broader federal protections, such as the Equal Protection Clause, First Amendment, and even landlord-tenant laws will continue to apply to state laws, ensuring that state action stays within certain bounds. Supreme Court precedent does not explicitly foreclose a statutory preemption view of federal authority; instead, it embodies the tension between an interest in a uniform rule on a national level, and states' interest in exercising police power to protect their citizens.[67]

An understanding of the basis for federal authority will influence how courts will assess substantive laws of the states, and will open up the debate about the proper allocation of authority between the various government entities. Federal delegation of authority to states will be permissible under the statutory preemption view, although it would be expressly suspect under a structural view. Even in the absence of delegation by the federal government, state and local enforcement of federal immigration laws would be permissible unless statutorily preempted under a statutory interpretation. If the constitution provides for state authority, it would not limit states to enforcement of existing law, but would also allow them to develop their own. Statutory preemption would permit states to innovate where the federal government has not already legislated, or where the federal government does not enforce. Currently most courts begin with the assumption that state laws are constitutionally proper to the extent they accord with traditional areas of state authority, such as health, safety, and other matters of local concern where Congress has not preempted through previous legislation. Structural preemption would distinguish these laws according to whether they can be labeled as alienage law or pure immigration law. Under the statutory preemption view, most state laws would be permitted, although the federal government would be able to preempt through congressional legislation.

VIEWPOINTS ON IMMIGRATION FEDERALISM

Even if state legislation is legally permissible, some scholars oppose the concept of immigration federalism and believe that individual rights will suffer under a "devolution" of immigration policy.[68] Other scholars are concerned that communities will see an increase in crime if immigrants learn to distrust local law enforcement agents.[69] Opponents of the development argue that there is a need for uniformity in immigration policy and that the national government is better able to identify and correct for market imperfections and failures, protect fundamental rights, and guard against a regulatory race to the bottom.

But gradually, scholars have come to embrace the inevitable trend of immigration federalism, and are willing to see the benefits of such a development. Immigration federalism provides the opportunity for innovation, a "quintessential force multiplier" in the resources available to address the issue,[70] and a "steam valve function" that allows states with strong anti-immigration leaning to have a voice without swaying all national policies.[71] States provide "laboratories of democracy," as they compete with each other for residents and resources, increasing political accountability and participation as they are able to address local needs and meet the demands of a smaller constituency.[72] The full development of divergent views on the benefits and costs of immigration allow for policies to be tested before enactment on a national scale.[73] State policies often fall on either side of national policy, as states have demonstrated both hostility and openness to noncitizens. While the federal government was developing policy to build a wall along the border of the United States, states such as California were working to provide in-state tuition to undocumented immigrants.[74] By allowing states to enact such policies, the federal government acknowledges the important economic and social stake that states and local governments have in immigration. Although many fear an increasing threat to individual rights, there is no reason to think the federal government is better at protecting such fundamental rights, and if anything, the states provide a check on such expansive power.[75]

CONCLUSION AND POLICY SUGGESTIONS

The 2012 decision in *Arizona v. United States*[76] has given grist to the mill of Americans who argue that immigration should be the exclusive purview of the federal government. Immigration is an issue that is continuing to increase in significance and volume. *Arizona* clearly places the onus on Congress to enforce immigration laws in a reasonable and timely fashion. Clear lines of accountability could spur grassroots movements to hold the institution accountable for what often seems like a gross dereliction of duties. Something must be done. The nation's immigrant population, both legal and illegal, reached 40 million in 2010, the largest number in the nation's history.[77] With the vast expansion of immigration throughout the country, negative externalities are no longer contained in border states, and certain communities have lost more than others.[78] Limited resources and a growing dependant population have left politicians with difficult decisions on how to allocate services to legal immigrants and residents as we enter into the twenty-first century.

State participation in immigration enforcement and policy has led some to question the legitimacy of such action, whereas others have seen the promise of a solution. Once we recognize that federal exclusivity is not constitutionally mandated, classic federalism arguments work well in determining the appropriate allocation of authority among levels of the government. The federal government may preempt states where it is necessary to have a unified policy, and broader constitutional provisions will ensure that state legislation protects individual rights. Since 1986, Congress has only been able to achieve piecemeal immigration reform. As a consequence, it is likely we will see state legislation continue to fill voids in immigration policy. As Cristina Rodriguez[79] argues, immigration is no longer a purely national issue, it is a state issue in the same vein as education, crime control, and the regulation of health, safety, and welfare; not only because immigration influences every one of those interests, but because managing the immigration movement itself is a state interest.

In order to achieve the beneficial partnership between local and federal, courts should assess potential conflicts between federal and state laws. Lawmakers should be encouraged to engage in federal-state-local cooperation, and Congress should restrain from overregulating the issue and thereby excluding state innovation. Integration and acceptance of new citizens must be taken on as a partnership. Although federal law will control who enters the country, states must play a necessary role in integrating new immigrants. We have a national interest in seeing laws upheld that reflect legitimate state interests, while not trampling on individual rights or the lofty goals and ambitions of a national policy that often seems vague and misguided.

Notes

1. Justice Stevens writing for the majority in *Arizona v. United States*, 132 S.Ct. 2492, 2510 (2012).
2. Malcolm Feeley and Edward Rubin, *Federalism: Political Identity and Tragic Compromise* (Ann Arbor: University of Michigan Press, 2008), 12.
3. National Conference of State Legislatures. "2011 Immigration Related Laws, Bills and Resolutions in the States: Jan.1–March 31, 2011." Retrieved from http://www.ncsl.org/default.aspx?TabId=13114.
4. Clare Huntington, "The Constitutional Dimension of Immigration Federalism," *Vanderbilt Law Review* 61 (2008), 790.
5. Hiroshi Motomura, "Federalism, International Human Rights, and Immigration Exceptionalism," *University of Colorado Law Review* 70 (1999), 1361; Michael J. Wishnie, "Laboratories of Bigotry? Devolution of Immigration Power, Equal Protection, and Federalism," *New York Law Review* 76 (2001), 493.
6. Michael J. Wishnie, "State and Local Police Enforcement of Immigration Laws," *University of Pennsylvania Constitutional Law Journal* 6 (2004), 1084; Motomura, "Federalism, International Human Rights, and Immigration Exceptionalism," 1361.
7. Linda Bosniak, "The Undocumented Immigrant" in *Debating Immigration*, ed. Carol Swain (New York: Cambridge University Press), 85–94.

8. Bosniak, "The Undocumented Immigrant," 86.

9. Bosniak, "The Undocumented Immigrant," 86–87.

10. Peter H. Schuck, "Taking Immigration Federalism Seriously," *University of Chicago Law Forum* (2007), retrieved from Social Science Research Network: http://ssrn.com/abstract=965338.

11. *Arizona v. United States*, 567 U.S. ___ (2012), retrieved from http://www.supremecourt.gov/opinions/11pdf/11-182.pdf.

12. See *Toll v. Moreno*, 458 U. S. 1, 10.

13. Tyler Anbinder, *Nativism and Slavery: The Northern Know Nothing and the Politics of the 1850s* (New York: Oxford University Press, 1992).

14. Chinese Exclusion Act, Sess. I, Chap. 126; 22 Stat. 58. 47th Congress; Approved May 6, 1882.

15. Roger Daniels, *Guarding the Golden Door* (New York City: Hill and Wang, 2004), chapter 1.

16. Daniels, *Guarding the Golden Door*; Alejandro Portes and Ruben Rumbaut, *A Portrait of Immigrant America*, third edition, revised (Berkeley, CA: University of California Press, 2006).

17. Portes and Rumbaut, *A Portrait of Immigrant America*, 12–38.

18. Carolyn Wong, *Lobbying for Inclusion: Rights Politics and the Making of Immigration Policy* (Stanford: Stanford University Press), 44–63.

19. Stephen Thomas Wagner, "The Lingering Death of the National Origins Quota System: A Political History of United States Immigration Policy, 1952–1965." PhD dissertation, Harvard University, Cambridge, MA (1986).

20. Wong, *Lobbying for Inclusion*, 61–62; Portes and Rumbaut, *A Portrait Immigrant America*, 12–63.

21. Wagner, "The Lingering Death of the National Origins Quota System," 464–465.

22. John D. Skrentny, "Obama's Immigration Reform: A Tough Sell for a Grand Bargain" in Theda Skocpol and Lawrence R. Jacobs (eds.) *Reaching for a New Deal* (New York: Russell Sage Foundation), 274.

23. Skrentny, "Obama's Immigration Reform," 270.

24. Wong, *Lobbying for Inclusion*, 68.

25. Wong, 95–132.

26. Daniel J. Tichenor, *Dividing Lines: The Politics of Immigration Control in America* (Princeton: Princeton University Press, 2002), 226–227.

27. Wong, *Lobbying for Inclusion*, 96; Skrentny, "Obama's Immigration Reform," 273–320.

28. Wong, *Lobbying for Inclusion*.

29. David M. Reimers, *Still the Golden Door: The Third World Comes to America* (New York: Columbia University Press, 1992).

30. Wong, *Lobbying for Inclusion*, 101.

31. Wong, *Lobbying for Inclusion*, 102.

32. Wong, *Lobbying for Inclusion*, 104.

33. The Immigration Act of 1990 (Pub.L. 101–649, 104 Stat. 4978, enacted November 29, 1990).

34. Douglas S. Massey, "Borderline Madness: America's Counterproductive Immigration Policy" in *Debating Immigration*, ed. Carol Swain (New York: Cambridge University Press, 2007), 132.

35. Massey, "Borderline Madness," 134–135.

36. Massey, 135.
37. Massey, 136–137.
38. Wong, *Lobbying for Inclusion*, 133.
39. Proposition 187 was ultimately overturned, but it is relevant in showing the rise of state action and its effect on national politics.
40. Peter Spiro uses this turn of events to indicate the need for the "steam-valve" function, discussed next.
41. Wong, *Lobbying for Inclusion*, 137.
42. Peter J. Spiro, "Learning to Live with Immigration Federalism," *Conneticut Law Review* 29 (2007), 1627.
43. Visa Law.Com. 2003. Retrieved from http://www.visalaw.com/03sep4/16sep403. html.
44. "Freedom Riders' Rally for Immigrant Rights," *The Chicago Tribune*. October 5, 2003.
45. Carol M. Swain, "Introduction" in *Debating Immigration*, ed. Carol Swain (New York: Cambridge University Press, 2007), 6–9.
46. Swain, "Introduction," 8.
47. Swain, "Introduction," 8–9.
48. "Immigration Bills Compared," *The Washington Post*, 2005, retrieved from http://www.washingtonpost.com/wp-dyn/content/custom/2006/05/26/CU2006052600 148.html.
49. "U.S. to Stop Deporting Some Illegal Immigrants," *The Wall Street Journal*, retrieved from http://online.wsj.com/article/SB10001424052702303822204577468343924 191180.html.
50. Immigration and Customs Enforcement, "Exercising Prosecutorial Discretion Consistent with the Civil Immigration Enforcement Priorities of the Agency for the Apprehension, Detention, and Removal of Aliens," 2011, retrieved from http://www.ice.gov/doclib/secure-communities/pdf/prosecutorial-discretion-memo.pdf.
51. Lamar Smith, "Obama Deportation Numbers a 'Trick,'" *Politico*, October 25, 2011, retrieved from http://www.politico.com/news/stories/1011/66805.html.
52. Smith, "Obama Deportation Numbers a 'Trick.'"
53. Cristina M. Rodriguez, "The Significance of Local in Immigration Regulation," *Michigan Law Review* 106 (2008), 569.
54. Ibid., 574.
55. Pew Hispanic Center, Jeffrey S. Passel, 2006. "The Size and Characteristics of the Unauthorized Migrant Population in the U.S., 2006," retrieved from http://pewhispanic.org/files/reports/61.pdf.
56. Steven A. Camarota, "A Record-Setting Decade of Immigration: 2000–2010," Center for Immigration Studies, October 2011, retrieved from http://cis.org/2000-2010-record-setting-decade-of-immigration.
57. Rodriguez, "The Significance of Local in Immigration Regulation," 579.
58. Schuck, "Taking Immigration Federalism Seriously," 79.
59. Huntington, "The Constitutional Dimension of Immigration Federalism," 578–579.
60. Schuck, "Taking Immigration Federalism Seriously," 60–61.
61. Immigration and Customs Enforcement, Fact Sheet: Section 287(g) Immigration and Nationality Act, U.S. Immigration and Customs Enforcement, 2011, retrieved from http://www.ice.gov/news/library/factsheets/287g.htm.

62. Office of Legal Counsel to the Attorney General, Jay S. Bybee, Assistant Attorney General, Non-Preemption of the Authority of State and Local Law Enforcement Officials to Arrest Aliens for Immigration Violations (2002).
63. Huntington, "The Constitutional Dimension of Immigration Federalism," 803–804.
64. Huntington, "The Constitutional Dimension of Immigration Federalism," 812–823.
65. Germany, Australia, Canada, and Switzerland allow subnational units to determine immigration policy. Schunk, "Taking Immigration Federalism Seriously," 67.
66. Where there is a desire to maintain consistent national policy, the federal government may preempt. Huntington cites *American Insurance Co. v. Garamendi* as an example of effective statutory preemption of undesirable state legislation. Huntington, "The Constitutional Dimension of Immigration Federalism," 817.
67. Huntington, "The Constitutional Dimension of Immigration Federalism," 824–827.
68. Wishnie, "Laboratories of Bigotry?" 493.
69. Orde F. Kittrie, "Federalism, Deportation, and Crime Victims Afraid to Call the Police," *Iowa Law Review* 91 (2006), 1449–1508.
70. Schuck, "Taking Immigration Federalism Seriously," 92.
71. Spiro argues that state action prevents a single state from pulling legislative reform in one direction – something he claims took place in the 1990s with California. While generally diminishing pressure on the structure as a whole, immigration federalism provides alternatives. Spiro explains it is "better from an alien's perspective to be driven from a hostile California into a receptive New York than to be shut out of the United States altogether." Spiro, "Learning to Live with Immigration Federalism," 1635.
72. Spiro, "Learning to Live with Immigration Federalism," 1627.
73. Huntington explains that in the case of Colorado, citizens who were virulently opposed any form of immigration changed their opinion once their ideas were put into practice, and they were able to experience actual costs and benefits of stricter laws. "The Constitutional Dimension of Immigration Federalism," 832.
74. Huntington, "The Constitutional Dimension of Immigration Federalism," 848.
75. Schuck, "Taking Immigration Federalism Seriously," 60.
76. *Arizona v. United States*, 132 S.Ct. 2492.
77. Camarota, "A Record Setting Decade of Immigration," 1.
78. George Borjas estimates that the least well off of our society face lower wages or lost jobs as the result of the increasing presence of undocumented workers in their communities. Borjas explains that for African American men in particular a 10 percent increase in competing laborers from illegal immigration leads to a 3 percent reduction in wage, and close to a 5 percent reduction in employment. George J. Borjas, "Immigration and the Economic Status of African-American Men." *Economica* 77 (2009), 255–282.
79. Rodriguez, "The Significance of Local in Immigration Regulation," 576–589.

9

Trade Politics and Reform

Judith Goldstein

INTRDUCTION[1]

In setting contemporary trade policy, Americans confront issues far afield from that imagined by the nation's Founders. The frontier in 1789 was sparsely populated, and although the new nation faced a British government willing and able to undermine commercial activity in the colonies, early elected officials worried little about international markets. Instead, they looked west, and America grew in isolated splendor. Isolationism, however, proved to be a short-lived policy. By the end of the nineteenth century, U.S. central decision makers had to deal with growing demands from constituents for access to foreign markets; by the mid-twentieth century, U.S. commercial policy had moved center stage as the United States orchestrated a widespread globalization in production and trade.

Creating that internationally oriented trade policy, however, was problematic. As the introduction to this volume sets out, most U.S. policies are constrained by decisions rendered long ago by America's Founders; in 1789, those Founders chose to give Congress the right to set tariffs. Instead of imagining tariffs as a foreign policy tool, tariffs were thought to be another tax. As result, high tariff barriers became the norm, used both to increase government coffers and facilitate rapid industrial development. By the end of the Civil War and demise of the southern pro-trade voting bloc, tariff setting had become the quintessential example of unfettered congressional logrolling. When the 1930 Smoot-Hawley tariff was making its way through Congress, more than 1,000 economists signed on to a document decrying its content. But as Schattschneider later wrote in his famous analysis of the act, congressional behavior was as predictable as it was problematic – in the face of powerful interest groups and the authority to set rates high tariffs were inevitable.[2]

Yet post–WWII tariff policy followed a path far different than what would have been thought from a reading of Schattschneider's book. The United States systemically changed its trade policy and opened its borders to foreign goods.

Instead of being the textbook example of poor public policy, trade politics became increasingly bipartisan and depoliticized. And although academics and pundits often cite the lack of forward movement in twenty-first century trade agreements as the first step down a slippery slope to the protectionism and economic decline associated with the Smoot-Hawley era, there is scant evidence of that happening. Looked at from the long view, the United States continues to have one of the most liberal trade policies in the world, and far more open than at any previous moment in U.S. history.

This chapter examines the oddity of post–WWII U.S. trade policy. As an empirical matter, America's borders are more open than ever before. Given increased congressional dissent, intense international competition, and partisan competition over policy and public discontent with America's trading partners, this "good" policy is an anomaly that needs explanation. To unravel the conundrum of good policy and bad politics, this chapter is organized around three questions.

Part one asks how the United States was able to get around the pro-protection bias found in the Constitution. This section argues that institutional changes dating to the interwar years made it more difficult for protectionist interest groups to effect policy when a web of international agreements, via both the WTO and a large number of preferential trade agreements, made it increasingly hard to close markets without a significant economic cost to constituents.

Part two begins with the current economic consensus; that is, that open trade is the best public policy, and asks to what extent these ideas influence the public policy process. I argue that three themes have repeatedly characterized all debate on legitimate trade policy. On one side are economists who argue uniformly that open markets serve the national interest. Although not arguing against the logic, a second line of debate focuses on issues of fair trade, where matters ranging from other nations' subsidies to currency manipulation to the lack of intellectual property protections are cited as leading to an unleveled playing field. The Democratic Party was a proponent of the first line of argument until the late 1980s, when they adopted the second; the Republicans argued the second, from their creation in the years before the Civil War until 1958, when they adopted the free trade position. For much of the post–World War II years, the parties agreed on the value of open borders; today, both parties worry about fair trade. They differ, however, on the third line of debate; that is, whether or not government should redistribute the gains from trade in order to compensate for job loss that results from opening the U.S. market. The fissures today revolve more around this issue than the other two.

Third, the chapter looks ahead and asks whether or not we should expect policy change. Given the difficulties with the Doha Round, the rise of anti-Chinese sentiment, and the partisan nature of the passage of the last three preferential trade agreements, the United States appears to have lost its commitment to the further opening of its borders. At the same time, both parties support increased use of sanctions for a variety of infractions, from antidumping to patents and copyrights, suggesting a move toward closure. The left of the Democratic Party and the right of the Republican Party are both critical of aspects of the globalization project, splitting a consensus among policy elites that has existed since the 1930s. This shift in domestic politics, opposed by just about every member of the economics community, is a bellwether of what some suggest is America's declining interest in providing international collective goods.

THE INSTITUTIONAL SETTING

Institutional Reform

All explanations of contemporary U.S. policy begin with events in the interwar years. Previous to the Depression, U.S. trade policy reflected the Article 2 grant of authority to Congress to set the tariff schedule. Given that tariffs are a "tax," initial authority for tariff bills go to the House of Representatives. Although a coequal with the Senate in legislative authority, House members answer to smaller constituencies and face significantly shorter electoral cycles.[3] It is well known that as district size increases in a representational system, leaders become more willing to think about the welfare of society as a whole, a reflection of their ability to make tradeoffs between competing groups with crosscutting interests.[4] Thus, the president who serves the largest constituency in the United States has historically been more willing to support free trade than has Congress. Among congressional representatives, the Senate is more free trade oriented than the House.[5]

With very small districts, House members have the greatest difficulty ignoring organized groups within their constituency; the granting to them of initial trade authority provides a simple explanation for early U.S. protectionism. Even though majorities existed in the United States for a more open trade policy, congressional representatives tended to heed the voice of import competing groups. When aggregated together, House votes became logrolls in which all interests were accommodated. The result was trade restrictions. Even with southern interests squarely in the pro-trade camp, the U.S. tariff schedule in the nineteenth century remained higher than that found in Europe.

Congress supported high tariffs throughout the nineteenth and early twentieth centuries, and enacted the Smoot-Hawley tariff in 1930. That tariff act marks a turning point in tariff history because of the economic decline that followed passage and the assumption that the two were related. The 1930 act both raised overall customs duties to more than 50 percent ad valorem (an amount not uncommon in the previous century) and was passed even though the revenue stream into government coffers, long the argument in defense of tariff hikes, had changed with the passage of the income tax in 1913. Most deleterious, after WWI the U.S. international footprint had grown rapidly; as the dollar took the place of the British pound, international borrowers were increasingly relying on access to the U.S. market to gain currency for loan repayment. Closing the

American market undercut the foundations of the financial system that had developed in the declining days of British hegemony and created economic hardship for most of the industrialized world.

The decision to return to the previous era of high tariffs was met by universal criticism and what many argue was retaliatory tariffs by trading partners causing, or at least aggravating, what would become the Great Depression. For American scholars, the height of the tariff wall and its relationship to the Great Depression was not the only source of criticism. For the next generation of academics, the process of passage became the epitome of how interest groups' involvement and congressional logrolling can undermine the policy process.

High tariffs and the onset of the Great Depression led to new majorities in Congress and the re-legislation of the tariff. The new act, however, changed the process of setting rates and not the rates themselves. Sidestepping Article 2 of the Constitution, the Reciprocal Trade Agreements Act of 1934 (RTAA) granted the president new authority to lower rates by up to 50 percent, if he received reciprocal reductions in a partner's tariff. The new treaties required no ex post congressional vote.[6] Between 1934 and 1947, when the General Agreement on Tariffs and Trade (GATT) came into force, the president used this authority to conclude thirty-two such agreements with twenty-eight countries.[7] This authority required regular congressional renewal and both Democratic and Republican majorities reauthorized the program.[8] When the GATT went into force on January 1, 1948, Congress continued to grant negotiating authority.[9] By 1962, trade was no longer a partisan issue and both parties had platforms that endorsed the trade liberalization program.[10]

The 1934 act dictated the form of tariff setting as well as its height, thus becoming the template for all future trade agreements. These early trade treaties were bilateral but their effect extended beyond the two nations. After 1923, the United States was bound by executive order to grant Most Favored Nation (MFN) privileges to our trading partners, and by the end of WWII, the United States had agreed to a large web of such MFN agreements. Thus, once the United States lowered rates for one nation as part of a bilateral process, others with whom we had an MFN agreement benefited immediately from the lower rate. The treaty process in the GATT was multilateral in essentially the same way. Negotiations occurred between dyads, but all members of the organization benefited because of the MFN agreement that accrued from signing onto the GATT itself.[11] Twenty-three nations, some of whom already had bilateral agreements with the United States, participated in the initial GATT negotiation. Thereafter, the organization grew rapidly.[12]

As well as being multilateral because of MFN provisions, the RTAA promoted worldwide tariff reductions because the executive was bound by law to negotiate *reciprocal* agreements, meaning that import access necessitated an immediate and monetarily equal export gain. Each agreement then guaranteed bilateral reductions in rates that were universally shared. As well, the reciprocity rule extended to parties withdrawing from the treaty that could have, but did not, lead to these agreements unraveling. When a nation reneged on a promise, the treaty partner that had been party to the original tariff reduction had the right to demand compensation, either in the form of a changed tariff to another product, or an increase in their own tariff schedule up to the lost revenue. In practice, a nation could, for political reasons, rescind a tariff by substituting an equivalent concession. However, moving a tariff concession to another product in the absence of a matching export deal was very difficult and thus rarely occurred.[13] The result was that treaty promises were rarely renegotiated or rescinded and the RTAA/GATT system stabilized commercial policy at low tariff rates.

The final structural rule of tariff reduction reflected congressional concern about what products would be open for reduction, and in hindsight proved to be an important factor in continued congressional support for liberalization. As part of a legislative compromise, the Roosevelt administration agreed to negotiate only on products to which the trading partner was the principal supplier. This rule reduced the number of potential reductions in any political district and increased the predictability of product choice. Thus, to know whether or not a particular treaty was going to effect constituents, the average congressman needed only to look at the import pattern of products in his or her district.[14]

Putting these rules together, trade liberalization occurred as a result of a process whereby nations initiated negotiations by asking for a change in the tariff of only a subset of products; that is, those in which they had a dominant share of the market.[15] The potential treaty partner would then look at the list of demands and make counteroffers. When a deal was struck, other nations would free ride on the tariff concession.[16] The benefit for small nations or those not at the table was that via MFN, they received a lowered rate without making a concession; the problem was that if you were not a participant, you could not dictate the products being reduced.

Two caveats are important for contemporary policy. First, congressional delegation to the President was not a form of abdication, although it has been so argued.[17] From the start, treaties occurred under the watchful eye of Congress. Congress kept the president on a short leash and renewals were a regular part of the trade agreements program, occurring four times before the creation of the GATT, and then regularly thereafter, whenever the president wanted to set up a new trade round. By the 1970s, Congress reasserted its centrality by mandating that negotiated agreements return to Congress for final approval. Further, Congress established the Office of the Special Trade Representative in 1962 to increase its oversight of the trade agreements program. That office was renamed the Office of the U.S. Trade Representative or USTR in 1979, and its head became the chief U.S. negotiator. In part, the intent of the office was to balance the power of the State Department and the perception that their civil servants were willing to undermine U.S. economic interests for larger foreign policy goals.[18] USTR joined the Commerce Department and the International Trade Commission (ITC) as the organizational support for U.S. trade policy setting.

Second, over time, all these agencies and Congress dealt less with tariffs and more with a range of other restrictions on the U.S. market. Legislated nontariff barriers (NTB), which include a large number of regulatory and other barriers to trade, were far less amenable to reciprocal reductions and less likely to be part of the early treaty process. As a result, congress retained substantial control on such trade barriers, even as tariffs were reduced. Increasingly, U.S. policy on free trade was deviating from that on fair trade, where fair trade because synonymous with the NTBs that congress supported in order to assure a level player field for U.S. producers.

On the free trade front, the president and Congress continued to endorse multilateral and bilateral agreements to open up markets. The GATT held eight rounds of trade talks, each begun with authorization from Congress to the president for American participation. Reciprocal reductions in tariffs were the focus of the first five rounds exclusively; the last three saw reductions in tariffs, but more centrally, began to deal with NTBs, now the more evident problem undermining trade flows. The shift in focus to fair trade concerns reflected a changed reality of border regulation. By the close of the last completed round, the Uruguay Round, tariffs in the developed world, on average, were below 5 percent; meanwhile, behind-the-border fair trade regulations remained the central impediment to the international flow of goods and services.

Negotiating away these trade barriers was difficult for the United States because behind the border, fair trade measures were deeply entrenched in U.S. law, even before the passage of the Smoot-Hawley tariff and the reforming of U.S. trade policy. For example, antidumping law, which protects producers from foreign imports sold at less than their real production costs, appeared in its modern form in 1921.[19] Although dumping involves corporations, countervailing duties, a second entrenched pro-protection law, protect American producers from unfair practices of foreign governments; Congress has provided such protections as far back as 1909. Similarly, section 337, which provides protections for intellectual property, was born out of legislation in the tariff act of 1922. Thus, although the United States has signed onto international rules on dumping, subsidies, and intellectual property protections that have focused on procedurals issues, domestic rules remain intact and under the watchful eye of Congress.[20]

Finding a majority in support of reform of these statutes is difficult, and Congress has routinely been unwilling to support changes in behind the border regulations, even when initialed by U.S. negotiators during trade rounds. In the Kennedy Round (1964–67), for example, negotiators returned to Congress with enabling legislation that included at least two measures that they felt were not in the president's domain: American Selling Price and Anti-Dumping rules. Neither was enacted. In anticipation of a reoccurrence of what Congress thought was an overzealous negotiating team, the Trade Act of 1974, which authorized the subsequent Tokyo Round (1973–79), pre-stated the need for final congressional approval of all GATT agreements. To appease the administration and signal to America's negotiating partners that congressional reassertion of authority would not lead to a permanent congressional veto of trade acts, Congress devised a new procedure called "fast track." Fast track was a commitment by Congress not to emasculate the initialed agreement; in practice, it was simply a promise that the trade bill would be considered as a whole, and not laden with particularistic amendments.

Fast track proved to be a successful innovation in presidential-congressional trade policymaking. In essence, fast track facilitated negotiations on trade rounds and bilateral agreements because it became a signal to treaty partners that there was a high probability that the agreement, once negotiated, would pass congressional muster. The procedure was used to approve the final Tokyo Round agreement in 1979, as well as the subsequent U.S.-Canada, North American Free Trade Association (NAFTA), Central America Free Trade Agreement (CAFTA), and Uruguay Round agreements. Although the procedure was created to preempt congressional logjams, it actually brought Congress center stage. Congress was now more central in the negotiating process and markup stage, and more resistant to executive foreign policy claims. By the turn of the century, instead of arguing about the trade agreements themselves, whether or not to give the president fast track approval had become the focus of debate. In 2002, Congress mustered support to renew fast track authority by two votes; the authority was renewed in 2005, but in 2007 that authority, now called Trade Promotion Authority (TPA), expired. Fast track is not needed to either negotiate or pass trade legislation. However, given past congressional resistance, U.S. credibility as a negotiating partner is far weaker in its absence. The three Free Trade Agreements (FTAs) that were signed into law in October 2011 with Korea, Colombia, and Panama were concluded before TPA expired, and before the Obama administration took office.[21] In the absence of TPA, there are no new agreements that have gone beyond the planning stage.

Mediating Partisan Politics and Unfair Trade Statutes

The United States has signed onto numerous international agreements that constrain trade policy today. These agreements mediate potential partisan swings in trade policy preferences, making commercial policy a far slower and more deliberate public policy than others in the congressional domain.[22] Thus, even though representatives have placed thousands of bills into the hopper that would have given tariff hikes to particular industries, they have rarely made it to the floor. The rare individual product bill that is enacted usually lowers a rate in response to a constituent need for some cheaper foreign product input needed in the production process, not the opposite.

The central constraint Congress faces from enacting trade-restricting legislation is potential punishment through the WTO dispute settlement system. If a nation believes that a trading partner has broken any part of the treaty, they can ask for consultation, and failing agreement, the creation of a panel of experts to hear the case. Decisions are binding, in that a nation is supposed to adhere to the decisions. There is an appellate process in place to hear appeals, but if that goes against the defendant, a change in policy is expected. If a nation does not adhere, the nation bringing the case has the right to retaliate, up to the amount of lost trade. This, too, however, must be authorized by the WTO. Under the GATT system, a nation could veto the creation of these panels; the WTO removed that right.

Congress was willing to go along with this set of rules because of a generalized belief that the United States was more often in adherence to WTO rules than were her trading partners. This has proved not to be the case. As of this writing, the US was a complainant in 107 cases since the WTO was created, and was a respondent in 121 cases. In addition, the United States participated in 114 other panels as a third party. This made the United States both the most likely target as well as the most likely complainant of any other member of the WTO. In fact, just about half of all cases involved the United States on one side or the other.

Few of these cases involved tariff policy. Rather, they more often dealt with those laws passed by congress that predated delegation of tariff setting-authority to the president. Most often, the United States is in court because of the administration of an unfair trade law, either antidumping, countervailing duty, or section 301 of the Trade Act of 1974.[23] As explained previously, these fair trade laws are politically and ideationally distinct from tariff regulation; as well, they have a different administrative structure. In unfair trade statutes, executive agencies are mandated to examine the technical aspects of whether or not a nation is out of compliance with a U.S. law. If a positive determination is made, neither congress nor the president can veto the finding. For example, if the Commerce Department and ITC concur that a product is sold at less than fair value and that the sale has caused harm to an American producer, the president has no authority to stop the additional duty on the dumped product.[24] America's trading partners have had numerous problems with the method used to assess both dumping and injury, and in 1994 the United States agreed to a clarified although not dissimilar standard. Still, Congress continues to mandate standards, and the agencies making the assessment of wrongful trade are answerable to congressional committees and not directly to the president.

Although the telling of the history of U.S. trade policy often focuses on high tariffs, unfair trade statutes such as antidumping are more longstanding and have increasingly become the chief means by which the United States protects its market. By the end of the 1970s, these statutes had risen in visibility and were increasingly seen as more problematic than tariffs for foreign exporters. In part, this reflected that even when the president felt that an unfair trade ruling adversely hurt an American ally or U.S. interest, he could do little other than cajole an industry to rescind its petition for aid. Large industries, such as steel, repeatedly filed petitions under these statutes claiming a need for help against a rising tide of imports; many of these cases were justified according to the letter of the law, although not its underlying intent: these industries most often lost market share not because of cheating but because others were more competitive. Given that they qualified for increased tariffs, often up to 100 percent, free trade oriented presidents repeatedly found themselves with limited tools to undercut a tariff hike. Voluntary Export Agreements grew as a response, although most everyone understood this to be a largely inefficient remedy.[25] From the perspective of the president, having a WTO panel rule against a U.S. action in this domain was not necessarily viewed negatively.[26]

In practice, neither party defends protectionism and most members of the legislature continue to believe that markets should dictate trade patterns, even when constituents pressure them for relief from imports. Consistent with their defense of free markets, however, legislators have limited patience for foreign practices that are at odds with the market-government relationship found in the United States.

As a result, the congressional shadow is most apparent in fair trade issues, and repeatedly, members of one chamber or the other have worried that the United States is being poorly served in Geneva. One bill, H.R. 496 (Rangel), proposed to create an Office of the Congressional Trade Enforcer that would itself investigate restrictive foreign trade practices and then call upon the USTR to take them to "court" in the WTO. Similarly, other legislation has proposed that there be recourse in the case of an adverse decision on dumping margins (2007), that the U.S. Court of International Trade be given primary jurisdiction in Section 301 cases, and a range of specific responses to harmful foreign practices. Most recently, the Senate has attempted to mandate a change in the Chinese exchange rate.

Presidents face political constraints in reforming unfair trade statutes, in part because congressional representatives on both sides of the aisle agree that the U.S. market must be protected from what they view as predatory behavior by trade partners. More generally, the congressional role in trade policy today is complex, often permeated by symbolic actions. When some trade problem is politicized, one house of Congress will respond with legislation, often at odds with treaty obligations. The president will then mediate the conflict by offering some alternative to the legislated response. This relationship was dubbed the "cry and sigh" syndrome by Robert Pastor.[27] According to Pastor, protectionists in congress regularly threaten to uproot open trade through some legislative action; the legislation or rabble-rousing is quelled, to the relief of the representatives themselves, by presidential action, or often, inaction.

In all these cases, the relationship between Congress, the president, and the WTO is more about symbols than real threats to the status quo. The United States is increasingly interdependent with foreign producers and consumers. And just as the original RTAA treaties were rarely renegotiated, the modern system is similarly stable because the norm of retaliation, inculcated in all treaties, means that any action on the part of Congress to protect one industry would lead to some harm to some other member's constituent. No congressman can predict, ex ante, what product will be hurt from retaliation against pro-protection legislation, creating a disincentive to move far from the current equilibrium. Strategic trading partners who understand electoral incentives in the United States will, in fact, target products and districts in disputes in order to quell congressional action. This practice of targeting particular groups in a trade dispute in order to mobilize anti-protection pressure is neither new nor unique to American politics. For example, in a 1995 U.S. case against the European Union (EU), the first product on the list of threatened sanctions was "cheese and curd," solely aimed to mobilize French farmers to pressure the EU to change course. Likewise, but in the other direction, representatives found it untenable to raise tariffs on Japanese Lexus producers in a Section 301 case because of resistance from Lexus dealers in their districts.[28]

In sum, the effect of globalized markets and an increasingly legalized and transparent international regime has been to change the nature of group politics in this issue area. The effect of international legalization has been policy stability; the unintended outcome, however, has been a reticence to expand international constraints by agreeing to "deeper" international rules, especially in the area of fair trade rules. I return to this point in Section 3.

THE IDEATIONAL LANDSCAPE

Most public policy debates are fueled by some uncertainty about what is the optimal policy for the nation. Elites debate the virtues of policies, and change often accompanies a shift in political control of government. The debate on trade policy exhibited this type of disagreement for the first 150 years of the nation's history. Democratic governments opened the border, whereas Republican governments raised the tariff. After the Great Depression, however, elites coalesced around one policy ideal, today espoused by just about every academic economist. That policy prescription is to keep your borders open, no matter what other nations do, if you want to increase welfare. Antidumping or fair trade laws that protect domestic producers are equally as problematic as a tariff – both, increase price and hurt consumers. If other countries want to sell the United States goods that are cheaper than production costs, economists see a buying opportunity.

The free trade position is unquestioned by academics,[29] is accepted by many policy elites, and makes little sense to the general public. When academics see protectionism, they decry rent-seeking groups who distort the political process.[30] In a recent letter to President Obama, for example, signed by the best-known trade economists in the nation, they urged the United States to close the Doha Round and pass the pending FTAs. "The fear of the labour unions that trade with the poor countries produced poor in the rich countries is mistaken," they explain.[31] Yet, these economists should not be surprised by rent-seeking behavior. If a voter works in a sector that benefits from trade openness, his wages will rise; the opposite occurs if that individual is in a sector that is uncompetitive with foreign producers. The job loser may benefit from cheaper and more diverse goods, but whether or not he can afford those products depends on whether or not the market creates new employment opportunities. In a perfect world a worker would find a new job although their wages might be less than before; in the real world, that of numerous transaction costs and workers with unequal skills, even that lesser job may not be available. Given the American form of political representation, job gains in California will do little to quell the discontent of the senator from Michigan. Trade is good in the aggregate but it is not equally good for everyone. Elected officials well familiar with the problems that followed the passage of the Smoot-Hawley Act may still find that advocating open trade is difficult.

Contemporary political elites were not the first to notice the distributional issues that accompany open borders. From the earliest debates in congress, three different lines of argument were offered for how to regulate trade. The first related to changing ideas about government regulation being developed in England. British ideas about open trade moved quickly across the Atlantic and were represented in legislative debate even before Britain opened its own borders in the 1840s. The Democratic Party and southern agricultural producers were early advocates of the free trade position. This was met by the more protectionist or mercantile position long defended by the British Crown. Whigs would adopt this line of argument, advocating a more interventionist government, and the Republican Party adopted that position after its creation. The Democratic Party retained its free trade position until the 1960s, and thereafter began to feel pressure from manufacturing constituents who competed with cheaper labor abroad. The Republican Party advocated closed borders until the 1950s, and only in 1960 did the party platform state that open trade was in the interest of the nation.

A second set of ideas developed as a response to British trade policy in the first half of the nineteenth century. The British worried about potential U.S. competition and pursued predatory trade policies to undercut manufacturing in the United States. American legislators were unsure of how to respond to British policies, especially after the War of 1812 and the resumption of trade. The debate about fair trade dates back to this time, with the Whig Party arguing that the United States needed to respond to British predatory policies in kind. The Democratic Party representatives argued against this position, fearing retaliation against southern cotton exports. With the rise of the Republican Party hegemony, however, a set of new laws were passed that protected the U.S. market against a variety of unfair trade practices, from the foreign use of subsidies to antidumping laws to protections of patents. By the time Congress delegated negotiating power to the president to lower tariffs, unfair trade laws were deeply institutionalized in legislation.

A third more uniquely American position came about as a result of early debates on the development of the relatively scarce American labor force, and whether or not the government needed to promote its development. Jefferson and Hamilton argued about the future of manufacturing in the United States, and in part, their positions reflected differing beliefs about the ideal society. Today, the parties continue to differ on the optimal relationship between government regulation and job growth. In regard to trade policy, they differ on how much to intervene in response to job losses due to foreign competition. The Democratic Party advocates Trade Adjustment Assistance (TAA) to both compensate and retrain workers. The Republican Party has been more reticent to sign on to such policies, in part reflecting differences in partisan preferences.

Trade politics in the United States has always reflected these three lines of thought, often in strange ways. Predatory practices in other nations were the focus of nineteenth-century debate, and today are the central issue in U.S.-China trade. The free trade position, comparatively, became ascendant only after Smoot-Hawley, when its proponents argued that protectionism caused the Great Depression. The slippery slope to protectionism is still a potent response on the part of supporters of globalization to any hint of U.S. policymakers wanting to close the U.S. market. The creation of the WTO in 1995 reflected that a majority still believed that open trade and deeper globalization was in the American interest. But although elected officials mostly agreed that open markets make economic sense, they also need to do something about job loss from foreign competition. The response by the Democratic Party was to legislate a TAA program, initially in 1962; its continued authorization is fundamental to Democratic Party support for trade treaties. Republicans today worry about unfair trade but support open trade, just not redistribution of the gain via TAA. Democrats shift the argument on free trade agreements, whether multilateral or bilateral, away from whether or not the agreement is economically sound to whether or not there are protections from job loss. Democrats agree with Republicans that fair trade is a problem. In fact, they advocate regulating a host of policies as part of the treaty process, from unionization to wage levels. As recent testimony shows, no one argues in defense of protectionism, even as they vote to retaliate against Chinese exchange-rate policy.

The trade policy debate today is somewhat unique in that it revolves less around policy options than about the state of the world. If the United States is faced by a nation that is breaking an antidumping rule, for example, there is no question about the response. The problem, however, is whether or not the dumping has occurred. Similarly, the United State has defined fair labor standards as a necessary requisite for a trading partner. But is Mexico keeping wages unfairly low, or does the wage difference reflect differences in productivity? The WTO makes it illegal for a nation to regulate a domestic policy to undermine a trade agreement, but is the Chinese exchange-rate peg a case of undermining its WTO obligations? More than in other issue areas, defining the problem to which the United States needs to respond is a central stumbling bloc for decision makers. This is not to say that once defined all problems have solutions. For example, Chinese infringement of intellectual property is recognized as problematic for U.S. interests yet given U.S.-Chinese interdependence the United States finds it difficult to respond without endangering its own producers.

What Do We Know about Popular Attitudes and Does It Matter?

Although academics and many elites embraced free trade ideals after the Great Depression, the public has been more reticent in believing in the benefits of open borders. The canonical position on public attitudes on trade policy is that it is determined by a voter's factor endowment. The notion of factor endowments derives from the economics of trade. According to classic theory, relative endowments in factors of production, land, labor, and capital determine the comparative advantage of that nation. When engaging in trade with another nation, products that are made with an abundant factor are assumed to be the cheapest and thus the most competitive, in part, because of reduced input costs. When markets are completely open, nations should, in theory, produce goods based on their abundant factor. This suggests that those employed in a scarce factor should be wary of global trade forces, whereas those who are employed in an industry based on the abundant factor should have the opposite interest.

Knowing a country's endowments leads to a set of predictions about political alignments on trade.[32] Given that labor has never been the abundant factor in the United States, it is not surprising that unions today have shown limited support for current trade agreements. The factor model, and even this prediction about the interest of labor, is complicated by a host of other variables. Labor, for example, can become competitive even in a labor-scare nation because of a capital and/or technology infusion. Technology serves to increase labor productivity; products made by workers can be enhanced by machinery, for example, and can lead to the production of goods that are as or more cheaply made than in nations with abundant labor. This helps explain why unions were not against the initial opening of the United States to trade; given U.S. technology, American workers, although scarce and relatively better paid, were more productive than were workers elsewhere for much of the twentieth century.

Factor endowments remain a good baseline, enabling us to ask questions about where individuals are employed as a prediction of their political position on trade, but factor endowment alone rarely explains all the variation we see in attitudes. Along with an examination of production factors, a number of other variables should be considered in a model of voter preferences on trade policy. For example, we know that many households are two earners and that the spouses are often in different occupations. Yet spouses tend to have the same political beliefs or at least vote for the same party. To predict attitudes in two-worker households, some aggregation mechanism must be assumed, even though the spouses' individual interests diverge. We also know that women are always less supportive of free trade than are men, no matter their occupation.[33] Gender differences exist, and are robust, even when we control for occupation category. Polls also suggest that the more risk averse a person, the more they question open trade policy. Risk acceptance may also be a characteristic that is not captured by any sector-specific attribute. In short, attitudes are complex even though occupation repeatedly appears to be associated with individual beliefs.

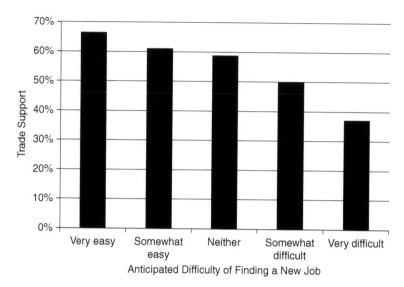

FIGURE 9.1. Trade Support by Labor Market Prospects

With that proviso, when Americans are asked about their beliefs about trade, the most robust finding from polls is that the more highly educated the individual is, the more likely he or she is to support free trade. The education effect remains at all income levels.[34] The finding may be a result of education itself; that is, if you take an economics class in any higher education establishment, you will be taught to value open markets. Alternately, the finding may reflect that education and job status is interrelated; those who are educated have job security because they are in competitive sectors.

Given the continued presence of underemployment and unemployment in the United States, the more important question may be the relationship between job *prospects* and trade attitudes. It is possible that attitudes are forward-looking and not just a reflection of current economic conditions. The data is instructive. Figure 9.1 suggests a strong relationship: the more insecure the person, the less supportive they are of U.S. trade policy. Not surprisingly, job insecurity leads to even less support for trade when both members of a household are worried about job prospects.[35] Still, it would be wrong to conclude that the public is anti-trade. Even among the very insecure, 40 percent say they support open trade.

The most recent economic downturn in 2008 led to shifting support for trade openness, but often in counterintuitive directions. In 2007, for example, before the financial meltdown, about 42.6 percent of Americans favored a reduced dependence on foreign markets; in 2009, only 37 percent of those same people favored market closure. The second result should not be interpreted as more support for open borders. What occurred was that more people answered that they just did not know what the U.S. policy should be. Recession seems to lead to uncertainty about trade – not necessarily a move to the protectionist camp.[36]

Some fissures in support have developed since 2007. In Figure 9.1, we looked more closely at respondents who had lost their jobs. Thirty-three percent of the newly unemployed had supported trade protection while employed; now, 40 percent supported an increase in trade barriers. Among those who remained employed throughout the recession, however, support for closure went the other direction, from 39 percent to 33 percent. When asked about welfare expansion, the reverse pattern emerged. Only 46 percent of this newly unemployed group had supported an expansion of welfare in 2007. In 2009, 65 percent of them said they supported welfare spending. Among those who had kept their jobs, however, support for welfare declined, from 48 percent to 44 percent.

We conclude from polling that trade policy preferences for the educated and elites remain pro-free trade, although pro-openness support begins to wane outside of these categories. Only a minority of the American public appears not to support liberal trade policies and/or globalization more generally. It is interesting to note that most voters know little and care less about most aspects of trade policy. They do, however, care about jobs. The recent passage of the three free trade agreements was supported only because they were argued to be about job creation. Although not totally untrue (some jobs will follow from trade), the net effect of the treaties will most likely be job loss in the United States. Still, politicians understood that the treaties needed to be argued to be about jobs and not access to either cheaper or better goods.

Given the importance of pro-job policies to the American electorate, and the association between job prospects and attitudes on trade we see in polls, support for globalization could easily wane if voters come to associate job loss with open borders. If job prospects decline, voters may well decide that open borders for goods and services are the cause of their unemployment, not unlike criticism of open immigration policy. Elites can try to explain the virtues of free trade, but in the absence of a vibrant economy, cheap goods may be no substitute for employment. The argument in defense of fair trade has always had more appeal to the general public; the case for free trade is far more elusive.

THE UNITED STATES IN AN INTERDEPENDENT WORLD

Our review of the history and politics of trade policymaking leads to three observations that inform analyses of policy reform in general. First, as the authors of this volume explain in their Introduction, policy is often constrained by founding documents. This is no truer than in the case of commercial policy. The administrative tools available for setting trade policy were fashioned for an earlier economic era, and they continue to act as a constraint on U.S. policymaking, even though America's place in the world has changed dramatically. Not only did the Framers create a bias toward protectionism by viewing tariffs as taxes, but because the House of Representatives was given a central role in setting policy most legislation on trade has focused on protecting the U.S. market from predatory foreign traders, not rent-seeking interest groups. Delegation of authority in 1934 to the executive was not a panacea, fixing the original design "flaw" for trade policymaking. The president has authority in that he has agenda control; but still, ultimate authority rests with congressional representatives whose interests are often particularistic and district focused.

Second, the ability of the United States to craft a policy that is in the interest of the country as a whole, not just in the interest of particular workers, firms, or regions, rests on the existence of a free trade coalition. The ideas on policy held by members of a coalition, as others in the volume suggest, are an important part of the explanation for the past stability of this coalition. In fact, the case of commercial policymaking is a textbook example of how the same institutional structures can lead to different policy outcomes when leaders ascribe to different worldviews. Today, the consensus on the value of open trade borders in both parties provides the balance against a pro-protection institutional bias. Presidential delegation alone cannot explain policy reform. Rather, reform is stable because of a shared belief that high tariffs lead to bad economic times. Whether true or not, even small shifts in the pro-protection direction lead critics to decry policy as the first step down a slippery slope toward another Great Depression.

Third, contemporary policy is constrained by a large number of agreements, both bilateral and multilateral, that deter unilateral action on the part of Congress. They are constraints not because they are international law but because reneging on an agreement leads to retaliation. It is the potential of retaliation targeted at a producer in the district of a representative that keeps that elected official wary of too much deviation from international agreements. Policy is stable because pressures from rent-seeking groups in one district are balanced by the potential harm to some producer in that or another district. In sum, trade policy outcomes are a function not only of agenda control by the president and the existence of a free trade ideology but also because of reelection concerns.

These three factors will determine just how Washington will respond to the changing interests of the U.S. economy. The interests of producers and consumers in the United States, however, are predicated not just on these domestic variables but also on the actions of external actors. Will China be socialized into the trading regime? Will WTO law defend U.S. producers? External trading patterns will continue to redistribute wealth in the United States and this will change both the power and preferences of political actors.

Changing interests and less-flexible domestic institutions suggest a pattern of trade policymaking that is more incremental than in the past. That pattern will be affected by events that are neither totally predictable nor in the hands of Washington. Four potentially important factors need consideration.

First, current international trade rules assume a type of trading partner. When the victors of WWII created the GATT, they shared a set of assumptions about the role of government and relationship between politics and markets. For fifty years, these nations dominated world trade and created a web of trading relationships with each other. The GATT/WTO was dominated by a U.S.-EU alliance and we shared a set of beliefs about the virtues of trade and the role of government in market transactions. Today, the WTO remains nominally controlled by this alliance, but trade flows have moved east and south. A set of developing nations (Brazil, Russia, India, and China) are now at the epicenter of economic activity. From the perspective of U.S. domestic law, these nations are not in compliance with the spirit of the trade regime. Industrial development occurred with far more government involvement than in the United States. As American firms find themselves unable to compete and unions attribute lost jobs to production in these nations, the United States will increasingly come to loggerheads with them over their practices. In particular, the rapid growth of China, both as an exporter and the location of U.S. foreign direct investment, has created doubts about the fundamental virtue of open markets with particular types of nations. Chinese policies, ranging from exchange rate controls to an aggressive policy of intellectual property transfer to labor policy, all suggest that the rules of market exchange are biased against U.S. worker and the U.S. economy.

Second, and related, the free trade policy consensus that has existed since 1958 and as is argued is key to a stable commercial policy, is eroding. In its place is a more precarious political lineup, a Baptist-bootlegger coalition of unlikely bedfellows. On the far right of the Republican Party are those who eschew international law and institutions as constraining U.S. autonomy. On the far left of the Democratic Party are those who see globalization as undermining U.S. jobs, the environment, and domestic production. They are equally as critical of the WTO regime but for very different reasons. The left sees the regime as encouraging cheap labor and undermining worker rights; the right sees the WTO injunctions as illegal constraints on U.S. law. Together, the far right and the far left are a potential future veto group, and they will make it difficult to get any forward-looking legislation through congress. Because both sides agree that the United States should leverage access to the U.S. market more forcefully as a means to get other nations, most recently China, to change their practices, the legislation that will gain majority support will be far more mercantile than at any time since the Great Depression. The United States may not be able to recreate the rules of the regime to its liking, but we are large enough to play the role of spoiler. This would be problematic, given the importance of a stable and open world economy for American firms and domestic economic growth.

Third, the political critique that the United States has been treated poorly under current international rules has implications for the future of the GATT/WTO liberalization project. In the absence of U.S. leadership, there will be limited or no new legislated trade rounds. If the Doha Round is ever closed it will be with minimal effect. In its place, the WTO will increasingly attempt to legislate via its judicial arm. Through the dispute settlement process, trade rules will be examined and often reinterpreted to increase trade flows. When these rulings challenge U.S. law, the anti-trade coalition will make it difficult for the United States to adhere. When they criticize other nations' practices but do not get adherence, critics will decry the futility of international law. An activist trade court in Geneva, whether ruling for or against the United States, is problematic for the United States. Not only will it raise legitimacy questions in Washington, it will focus attention on the lack of correspondence between the size of the member's economy and voting rights in the ever-growing WTO.

The alternatives to the multilateral trading system are equally problematic. Over the last twenty years, nations have increasingly signed onto regional trade agreements, many of which counter aspects of WTO law. In the United States, NAFTA, CAFTA, and the more recent three FTAs regulate aspects of trade and reduce U.S. barriers beyond what has occurred in the WTO. For many nations, their leaders may view these agreements as akin to insurance – a hedge against decisions they may dislike in the WTO. This disemboweling of the system into smaller, often regional, units may be the future of the international trading system. This is not in the interest of the United States; the alternative, however, of either support for the current multilateral system or an expansion of the role of the WTO has waning political support.

Fourth, growing market interdependence means that external shocks will more quickly affect the U.S. economy. The U.S. government has limited means to deal with these market fluctuations. Thus, even small shocks will have substantial impact on employment. The erosion of the safety net and absence of consensus on support for programs such as TAA means that trade policy itself will become the focus of the ire of the unemployed, even if unjustified. Furthermore, firms have become increasingly international and thus vulnerable to economic tsunamis – there are few, if any, products on the U.S. market that are wholly American made. Workers and firms have recourse when hurt by market conditions. They can, and do, turn to legal remedies in order to get government support against market downturns. These remedies, however, are all in the direction of closing the U.S. market.

Policy Implications and Recommendations

Putting all this together, what is the best policy given the changing nature of domestic politics and international trading landscape? Let us assume that the goal of trade policy is twofold: first, policy should provide the widest array of goods and services to the U.S. public; second, policy should assure that U.S. producers and their products are not discriminated against abroad. We know that the first best method of attaining this goal is to allow markets, and not governments, to set prices, but two problems exist. First, there exists an institutional bias toward intervention – Congress has an incentive to use its legislative authority to increase border measures of many sorts, in response to constituent pressure to deal with unemployment at home, and discrimination against U.S. firms abroad. And second, we are not interacting with nations who abide by laissez-faire strictures. This may be most evident in U.S.-China trade but other nations, as well, regularly support their domestic industries. Only in academic textbooks does the first best condition of market-driven trade exist. Policy must reflect not only what we know about market mechanisms, but also what policymakers can sell to the voting public.

This suggests two responses. First, policymakers must recognize that trade always leads to some individual losing his or her job. New jobs will be created but they will rarely be those that the unemployed can aspire to. As suggested, trade is good in the aggregate, but not good for everyone. Policy needs to address the interests of those hurt by trade, if not for normative reasons then because the losers are a potential political force. The losers from trade need to be either compensated and/or retrained. Retooling, expanded unemployment insurance, and relocation services are inexpensive ways to ensure continued support for open markets. The easiest and best assurance against future protectionism is an expanded set of options for the unemployed that Congress can use to aid constituents. In their absence, Congress will respond with the tools at their discretion and that is to close the U.S. market.

Second, to assure majority support for globalization, voters cannot think that other members of the trading community are treating the United States unfairly. As detailed previously, there is a long tradition in American law defending fair trade, and American support for open markets evaporates in the face of the perception of other nations cheating. Trade must look free and fair – the United States should punish trade partners who break the trading regime rules. Yet such retaliation, even in the face of a clear infringement of free trade norms, sits poorly with most elites. Many U.S. policymakers believe that even a *single* defection by the United States could undermine the trading regime. This is the ideological baggage we carry from Smoot-Hawley – it is the fear that any pro-protection legislation will lead to an unstoppable flow of higher barriers to trade. This fear is important because it is the glue that has kept the free trade coalition together. This fear, however, is outdated. The trading regime institutionalized retaliation as a method to reenforce open trade rules. Retaliation is sanctioned and expected; it is also limited in use to forestall that slippery slope.

As a result of a fear of a protectionist tidal wave, the United States rarely plays tit for tat, more often selecting the cooperative move in the canonical prisoner's dilemma (PD) game; comparatively, what China has done is "defect" on every move. The result, in that dyad, is that the United States has cheap goods but China has market power, which is used against U.S. producers both in the Chinese and U.S. markets. Logic suggests that periodic U.S. retaliation, or threat of retaliation, would be the correct policy response; tit for tat should encourage the Chinese to be more cooperative, even if they complain and take the case to the WTO. As a nonmarket economy, China will have a difficult time arguing that the United States is not within its right to protect its market against government subsidies and selling prices that are substantially below production costs.

Retaliation, of course, must be viewed as a second best strategy. In a globalized world, retaliation is difficult; it often hurts a domestic constituency as much as some producer in the target nation. When countries renege on trade agreements in today's interdependent market, renegotiation and arbitration are the more common responses. Although students are often taught that trade negotiations are akin to a PD game, that metaphor is applicable only to a small number of U.S. trade partners, of which China may be the most problematic. The game theoretic metaphor that is more fitting to current utilities and the vast majority of America's trading partners is a battle of the sexes. Here, both sides want to cooperate but they differ in the exact nature of that cooperation. Being off the equilibrium path is painful and no nation wants to be there. In this strategic environment, negotiations are better than threats, and retaliation is not useful.

General Conclusions

Consideration of the history and politics of trade policymaking suggests some general conclusions beyond commercial policy. As the editors of this volume explain in their Introduction, the growth of government since the 1930s has lead to a vast and changing array of policy interventions. Although the conventional wisdom may remain that the role of government is to "internalize negative externalities," the editors rightly point out that the scope of problems, or externalities, now considered within the range of legitimate interventions may have expanded beyond the capacity of governments. Trade policymaking is an exception to this observation. Trade works best when government does the least in terms of border controls and concentrates instead on ameliorating, not ignoring, the domestic dislocation that follows from this most efficient policy. Thus commercial policy is an important counterpoint to many of the cases in this volume. Instead of more government intervention over time, there has been less; instead of institutions increasingly pushing out market actors, the twentieth century saw a downsizing of the government's role in protecting particular U.S. producers. In part, the answer is functional. A great nation needs markets, and U.S. jobs and growth depended upon trade liberalization. But the politics leading to the "right" outcome still begs explanation.

As Jacobs and Page argued in 2005, three groups of actors, of different weights, have input into foreign policy.[37] As in this chapter, they consider groups, elite ideas, and voters. In their analysis, business groups appeared the most relevant. Labor had some affect, but less than business. This chapter confirms the importance of all three but suggests that institutional arrangements mediate these forces in somewhat counterintuitive ways. Even with a shared ideology and business support, trade policy could have been hijacked by those who do not share in the riches of the world economy. And today, increasing mobilization of labor unions, widespread job dislocations, and/or illegitimate behavior by our trading partners could lead congress to re-intervene. Although Warren rightly points out in Chapter 5 in this volume that the power of organized labor has receded, they still supply a counter ideology that connects trade and job losses that could serve to mobilize public opinion. Globalization is not good for everyone, and there is a possible majority that could make the connection between job loss and trade liberalization, even in an era of declining union power. The lack of job creation remains the central problem to be faced by those who endorse current U.S. commercial policy.

In conclusion then, two policy changes should be considered as a means to increase public support for continued U.S. participation in global markets. First, Congress needs to enact programs to counter jobs lost; second, the policy elite should *not* discourage congressional action that defends fair trade statutes that are consistent with the treaty obligations of America's trading partners. Fear of job loss undermines support for trade openness; similarly, predatory competition will provide fuel for politicians who incite xenophobia in the voting public. Trade policy is one of the few examples of consistently good policy emanating from Washington. It needs to be re-enforced, taking into account the changing nature of politics both at home and abroad.

Notes

1. Special thanks goes to Terry Moe and Robert Gulotty for many of the ideas in the chapter. As well, I received valuable comments from the authors of this volume, participants in the conference, and the volume reviewers.
2. Schatschneider, E. E., *Politics, Pressures and the Tariff*. New York: Prentice Hall, 1935.
3. Conconi, Paola, Giovanni Facchini, and Maurizio Zanardi, "Policymakers' Horizon and Trade Reforms," Development Working Papers 311, Centro Studi Luca d'Agliano, University of Milano, 2011.
4. The relationship between district size and trade politics has shown up consistently in numerous empirical studies. E.g., McGillivry, Fiona, *Privileging Industry: The Comparative Politics of Trade and Industrial Policy*. Princeton: Princeton University Press, 2004; Milner, Helen, "Democratic Politics and International Trade Negotiations: Elections and Divided Government as Constraints on Trade Liberalization," *Journal of Conflict Resolution* 41(1): 117–46, 1997; Verdier, Daniel, *Democracy and International Trade*. Princeton: Princeton University Press, 1994; Bailey, Michael, Judith Goldstein, and Barry Weingast, "The Institutional Roots of American Trade Policy: Politics, Coalitions, and International Trade," *World Politics* 49(3): 309–38, 1997.
5. Although agreeing that there is a difference among the branches of government on trade preferences, Karol suggests the cause may not be constituency size. Some alternative mechanisms suggested are term length, role of campaign finance, and chamber size. Chamber size and collective action issues are also an argument made in Goldstein and Gulotty, 2013. See: David Karol, "Does Constituency Size Affect Elected Officials' Trade Policy Preferences?" *Journal of Politics*, volume 69, issue 2, May 2007.
6. Ultimately defended in the courts a generation later.
7. On the congressional role in tariff setting, see, Goldstein, Judith and Robert Gulotty, "America and Trade Liberalization: The Limits of Institutional Reform," *International Organization*, Spring 2014.

8. The RTAA program was renewed in 1937, 1949, 1943, and 1945.
9. GATT participation was authorized in 1948, 1949, 1951, 1954, 1955, 1958, and 1962.
10. As well as both parties endorsing free trade, open markets were controlled in the House by the chair of the Ways and Means Committee, Wilbur Mills, who "would not let a Democrat on Ways and Means unless he was for the trade program, against cutting the oil depletion allowance and for Medicare." Given that the one example of this recruitment process not working perfectly on trade was that Aime Forand from Rhode Island was on the committee, "it was nearly perfect, as shown by the voting record of the Committee Democrats through the 1957–1967 period." Manley, John, *The Politics of Finance.* Boston: Little Brown, 1970, p. 26. By the time the 1962 Act was signed by Kennedy (10/11/62) he would declare that "this act is, therefore, an important new weapon to advance the cause of freedom."
11. Non–GATT-participating nations with whom the United States had a bilateral agreement benefited from these changes in the U.S. schedule, as well, as all the bilateral agreements included MFN provisions.
12. New treaty partners in the GATT who did not have agreements with the United States via the RTAA process were: Australia, Burma, Ceylon, Chile, India, Pakistan, Lebanon, New Zealand, Norway, Southern Rhodesia, Syria, and Union of South Africa.
13. The exception to this rule was in Australia, where a federal tariff board was able to respond to import surges by moving tariff concessions onto other products. No other major trading nation supported such centralized authority.
14. When congress entertained the original bill sponsored by the State Department that allowed the president to negotiate to open the U.S. market, the members of the Ways and Means Committee had balked at treaties, less because it gave the president a new authority (treaties were always in the president's domain) but because the treaties would be shared with others via MFN agreements. The committee worried about free riding on the part of nations who did not give reciprocal access. Hull's response was to explain the notion of a "chief supplier," and he promised a treaty would only be on a product with a nation that was the low-cost producer. Explaining that the world economy was tied into a "hard knot," the procedure was at best limited, "operating by singling out a leading commodity we buy from one country and ascertaining whether we can enter into, not hurtful relations in trade arrangements that would be a loss to us, but arrangements that would be equally profitable to us and other countries." See Hearings Before the Committee on Ways and Means, Reciprocal Trade Agreements Act, 73rd Congress, second session, no. 1, March 8, 1934 (15).
15. One of the most underappreciated reasons for the stability of the RTAA treaty process was that almost a majority of the most highly protected products in the 1930 act had Germany as its principal supplier. By the time the United States began negotiations under the new act, U.S.-German relations precluded a treaty to open up the market in those products. As a result, protections remained on the most highly organized product groups. Although unintentional, not having to face these groups allowed early liberalization to succeed and gain more generalized political support.
16. The rule, which meant that the smaller nations rarely got the products they exported onto the negotiations agenda, led to developing world complaints in ensuing years.

Even with preferential tariffs, many developing nation products were not granted access via this process.

17. Numerous scholars have offered explanations for delegation in 1934. For a complete analysis and some empirical tests, see, Goldstein and Gulotty, 2012.

18. Irwin, Douglas, *Free Trade Under Fire*. Princeton: Princeton University Press, 2002, p. 171.

19. The law made its first appearance in Section 5 of the Federal Trade Commission Act of 1914 and was reformed after a 1919 report by the U.S. Tariff Commission that suggested the need for more protections.

20. Along with section 301 cases, these three laws are the most often used by U.S. producers hurt by trade competition.

21. There are seventeen in-force FTAs: Australia, Bahrain, Canada, Chile, Costa Rica, Dominican Republic, El Salvador, Guatemala, Honduras, Israel, Jordan, Mexico, Morocco, Nicaragua, Oman, Peru, and Singapore. As with WTO agreements, these open trade in many but not all industry categories. Often they extend policy constraints and opportunities to investment-access issues areas, as well.

22. Bailey, Goldstein, and Weingast, 1997.

23. Section 301 is used by the USTR to retaliate against practices felt to undermine U.S. exporters' access to foreign markets. The legislation gained majority support as a way to provide ailing U.S. businesses with aid that was otherwise unavailable because of the injury requirements in earlier unfair trade laws. The law first appeared in 1974, and again in 1988 as Super 301 legislation. Super 301 was meant to spur USTR to identify and prosecute unfair trade activities, an attempt by Congress to force the president to be more aggressive. Its use has been challenged in the WTO on the grounds that it is a unilateral action in violation of the multilateral provisions in the WTO.

24. Until 1974, the U.S. Treasury Department evaluated whether or not products were being dumped onto the U.S. market. Because Congress felt that Treasury's interest had deviated from their own, they moved jurisdiction to Commerce. In both cases, the ITC, a congressional agent, ruled on whether or not injury had occurred as a result of a product being dumped into the U.S. market.

25. Voluntary Export Agreements on cars, textiles, and steel, among others, were agreements by the exporter to restrain their own exports into the U.S. market. The effect was akin to a tariff; that is, it raised the domestic price, but the exporter not the United States reaped the "rent."

26. One of the clearest cases of this involved President Bush and steel tariffs. As a free trader, his hand was forced during the 2004 campaign to grant aid. When the WTO ruled against the United States, the United States quickly concurred.

27. Pastor, Robert, *Congress and the Politics of US Foreign Economic Policy, 1929–1976*. Berkeley: University of California Press, 1980.

28. Cited in Goldstein, Judith and Lisa Martin, "Legalization, Trade Liberalization and Domestic Politics: A Cautionary Note," *International Organization* 54 (3): 603–32, 2000.

29. There are exceptions, the best know of which is Dani Rodrick, who has criticized aspects of the trading regime agenda as problematic for developing nations. Rodrick, Dani, *One Economics Many Recipes*. Princeton: Princeton University Press, 2007.

30. Grossman, Gene and Elhanan Helpman, "Protection for Sale," *American Economic Review* 84 (4): 833–50, 1994.

31. Letter dated August 31, 2011, on the letterhead of Jagdish Bhagwati of Columbia University.

32. Ronald Rogowski uses the Stolper-Samuelson theorem, based on the Heckscher-Ohlin trade theory to derive predictions of trade policy preference in *Commerce and Coalitions: How Trade Affects Domestic Political Alignments*. Princeton: Princeton University Press, 1989.

33. Burgoon and Hiscox, "The Mysterious Case of Female Protectionism." Working Paper, Harvard University, 2003.

34. Scheve, K. F. and M. J. Slaughter, "What Determines Individual Trade-Policy Preferences?" *Journal of International Economics* 54 (2):267–292, 2001; Scheve, K. F. and M. J. Slaughter, "Economic Insecurity and the Globalization of Production," *American Journal of Political Science* 48 (4):662–674, 2004; Mayda, A. M. and D. Rodrik, "Why Are Some People (and Countries) More Protectionist than Others?" *European Economic Review* 49 (6): 1393–1430, 2005.

35. Goldstein, Judith, Yotam Margalit, and Doug Rivers, "Household Attitudes on Trade: How Do Families Reconcile Competing Interests in the World Economy?" MS. Stanford University, 2010.

36. Goldstein, et al., 2010.

37. Jacobs, Lawrence R. and Benjamin I. Page, "Who Influences U.S. Foreign Policy?" *American Political Science Review* 99: 107–124, February 2005.

10

The Politics of Intelligence Reform

Richard H. Immerman

The Intelligence Reform and Terrorism Prevention Act (IRTPA) is "the most dramatic reform of our nation's intelligence capabilities since President Harry S. Truman signed the National Security Act of 1947," remarked President George W. Bush when signing the legislation on December 17, 2004.[1] He was right. Although the effectiveness of IRTPA remains to be determined, the legislation's intent was ambitious and far-reaching.

Bush left unmentioned that most of IRTPA's initiatives had been proposed previously – and repeatedly. Intelligence reform has been a recurrent theme on Capitol Hill since the establishment of the Central Intelligence Agency (CIA) at the outset of the Cold War. Over the subsequent sixty-five years, approximately twenty commissions, committees, and panels recommended improvements to the structure, mission, and operations of the CIA and other components of the intelligence community (IC). Prescriptions to strengthen community management in order to enhance coordination and integration among the disparate elements, a linchpin of IRPTA, which a historian in the Office of the Director of National Intelligence described as the "unfinished business of 1947," were common and frequent.[2] So, too, were proposals to promote information sharing and eliminate stovepipes, fortify congressional oversight, redistribute the budget and make it more transparent, improve the relationship between intelligence producers and consumers at all levels and between the foreign and law enforcement communities, and address other fundamental problems. These proposals received serious attention and often the support of experts and veteran officials. In almost all cases until 2004, nevertheless, those with the capacity to enact or institute major reforms either rejected the recommendations or gravely diluted them. Even the impact of IRTPA, contemporary evidence suggests, will be less transformative than its proponents intended, and many close observers of and commentators on America's national security architecture argue is necessary.

The dysfunctions that have plagued the IC and been identified by reformers decade after decade can be attributed to the politics of intelligence. And the failure, either through legislation or executive order, to impose remedies, or for that matter implement substantive measures that directly address the pathologies, can be attributed to the politics of intelligence reform. A peacetime, civilian government agency dedicated to secrecy, spying, stealing, and other unsavory conduct has never fit comfortably next to Americans' devotion to democracy, civil liberties, transparency, and concomitant ideals and values. Creating one, therefore, required the right conditions – first a crisis, then a threat of an even greater crisis – to mobilize policymakers and their constituents. This formula explains the bargaining and compromises that produced a misshapen structure and an ambiguous mission.

Within this inhospitable political climate, moreover, reforms aimed at improving the effectiveness of an arm of the national security state which the public intrinsically mistrusts, and which much of the time operates hidden from its view, are a hard sell to presidents, the chairs of powerful congressional committees, and party leaders – those capable of generating change. Both the executive and legislative branches require incentives, normatively the shock of an external threat but, as we will see, on occasion a severe domestic crisis, to accept the political risks and take on the bureaucratic challenges inherent in proposing to reform an unpopular institution and acting to in unison to the degree necessary. Decreasing the likelihood of instituting effective reform, partisanship and vested individual and organizational interests must be mitigated if not overcome. These conditions are similar to those identified in the contribution to this volume by Jennifer Merolla and Paul Pulido on reforming Homeland Security and Terrorism policy. Yet because officials and voters within and beyond the Beltway commonly perceive the threats and crises with the potential to drive intelligence reform as foreign and indirect, the conditions are more rarely met.[3] As a consequence, the IC muddled, and still muddles, through, with many of the same flaws and deficiencies. By exploring reform efforts from the CIA's origin to the present, this chapter tells the story of that predicable failure to manage intelligence reform.

OVERCOMING THE NATIONAL AVERSION TO THE INTELLIGENCE ENTERPRISE

The very notion of intelligence – a codeword to most Americans for espionage and covert operations, not to mention cloaks, daggers, and rogue elephants – is laden with intense emotion in the United States. For that reason, politics has incessantly pervaded the intelligence enterprise, and the creation of the CIA itself could only come about through revolutionary reform of not only the national security bureaucracy but also the thinking about national security. Despite deep roots in U.S. history, extending to Nathan Hale and the Culper Ring during America's revolution through the origins of the Office of Naval Intelligence (ONI) and Division of Military Intelligence (later G-2) during America's "rise to globalism" in the late nineteenth century to contemporary controversies over enhanced interrogation techniques and targeted assassinations, intelligence connotes un-American behavior and values. "Gentlemen do not read each other's mail," allegedly uttered Secretary of State Henry Stimson in 1929 as he shut down Herbert Yardley's codebreaking unit, the ominously named Black Chamber. Polling data consistently reveal that the American public respects and trusts intelligence agencies less than other institutions related to national security. And accompanying this negative image is often a modest estimate of intelligence's value and the judgment that the agencies are more times than not deficient in their performance. In sum, from America's founding, intelligence as a concept and institution has received insufficient or at best intermittent support from essential domestic constituencies.[4]

This political culture provided the framework for the CIA's establishment as part of the National Security Act of 1947. It took the exigencies of World War II, specifically Japan's surprise attack on Pearl Harbor and the threat to the survival of the United States and its allies posed by Nazi Germany, for Franklin D. Roosevelt (FDR) to set up the Office of Strategic Services (OSS) under William Donovan. Even then the decision was difficult. Roosevelt quietly asked Donovan to consult with the British and present him with a draft plan to create an intelligence service. After that the president relied on his powers as commander in chief to establish the OSS in June 1942.[5] The decision of FDR's successor, Harry S. Truman, to support making the OSS or another stand-alone variation of it permanent was more difficult. Washington is a political town in which virtually any initiative confronts entrenched interests opposed to it. During wartime, the Army's G-2, the ONI, the Federal Bureau of Investigation (FBI), and the Department of State protested what each considered Donovan's encroachments on their turf. Political leaders and operatives with eyes on the White House, moreover, and not just Republicans, worried that Donovan had ambitions similar to theirs.[6]

This collision of interests and ambitions intensified at the end of the war when Donovan proposed to institutionalize an autonomous and centralized intelligence organization with its own budget and a director who reported directly to the president.[7] His best chance lay with FDR, who, albeit with reservations, appeared sympathetic. If Roosevelt placed the power of the presidency and his personal popularity behind establishing a permanent central intelligence agency, he very well could override political and bureaucratic opposition. But FDR's death unleashed multiple pockets of resistance. In the words of one astute commentator, "Politics made for strange bedfellows" in this context. "Between November 1944 and September 1945, the departments of State, War, the Navy, and Justice joined forces against the Donovan plan." As an "accidental president" who would have to manage America's postwar readjustment by filling the shoes of the four-times elected FDR, Truman faced enough domestic challenges without taking on this united front. On September 20, 1945, he ordered the abolition of the OSS, to take effect in less than two weeks. Truman divided the responsibilities for intelligence collection and counterintelligence on the one hand and evaluation on the other between the Departments of War and State, respectively.[8]

Still, the intelligence failure of December 7, 1941, all but assured further reform. The 1955 Hoover Commission only slightly exaggerated when it wrote, "The CIA may well attribute its existence to the surprise attack on Pearl Harbor." The line between 1941 and 1947 nevertheless could not have been more circuitous. Truman, along with Secretary of State James Byrnes and James Forrestal, the powerful secretary of the navy, appreciated the value of a coordinating mechanism, but for different reasons they wanted it to be weak. Byrnes and Forrestal jealously guarded the prerogatives and responsibilities of their departments. Truman fretted over the possibility that a peacetime nest of civilian spies would turn into an American "Gestapo," incapable of respecting the boundary between a liberal democracy and police state. He also recognized that Republicans in Congress, no longer confronted with FDR in the White House, would resume their attack on the New Deal by railing against adding to the already overextended government bureaucracy.[9]

After heated debate and bargaining, described by one participant as "tougher than I'd seen before; as tough as anything I saw afterwards," in January 1946 Truman, by presidential directive, established a National Intelligence Authority (NIA). Comprising the NIA were representatives of the secretaries of war, navy, and state as well as the president. The directive charged it with supervising a Central Intelligence Group (CIG). This CIG would take responsibility for performing the functions necessary to provide the White House and managers of the nation's security with "authoritative information on conditions and developments in the outside world." Yet those departments that formed the backbone of the national security state would "continue to collect, evaluate, correlate, and disseminate departmental intelligence."[10]

The intent of the 1947 National Security Act was to reform this crazy-quilt apparatus, which itself was the product of an effort, as one CIA historian has written, to "reform the intelligence establishment that had grown so rapidly and haphazardly during the national emergency [World War II]."[11] Initially under the direction of Rear Admiral Sidney Souers (called the Director of Central Intelligence, DCI), the CIG limped along, beset by bureaucratic politics and unsure of its mission, below the public's radar, and regularly ignored by the president and Congress. But after only a half-year as DCI, Lt. General Hoyt Vandenberg succeeded Souers. Vandenberg had no intention of deferring to department heads and serving merely as a custodian for the NIA. He had grander plans – for himself (he saw this position as a stepping stone to commanding an independent Air Force) and the CIG. And in his corner was his uncle, Senator Arthur Vandenberg, the ranking Republican on the Senate Foreign Relations Committee and pivotal to whatever bipartisan support Truman could engender on Capitol Hill. This support became that much more vital when in November 1946 the Republicans gained control of Congress. Truman's selection of

Vandenberg represented a watershed in the reform process, underscoring that individuals do matter. In the words of the history of the CIA prepared for use by Frank Church's Senate Select Committee to Study Government Operations with Respect to Intelligence Activities in 1975, "The appointment of Lieutenant General Hoyt Vandenberg as DCI on June 10, 1946 marked the beginning of CIG's gradual development as an independent intelligence producer."[12]

Vandenberg's opening salvo was to garner an independent budget. He insisted that each department represented on the NIA earmark appropriations for the CIG and empower him, as DCI, to disperse them. This allowed him to purchase materiel and hire personnel. The department secretaries objected; Truman backed Vandenberg. From that meager beginning Vandenberg incrementally accrued greater authority for the CIG, chipping away at the responsibilities of the State, War, and Navy Departments, and the FBI. His goal was real reform: the centralization of U.S. intelligence and institutionalization of its role in the formulation of national security policy.[13]

Vandenberg's breakthrough came in early 1947. Months earlier he had established within the CIG the Office of Reports and Estimates (ORE) for the purpose of providing the fulcrum of the national security machinery, the president, with what he defined as strategic intelligence. By this time, the intensification of the Cold War, meaning the deterioration of U.S. relations with the Soviet Union, concomitant perception of an increased Soviet threat, and collapse of whatever remained of FDR's hope for a cooperative global order, underscored the administration's vital need for strategic intelligence even as it eroded opposition to the centralization of its production. In February 1947 George Kennan published his "X" article in *Foreign Affairs*. That same month Vandenberg received the NIA's endorsement of the CIG's responsibility for "all-source" strategic intelligence. It charged ORE with producing

composite intelligence, *interdepartmental in character*, which is required by the President and other high officers and staffs to assist them in determining policies with respect to national planning and security in peace and war and for the advancement of broad national policy. It is in that political-economic-military area of concern to more than one agency, must be objective, and *must transcend the exclusive competence of any one department* [sic].[14]

This reification of a central intelligence agency's contribution to national security exacerbated the politics of intelligence reform. Although the opposition of the State, Navy, and War Departments (and the FBI) to the CIG's aggrandizement eroded, it did not dissipate completely. They continued to defend their respective turfs even as the salience of two other political dynamics intensified, both of which curbed centralizing intelligence in the first place. The first was a function of the first customer himself, the president, for whom the growing CIG was designed to serve most of all. As alluded to briefly, Truman was among those Americans with an inherent distaste for and distrust of intelligence. Having had paltry previous experience as a customer, like many in the United States he viewed intelligence operations as incompatible with democratic practices. "You must always be careful to keep [national defense] under the control of officers who are elected by the people," he commented at an off-the-record press conference. As president it was his responsibility to "guard against a Gestapo."[15]

With images of Nazi goose-stepping still fresh, this Gestapo metaphor was ubiquitous in and out of Washington. The metaphor by itself deterred empowering the intelligence enterprise by bringing the disparate elements under centralized management. But a second dynamic exacerbated its effect. The Gestapo metaphor became a political weapon. With the formidable FDR replaced by the untested and politically vulnerable Truman, conservatives took dead aim at the FDR legacy. They sought to cast proposals to set up a bigger and better intelligence bureaucracy as a gambit to create one last New Deal agency. FDR's critics maintained that a central intelligence agency would be bloated and unwieldy. It would also, as attested to by the demographics of the OSS, be elitist and liberal, which to their way of thinking added up to totalitarian.[16]

The fearmongering that linked a permanent organization that centralized intelligence to institutions such as the Gestapo and concepts such as totalitarianism circulated throughout the two-year interval between the defeat of Germany and the proposed legislation to establish the CIA. The most avid proponent was Walter Trohan. Trohan wrote for the *Chicago Tribune*, the mouthpiece for its proprietor, the venomous anti-New Dealer and dyed-in-the wool isolationist, Colonel Robert McCormick. Trohan learned of Donovan's proposal to make the OSS permanent at the time of the Yalta Conference. Interpreting it as evidence of a conspiracy to turn the United States into a totalitarian state, beginning on February 9, 1945, he published his finding in the *Tribune* and other newspapers published by McCormick or his like-minded cousin, Eleanor "Cissy" Patterson. The headlines were like hammers, ranging from "New Deal Plans Super Spy System" to "New Dean Plans to Spy on World and Home Folks; Super Gestapo Agency is Under Consideration." Trohan claimed that FDR sought to create an "all powerful intelligence service" that would not only "spy on the postwar world" but also "pry into the lives of citizens at home." For two years Trohan, egged on by McCormick and supported by antiliberals such as the State Department's Sprouille Braden and FBI Director J. Edgar Hoover, who not uncoincidentally were jealous of their own fiefdoms, waged his war (it remains undocumented who leaked information to Trohan). As late as June 1947, when the National Security Act was before Congress, he wrote, "Agents of the CIG have begun operations on the pattern of the Soviet secret police, the MVD, or Nazi gestapo agents."[17]

The McCormick clan's political motivations and ideological dispositions were mutually reinforcing. Then there were those in Congress who like Truman sympathized with the New Deal but feared a central intelligence agency's potential to subvert Americans' civil rights and liberties. For others, primarily Republicans, the reverse was true. They could tolerate almost anything in the interest of national security but considered another bloated bureaucracy intolerable.

THE CENTRAL INTELLIGENCE AGENCY AND MISSION CREEP

Thus, there was resistance to establishing a powerful central intelligence agency in both the executive and legislative branches of government that cut across party lines and influenced public opinion. Yet with the World War II Grand Alliance declared officially dead and the Soviet threat to peace, prosperity, and liberty articulated in the gravest terms in the president's "Truman Doctrine" address to a joint session of Congress in March 1947, these forces were insufficiently powerful or united to halt the momentum for reform. Unwilling to go on record as opposed to an initiative framed as vital to the nation's security, the White House, bureaucracy, and legislature muted their reservations and defined institutional reform (sanctioning a central intelligence agency) as a requisite for policy reform (more effective containment of communism). But even then, they buried establishing the CIA in a single brief section of the comprehensive 1947 National Security Act that devoted much more attention to creating a National Security Council (NSC) and National Military Establishment headed by a Secretary of Defense and comprised of a merged Department of War, Navy, and new Department of the Air Force.[18]

Further, given the paucity of grassroots support for a civilian intelligence agency, the president's anxiety about the consequences of setting one up, the departments' reluctant acquiescence, and the continued opposition of many in Congress, the reform was predictably restrained. The director of central intelligence could exercise only marginal influence over intelligence activities that remained the purview of the military services and other departments. This was partially because of limited personnel and authorities, partially because the CIA was placed under the supervision of the NSC but was not a member of it, and partially, indeed primarily, because of budgetary allocations. Power and influence follow the money, and the military had most of it – even before the advent of extremely expensive technologies. Truman had no qualms about leaving the military services with the bulk of the intelligence budget in return for their support for creating the National Military Establishment. The legislation did grant the new agency a robust analytic function, a legacy of Vandenberg's tenure. But even in this sphere, its precise responsibilities were stipulated only in the most general terms, and thus its capability to manage analysis across the community was circumscribed. The CIA's initial organization provided the impetus for the decades of reform efforts that would ensue: rather than centralizing the IC, it institutionalized a confederation.[19]

The one section in the National Security Act devoted to establishing the CIA, which Truman signed into law on July 26, 1947, did not even explicitly endow the agency with the capability to collect intelligence. It did, however, include an elastic clause which provided the space for the agency's development over the subsequent decades into the "company" so familiar today. The agency, read the legislation, should perform "such additional services of common concern as the National Security Council determines can be more efficiently accomplished centrally." This phrase "additional services of common concern" opened the door to more intense bureaucratic wrangling. Nevertheless, in light of such indicators of an increased threat as the communist coup in Czechoslovakia and Berlin blockade in 1948, the "fall" of China and successful Soviet test of an atomic device in 1949, and the outbreak of the Korean War in 1950, the predictable outcome of the elastic clause was a steady accretion of the CIA's responsibilities.[20]

Truman's close advisor Clark Clifford claims in his memoir that both Congress and the president understood that the elastic (what Clifford calls the "catchall") clause granted the CIA license not only to spy and otherwise clandestinely collect intelligence, but also to plan and execute covert and paramilitary actions.[21] Extant evidence does not support Clifford's claim, which he made some thirty-five years after the fact and which runs counter to the dynamics of the intelligence reform effort. Legendary CIA general counsel Lawrence Houston emphatically rejects it: There was not "any thought in the minds of Congress that the Central Intelligence Agency under this authority would take positive action for subversion and sabotage," he wrote at the time for the record.[22] But the trajectory of the Cold War crisis may well have influenced the authors and ratifiers of the legislation to leave that possibility open for the future. The fact of the matter is that by the end of the 1950s, the CIA's responsibilities did envelope the conduct of political warfare and covert operations for the purpose of affecting political change in the international environment as well as collecting secret information on that international environment. With the exception of the 1949 Central Intelligence Agency Act, which allowed the CIA to operate under a greater cloak of secrecy by exempting it from the need to disclose publicly its activities, budget, and personnel, Congress was precluded from the process by which the agency acquired the additional authority to employ "all means ... short of war." The CIA augmented its mission through presidentially sanctioned NSC directives and to a remarkable extent by default.[23]

Initially, management of the range of covert operations (propaganda and psychological warfare, sabotage, support for resistance movements, and more) was uncomfortably shared between the CIA and State Department through the anodyne-named Office of Policy Coordination (OPC). Dual management was tantamount to almost no management, allowing OPC Director Frank Wisner to exploit the shocks to American security between 1948 and 1950 to rapidly expand its size and scope. Its personnel and budget ballooned, and as the authors of an internal CIA history argue, the "OPC achieved an institutional independence that was unimaginable at the time of its inception." Appointed DCI in 1950, Walter Bedell Smith deemed Wisner's independence intolerable, was "dumbfounded" by the OPC's accretion of power and responsibility, and judged its expansion detrimental to the CIA's core mission of analysis and collection. Demonstrating again the ad hoc character of intelligence reform, he virtually by fiat made the OPC exclusively the CIA's and folded it into a newly established Directorate of Plans (DP). As a result, in the antiseptic words of the Church Committee a quarter-century later, the CIA evolved "into a far different organization from that envisioned in 1947."[24]

At odds with the initial aims of intelligence reform, this evolution was a function of the nexus between personalities and politics. Key players such as Wisner and Smith were strong individuals eager to take ownership of their institutions. So, too, was Allen Dulles. Smith had appointed Dulles the CIA's first deputy director for plans. When Dulles became Dwight D. Eisenhower's DCI in 1953, he was determined to continue the agency's tremendous growth spurt, particularly within the DP. He received the support of Eisenhower, and equally importantly, John Foster Dulles, his brother and the secretary of state. This was the apex of the Cold War, when the Soviets gained a thermonuclear and intercontinental ballistic missile capability, Joseph McCarthy charged the State Department with harboring communists, and Americans practiced duck-and-cover exercises. The public wanted only to know, or to think, that the CIA was helping make them safe; they did not care how. The same held true for Congress. This was the era of "Congressional undersight," when except for a select few senators and representatives that chaired or served on understaffed subcommittees of the Armed Services and Appropriations Committees of each House, members of both chambers avoided asking questions lest they be held accountable for the answers.[25]

Under the leadership of Allen Dulles and the concurrence of elite policy-makers, therefore, the distortion of the post–World War II intelligence reform accelerated. Early successes against feeble opponents, such as in Iran and Guatemala, provided impetus for more covert operations, even as they produced within the agency, administration, and Congress (at least those with a "need to know") an inflated estimate of the CIA's capabilities. Identified primarily with Montana's Senator Mike Mansfield, proposals for reform, or perhaps more accurately to resurrect the principles and goals of the initial reform effort, surfaced periodically, largely in the form of increased congressional oversight. But politics continually intervened to thwart action. Early on, the Eisenhower White House vigorously opposed congressional "interference" in intelligence operations lest it provide an opportunity for McCarthy-like investigations. This rationale for opposing congressional oversight outlived McCarthy. The longer he held office, the more convinced Eisenhower became that politics did not stop at the water's edge. His successors were never under the illusion that they did. In truth, executive opposition to congressional oversight was hardly necessary. Americans trusted Eisenhower, America's last true hero, to keep them safe. What is more, the Cold War crisis in global politics was the cornerstone for the imperial presidency. Legislators increasingly deferred to the executive, especially when confronted with Cold War initiatives. There were few votes to be won in home states by opposing presidential policies and programs designed to promote national security, and the CIA was an executive agency. There was insufficient incentive to take on intelligence reform, even after the Soviet shoot down of a U-2 spy plane scuttled the 1960 Paris summit and covert effort to overthrow Cuba's Fidel Castro in 1961 imploded on the beaches of the Bay of Pigs.[26]

VIETNAM, THE FAMILY JEWELS, AND THE CHURCH COMMITTEE HEARINGS

This condition – and environment – was dramatically transformed in the late 1960s and early 1970s. The escalation of the Vietnam War and the protests against it, coupled with the muckraking journalism typified by the revelation by the *New York Times* and *Ramparts* magazine in 1967 that the CIA secretly funded the National Student Associate and other nongovernmental organizations, brought unwanted attention to the agency. The result was the generation of a different kind of crisis even as the Cold War consensus centered on the threat of communism unraveled. And as the CIA's veil of secrecy and protective shield disintegrated, public and congressional support diminished. Its association with the presidency became part of its problem, not solution. Defining the CIA through the lens of its covert projects in Vietnam, epitomized by Operation Phoenix, opponents of the war tied it to the worst exemplars of America's immoral conduct. Advocates of the war criticized the agency for insufficient enthusiasm for the effort and inadequate reporting and estimating. The "war dealt a double whammy to the CIA," writes Anne Kahn. The effect was to make it more vulnerable to Richard Nixon's hostility. Nixon never liked or trusted the CIA. But it was his disrespect for the U.S. Constitution more than for the CIA that turned 1975 into the "Year of Intelligence," or as it was known within the agency, the "Year of the Firestorm," and instigated the most concerted effort toward reform since 1947.[27]

What drove the months of hearings, hundreds of interviews, and scrutiny of thousands of pages of documents that produced reports from both houses recommending a litany of reforms were not the CIA's inefficiency and very mixed record of addressing an external threat – the normative drivers of intelligence reform. The impetus in 1974 reflected internal, domestic dynamics: the revelations of CIA abuses and the polarized politics that were so intertwined with those abuses. Further, taking the lead were Congress, the press, and the public, not the president and his elite team of advisors. It therefore was both appropriate and ironic that long before he was consumed by the Watergate scandal, Nixon, convinced that the CIA was a "refuge for Ivy League intellectuals" that had contributed more to Kennedy's victory in the 1960 election than to America's national security, sought to institute a series of reforms to change its organization and way of doing business. "Intelligence reform won't save a lot of money but will do a helluva lot for my morale," he explained to his lieutenant, H. R. "Bob" Halderman. Nixon was only partially correct.[28]

The reforms that Nixon sought were symptomatic of the poisonous politics that would precipitate congressional calls for reform and frustrate real reformers. The president's motives were mixed – and as personal as they were political. The common denominator was his judgment that the IC suffered from inherent flaws. For one thing, it focused on the wrong enemy. Confident in his skill at geopolitical gamesmanship, Nixon identified the greatest threats to the United States as emanating from foreign agents that were posing as domestic radicals and infiltrating antiwar, civil rights, and parallel organizations. Moreover, the president considered the CIA's process for evaluating strategic threats, which was located primarily in its Office of National Estimates, as cost ineffective, poorly managed, and insufficiently committed to serving the White House (or put another way, insufficiently politicized).

As a consequence of the political environment of the 1970s, Nixon lost control of the reform agenda. Within a year of his taking office, gun-toting African Americans occupied the student union at Cornell University and a half-million demonstrators marched on Washington to protest the Vietnam War. Nixon attributed such outrages to subversive foreign influences, but the FBI could not provide corroborating intelligence. The president assigned Tom Charles Huston, his internal security aide, to develop a better mechanism. The CIA, National Security Agency (NSA), and Defense Intelligence Agency (DIA) all signed onto Huston's plan, which authorized the IC to intensify domestic surveillance by opening mail, electronically eavesdropping on phone conversations, entering homes and business illegally, and more. Virtually at the same time Nixon instructed James Schlesinger, then the assistant director of the Office of Management and Budget, to evaluate the entire IC.[29]

Nixon's approval of the Huston Plan and its endorsement by the CIA, NSA, and DIA meant nothing to J. Edgar Hoover. One of the most serious dysfunctions of the IC that the reform effort has never satisfactory addressed is that it is a confederation. For decades the FBI was Hoover's fiefdom, and at the age of seventy-five he had his legacy to consider. Accordingly, he deemed any proposed reform of domestic intelligence that did not originate with him an end-run. That was intolerable. That the reform was illegal made it more intolerable. Hoover had been engaged in these kinds of activities since the 1950s. Huston's proposal, which would involve multiple and uncoordinated new actors, increased the risk of exposing past transgressions even as it implicated the FBI in fresh ones. Hoover's reputation, carefully constructed over almost a half-century, could be shattered. Recognizing he could not overcome what was essentially Hoover's veto, Nixon aborted the Huston Plan. He went ahead with his plans to overhaul the IC, however. Among the faults Schlesinger found were that the DCI's "theoretical control of the community was an impolite fiction ... the total cost of intelligence ... was at least twice the figure formally submitted to Congress; that intelligence estimates too often hid differing judgments in bland compromise ... and that technical intelligence far surpassed political intelligence in quality." The "main hope" for remedying these and multiple other serious deficiencies, read the introduction, "lies in a fundamental reform of the IC's decisionmaking bodies and procedures."[30]

Using the report as his club, at the end of 1971 Nixon proposed a radical reorganization, the centerpiece of which vested the DCI with vast new authority to manage the community. But Helms did not like to manage, and Nixon did not like Helms. Within weeks of his reelection, he replaced him with none other than Schlesinger. Schlesinger had virtually no support within the IC, and he did little to generate it. Nevertheless, he sought immediately to institute a "program of draconian reform." The key components were downsizing CIA personnel drastically, renaming the DP the Directorate of Operations, and strengthening the DCI's community management responsibilities and supervision of the Office of National Estimates. But Nixon gave Schlesinger little time to implement the reforms. In spring 1973 he appointed him secretary of defense and promoted his deputy, William Colby, to DCI.[31]

Nixon, Schlesinger, nor Colby imagined the blowback their reform effort would trigger. A few months prior to Schlesinger's appointment as DCI, a five-member team in the pay of the Committee to Re-Elect the President broke into the headquarters of the Democratic National Committee at the Watergate Complex in Washington in an effort to intercept their communications. Any CIA connection to this "third rate burglary" seemed extremely far-fetched. And there was none – at first. Part of the reason Nixon fired Helms from the directorship of the CIA was his refusal to interpose the CIA between the White House and the FBI investigation of the break-in. About that Schlesinger was unaware. But he was aware that the burglars included CIA veterans. That prompted the new DCI to instruct his deputy, Colby, to survey agency personnel to compile a record of past behavior that was not authorized by its charter. The resultant product came to be called the "Family Jewels."[32]

Schlesinger and Colby intended to keep the report secret from Congress and the public. But the early 1970s was an extraordinary time in U.S. politics. Despite Nixon's landslide reelection and the signing of the Paris Treaty ending the Vietnam War in January 1973, American society remained profoundly polarized. Large swaths of the population spanning the political spectrum harbored a deep distrust if not hostile attitude toward the government. This dynamic encouraged revisionist scholarship, muckraking journalism, and a slew of authors, filmmakers, and artists who challenged societal norms. Within this charged atmosphere, the CIA was a particularly exposed target. This was in no small measure due to its uneasy relationship with American democracy that a quarter-century of Cold War rhetoric had not dissipated. Thus, since its inception the CIA had served as a convenient scapegoat when things went wrong. Its politicization during the Vietnam War added some justification to this scapegoating. Exacerbating its vulnerability was the fracturing of the Cold War consensus and instability produced by the rapid succession of DCIs from

Helms to Schlesinger to Colby (and soon George H. W. Bush). But perhaps the most salient catalyst for efforts toward intelligence reform was the CIA's association with the "imperial presidency." Even though Congress was primarily responsible for its failure to oversee the IC, it identified this neglect as symptomatic of an unconstitutional erosion of its prerogatives. Much of the public agreed.[33]

This perfect storm of domestic phenomena, aggravated by the international environment but now largely dissociated from it, produced the Year of Intelligence. In December 1974, in the wake of the Watergate hearings, the indictment of multiple White House officials, and the resignation of Richard Nixon, Seymour Hersh, whose exposé of the My Lai Massacre won a Pulitzer prize, published a *New York Times* article under the four-column headline, "Huge C.I.A. Operation Reported in U.S. against Antiwar Forces, Other Dissidents in Nixon Years." Drawing on information from the Family Jewels report, he revealed the stillborn Huston Plan. He also disclosed Operation MHCHAOS, a program begun by Lyndon Johnson, expanded by Nixon, and run by the long-time and many suspected paranoid head of the agency's counterintelligence unit, James Jesus Angleton. Hersh described MHCHAOS as a "massive, illegal, domestic intelligence operation" that violated the CIA charter by targeting the "antiwar movement and other dissident groups." He claimed that he likewise had evidence of illegal CIA surveillance of suspected foreign intelligence agents in the United Stated that dated to the 1950s. Writing that a "possible Watergate link is but one of many questions posed by disclosures about the CIA," Hersh concluded that only a congressional hearing could "unravel" the web of deceit.[34]

The political climate in which Hersh was reporting all but assured he would be preaching to the choir. His article a few months earlier on the CIA's efforts to subvert the government of the by-then-overthrown government of Chile's Salvadore Allende had already generated legislation to increase congressional oversight. Enacted less than two weeks after Hersh's Family Jewels piece, the [Harold] Hughes-[Leo] Ryan Act, an amendment to the Foreign Assistance Act of 1961, required the president to report all covert operations to one if not more congressional committees and prohibited the expenditure of CIA funds unless authorized by a presidential "finding." It was, Loch Johnson observes, "the first measure since the creation of the CIA in 1947 to place formal controls on the Agency." But it turned out to be just a step on the road to more substantive proposals for reform.[35]

Hersh had let the cat out of the bag. In an effort to co-opt congressional initiatives even as he allowed America "time to heal" following the Watergate revelations, President Gerald Ford established a blue-ribbon commission under Vice President Nelson Rockefeller to investigate Hersh's allegations. Congress was not satisfied. Elected only months after Nixon's resignation, the "Fighting 94th" was overwhelmingly Democratic. This Congress also counted among its ranks ten freshman senators and seventy-five freshman representatives committed to fixing what was manifestly broken. In January 1975 the Senate mandated the establishment of a Select Committee to Study Governmental Operations with Respect to Intelligence Operations, chaired by the Democrats' senator from Idaho, Frank Church. The next month the House followed suit. The House Select Committee on Intelligence was initially chaired by Lucien Nedzi (D-MI), but five months later it was reconstituted and New York Democrat Otis Pike replaced Nedzi.[36]

By spring the Church Committee had started to call witnesses – a who's who of CIA and government officials – and its staff had begun to pour through volumes of classified materials. Its charge, as interpreted by its chairman, was to focus on the abuses of the Nixon administration highlighted by Hersh. That was fine with Church. An admirer of his forerunner as Idaho's senator, the progressive isolationist William Borah, he abhorred state misconduct, government secrecy, and an interventionist foreign policy. He associated the Nixon administration and the CIA with all three. Church was equally motivated by his political ambitions, however. He had sought the committee's chairmanship as a springboard to campaign for the presidency in 1976. Even as he appeared above politics, Church imagined, he would become a Democratic darling by painting Ford with a Nixonian brush.[37]

Events conspired against such calculated partisanship. In June the White House released portions of the Rockefeller Commission's report. It confirmed and elaborated upon the CIA's domestic spying exposed in Hersh's article, and it included insight on covert operations, surreptitious drug testing on human subjects, and parallel abuses. What it omitted was any reference to assassinations. In a television broadcast that February, the journalist Daniel Schorr had broken the news that Ford had inadvertently leaked that the Family Jewels contained explosive material on U.S. plots to assassinate foreign leaders. The Rockefeller Commission Report was silent on this bombshell; Ford had ordered that the findings remain classified. But Schorr's public disclosure of the plots' existence compelled the Church Committee to add an investigation of them to its agenda. For Church this was inconvenient. Among the targets for assassination were South Vietnam's Ngo Dinh Diem (who was actually not a U.S. target) and Cuba's Fidel Castro. The planning took place not under the deposed Republican Richard Nixon but the martyred Democrat John Kennedy.[38]

By sensationalizing the hearings, the revelations about assassinations politicized them. Or it further politicized them. Although the testimony and staff research uncovered robust evidence of the CIA's complicity in assassination plots, the bureaucratically-engineered shield of plausible deniability prevented the Church Committee from determining that any president had explicitly authorized an assassination. Church was relieved. The ethical quagmire Nixon had dug for Republicans was adequate without adding the CIA's transgressions, and by portraying the CIA as an out of control "Rogue Elephant," he could keep Kennedy's reputation out of harm's way. In the House, however, Pike challenged the rogue elephant metaphor by proposing a systemic explanation for the

CIA's misdeeds that implicated the executive and legislative branches as well as both parties. The result was to make enemies up and down Pennsylvania Avenue and across both chambers' aisle. On January 23, 1976, the committee voted to reject more than 100 deletions from the report insisted on by the CIA. On January 30, the full House voted against its public release. But from a still unidentified source, Daniel Schorr received a copy. On February 16, the *Village Voice* published the unexpurgated report.[39]

Each of the reports expressed a number of well-founded recommendations, beginning with but going beyond the establishment of standing oversight committees. Other suggestions included making transparent the intelligence budget; obliging the Government Accounting Office to audit the CIA; approving a legislative charter for the NSA; requiring court orders before the FBI infiltrates domestic organizations; and requiring the president to notify Congress in writing within forty-eight hours of a covert operation, restricting their scope and prohibiting assassinations. The Pike Committee even proposed placing the DCI under the supervision of a community intelligence tsar. Yet the politics that suffused each of the committees and their relationships with the White House eviscerated the reports' impact. The attention the Church Committee paid to assassinations and other CIA abuses combined with its chairman's political agenda to generate a report more focused on the past than the future. The Pike Committee's report's perspective was more structural, but its report became a victim of partisan warfare and executive branch intervention. Its unauthorized release undermined its legitimacy, and the goal of the Ford White House was containment. With few exceptions, moreover, the public read the headlines, not the fine print.[40]

The end results, accordingly, were moderate. The Senate established its permanent Select Committee on Intelligence (SSCI) in 1976, the same year that President Ford issued Executive Order 11905, U.S. Foreign Intelligence Activities. Its provisions included the creation of a Committee on Foreign Intelligence to prepare and manage the budget and otherwise supervise the National Foreign Intelligence Program (NFIB), and an Intelligence Oversight Board. A year later the House stood up its Permanent Select Committee on Intelligence (HPSCI). Two decades after it was proposed by Mike Mansfield and others, congressional oversight was institutionalized. The Foreign Intelligence Surveillance Act of 1978 mandated strict procedures for electronic surveillance and other methods of collecting information on suspected agents of foreign powers operating on U.S. soil. Then in 1980, President Jimmy Carter signed the Intelligence Oversight Act, making the IC responsible for ensuring that the SSCI and HPSCI receive timely and comprehensive notification about significant intelligence activities, particularly covert actions.[41]

Although constructive and progressive, these reforms, promoted by mixed constituencies with mixed motives but uniformly opposed by the officials within the IC who would be most affected by them, fell far short of the aims of ambitious reformers in the heady days following Watergate. Some argued that they were even counterproductive. Who received prior notifications of and briefings about intelligence activities was determined previously by informal arrangements and was somewhat flexible. The 1980 legislations specifically mandated the briefings of SSCI and HPSCI members. Excluded were each chamber's armed forces, foreign affairs, appropriations, and other committees. Unlike SSCI and HPSCI, these other committees' relations with the IC were more distant, and therefore less comfortable. This feature led one scholar to lament that the Intelligence Oversight Act was "a victory for executive secrecy." Moreover, shortly after the enactment of the Intelligence Oversight Act, Ronald Reagan appointed the OSS veteran William Casey DCI and made him the first occupier of that office to hold Cabinet rank. The covert projects Casey pursued, particularly but not exclusively with regard to Central America and Iran, revealed that the 1980 legislation was susceptible to interpretation and evasion, and the oversight mechanism was hardly foolproof.[42]

INERTIA AND THE END OF THE COLD WAR

Casey's behavior revealed no less that the end of the "Year of Intelligence" slammed shut the political window for further reform. Ford's pardon allowed Nixon – and Watergate – to retreat if not fade from the public memory, along with the Vietnam War, overthrow of Allende, and marches on Washington. The public ire that precipitated Nixon's downfall and the hearings was now directed toward Schorr and Hersh as much as government institutions. Even the civil rights movement seemed more subdued, signaling once again that American political culture is not conducive to sustained reform. Impressing on congressional and public critics the dangers confronted by agency personnel even as it underscored the risks to the secret world of intelligence of too much transparency, the December 23, 1975, assassination of Richard Welch, the station chief in Athens, all but sealed the fate of reform by returning domestic attention to the global threat – the reason the CIA was created in the first place.

Not even Iran Contra could revive the reform impulse. The hearings over the scandal achieved next to nothing. Directed by an incompetent colonel with little experience in intelligence from the White House basement, possibly without the knowledge of a detached and admittedly forgetful president, Iran Contra's interlocking operations were so outrageous from beginning to end as to defy systemic reform. Identifying, indicting, and in some cases even convicting the outliers culpable for this keystone-cops-type venture seemed the appropriate fix. Furthermore, for most of the public, Congress, and even the press, what mattered most was that after a half-century the Cold War wound down to a triumphalist end. For that achievement, Reagan, George H. W. Bush, and the foreign policy establishment received a pass for what appeared as comparatively petty dalliances in Iran or Central America. Within and beyond the beltway, the salience of the IC faded. Its poor performance in estimating the prospects for a revolution in Iran was all but forgotten, its operations in Afghanistan ignored, and its contributions to ending the Cold War dismissed or criticized.

Whatever vestigial sentiment remained for intelligence reform disintegrated during the Clinton years. Senator Patrick Moynihan of New York did propose legislation – to abolish the CIA, not reform it. Moynihan knew the proposal was dead on arrival. He wanted to make the point that an institution committed to secrecy had no place in a democratic society, and its influence on the outcome of the Cold War had been negligible. "The Soviet Empire did not fall apart because the spooks had bugged the men's room in the Kremlin or put broken glass in Mrs. Brezhnev's bath, but because running a huge closed repressive society in the 1980s had become – economically, socially and militarily, and technologically – impossible," he thundered when introducing the Abolition of the Central Intelligence Act of 1995.[43]

Moynihan's bill generated scant support; reforming let alone abolishing America's intelligence establishment was far down on the list of everyone's priorities, perhaps President Bill Clinton's most of all. But there were those in Congress and the public who expected, and indeed insisted on, receiving a peace dividend from "winning" the Cold War. Such a benefit was likely to gain the support of the White House, which cared most about domestic matters and economic growth. According to this viewpoint, the CIA did not need to be abolished in order to obtain the "dividend" of drastically reducing its budget. On the other side, and cutting across party lines, a minority in Congress with long-standing interest and expertise in security issues, such as John Warner, Sam Nunn, Porter Goss, and Bob Kerrey, feared the effects of Moynihan- and peace-dividend-type thinking on intelligence capabilities. They agreed that the end of the Cold War provided an opportunity to reexamine the CIA – and the rest of the IC. But the goal was to readjust its structure and mission to correspond to new conditions. The CIA was established in response to Pearl Harbor and in anticipation of a long Cold War. It now needed to adapt to a different environment.

Having earned a reputation as an authority on defense over some two decades representing Wisconsin in Congress, Leslie ("Les") Aspin sympathized with this minority. But he had a personal motive, as well, to promote intelligence reform. Aspin had resigned his seat in the House in 1993 to accept Clinton's appointment as secretary of defense. But his tenure was beset with difficulties from the start, with controversies erupting over the budget and base closings, homosexuals in the military, and finally, the deaths of eighteen servicemen in Mogadishu, Somalia. After but one year Clinton replaced Aspin with William Perry. To soften the blow, Clinton made Aspin chair of the President's Foreign Intelligence Advisory Board (PFIAB, renamed the President's Intelligence Advisory Board, PIAB, in 2008). The intellectually restless Aspin made intelligence reform his mission.

The aim to reduce intelligence spending, adapt the CIA to the post–Cold War environment, or in Aspin's case, to lend substance to his position as PFIAB chair, were neither individually nor collectively sufficient to produce significant reform. This is not surprising. In 1994, external threats seemed to be no more than irritants, and there was nothing remotely resembling the internal crisis associated with Vietnam and Watergate. With the exception of those who followed the arrest and conviction of the CIA's Aldrich Ames for treason, the public paid no attention to the IC. Then in 1995 Aspin died and Harold Brown, another former secretary of defense, took over as commission chair. These conditions were not conducive to overcoming the differing agendas and institutional inertia.

For more than a year the Aspin-Brown Commission, drawing on dozens of formal testimonies, hundreds of other interviews, and thousands of pages of documentation, examined nineteen of the most fundamental issues confronting the IC. Most of these, relating to roles and missions; structure, coordination, and management; budget and resources; and oversight and accountability had been long-standing concerns. In March 1996 it produced a 200 page report with 39 proposals for reform. It provoked a great deal of resistance, especially from most veterans of the IC and entrenched bureaucratic interests, the Pentagon above all, and their congressional allies. Given the context in which the study took place, the report predictably generated nothing close to the enthusiasm or sense of urgency to overcome this resistance. The effort at intelligence reform in 1994–96 failed.[44]

9/11, WEAPONS OF MASS DESTRUCTION, GLOBAL WAR ON TERROR, AND THE INTELLIGENCE REFORM AND TERRORISM PREVENTION ACT

Although mostly underappreciated and largely divorced from the nation's political pulse, the conditions for generating the political will required for intelligence reform, unfortunately, began to remerge shortly after the stillborn Aspin-Brown recommendations. A June 1996 terrorist bombing of the military barracks at Khobar Towers in Saudi Arabia that cost the lives of nineteen U.S. servicemen was one catalyst. The appointment a year later of George Tenet as DCI was another. Tenet was a skilled bureaucrat and a political centrist without party ties. Prior to becoming the agency's deputy director under his predecessor, John Deutch, he had served on the staffs of the SSCI and the NSC. Tenet recognized that in order to safeguard American security on the one hand and restore the CIA's reputation, budget, and élan on the other, the agency had to reorient its emphases. A renewed external threat, global terrorism, provided the opportunity, and soon, the support. Tenet immediately began to position the CIA at the forefront of what he argued had to be a much more aggressive and concerted effort to confront international terrorism, the proliferation of weapons of mass destruction, and other unconventional threats to U.S. security far removed from dynamics associated with the Cold War.[45]

Intelligence reform was not on Tenet's agenda, nor was it on that of the president or Congress, let alone the public. The DCI focused his attention and bureaucratic skill on elevating appropriations in order to boost the recruitment of personnel. He also fiddled with the organizational chart. But virtually every one of Tenet's initiatives targeted the CIA's Directorate of Operations (DO). As had been the case since covert operations became a CIA responsibility in the interval between the enactment of the 1947 National Security Act and the outbreak of the Korean War, the agency's DO tail wagged the IC dog. Not only did Tenet leave the analytic side of the IC essentially untouched, he also paid short shrift to his community-management role. Focusing on the CIA, he made little effort to enhance the IC's integration and foster collaboration among the elements. To Tenet, the Pentagon was as off limits, as was the FBI and other agencies of law enforcement. This state of affairs did not change after the 1998 terrorist bombings of the U.S embassies in Kenya and Tanzania, after al Qaeda attacked the *U.S.S. Cole*, docked in the harbor of Aden, Yemen, in October 2000, or even after it destroyed both of the Twin Towers in New York and flew a plane into the Pentagon soon thereafter.

Indeed, notwithstanding representations of the 9/11 tragedy as a colossal intelligence failure, demands to hold the IC accountable were at first muted. Americans, including those in Congress, appeared more intent on uniting in their grief and anger than apportioning blame. Further, the night of the attack and in a series of follow-on speeches, President George W. Bush gave voice to the American quest for revenge, and on that purpose the CIA soon began to make amends. Operation ENDURING FREEDOM was the plan of the CIA, not the Pentagon. Its agents in the field quickly reestablished contacts with the Northern Alliance's warlords, provided them with intelligence, money, and materials, supplied U.S. forces with "actionable" intelligence (including bombing targets), and otherwise served valiantly. By the time Bush and the Congress established the National Commission on Terrorist Attacks Upon the United States (9/11 Commission) after Thanksgiving in 2002 (and even then it did not begin work until spring 2003), Bush declared Mission Accomplished in Afghanistan and ceased operations there.[46]

But then everything fell apart for the IC. Had ENDURING FREEDOM ended with the defeat of the Taliban, the death (or better yet capture) of Osama bin Laden, and the destruction of al Qaeda, the 9/11 Commission report probably would have taken its place next to the many preceding studies and proposals for reform. Its impact would have been at most marginal. Conversely, had the president pushed for intelligence reform in 2002, with his popularity exceptionally high and the attack on American soil fresh in the minds of a relatively united Congress and public, the reforms may well have been more effective, particularly in promoting information sharing and interagency integration. A commission headed by former two-time national security advisor Lt. General Brent Scowcroft issued a report that anticipated many of the provisions of the 2004 reform legislation. But the White House had neither the time nor inclination to take on the issue, because the administration's goals went beyond Afghanistan – and even al Qaeda. Declaring a Global War on Terror, Bush sought regime change in Iraq.[47]

With reluctance and trepidation, the IC facilitated executing the administration's agenda. Alert to Bush's predisposition to invade Iraq, unaware of evidence disconfirming the premise that Saddam Hussein had a hidden cache of chemical and biological weapons and was seeking to reconstitute a nuclear program, misled by "Iraq's intransigence and deceptive practices," and sensitive to its earlier failure to detect Iraq's nuclear program, on instructions from Congress the National Intelligence Council (NIC) on October 30, 2002, published a hastily drafted and flawed National Intelligence Estimate (NIE). Based on extant "off the shelf" products, conflating "fact" with assumptions, and failing to identify gaps in intelligence or provide insight on the reliability of sources, "Iraq's Continuing Programs for Weapons of Mass Destruction" violated many of the cardinal principles of analytic tradecraft. The NIE served as a justification, although not a precipitant, for Bush's decision to go to war in March 2003. Then, under great pressure from Congress and the press in the aftermath of the invasion, in July 2003 the White House released the NIE's Key Judgments and an uncoordinated unclassified White Paper that Congress had insisted the NIC produce. The White Paper exacerbated the NIE's shortcomings by omitting the caveats, qualifiers, and dissents. The *New York Times*, correctly, albeit simplistically, declared the NIE "one of the most flawed documents in the history of American intelligence." When the War in Iraq took a turn for the worse, and from there conditions rapidly deteriorated further, the IC with its NIE became *a* if not *the* scapegoat.[48]

In sum, it was not the connection between the IC's intelligence failure, the 9/11 tragedy, and the threat of future attacks that was the primary driver of intelligence reform. Rather, it was the political finger-pointing and blame game that attended the Iraq War. Attesting to the adage that in the political world of Washington "there are only two possibilities: policy success and intelligence failure," critics and advocates of the war alike held the NIE responsible for their postures. They claimed that the estimate, which in truth only a handful of individuals had read, either misled them by exaggerating Saddam's Hussein's threat or by failing to expose the threat's hollowness. Meanwhile, led by families, especially widows, of the 9/11 tragedy who were persuaded that their loved ones would have lived had the IC simply "connected the dots," they actively promoted intelligence reform.[49]

Within this context, the 9/11 Commission proceeded toward producing its report. Some observers argue that Philip Zelikow used his position as the commission's executive director to direct its findings toward indicting the IC and exonerating the White House. Zelikow had coauthored a book with Condoleeza Rice on German reunification based on their experiences together as NSC staffers under George H.W. Bush, he had served on George W. Bush's transition team and PFIAB, and he had headed Bush's Markle Task Force on

National Security in the Information Age. Perhaps Zelikow did want to shield the administration. If so, he was frustrated by its bipartisan composition, which limited his ability to shape the conclusions.[50]

The report was politicized, but for that Democrats contributed no less than Republicans. The 9/11 Commission issued its final report in June 2004, when the looming presidential election accelerated the growing polarization of politics. In addition, almost exactly a year before, three months after Bush gave the green light to the invasion of Iraq and the 9/11 Commission opened its hearings, the SSCI began to investigate, in the words of its vice chair, Jay Rockefeller, "the accuracy of our pre-war intelligence and the use of that intelligence by the Executive." It issued its report in July 2004. The lockstep progress of the 9/11 Commission and SSCI's examination of the pre–Iraq War intelligence in fundamental ways fused the two disparate events. And with regard to the latter, Democrats, many of whom had supported the invasion and were reluctant to be exposed for failing rigorously to interrogate the 2002 NIE, were as eager as Republicans to lay the blame primarily on the IC. Accordingly, both parties, misleadingly claiming a spirit of bipartisanship, supported scapegoating the IC in both reports.[51]

Within six months of the release of the reports and notwithstanding the bitter and nail-biting 2004 election, this unholy alliance of Republicans and Democrats, spurred on by the 9/11 families and with the White House remaining passively on the sidelines, held sufficiently to hammer out the IRTPA. Its centerpiece was the establishment of the Director of National Intelligence (DNI). The Office of the Director of National Intelligence (ODNI) would not collect intelligence nor – with the exception of NIE and the President's Daily Brief, both community products – would it produce finished intelligence. Rather, theoretically halving the DCI's role, it would be responsible for managing the sixteen elements that comprised the IC, fostering greater collaboration and information sharing among them, and improving the element's capabilities individually and collectively.[52]

Establishing the DNI was not a new idea. It has been proposed multiple times previously. In 1989, Senator Arlen Specter had actually introduced legislation to establish a position with that very title. Although Specter garnered little support, the concept resurfaced during the Aspin-Brown and Scowcroft commission inquiries and, sandwiched between them, a 1998 commission that former Vice Chairman of the Joint Chiefs of Staff Admiral David Jeremiah (USN, ret.) led to investigate the IC's failure to detect India's nuclear test. The same was true with other key features of IRTPA. But in the latter half of 2004, both Republicans and Democrats saw it in their respective political interest to initiate intelligence reform. The American public, still reeling from the 9/11 attacks, fearing another, observing the rising body count in Iraq, and enraged by the absence of a cache of WMD, demanded it or, at the very least, was receptive to it. Opponents, moreover, especially high-ranking or veteran intelligence officials, had been discredited. Only these conditions enabled decades of bureaucratic and

institutional resistance to be overcome. The enactment of IRTPA is testament
that in the political world of Washington, there really are only policy successes
and intelligence failures.[53]

It is too early to assess the consequences of the 2004 reform legislation. In
order to collect the necessary votes in the face of vested interests and conflicting
perspectives, the authors finessed most of the details. They left responsibilities,
much of the reorganization, and even location for future deliberations and
decisions, despite the law extending to hundreds of pages. Further, as one
observer notes, "the result is a job [the DNI] whose responsibilities and expectations exceed its authorities."[54] The CIA continues to resist integration, the
Pentagon still commands the bulk of the intelligence budget, individual elements
hoard information only slightly less than before, collectors remain distrustful of
analysts, and all but one of the IC elements reports to a cabinet-level official, not
the DNI. Congress is miserly in committing resources to the ODNI lest it evolve
into another bloated bureaucracy, and IRTPA left both chambers' capacity for
oversight untouched. The primary reform of covert operations was a name
change. There are signs that the legislation has had positive effects, but not
enough to generate optimism. And the prospects for future reform are dim. It
took virtually a unique confluence of events, threats, and individuals between
2001 and 2004 to open the political window required to enact IRTPA. That
window seems closed – tightly.[55]

ACKNOWLEDGMENTS

For their advice and criticism, I thank the organizers of and participants in the
Miller Center conference and my Temple colleague, David Farber. Although I
served in the Office of the Director of National Intelligence, the views expressed
in this publication are my own and do not imply endorsement of ODNI or any
other U.S. government agency.

Notes

1. "President Signs Intelligence Reform and Terrorism Prevent Act," December 17, 2004,
   retrieved from http://georgewbush-whitehouse.archives.gov/news/releases/2004/12/
   20041217-1.html, accessed on September 26, 2011.
2. Laurie West Van Hook, "Reforming Intelligence: The Passage of the Intelligence
   Reform and Terrorism Prevention Act" (Washington: Office of the Director of
   National Intelligence and National Intelligence University, 2009), retrieved from
   http://www.fas.org/irp/dni/reform.pdf, accessed on September 24, 2011. See also
   Michael Warner and J. Kenneth McDonald, "U.S. Intelligence Community Studies
   Since 1947" (Washington: Strategic Management Issues Office and Center for the
   Study of Intelligence, 2005).
3. Jennifer L. Merolla and Paul Pulido, "Follow the Leader: Major Policy Changes to
   Homeland Security and Terrorism Policy," Chapter 11.
4. David Rudgers, *Creating the Secret State: The Origins of the Central Intelligence Agency,
   1943-1947* (Lawrence: University of Kansas Press, 2000), 5; McGeorge Bundy and

Henry Stimson, *On Active Duty* (NY: Harper & Brothers, 1947), 188; Paul R. Pillar, *Intelligence and U.S. Foreign Policy: Iraq, 9/11, and Misguided Reform* (NY: Columbia, 2011), 179.

5. A year earlier FDR had appointed Donovan to lead an Office of the Coordinator of Information.

6. Thomas F. Troy, *Donovan and the CIA* (Frederick, MD: University Publications of America, 1981), 23–70; Rudgers, *Creating the Secret State*, 15–32.

7. Donovan's memorandum to FDR of November 18, 1944, in Troy, *Donovan and the CIA*, 445–47.

8. Amy B. Zegart, *Flawed by Design: The Evolution of the CIA, JCS, and NSC* (Stanford: Stanford University Press, 1999), 175.

9. Harry Howe Ransom, *The Intelligence Establishment* (Cambridge: Harvard University Press, 1970), 60; Rhodri Jeffreys-Jones, *The CIA and American Democracy* (New Haven: Yale University Press, 1989), 30; Anne Karelekas, *History of the Central Intelligence Agency*, in *The Central Intelligence Agency: History and Documents*, ed. William M. Leary (University, AL: University of Alabama Press, 1984), 20–21.

10. Rudgers, *Creating the Secret State*, 63–64; Harry S. Truman to the Secretaries of State, War, and Navy, January 22, 1946, in Leary, *Central Intelligence Agency*, 126–27.

11. *Central Intelligence: Origin and Evolution*, ed. Michael Warner (Washington, DC: Center for the Study of Intelligence, 2001), 2.

12. Karelekas, *History of the Central Intelligence Agency*, 22.

13. Ibid., 22–23.

14. "X" (George Kennan), "The Sources of Soviet Conduct," *Foreign Affairs* 25 (July 1947): 566–82; Vandenberg memorandum for the Assistant Director for Special Operations [David Galloway], "Functions of the Office of Special Operations," October 25, 1946, in *The CIA under Harry Truman*, ed. Michael Warner (Washington, DC: Center for the Study of Intelligence, 1994), 87; Minutes of the Meeting of the National Intelligence Authority, February 12, 1947, ibid., 113–21 (author's emphasis).

15. David M. Barrett, *The CIA and Congress: The Untold Story from Truman to Kennedy* (Lawrence: University of Kansas Press, 2005), 21; Jeffreys-Jones, *The CIA and American Democracy*, 29–30.

16. Burton Hersh, *The Old Boys: American Elite and the Origins of the CIA* (NY: Charles Scribner's Sons, 1992); Evan Thomas, *The Very Best Men: Four Who Dared: The Early Years of the CIA* (NY: Simon & Schuster, 1996).

17. Douglas Waller, *Wild Bill Donovan: The Spymaster Who Created the OSS and Modern American Espionage* (NY: Free Press, 2011), 304–12; Jeffreys-Jones, *CIA and American Democracy*, 30–33.

18. President Harry S. Truman's Address Before a Joint Session of Congress, March 12, 1947, retrieved from http://avalon.law.yale.edu/20th_century/trudoc.asp, accessed on August 20, 2012; The National Security Act of 1947, retrieved from http://www.google.com/url?sa=t&rct=j&q=&esrc=s&source=web&cd=3&ved=0CCoQFjAC&url=http%3A%2F%2Fwww.drworley.org%2FNSPcommon%2FEarly%2520Cold%2520War%2F1947%2520National%2520Security%2520Act.doc&ei=QZYyUKLuNYH4ogHUooHwBQ&usg=AFQjCNEygfp3cppoU6ohHo4IJCJJ71-DnQ, accessed on August 20, 2012.

19. John J. Rosenwasser and Michael Warner, "History of the Interagency Process for Foreign Relations in the United States: Murphy's Law?" in *The National Security Enterprise: Navigating the Labyrinth*, ed., Roger Z. George and Harvey Rishikof (Washington, DC: Georgetown University Press, 2011), 20; Zegart, *Flawed by Design*, 184.

20. National Security Act of 1947, July 26, 1947, excerpts pertaining to establishment of CIA, its responsibilities and those of the Director, and abolition of NIA and CIG, in Warner, *The CIA under Truman*, 131–35.

21. Clark Clifford with Richard Holbrooke, *Counsel to the President: A Memoir* (New York: Random House, 1991), 169–70.

22. Memorandum by CIA General Counsel Lawrence Houston to the DCI, September 25, 1947, *Foreign Relations of the United States, 1945–1950: Emergence of the Intelligence Establishment* (Washington, DC: GOP, 1996): 622–23 (hereafter *FRUS, Intelligence*).

23. George Kennan defined political warfare as "all means . . . short of war." See Policy Planning Staff Memorandum, May 4, 1948, ibid., 269–72.

24. Loch K. Johnson, *America's Secret Power: The CIA in a Democratic Society* (NY: Oxford, 1989), 36–37; "Office of Policy Coordination," 1948–52, p. 22, retrieved from http://www.foia.cia.gov/sites/default/files/document_conversions/89801/DOC_0000104823.pdf; Karalekas, *History of the Central Intelligence Agency*, 43–44; 50–53; United States Senate, 94th Congress, 2nd Session, *Final Report of the Select Committee to Study Governmental Operations with Respect to Intelligence Activities* [*Church Committee Report*], Book IV (Washington, DC: GPO, 1976), 31.

25. Barrett, *The CIA and Congress*, 447–59; Zegart, *Flawed by Design*, 193.

26. Stephen E. Ambrose with Richard H. Immerman, *Ike's Spies: Eisenhower and the Espionage Establishment* (Garden City, NY: Doubleday, 1981), 187–88; Frank Smist, *Congress Oversees the United States Intelligence Community, 1947–1989* (Knoxville: University of Tennessee Press, 1990).

27. Neil Sheehan, "A Student Group Concedes It Took Funds from C.I.A.," *New York Times*, February 14, 1967; Sol Stern. "A Short Account of International Student Politics & the Cold War with Particular Reference to the NSA, CIA, Etc." *Ramparts* 5 (March 1967): 29–39; Tity de Vries, "The 1967 Central Intelligence Agency Scandal: Catalyst in a Transforming Relationship Between State and People," *Journal of American History* 98 (March 2012): 1075–92; Anne Hessing Cahn, *Killing Détente: The Right Attacks the CIA* (University Park, PA: Pennsylvania State University Press, 1998), 71–72; Johnson, *America's Secret Power*, 3–5.

28. Cahn: *Killing Détente*, 74.

29. *Church Committee Report*, book III: 921–82.

30. Kahn, *Killing Détente*, 76–78, "A Review of the Intelligence Community," March 10, 1971, retrieved from http://www.gwu.edu/~nsarchiv/NSAEBB/NSAEBB144/document%204.pdf, accessed on September 24, 2012.

31. Jeffreys-Jones, *The CIA and American Democracy*, 191–92; Douglas F. Garthoff, *Directors of Central Intelligence as Leaders of the U.S. Intelligence Community, 1946–2005* (Washington, DC: Potomac Books, 2007), 65–75.

32. The "Family Jewels" report, retrieved from http://www.gwu.edu/~nsarchiv/NSAEBB/NSAEBB222/family_jewels_full_ocr.pdf, accessed on October 6, 2011. See also, John Prados, *The Family Jewels: The CIA, Secrecy, and Presidential Power* (Austin: University of Texas Press, 2013).

33. *America in the Seventies*, ed. Beth Bailey and David Farber (Lawrence: University Press of Kansas, 2004).
34. Seymour M. Hersh, "Huge C.I.A. Operation Reported in U.S. against Antiwar Forces, Other Dissidents in Nixon Years," *New York Times*, December 22, 1974.
35. Seymour M. Hersh, "C.I.A. Chief Tells House of $8 Million Campaign against Allende in '70–'73," *New York Times*, September 8, 1974; Johnson, *America's Secret Power*, 207.
36. Kathryn S. Olmstead, *Challenging the Secret Government: The Post-Watergate Investigations of the CIA and FBI* (Chapel Hill: University of North Carolina Press, 1996), 48–58. See also Loch K. Johnson, *A Season of Inquiry: The Senate Intelligence Investigation* (Lexington: University Press of Kentucky), 1985.
37. LeRoy Ashby and Rod Gramer, *Fighting the Odds: The Life of Senator Frank Church* (Pullman: Washington State University Press, 1994), 472.
38. Cahn, *Killing Détente*, 78–81.
39. Olmstead, *Challenging the Secret Government*, 85–167; Christopher Andrew, *For the President's Eyes Only: Secret Intelligence and the American Presidency from Washington to Bush* (NY: HarperCollins, 1995), 413–20; Gerald K. Haines, "Looking for a Rogue Elephant: The Pike Committee Investigations and the CIA," *CSI* (Winter 1998–99): 81–92.
40. Olmstead, *Challenging the Secret Government*, 163–76; Haines, "Looking for a Rogue Elephant."
41. Garthoff, *Directors of Central Intelligence*, 295–96; Executive Order 11905: United States Foreign Intelligence Activities, retrieved from http://www.ford.utexas.edu/library/speeches/760110e.htm#SEC, accessed on October 7, 2011; Johnson, *America's Secret Power*, 209.
42. Olmsted, *Challenging the Secret Government*, 176–79; Theodore Draper, *A Very Thin Line: The Iran Contra Affairs* (NY: Hill & Wang, 1991); Bob Woodward, *Veil: The Secret Wars of the C.I.A., 1981–1987* (NY: Simon & Schuster, 1987).
43. Moynihan's Abolition of the Central Intelligence Agency Act and his speech introducing it on January 4, 1995, retrieved from http://www.fas.org/irp/s126.htm, accessed on October 10, 2011.
44. For a detailed study of the Aspin-Brown Commission, see Loch K. Johnson, *The Threat on the Horizon: An Inside Account of America's Search for Security After the Cold War* (NY: Oxford University Press, 2011).
45. James Risen, "Failures on Terrorism Are Seen Shaping Tenet's Legacy," *New York Times*, June 4, 2004.
46. Bob Woodward, *Bush at War* (NY: Simon & Schuster, 2002); Peter L. Bergen, *The Longest War: The Enduring Conflict Between American and al-Qaeda* (NY: Free Press, 2011), 3–85.
47. Garthoff, *Directors of Central Intelligence*, 274.
48. National Intelligence Estimate [sanitized], "Iraq's Continuing Programs for Weapons of Mass Destruction," 30 October 2002, retrieved from http://www.fas.org/irp/cia/product/iraq-wmd-nie.pdf; "Misreading Intentions: Iraq's Reactions to Created Picture of Deception," retrieved from http://www.gwu.edu/~nsarchiv/news/20120905/CIA-Iraq.pdf; Key Judgments from NIE on "Iraq's Continuing Programs for Weapons of Mass Destruction," retrieved from http://www.fas.org/irp/cia/product/iraq-wmd.html; "Iraq's Weapons of Mass Destruction Programs [White Paper],"

October 2002, rerieved from https://www.cia.gov/library/reports/general-reports-1/iraq_wmd/Iraq_Oct_2002.pdf, all accessed on August 23, 2012; David Barstow, William J. Broad, and Jeff Gerth, "How the White House Embraced Disputed Arms Intelligence," *New York Times*, October 3, 2004.

49. Thomas Fingar, "Office of the Director of National Intelligence: Promising Start Despite Ambiguity, Ambivalence, and Animosity," in George and Rishikof, *The National Security Enterprise: Navigating the Labyrinth* (Washington, DC: Georgetown University Press, 2011), 140–41; Thomas Fingar, *Reducing Uncertainty: Intelligence Analysis and National Security* (Stanford: Stanford University Press, 2011), 89–108; "9/11 Families Plead for Intelligence Form," *CNN Politics*, August 17, 2004, retrieved from http://articles.cnn.com/2004-08-17/politics/911.families_1_intelligence-reform-terror-attacks-mary-fetchet?_s=PM:ALLPOLITICS, accessed on August 23, 2012.

50. Philip Shenon, *The Commission: The Uncensored History of the 9/11 Commission* (NY: Twelve, 2008).

51. *The 9/11 Commission Report: The Final Report of the National Commission on Terrorist Attacks Upon the United States* (NY: Norton, 2004); Statement by Jay Rockefeller, *Congressional Record*, July 17, 2003 (Senate), Page S9580-S9581, retrieved from http://www.fas.org/irp/congress/2003_cr/s071703.html, accessed on October 13, 2011; U.S. Senate, Select Committee on Intelligence, *Report on the U.S. Intelligence Community's Prewar Intelligence Assessments on Iraq*, retrieved from http://web.mit.edu/simsong/www/iraqreport2-textunder.pdf, accessed on October 13, 2011.

52. Public Law 108–458, *The Intelligence Reform and Terrorism Prevention Act*, December 17, 2004, retrieved from http://www.intelligence.senate.gov/laws/pl108-458.pdf.

53. Garthoff, *Directors of Central Intelligence*, 176, 272–74.

54. Pillar, *Intelligence and U.S. Foreign Policy*, 296.

55. Richard H. Immerman, "Transforming Analysis: The Intelligence Community's Best Kept Secret," *Intelligence and National Security* 26 (April–June 2011): 159–81.

Follow the Leader

Major Changes to Homeland Security and Terrorism Policy

Jennifer L. Merolla and Paul Pulido

Taking off our shoes at airports, walking through body scanners, packing liquids less than 3 ounces in a Ziploc bag – these are all things that have become "the new normal," to quote Dick Cheney,[1] in a post-9/11 world. Many of these policy changes occurred without much fanfare among the American public, who prioritized security after hijacked planes crashed into the World Trade Center and the Pentagon. Although there was more controversy surrounding the introduction of body scanners, the public has now accepted this new norm, even over a decade out from 9/11, when there have not been other attacks on U.S. soil.

Although many Americans were willing to cede some intrusions on privacy and inconvenience with the new Transportation Security Administration regime, other policy changes enacted in response to 9/11 were far more extensive with respect to government administration, government surveillance of terrorist suspects, and how the government handles alleged terrorists in custody. Shortly after the events of 9/11, Congress approved a new department of homeland security whose first secretary was Tom Ridge. The government relaxed requirements for wiretapping suspected terrorists (even U.S. citizens) on U.S. soil by reducing judicial barriers on the scope and specificity requirements of warrants. Racial profiling of Arab and Muslim individuals increased post-9/11. These are but a handful of the major shifts in homeland security and terrorism policy in a post-9/11 world.

The policy changes instituted post-9/11 are the most salient given that we are over a decade away from the events of that day and the threat of international terrorism has persisted. Although there has not been another attack on U.S. soil, U.S. interests abroad have been attacked in countries from Saudi Arabia to Pakistan, and some attempted attacks have been foiled. That being said, there have been other important policy changes to homeland security and terrorism policy since the end of World War II that predate these changes. As Immerman discusses in Chapter 10, the creation of the Central Intelligence

Agency (CIA) reflected the changing nature of security norms; intelligence gathering sought to prevent full-scale war with the USSR. The growth in hijacking strategies in the '70s and '80s also led to major changes in airport security.

In this chapter we seek to understand the political factors that led to some of these major policy shifts in homeland security and terrorism policy. More specifically, we will consider the role played by external events, the president, Congress, the bureaucracy, and the public. As we review major policy changes, a common thread will emerge across many of the changes, one in which we observe policy coming on the heels of terrorist incidents, being led by the president (along with the bureaucracy), with Congress being supportive, and the public generally showing high levels of support. Deviations from this pattern generally occur when policy changes do not fall on the heels of a specific terrorist incident, and spill into domestic politics.

In the next section we briefly discuss the ways in which external events and all of these actors might influence major policy changes on homeland security and terrorism. Following that, we identify the major changes in policy that have occurred between 1945 and the present. The third part of the chapter provides a detailed discussion of the major policy changes that we identified with a careful focus on the factors noted previously. We conclude by discussing some implications that changes in terrorism and homeland security policy may have for the quality of democracy.

POLITICAL FORCES THAT INFLUENCE HOMELAND SECURITY AND TERRORISM POLICY

The confluence of several factors may lead to major policy changes related to terrorism and homeland security. We consider the role of factors internal and external to the U.S. context, as we are dealing with policies relevant to foreign affairs.

External Factors

One of the most important factors relevant for major policy changes in terrorism and homeland security is the presence of external threats. Because these policies typically involve some trade-off between individual liberty and security, democratic societies are generally only likely to support changes when there is a salient threat. In fact, considering security threats more broadly, major policy changes have often occurred in tandem with conditions of conflict.[2] For example, during World War II, security concerns lead to the internment of countless Japanese Americans. The Red Scare and McCarthy's "witch hunts" utilized invasive

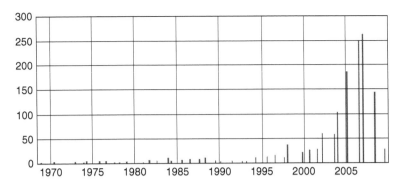

FIGURE 11.1. Total Number of Terrorist Incidents, 1968–2009
Source: RAND Database of Worldwide Terrorism Incidents

tactics that set the stage for future debates on the degree to which government should have access to citizens' personal information.

If we consider the presence of the threat of international terrorism, the number of attacks, as well as the lethality of attacks has increased over time. In Figure 11.1, we present the number of terrorist incidents around the globe from late 1968 to 2009 compiled from the RAND Corporation. Although the number of incidents is fairly low in the 1960s, 1970s, and 1980s, we start to observe more of an increase in the 1990s, and exponential growth in the 2000s.

The nature of these attacks has also varied over time. William Shugart outlines three waves of terrorism since the end of World War II.[3] The first wave of terrorist incidents in the 1940s and 1950s was primarily targeted within colonial societies. Terrorist violence took the shape of ethnic separatism and national liberation, with former colonial subjects rallying for their own independent rule. Because this wave of terrorism did not attack U.S. targets, we would not expect much of a response from the U.S. policy community.

The second wave of terrorism began on July 22, 1968, with a Palestinian hijacking of an El Al flight from Rome to Tel Aviv. Shugart explains:

Terrorism was elevated to the international stage over the next two decades as ethno-national movements in the Netherlands, Turkey, and elsewhere attempted to duplicate the Palestinian Liberation Organization's success in galvanizing public opinion. Fueled by opposition to the Vietnam War ... and anti-Americanism in general, left-wing terrorist groups in Europe and North America ... waged campaigns of political assassinations, bombings, and hijackings that continued until the fall of the Berlin Wall.[4]

Violence in this wave was a truly international experience, as almost every corner of the globe was affected by some antiestablishment or antigovernment group, and targets shifted from political and military targets to include civilian populations. With U.S. interests being targeted, we begin to see responses from the U.S. government.

Shugart highlights the 1979 Iranian Revolution as the beginning of the third wave of terrorism, which is dominated by radical, extremist Islamic groups. Two key grievances fuel the third wave of terrorism: anger over the creation of the Israeli state after World War II and contempt for blasphemers and "betrayers of Islam." For Shugart, the Afghan War was particularly important due to the fact that resources expended by both the United States and Soviet Union provided skills and training that would ultimately give rise to the Taliban, al-Qaeda, and Osama bin Laden. It is in response to this third wave of terrorism that we have observed the most dramatic shifts in homeland security and terrorism policy, particularly following the events of 9/11. As we discuss the major policy changes in more detail, we will more explicitly discuss the role of external events in affecting proposed changes.

Public

Many of the policy changes related to homeland security and terrorism deal with some restrictions on civil liberties. Americans are typically very supportive of democratic values and civil liberties in the abstract.[5] In fact, support is so high that many survey organizations do not even ask these types of questions in surveys. However, another important finding is that support in practice tends to be much lower, particularly in a context of threat.[6]

According to Merolla and Zechmeister, conditions of national security threat elicit a range of negative emotions, such as anxiety, fear, and even anger.[7] In order to cope with the negative emotions that arise from the threat context, individuals may adopt a number of coping strategies, some of which are relevant for politics. One way in which individuals seek to cope with the threat is to become more authoritarian, which enables them to feel a greater sense of control. With respect to the policies we explore in this chapter, this means that they will be more inclined to support civil liberties tradeoffs in the name of security, and will be more inclined to support restrictions on liberties for out-groups. Another coping strategy is to look for a leader to save them from the crisis context and throw their support behind that leader. In the U.S. context, we would therefore expect citizens to rally around the president when they are concerned about national security threats.

With respect to the first strategy of coping, a long line of literature demonstrates that individuals become more negative toward out-groups in times of national security threat. For example, in his classic study of political tolerance, Stouffer showed that those in the United States who perceived a higher threat from Communists exhibited lower levels of tolerance.[8] We see a similar pattern on the issue of terrorism. For example, Huddy and colleagues[9] demonstrated a relationship between those with high levels of worry about future attacks and willingness to increase surveillance on Arabs and Arab Americans, increase security checks on Arab visitors, and decrease visas to Arab countries. Scholars also find that individuals are more willing to trade civil liberties for more security in a context of national security crisis.[10] For example, Huddy et al. showed that individuals worried about national terrorist attacks were more supportive of a national identification card, government monitoring of phones and email, and were more concerned that government would not enact strong enough antiterrorism measures.[11]

With respect to the second means of coping with threat, there is a vast array of evidence that sitting presidents receive a boost in approval, across many issue domains, when there is a dramatic foreign policy event.[12] Scholars have documented a similar relationship between terrorist attacks and approval of the president.[13] At least with respect to terrorism, extant research has found that Republican incumbents, in particular George W. Bush, have benefited not just following 9/11, but even under conditions in which terror threat was salient.[14] We would therefore expect to see that the public is likely to be very supportive of the president whenever the threat of terrorism is highly salient, which should improve the president's chances of making policy changes.

Political Elites

The presence of a threat combined with strong public support often results in major policy changes being drafted by the president along with the bureaucracy with strong bipartisan support in Congress. There are several reasons why we observe this pattern among political elites. For one, as commander in chief of the military, the public, as well as other elites, look to presidential leadership in the context of a salient threat such as terrorism. Second, because much of the expertise on national security lies with the executive branch, other elites are more likely to defer on matters related to national security interests. The president is therefore expected to be ready with a plan of action to defend the nation and its interests, both domestically and abroad. Third, there is generally a sense among elites that in a time of threat it is important to maintain a sense of cohesion to ease concerns among the public. Finally, it is not generally in the interests of Congress to challenge the president on national security policy, particularly early in the stages of a crisis context.

To elaborate on the first two points, the public often rallies behind the sitting president whenever there is a security threat. As we articulated, in this type of context the public looks to a leader to save them from the crisis context, and they are inclined to throw support to the sitting president.[15] Even other political elites will look to the president to take the lead on national security issues. According to the two-presidencies thesis, first articulated by Wildavsky, Congress is likely to defer to the president on foreign policy (but not in the domestic policy arena), in part due to the possession of privileged information, expanded powers in foreign affairs, weak foreign policy opposition, and the zero-sum nature of

international affairs.[16] Furthermore, in the event of an actual crisis, the legislative process is generally not swift enough to have a careful consideration and
deliberation on "needed" policy changes, so they will tend to defer to the
president and bureaucracy in crafting policy in this arena. Often, the two-
presidencies thesis suggests a depoliticized process. As Goldstein notes in
Chapter 9, trade foreign policy is bipartisan, not unlike security policy.
However, partisan tensions arise in trade policy when elites discuss domestic
distribution of trade benefits, similar to contentious debates over externalities
resulting from antiterrorism measures.

Related to the second point, the president often relies heavily on the
bureaucracy in crafting national security legislation and policies because
they have the highest level of expertise in this issue area. As Kingdon argued
long ago, the bureaucracy often has policy solutions ready when a policy
problem arises.[17] This has particularly been the case in contexts of national
security threat. According to Naftali, low- and mid-level meetings among
bureaucrats have been taking place since the start of Nixon's presidency,
ready to address the perceived growing threat of substate actors. The role of
the bureaucracy intensified, as the threat of terrorism grew larger in the 1990s
and into the 2000s.[18]

On the third and fourth points, at the onset of any national security incident,
we typically see consensual policies and messages sent by elites. According to
Relyea, immediately after a terrorist attack, Congress may provide undivided,
bipartisan support as a sign of solidarity.[19] Congress may also agree in principle
with the policies forwarded by the president or bureaucracy in order to
strengthen a sense of national security. In times of crisis, dissent may only add
to the public sense of panic and chaos, and a united front serves to bolster the
mood of the people. The rhetoric during these times highlights the need for all
Americans to come together to confront the threat. Opposition, regardless of
partisanship or ideology, to this sentiment is perceived as a threat to group
cohesion; from a practical standpoint this may doom a political career.
Members of Congress concerned with reelection would therefore not be very
inclined to go against a president with high levels of popular support. Previous
studies have shown that public opinion and congressional support can reflect
"rally around the flag" effects, elevating bipartisan support on security measures
and impacting public opinion favorably toward the president.[20] We generally do
not observe any challenges to presidential policies until later in the crisis, as
public support for conflict might wane.[21] We should note that these effects,
especially early in a crisis, can obtain even in otherwise highly partisan contexts.
After all, dramatic changes were made to homeland security policy with hardly
any congressional opposition after the events of 9/11, even though the period
was characterized by high levels of party polarization.[22]

Just as partisanship tends to be weaker given a salient homeland security
threat, interest groups are also typically weaker than they are in the domestic
policy arena. Interest group actions might arise when the threat has receded,

especially if proposed policies start to intersect with domestic politics and have negative residual effects on certain groups.[23] For example, Haney and Vanderbush show how the Cuban American National Foundation formed in reaction to post–Cold War U.S. foreign policy interactions with Cuba, primarily due to adverse domestic impacts on Cuban American community.[24]

Later in the chapter, we will carefully consider the role of the president, bureaucracy, and Congress for each major policy change in homeland security and terrorism policy that we identified. Important for our purposes will be to see whether the trend of presidential leadership and bipartisan congressional support holds across most of the policy changes.

GENERAL LOOK AT MAJOR POLICY CHANGES

We began the process of identifying major policy changes by searching on the govtrack.us Web site, THOMAS online, Congressional Quarterly, and the House and Senate online roll-call records using the following search terms: "security," "terrorism," "safety," "threat," "homeland," and "defense." After developing a comprehensive list of bills, we selected policies for analysis by consulting *Congressional Quarterly*'s list of critical pieces of legislation, and those pieces of legislation most identified throughout existing literature by scholars on history and counterterrorism, such as Falkenrath and Naftali. Policies were further filtered based on the degree to which the policy represented major changes to both governmental affairs *and* daily public life. This excludes laws such as chemical and biological weapons acts, which specifically target wartime combat conduct, and funding measures specifically for programs isolating international counterterrorism.

This process revealed nine major proposed policy changes to homeland security and terrorism policy. All of these laws are listed in Table 11.1.

TABLE 11.1. *List of Major Policy Changes*

Year	Policy
1947	National Security Act
1974	Anti-Hijacking Bill
1985	International Security and Development Cooperation Act (Sky Marshals)
1988	Terrorist Firearms Detection (via Omnibus Drug Control Act)
1989	Comprehensive Airport Security
1994	Violent Crime and Law Enforcement Act
2001	Aviation Security Act
2001	PATRIOT Act
2002	Homeland Security Act

Before we turn to a detailed discussion of each policy, we note some general patterns on our primary factors. First, almost all of these proposed major changes followed on the heels of terrorist attacks targeting U.S. interests. The only exceptions include the National Security Act in 1947, which was a reaction to WWII, and the aviation security measures during the 1980s, which were not responses to a specific event but a string of ongoing terrorist incidents, notably attacks abroad. With respect to the public, available public opinion data shows strong support for the policies, as well as strong support for the president around the time legislation was being considered. Finally, the majority of the major policy changes were initiated by the president, in close consultation with the bureaucracy, and strong bipartisan support in Congress.

To preview some of this pattern, Tables 11.2 and 11.3 show levels of bipartisan support for the major policies identified above, for the House and Senate, respectively. Two exceptions, however, are reflected in this data. One notable exception is the Violent Crime and Law Enforcement Act of 1994, which passed but not with much bipartisan support. Furthermore, the aviation security measures in the 1980's are also a slightly different case since some of the measures did not get a final vote in the Senate, one of the few failed attempts at national security and homeland security policy. We discuss these exceptions more in the next section, where we detail each major policy change.

TABLE 11.2. *U.S. House Votes on Major Policy Changes*

Policy	Dem Vote Yes	Dem Vote No	Rep Vote Yes	Rep Vote No	Total Yes	Total No
Anti-Hijacking Bill	198	2	156	0	354	2
International Security and Development Cooperation Act	152	92	110	69	262	161
Terrorist Firearms Detection (via Omnibus Drug Control Act)	196	11	150	0	346	11
Aviation Security Act of 1989	248	2	144	29	392	31
Violent Crime and Law Enforcement Act	188	64	46	131	234	195
Aviation and Transportation Security Act	200	0	207	9	407	9
PATRIOT Act	145	62	210	3	357	66
Homeland Security Act	88	120	206	10	294	130

TABLE 11.3. *U.S. Senate Votes on Major Policy Changes*

Policy	Dem Vote Yes	Dem Vote No	Rep Vote Yes	Rep Vote No	Total Yes	Total No
Anti-Hijacking Bill	41	0	32	0	75	0
International Security and Development Cooperation Act	35	11	69	8	75	19
Terrorist Firearms Detection (via Omnibus Drug Control Act)	49	1	38	2	87	3
Aviation Security Act of 1989	N/A	N/A	N/A	N/A	N/A	N/A
Violent Crime and Law Enforcement Act	55	2	6	36	61	38
Aviation and Transportation Security Act	50	0	49	0	99	0
PATRIOT Act	48	1	49	0	98	1
Homeland Security Act	41	8	48	0	89	8

DETAILED EXAMINATION OF POLICY CHANGES

National Security Act of 1947

The National Security Act of 1947 represented a major change in the policy direction of the United States. The various branches of the military would be unified into the National Military Establishment, later to become the Department of Defense, and the most critical aspect of this law was the creation of the CIA. This law represented a major policy change because, as Hansen points out, intelligence had previously been perceived to be a wartime event; the CIA would conduct business during peacetime as well, and would become a critical player in the fight against domestic and international terrorism.[25] The chapter by Immerman (Chapter 10) provides a very rich and detailed review of the politics that led to the National Security Act of 1947, so we will not reiterate them here. All we will add is that the adoption of the law reflects many of the forces that we have noted. First, it was in response to lessons learned after the bombing of Pearl Harbor and the growing communist threat.[26] That being said, because the threat was not as imminent, the president did face some tensions with Congress and the bureaucracy.[27] As Immerman details, although congress agreed that streamlining and strengthening intelligence gathering was important, they were hesitant to overly empower an executive department, and different departments in the bureaucracy were concerned with protecting their budgets.

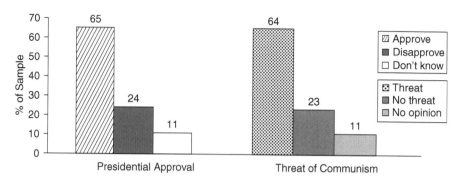

FIGURE 11.2. Presidential Approval and Perceiving Communism as a Threat, May 1947
Source: Gallup

Congress certainly had an incentive to work with the president because public opinion at the time showed concern about the threat of communism and strong support for Truman. Figure 11.2 shows Gallup data on Truman's presidential approval ratings around the time of this legislation and public opinion on the threat of communism. Truman's approval ratings were quite high, at 65 percent, and 64 percent of the public perceived communism as a credible threat to the United States. Thus, the president certainly had leverage with Congress and the bureaucracy in pushing this major policy change, and a compromise was ultimately reached before the bill reached the floor.

Anti-Hijacking Bill of 1974

We do not observe another major change to homeland security and terrorism policy until the mid-1970s. The Anti-Hijacking Bill of 1974 consolidated many of the piecemeal features that had been established since the 1960s, when hijacking quite visibly reemerged into public view. The bill made it a crime to carry weapons onto aircraft, solidified the air marshal program, and made security screenings of passengers and luggage mandatory at all airports. This represented a major change, particularly for the public, because the bill represents the dawn of "inconveniences" for air travel. The bill also represents a moment in which the response to a crisis event highlighted the trade-off between civil liberties and security. Crenshaw suggests that the notion of the invasion of privacy entered the public consciousness because of these mandatory searches.[28]

Certainly, external factors played a significant role in the passage of this bill. Hijackings of American airliners began in 1961, which Hansen explains prompted Congress to pass a law forbidding the possession of weapons on a flight.[29] However, the initial infrequency did not result in further responses from U.S. lawmakers. But the end of the 1960s and early 1970s saw a major spike in the occurrence of airline hijackings. Hansen points out that Fidel Castro quickly viewed hijackings as a way to punctuate his political goals, and subsequently, pro-Castro militants began hijacking American airliners.[30] Nixon reacted quickly to the Cuban-based hijackings, with an emergency directive establishing the air marshal program in 1968.[31] Hansen points to two violent and highly publicized hijackings in the early 1970s prompting further evaluation of the safety and security of American airports.[32] The first was the D.B. Cooper airline hijacking, in which Cooper escaped with $200,000 and simply disappeared. The second involved three armed, violent criminals who overtook a plane and threatened to crash it into a nuclear plant if they were not given $10 million. Naftali points to a third incident, which was a coordinated effort by militant, anti-Israel Palestinian extremists to hijack four airplanes in order to disseminate their political goals.[33] After letting the passengers go, the terrorists detonated explosives inside, completely destroying the plane. In response to these events, Nixon issued another emergency directive in 1973, initiating the first iteration of airline security screenings of passengers and their luggage, but with such threats failing to recede, more comprehensive solutions were sought through legislation.

The president, along with the bureaucracy, played a vital role in the Anti-Hijacking Bill. Nixon's executive orders for airport security and his successful 1972 pact with Cuba to reduce the number of air hijackings gave him fuel to pressure Congress to pass airport security legislation.[34] The bill was primarily formulated by consolidating Nixon's directives establishing the air marshal program and mandating that all airports screen all passengers and luggage. An interagency counterterrorism group, comprised of representatives from the CIA and Federal Bureau of Investigation, which met regularly starting in 1972,[35] privately briefed the president on terrorism developments and made recommendations on the validity of threats while also submitting appropriate covert and overt responses. Other members of the bureaucracy, particularly those dealing with airline regulations, were less receptive. Bailey points to congressional and private pressure throughout the 1960s and 1970s on regulatory agencies to keep government interference in airline affairs to a minimum, as the focus was on cost reduction and efficiency.[36]

Although the bill had bipartisan support, Crenshaw points out that it also had some critics.[37] Congressional opponents were concerned about the logistics of the plan, fearing both the cost and the simple ability to effectively carry out searches without creating massive delays. However, the far more immediate threat of future hijackings created enough bipartisan support in order to push this bill through with almost unanimous support in both chambers, 354-2 in the House and 75-0 in the Senate.

These votes illustrate the relative weakness of party tensions with respect to domestic security policy. McCormick and Wittkopf analyze congressional voting patterns during the Cold War and point out moments of bipartisanship.[38] Overall, the Nixon presidency had relatively strong bipartisanship on foreign policy, with generally equal amounts of support from liberals and conservatives. Essentially in the thick of the Cold War, policy makers seemed to agree that security and containment were of utmost importance, and were willing to put aside budget concerns, which may have led to more partisan division.

It is likely that elected officials were also reacting to support for Nixon and public opinion on hijackings. Nixon's approval ratings were in the 57 percent to 62 percent range around the time of his directives and around the time during which the Anti-Hijacking Bill was passed. He therefore had enough perceived popularity to push for legislation. The available public opinion data showed that individuals wanted stiff penalties for hijackers, suggesting enough concern existed regarding airline safety. A 1970 poll by the Gallup organization asked respondents what they felt was an appropriate penalty for multiple crimes. A vast majority of the public thought that hijackers should face a harsh sentence (including more than ten years in prison up through death), whereas only 26 percent indicated less than ten years in prison. Two years after passage of the act, as hijackings continued, the public registered even stronger opinions. In a Cambridge Reports/National Omnibus Survey in July of 1976, 75 percent of respondents agreed with the following statement: "The tremendous increase in airplane hijacking and other forms of random violence and terrorism only show that if these terrorist groups had nuclear weapons they would not hesitate to use them." In a Harris Survey that same year, 74 percent of the sample thought the United States should take the lead in setting up an international police force that would crack down on hijackers and guerrillas who take violent action around the world. These opinions reflect not only the sense of threat that the public perceived from the hijackings, but also the tendency to adopt more authoritarian attitudes in the presence of threat. They also certainly foreshadow the public's support of the more intense policies that would be instituted post-9/11.

Aviation Security Legislation in the 1980s

Legislation during the 1970s would certainly not be the last iteration of airline security measures. Three pieces of legislation sought to further bolster security at airports in the 1980s. Under Reagan, the 1985 International Security and Development Cooperation Act expanded the scope and enforcement powers of the sky marshals. The Terrorism Firearms Detection Act, started under Reagan's tenure and meant to address gun restrictions, would end up folded into other legislation during the next administration. Under Bush, The Aviation Security Act of 1989 would attempt to encompass two vital provisions that had been debated throughout the 1980s: the gun restrictions of the Terrorism Firearms Detection Act, and broader research funding for airport security technology such as improved metal detectors and scanners. These were important developments because, as Crenshaw and Bailey note, the trend of increased government intervention into airports continued into the 1980s.[39] Bailey explains that this trend went against private interests that sought to reduce government involvement in airline business.[40] Furthermore, the advent of metal detectors as a security measure continued the discussion about the tradeoffs between security and privacy.

Yet again, external events triggered continued attention to security concerns. Cooper and Crenshaw point to the increasingly violent and indiscriminant nature of airline hijackings.[41] Rather than hostage situations, hijackers sought to create as much destruction and chaos as possible, often by taking explosives on board and detonating the aircraft. Hansen paints the Palestinian hijacking and destruction of four planes as a precursor to developments in the 1980s.[42] At that time, the highest profile incident was the Lockerbie bombing, in which terrorists hijacked a plane and set off explosives midair, killing all 259 passengers. These incidents seemed to enter the public consciousness. There were sharp declines in airline travel during the 1980s, and this had a strong economic impact on tourism-related businesses.[43] A majority of Americans polled consistently viewed terrorism as either a serious or very serious threat.[44] That being said, there was not a specific event that prompted the legislation in the 1980s.

According to Naftali's analysis, Reagan played a significant role on homeland security during the 1980s. Initially, low- and mid-level intelligence meetings occurred weekly, as far back as the Nixon administration, regarding terrorism. He contends, however, that terrorism was viewed as a politically volatile issue, and the high-level bureaucrats shielded the president from the plans and recommendations of these weekly briefings.[45] This changed with the escalating magnitude of terrorist incidents. Responding to increased public concern over terrorism, Reagan upgraded the role of his counterterrorism experts to inform domestic and international security policy. In response to the escalating international violence of the Abu Nidal organization, Reagan sought a stronger mandate for counterterrorism in general. Duane Clarridge, a high-ranking CIA official, sought to expand the offensive scope of the CIA while also enabling a stronger informative role directly to the president. And, in this round of aviation legislation, the airline regulatory agencies seemed much more receptive to changes, in part because the destructiveness of terrorist incidents created a much more damaging economic threat to the airlines.[46]

One major piece of legislation that Reagan pushed for during his term was the International Security and Development Cooperation Act, which expanded and enhanced the sky marshall program originally set forth in the Nixon administration. This bill also contained measures on international counterterrorism and foreign aid for democratic development. Reagan had a high degree of political capital when pushing this bill forward in that public concern about terrorism was elevated and his approval ratings, according to Gallup polls, were in the high 50s and low 60s range. Although there was broad support for the sky marshall aspect of the bill on Capitol Hill, some members of Congress were less enthusiastic about the foreign policy aspects, particularly those that dictated which countries would receive development aid and which were isolated as adversarial.[47] Still in the shadow of the Cold War, a coalition of Democratic and Republican members of Congress had difficulty supporting development in Third World countries, particularly those that had previously shown hostilities to democracy. Republicans viewed aid in this sense as taking a softer approach in foreign policy; Democrats had issues supporting human rights violators. The nature of development assistance for democratically questionable states was a volatile issue, particularly given that the Iran-Contra scandal would soon rock the headlines. Therefore, although the bill passed by a comfortable margin in both chambers (House vote 262-161, Senate vote 75-19), it did not have the near unanimous support that is characteristic of some of the other policy changes.

The next important piece of legislation on terrorism and homeland security in the 1980s was the Terrorism Firearms Detection Act, during Reagan's tenure. German weapon manufacturers had begun producing guns made almost entirely out of plastic, from small pistols to submachine guns. These weapons were lauded for their light weight, but could pass through metal detectors without setting off alarms. Weapons of this nature were transported by the drug cartels and utilized by terrorists in their hijackings. The intent of the proposed bill was to set a minimum metal component standard for imported and exported guns into the United States. Even though Reagan's approval ratings had dipped into the low 50s, given strong support for an omnibus drug trafficking law being considered close to this time, the airport weapon bans and terrorist weapons detection act ended up being folded into this legislation, and the omnibus bill became law with almost unanimous support in both chambers on October 21, 1988 (House vote 346-11, Senate vote 87-3). This particular bill was also clearly related to security-related concerns and did not dip into existing partisan cleavages, so it enjoyed broad support.

The final proposed policy change, under new president George H.W. Bush, was the comprehensive Aviation Security Act, which provided funding for research and development for detection technology, set minimum standards for security personnel, and included stipulations for continued research, development, and deployment of security technology. The proposed Aviation Security Act was meant to consolidate many piecemeal standards set in motion by the bureaucracy during the 1980s. Additionally, it was meant to be a sign that the government was taking action against the rising magnitude of terrorist violence. Even though Bush had high levels of approval at the time the bill was being considered – in the high 60s – it never reached the Senate for approval, primarily due to debates over the amount of funding. Politicians agreed in principle about the need to bolster airport security. For example, the primary sponsors of the bill emphasized the fact that terrorism was a direct attack on the American people, and that the government should address airport security. Opposition arose in the Ways and Means Committee, where all of the issues centered around how much public funding should be relegated to the airports in the form of research and development grants. Furthermore, newly elected President Bush opposed excess spending in order to be consistent with his conservative fiscal policy. Although the Aviation Security Act did not reach a Senate vote, agencies and subagencies within the bureaucracy began more vigilantly implementing and enforcing safety recommendations, such as mandating metal detectors. At that time, the bill unofficially went into effect; the only pieces missing were federal grants into technological research.

Partisan divisions played a more prominent role in homeland security legislation during this time period compared to the legislation during the 1970s. Under Reagan, the vote on the International Security and Development Cooperation Act was not near unanimous, and the Aviation Security Act under Bush did not make it to a Senate vote. We believe two key features of the legislation in the 1980s may have accounted for this observation. First, bipartisan support is often strongest in reaction to a crisis event. Proposed policy changes during this time period were not in response to a particular event, but rather a looming threat, and were more proactive in nature. Second, Souva and Rohde found strong partisan divisions in foreign policy throughout the 1980s, particularly in areas involving defense and security.[48] This coupled with the fact that many of the policies spilled over into domestic politics, particularly partisan debates over government spending, created a more partisan climate on homeland security policy. Given the blending of foreign and domestic policy, it was less likely that Congress would defer to the president.[49]

Further laying the foundations for Homeland Security legislation in the twenty-first century, these aviation policies mark the start of convergence under the two-presidencies thesis. As Peppers and Parsons both contend, the realms of foreign and domestic policy could no longer so easily be kept separate. Previously, issues such as airline security could easily be tied to foreign policy. The escalating violence prompted security measures that began encroaching on domestic rights, slowly blurring the line between domestic and foreign policy. These spillover effects and blurred lines weakened the president's ability to drive foreign policy because of the ideological political battles that had to be fought on the domestic dimension.

Violent Crime Control and Law Enforcement Act of 1994

The large publicity of the Unabomber and the first bombing of the World Trade Center were key elements in the passage of the Violent Crime Control and Law Enforcement Act of 1994. The bill was initially aimed at increasing funding for police officers and other bureaucratic reorganizations, but the form of the bill that passed included a great deal of antiterrorism measures. The bill included provisions against aiding and abetting terrorists, falsifying identification documents, and listed terrorism as a capital crime. Furthermore, the bill included language that added further penalties for using nuclear, chemical, or biological weapons in conducting terrorist activity. Also important, yet not directly related to terrorism and homeland security, the act expanded the crimes punishable by death, included a ban on assault weapons, created even harsher penalties for domestic violence against women, contained stricter sentencing guidelines, and included the three strikes law for repeat offenders.

Kim contends that crime control and prevention was a top priority for Clinton during his first term, to counter the perception that Democrats are soft on crime, and this bill initially served this purpose.[50] The bill met with opposition from

Republicans and conservative Democrats, as well as some segments of the public after the highly publicized Rodney King incident. Survey and experimental data reflect backlash against law enforcement due to perceptions of racial discrimination on the part of police officers in the King incident, which forced Clinton to reframe the bill as crime prevention instead of punishment.[51] In Congress, the provisions for stricter penalties in the bill enticed conservatives but was opposed by liberals in Clinton's party; on the other hand, provisions for greater gun control and pork spending for youth programs fostered tensions from the very same conservatives but appealed to members of Clinton's own party. Passage of the bill therefore was going to be an uphill battle.

The first bombing of the World Trade Center changed the ball game with respect to this bill. Despite the very salient nature of terrorism as a threat, most actions had occurred abroad, and any domestic events were often dismissed as the isolated actions of a loner. According to Naftali and Zegart, the bombing of the World Trade Center shifted these conceptions.[52]

Cooper points out how, in response to the wave of terrorist incidents, President Clinton received a moment of bipartisan support, and a boost in presidential approval ratings.[53] Immediately after the bombing of the World Trade Center, the president issued a statement that he would turn the full resources of the government to pursuing those responsible and bolstering security for the country. Shortly afterward, antiterrorism language entered the bill, as Clinton viewed a governmental response as a law enforcement issue.[54] Haass notes that elements in the bill on foreign policy and counter-terrorism allowed Clinton to form a congressional support base.[55] Kuzma's analysis further suggests that the terrorist attacks in the early 1990s provided a sizable enough reason for Clinton to effectively sway Congressional opposition into enough support for this bill.[56] For example, Senator Orrin Hatch, one of six Republicans who supported the bill, deflected criticism by noting the antiterrorism language of the bill.[57] Although the bill passed by a comfortable margin (House vote 234-195, Senate vote 61-38), the terrorism provisions alone did not lead to the type of unanimous vote characteristic of some of the other major legislation on homeland security and terrorism.

Public concern about terrorism likely played an important role in persuading some hesitant members of Congress to ultimately support the legislation. Before the World Trade Center bombing, the American public did not view terrorism as a primary concern. However, after the bombing, the public's concern about terrorism increased. In Figure 11.3, we present the public's perceptions of the threat of weapons of mass destruction and terrorism using data from Time/CNN. A majority of the public, 54 percent, perceived an extreme threat from terrorism, whereas only 27 percent perceived a moderate threat. Furthermore, President Clinton's approval rating spiked to 59 percent following the bombing, which afforded him some political capital in pushing through the legislation. Another interesting thing to look at is public approval of Clinton across different issues, which we display in Figure 11.4. Positive perception of

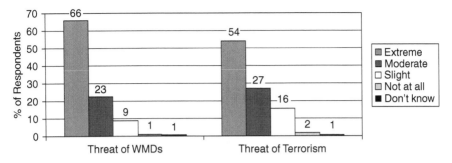

FIGURE 11.3. Perceptions of Terrorist Threat and Weapons of Mass Destruction, 1994
Source: Time/CNN

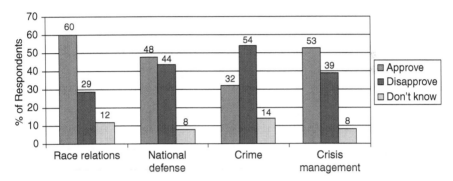

FIGURE 11.4. Clinton Approval on Different Issues
Source: Gallup

Clinton's crisis management style is suggestive of public support with respect to the terrorist incidents. Meanwhile, public perception of Clinton's handling of crime is quite low, suggesting that terrorism played a major role in drumming up enough support to overcome partisan opposition to the bill.

The Violent Crime Control and Law Enforcement Act represents an interesting moment in the intersection of the two-presidencies thesis. Although major portions of this law addressed security issues that can be traced to foreign policy, other aspects touched more on domestic crime policy. Thus, Clinton was able to use the blurring of foreign and domestic policy to aid in passing a domestic policy priority that otherwise would have failed.

Legislation after 9/11

On September 11, 2001, terrorists hijacked airplanes, crashing two into the World Trade Center and one into the Pentagon. An additional hijacked plane did not make it to its intended target, with passengers fighting their captors;

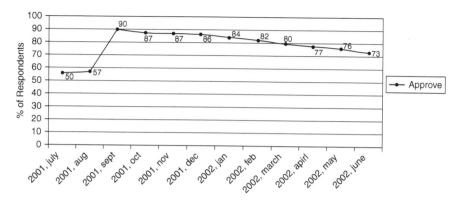

FIGURE 11.5. Bush II Approval Ratings
Source: Gallup

unfortunately, that plane and its passengers would also be lost in Shankesville, PA. Estimates suggest that nearly 3,000 people lost their lives in the most devastating and coordinated terrorist attacks on U.S. soil. This major external event sparked several pieces of legislation to deal with protecting the homeland in the face of a continued threat of terrorism. The event also led to a proactive campaign to target terrorists abroad, leading most notably to the Afghanistan war, but also to drone attacks in Pakistan and Yemen, and it was also used as a justification for the Iraq war.

As Merolla and Zechmeister document, worry about terrorism was high in the immediate aftermath of 9/11 and stayed fairly high through much of 2007.[58] The public showed a huge increase in support for George W. Bush following the events of 9/11. In Figure 11.5, we can see that Bush's approval ratings jumped from 57 percent in August 2001 to 90 percent in September 2001. The approval rating showed a slow decline over time, but remained in the 70s throughout 2002. Most of the major changes to homeland security and terrorism policy that transpired occurred in the window from 2001 to 2002. With such strong support from the public and the threat of terrorism very salient, it is not surprising that many of the major pieces of legislation met with little opposition in Congress.

PATRIOT Act

The PATRIOT Act, signed into law on October 26, 2001, was a measure that sought to enhance the enforcement arm of the American government. This bill allowed the Department of Justice and the Department of Homeland Security (DHS) to restrict information that was once viewed as public such as non-disclosure of the names of individuals who were detained and closure of immigration hearings. The bill also restricted due process for individuals deemed to be of interest due to potential terrorism links, gave law enforcement the ability to suspend habeas corpus if the individual is deemed to be an enemy national due to suspected terrorist activity, and expanded the Foreign Intelligence Surveillance Act for wiretaps, electronic, and physical searches. In short, the bill massively expanded powers through which the government could monitor and detain individuals on nothing more than a suspicion of terrorist activity.[59]

Reports quickly arose about the rampant spread of racial profiling and discrimination. Baker notes that just eight weeks after the passage of the act, 1,147 individuals were detained under the provisions of the PATRIOT Act; another 5,000 were interrogated to reportedly such varying degrees that John Ashcroft had to make a public statement defending against public accusations of racial profiling; and the Bush administration had yet to formally declare a "War on Terror," instead only isolating Al-Qaeda as the primary target.[60]

President Bush enjoyed a great deal of congressional and public support for this legislation in the early stages after the attacks. Farrier notes unanimous congressional agreement with Bush that the scope of the executive needed to be expanded in order to sufficiently address vulnerabilities of the system.[61] Bush spearheaded the movement to get support, but relied on the expertise of the bureaucracy to formulate the specific legislation.

Masci and Marshall point out relatively little opposition to expanding the scope of the federal government to address terrorism.[62] Attorney General John Ashcroft played a major role initiating bureaucratic restructuring meant to bolster investigative methods and detain suspects. Masci and Jost further highlight the relative ease with which Congress accepted these proposals.[63] The PATRIOT Act ultimately endowed the bureaucracy with most of Ashcroft's recommendations, due to pressures to appear tough and decisive on antiterrorist programs. In conjunction with the Homeland Security Act, the PATRIOT Act was deemed a necessary step in order to provide powerful tools for the newly reorganized bureaucracy. Ashcroft not only had a strong hand in formulating much of the legislation, but also lobbied hard for quick passage of the bill.

Farrier notes that, rather than acting as the gatekeeper of debate and deliberation, much of the negotiation behind the PATRIOT Act took place in the 11th hour (House vote 357-66, Senate Vote 98-1).[64] The bill was almost unanimously supported by both chambers; with only sixty-two House Democrats and three House Republicans opposing the bill, and only one member of the Senate, Democrat Russ Feingold, who cited violations of civil liberties. Because of political and social pressures to swiftly and decisively address terrorism, Farrier suggests that the normal process of negotiation would be sidestepped in the interest of national security, and Congress essentially skirted their immediate duties in the hopes of being able to review and modify the law after the fact.[65]

Overall, public opinion data suggests that, in the aftermath of the terrorist attacks, Americans were willing to make sacrifices in order to bolster security.

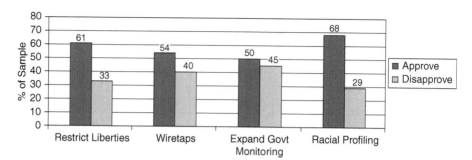

FIGURE 11.6. Support for Elements Relevant to the PATRIOT Act, September 2001
Source: LA Times 09/13/01

Figure 11.6 shows data from an *LA Times* poll of the nation taken on Sept. 13. The results show that 61 percent of respondents were willing to sacrifice civil liberties in order to achieve these ends; 54 percent supported the use of wiretaps, 50 percent supported expanding the government's role in information and technological monitoring; and a surprising 68 percent of the sample supported the use of racial profiling. A few years after passage, polling organizations began to ask more directly about the PATRIOT Act, and support was also high. In a Fox News/Opinion dynamics poll in July 2003, 55 percent of the sample indicated that the PATRIOT Act is a good thing for America, whereas only 27 percent said it was a bad thing for America. In a Gallup/CNN/*USA Today* poll in August 2003, 48 percent of the sample indicated that the PATRIOT Act is about right in the degree to which it restricts civil liberties in order to fight terrorism, whereas 21 percent said is does not go far enough (only 22 percent said too far). As we noted earlier, scholarly research has demonstrated a strong link between worry about terrorist attacks and a willingness to trade liberty for more security.[66] Even as of February 2011, in a PEW weekly interest news poll, a plurality of the public, 42 percent said that the PATRIOT Act is a necessary tool to fight terrorism, compared to 34 percent who say it goes too far and poses a threat to civil liberties (11 percent say do not know).

Aviation and Transportation Security Act

The Aviation and Transportation Security Act, signed into law on November 19, 2001, entailed a complete overhaul of the aviation system. Hansen and Bailey both outline how the act substantially increased government oversight of airport security. Airport screeners became government employees under the Transportation Security Authority, far stricter guidelines of screenings would be implemented, extra airline taxes and fees were added to ticket prices, and for a time, a military presence could be seen at every airport.[67] The entirety of the law represented a massive paradigm shift for the public and airline businesses. On the business side, this piece of legislation represented more encroachment of the government into private affairs, but with due cause. For the public, new guidelines further encroached on civil liberties. Individuals were required to unpack their luggage in order to conduct screenings, which many saw as a violation of their privacy. Baker highlights numerous cases of racial profiling as security personnel targeted individuals from certain racial and ethnic backgrounds for "extra" screening procedures, which sometimes entailed hours of detention in airport holding areas coupled with interrogations.[68]

Bureaucratic experts played a key role in helping formulate the legislation. Even before the events of 9/11, Zegart suggests that members of the bureaucracy had anticipated a need for reorganization.[69] Counterterrorism working groups included airport safety as part of their systemic analysis, including recommendations on both intelligence and domestic security reform. Thus, plans had already existed for strengthening and reorganization, but were stymied pre-9/11 by old-guard resistance.[70] Thus, in the wake of the attacks, solutions were already available and had been waiting to attach themselves to a problem, very akin to Kingdon's classic treatment of policy making.[71]

President Bush ardently spearheaded the passage of all antiterrorism legislation immediately after 9/11, and the Aviation and Transportation Security Act would be no different. The pursuit of aviation legislation followed roughly the same path as the PATRIOT Act, although some debate over the details occurred in Congress. One key contention was whether security training, screening, and background checks should take precedent or whether the focus should be on developing better technology. In any event, however, Congress recognized the immediacy of the situation and passed the law with an eye toward modifications in the future (House Vote 407-9, Senate Vote 99-0).

Given the close proximity of all counterterrorism legislation immediately after the attacks on 9/11, public opinion essentially acted in a similar fashion for all of these pieces of legislation. Fear of travel was clearly revealed in that the volume of domestic flights dropped by nearly 40 percent in the days and weeks after 9/11.[72] Furthermore, survey data show that Americans had serious concerns about the safety and security of the country while also demanding that the government act even if it meant sacrificing civil liberties. Other questions from the *LA Times* poll taken a few days after 9/11 suggest that individuals were quite dissatisfied with the status of aviation security. For example, 82 percent of the sample disapproved of airport security. At the same time, 95 percent of the sample approved of the new airport security measures. These public opinion trends show that in the aftermath of a crisis event, individuals resoundingly supported stricter security protocols at airports. Although there has not been another attack on U.S. soil since 9/11, several foiled attacks on U.S. planes have meant that the public remains accepting of more intensive screening, with the most recent addition being body scanners.

Homeland Security Act

The Homeland Security Act, signed into law on November 25, 2002, reorganized the government in a number of significant ways. Donley and Pollard explain that the creation of the DHS sought to streamline the avenues of communication between all of the major branches of law enforcement and intelligence gathering.[73] This umbrella was also meant to have a direct line to inform the president on the most current trends and events related to counterterrorism and the security of domestic interests. The creation of the DHS also entailed a restructuring of law enforcement, as the act created a new dimension of security to law enforcement. Donley notes the call for unified goals and strategies starting from the DHS and downward to all the agencies and subagencies now reorganized under the DHS. The unification of these agencies is significant given the disjointed and disconnected nature of law enforcement and intelligence gathering before 9/11, which some argue contributed to the security failure in preventing the airline hijackings.[74] The Homeland Security Act also had a significant impact on the American public. Before 9/11, no one had even conceived of the notion of "homeland security"; the term rapidly became ubiquitous and the publicized focus on intelligence failure and the need for vigilance made sacrifices for the sake of security much more palatable.[75]

President Bush played a significant role in pursuing this legislation. Gordon underscores the role of the executive in providing organization, management, control, and coordination in response to a crisis of national security.[76] President Bush acted in such a manner, decisively pushing for legislation to address the failures of the previous system, simultaneously using national security directives to speed up legislation to comprehensively attend to the wide range of issues created by the terrorist attacks. The legislation itself was developed given recommendations from the bureaucracy. According to Wise, an evaluation committee pointed out the disjointed nature of the intelligence and security apparatus and recommended the creation of a unifying agency to streamline the process.[77]

Wise further notes that Congress was not as willing to unanimously support legislation that was simply placed in front of them, especially one creating a new department.[78] Although they agreed that an overhaul of the system was necessary, Congress played the role of the debate forum over the proper ways to address security and intelligence. Even though the concept of agency unification was agreeable in theory, members of both parties gave pause as to the degree, and there were some debates over the allocation of funding.[79] The general public seemed receptive to calls for reorganization. In the LA Times poll cited earlier, 51 percent of respondents disapproved of the current state of American intelligence, and by November 2002, a Gallup poll reported a 60 percent approval rating for Director Tom Ridge. However, there was labor union opposition to certain provisions of the bill, namely further limits on whistleblower protections and collective bargaining rights.[80] That being said, the bill received a fairly high level of bipartisan support (House vote 229-121, Senate Vote 89-8).

The political landscape surrounding the bill helps explain the high levels of bipartisan support, even in light of some of the debates that emerged. The bill passed on the heels of the 2002 congressional elections. Jacobson explains that Bush's decisive action immediately after the attacks of 9/11 rallied the nation behind him, which translated into a great deal of momentum for his national security policies and party in the 2002 midterm elections.[81] According to Brook and King, some of the issues surrounding labor union opposition came to the forefront in Senate election battles, as public attention viewed the sides as "national security" versus "workers' rights."[82] Bush backed candidates who supported the bill and labeled those against it – mostly Democrats and a very small number of Republicans – as "unpatriotic." Republicans gained more seats during the election, and as a result, the bill passed with relatively minor concessions given to labor unions.

DISCUSSION AND CONCLUSIONS

We identified nine major policy changes to homeland security and terrorism in the post–WWII era. Only one of these pieces of legislation was not directly relevant to terrorism, the National Security Act, which came on the heels of WWII. However, the CIA would come to play an important role in combatting terrorism in the future, and the creation of the agency was meant to protect homeland security. Most of the important policy changes through the 1970s and 1980s had to do with airport security in light of an increase in the number of hijackings. Policy changes in the 1990s dealt more with harsher sentences for terrorists. The most dramatic changes would come with the devastating events of 9/11, which led to more security reorganization, airport security measures, and policy changes that were more extensive with respect to civil liberty and security tradeoffs.

As we indicated at the start of this chapter, we believe that major policy changes in homeland security and terrorism are often characterized by several characteristics: the presence of a salient external threat, public concern about the threat and strong approval for the president, president-initiated legislation (often in close consultation with the bureaucracy), and bipartisan support in Congress. Across almost all of these pieces of legislation, we find that these characteristics were all present. With so few events, it is difficult to systematically test whether all of these factors need to be present for major policy change. However, the pattern is certainly suggestive, and we only see a few deviations. One important exception was the Aviation Security Act of 1989, which failed to get a vote in the Senate because of funding issues, as well as the other pieces of legislation in the 1980s, only one of which became law as its own bill. However, all three pieces of legislation that were proposed did not coincide with a specific external threat, thus a key factor was missing. Another important exception was the Violent Crime and Law Enforcement Act. One reason why this bill did not follow the standard pattern was that the original bill was geared more toward fighting crime in general, rather than terrorism specifically. In fact, it was only after the World Trade Center bombing that Clinton was able to build a strong enough coalition to pass the legislation through, and mostly because of incorporating the anti-terrorism provisions.

In many ways, these policies are quite different from the route typically taken for domestic policy reform, stemming from the fact that these policies are often emergency responses. Many of the policies were characterized by much higher levels of bipartisan support than is typically seen in domestic policy reform. This bipartisanship broke down in some of the cases in which the president was not acting in response to a particular threat. That congress is often willing to let the president lead in the domain of foreign policy in the presence of a salient threat tends to support the two-presidencies thesis. However, the lines of foreign and domestic policy were blurred in cases in which the external threat was not as salient, and bipartisanship broke down.

In other ways, these changes are similar to general theories of policy change. The president often takes an active role in major policy changes, and this was clear in all of the cases we examined. Furthermore, the president often relied heavily on the bureaucracy, which was already armed with potential solutions, a trend that Kindgon noted in early work on the policy process. Furthermore, these major policy changes were often supported by public opinion, which is also characteristic of major policy changes.

One important feature of these major policy changes is that they have tended to build on each other over time. In times of war, restrictions on civil liberties are usually lifted at the conclusion of hostilities. One problem with the war on terrorism is that there is no clear end date in sight; thus, these policies are more likely to stay on the books.[83] Stone reflects on this quite succinctly:

As we have seen, a saving "grace" of America's past excesses is that they were of "short" duration and that, once the crisis passes, the nation returned to equilibrium. A war of indefinite duration, however, compounds the dangers both by extending the period during which civil liberties are "suspended" and by increasing the risk that "emergency" restrictions will become a permanent fixture of American life.[84]

Since Stone's writing, the Obama administration no longer uses the term "war on terror," and there have been some modifications to some of the policies that are most restrictive of civil liberties. For example, the PATRIOT Act was modified to reinstate some limits on the availability and government accessibility of personal information, particularly of foreign nationals. In 2009, the Supreme Court lamented the ambiguity of the term "enemy combatants," noting it added another complex legal layer as to which rights were afforded to prisoners. Subsequently, the Obama administration dropped usage of the term. Even though there has been some shift back to pre-9/11 policies, almost all of the changes to airport security have remained on the books, and have become arguably more invasive of personal privacy. The DHS is certainly not dissolving anytime soon. So long as the threat of terrorism remains present and salient among the public, it is not likely that these policies will revert to the pre-9/11 period anytime soon.

Notes

1. Cheney made this reference to a Republican fund-raising crowd (*Associated Press*, Oct. 25, 2001).
2. Masci, David, and Patrick Marshall. 2001. "Civil Liberties in Wartime." *Congressional Quarterly Researcher* 14: 1017–1040.
3. Shugart, William II. 2006. "An Analytical History of Terrorism, 1945–2000." *Public Choice* 128(1): 7–39.
4. Ibid., p. 8. Shugart lumps many of the groups such as the Black Panthers or the Italian Red Brigade into such "social justice" groups, explaining that the cultural climate of the 1960s and 1970s emboldened anti-system actors; these individuals "turned their pacifist sympathies for the downtrodden into rage against the imperialist 'system' that oppressed them."
5. Jackman, Mary R. 1978. "General and Applied Tolerance: Does Education Increase Commitment to Racial Integration?" *American Journal of Political Science* 22(2): 302–324; Marcus, George E., John L. Sullivan, Elizabeth Theiss-Morse, and Sandra L. Wood. 1995. *With Malice Toward Some*. New York: Cambridge University Press; McClosky, Herbert. 1964. "Consensus and Ideology in American Politics." *American Political Science Review* 58: 361–382; Stouffer, Samuel. 1955. *Communism, Conformity, and Civil Liberties*. New York: Double Day.
6. Stouffer, Samuel. 1955; Sullivan, John L., James Pierson, and George E. Marcus. 1982. *Political Tolerance and American Democracy*. Chicago: University of Chicago Press; Marcus, George E., et al., 1995.
7. Merolla, Jennifer L., and Elizabeth J. Zechmeister. 2009. *Democracy at Risk: How Terrorist Threats Affect the Public*. Chicago: University of Chicago Press.
8. Stouffer, 1955.
9. Huddy, Leonie, Stanley Feldman, Charles Taber, and Gallya Lahav. 2005. "Threat, Anxiety, and Support of Antiterrorism Policies." *American Journal of Political Science* 49(3): 593–608.
10. Davis, Darren W. 2007. *Negative Liberty: Public Opinion and the Terrorist Attacks on America*. New York: Russell Sage Foundation; Davis, Darren W., and Brian D. Silver. 2004. "Civil Liberties vs. Security: Public Opinion in the Context of the Terrorist Attacks on America." *American Journal of Political Science* 48(1): 28–46; Huddy, et al., 2005; Merolla and Zechmeister, 2009.
11. Huddy, et al., 2005.
12. Bowen, Gordon L. 1989. "Presidential Action and Public Opinion about U.S. Nicaraguan Policy: Limits to the 'Rally Round the Flag' Syndrome." *PS: Political Science and Politics* 22(4): 793–800; Brody, Richard. 1991. *Assessing the President: The Media, Elite Opinion, and Public Support*. Stanford: Stanford University Press; Kernell, Samuel. 1978. "Explaining Presidential Popularity." *American Political Science Review*: 506–522; Mueller, John E. 1970. "Presidential Popularity from Truman to Johnson." *American Political Science Review* 64(1): 18–34; Mueller, John E. 1973. *War, Presidents, and Public Opinion*. New York: John Wiley; MacKuen, Michael A. 1983. "Political Drama, Economic Conditions, and

the Dynamics of Presidential Popularity." *American Journal of Political Science* 27: 165–192; Newman, Brian. 2002. "Bill Clinton's Approval Ratings: The More Things Change, the More They Stay the Same." *Political Research Quarterly* 55: 781–804; Ostrom, Charles W. Jr., and Dennis M. Simon. 1985. "Promise and Performance: A Dynamic Model of Presidential Popularity." *American Political Science Review* 79: 334–358; Ostrom, Charles W. Jr., and Dennis M. Simon. 1989. "The Man in the Teflon Suit: The Environmental Connection, Political Drama, and Popular Support in the Reagan Presidency." *Public Opinion Quarterly* 53: 353–387.

13. Kam, Cindy D., and Jennifer M. Ramos. 2008. "Joining and Leaving the Rally: Understanding the Surge and Decline in Presidential Approval Following 9/11." *Public Opinion Quarterly* 72: 619–650; Hetherington, Marc J., and Michael Nelson. 2003. "Anatomy of a Rally Effect: George W. Bush and the War on Terrorism." *PS: Political Science and Politics* 36: 37–42.

14. Berinksy, Adam J. 2009. *In Time of War: Understanding American Public Opinion from World War II to Iraq.* Chicago: University of Chicago Press; Merolla, Jennifer L., Jennifer M. Ramos, and Elizabeth J. Zechmeister. 2007. "Crisis, Charisma, and Consequences: Evidence from the 2004 U.S. Presidential Election." *Journal of Politics* 69(1): 30–42; Merolla and Zechmeister, 2009.

15. Ibid.

16. Wildavsky, Aaron. 1975. "The Two Presidencies," in Wildavsky, ed. *Perspectives on the Presidency,* New York: Little Brown and Co.

17. Kingdon, John. 1984. *Agendas, Alternatives, and Public Policies.* New York: Little Brown and Co.

18. Naftali, Timothy. 2005. "US Counterterrorism before Bin Laden." *International Journal* 60(1): 25–34.

19. Relyea, Harold. 2003. "Organizing for Homeland Security." *Presidential Studies Quarterly* 33(3): 602–624.

20. Colaresi, Michael. 2007. "The Benefit of the Doubt: Testing an Informational Theory of the Rally Effect." *International Organization* 61(1): 99–143; Norpoth, Helmut, and Sidman, Andrew. 2007. "Mission Accomplished: The Wartime Election of 2004." *Political Behavior* 29(2): 175–195; Oneal, John, and Bryan, Anna. 1995. "The Rally Round the Flag Effect in US Foreign Policy Crises." *Political Behavior* 17(4): 379–401; Casey, Steven. 2002. "Red, White, and Bush." *Foreign Policy* 128: 90–91; Norrander, Barbara, and Clyde Wilcox. 1993. "Rallying Around the Flag and Partisan Change: The Case of the Persian Gulf War." *Political Research Quarterly* 46(4): 759–770; Souva, Mark, and David Rohde. 2007. "Elite Opinion Differences and Partisanship in Congressional Foreign Policy." *Political Research Quarterly* 60(1): 113–123.

21. Mueller, John E. 1973. *War, Presidents, and Public Opinion.* New York: John Wiley.

22. Abramowitz, Alan, and Walter Stone. 2004. "The Bush Effect: Polarization, Turnout, and Activism in the 2004 Election." *Presidential Studies Quarterly* 36(2): 141–154.

23. Clark, David. 2001. "Trading Butter for Guns: Domestic Imperatives for Foreign Policy Substitutes." *The Journal of Conflict Resolution,* 45(5): 637.

24. Haney, Patrick, and Walt Vanderbush. 1999. "The Role of Ethnic Interest Groups in US Foreign Policy: The Case of the Cuban American National Foundation." *International Studies Quarterly* 43(2): 345–346.

25. Hansen, B. 2002. "Future of the Airline Industry." *Congressional Quarterly Researcher* 12: 545–568.
26. Ibid.
27. Stevenson, Charles. 2008. "Underlying Assumptions of the National Security Act of 1947." *Joint Force Quarterly* 48(1): 129–133.
28. Crenshaw, William. 1988. "Civil Aviation: Target for Terrorism." *Annals of the American Academy of Political and Social Science* 498: 60–69.
29. Hansen, 2002.
30. Ibid.
31. Mayer and Price (2002) suggest that presidents are likely to issue executive orders and directives in order to appear strong amidst unexpected emergencies.
32. Ibid.
33. Naftali, 2004.
34. Crenshaw, 1988.
35. Naftali, 2004.
36. Bailey, Elizabeth. 2002. "Aviation Policy: Past and Present." *Southern Economic Journal* 69(1): 12–20; Frederickson, H. George, and Todd R. LaPorte. 2002. "Airport Security, High Reliability, and the Problem of Rationality." *Public Administration Review* 62: 33–43.
37. Crenshaw, 1988.
38. Wittkopf, Eugene, and James McCormick. 1990. "The Cold War Consensus: Did It Exist?" *Polity* 22(4): 627–653.
39. Crenshaw, 1988; Bailey, 2002.
40. Ibid.
41. Cooper, Mary. 1995. "Combating Terrorism." *Congressional Quarterly Researcher* 5: 633–656; Crenshaw, 1988.
42. Hansen, 2002.
43. Cooper, 1995; Crenshaw, 1988.
44. Kuzma, Lynn. 2000. "Trends: Terrorism in the United States." *The Public Opinion Quarterly* 64(1): 90–105.
45. Naftali, 2004.
46. Crenshaw (1988) further explains that improving security efficiency and effectiveness became part of regulatory agencies' mission statements, which was a stark contrast to the hands-off pressures of the past.
47. Naftali, 2004.
48. Souva and Rhode, 2007.
49. Parsons, Karen. 1994. "Exploring the 'Two Presidencies' Phenomenon: New Evidence from the Truman Administration." *Presidential Studies Quarterly* 24(3): 495–514; Peppers, Donald. 1975. "The Two Presidencies: Eight Years Later," in Wildavsky, Aaron (ed.). *Perspectives on the Presidency*, New York: Little Brown and Co, pp. 462–71.
50. Kim, Claire Jean. 2002. "Managing the Racial Breach: Clinton, Black-White Polarization, and the Race Initiative." *Political Science Quarterly* 117(1): 55–79.
51. Sigelman, Lee, et al., 1997. "Police Brutality and Public Perceptions of Racial Discrimination: A Tale of Two Beatings." *Political Research Quarterly* 50(4): 777–791; Holian, David. 2004. "He's Stealing My Issues! Clinton's Crime Rhetoric and the Dynamics of Issue Ownership." *Political Behavior* 26(2): 95–124.

52. Naftali, 2004; Zegart, Amy. 2005. "September 11 and the Adaptation Failure of US Intelligence Agencies." *International Security* 29(4): 78–111.
53. Cooper, 1995.
54. Smith, Sally. 2007. *For Love of Politics: Bill and Hillary Clinton: The White House Years*. New York: Random House.
55. Haass, Richard. 1997. "Fatal Distraction: Bill Clinton's Foreign Policy." *Foreign Policy* 108: 112–123.
56. Kuzma, 2000.
57. CBS, "Face the Nation," August 15, 1993.
58. Merolla and Zechmeister, 2009.
59. The decision to use Guantanamo Bay came after the PATRIOT Act, essentially as a logistical solution that starkly highlights the degree to which civil liberties were sacrificed. The site was chosen because enemy combatants were located outside the legal jurisdiction of the United States, adding another complicated layer to withholding these civil liberties.
60. Baker, Nancy. 2003. "National Security versus Civil Liberties." *Presidential Studies Quarterly* 33(3): 547–567.
61. Farrier, Jasmine. 2007. "The PATRIOT Act's Institutional Story: More Evidence of Congressional Ambivalence." *Political Science and Politics* 40(1): 93–97.
62. Masci and Marshall, 2001.
63. Masci, D., and K. Jost. 2001. "War on Terrorism." *Congressional Quarterly Researcher* 11: 817–848.
64. Farrier, 2007.
65. Ibid.
66. Davis, 2007; Davis and Silver, 2004; Huddy, et al., 2005; Merolla and Zechmeister, 2009.
67. Hansen, 2002; Bailey, 2002.
68. Baker, 2003.
69. Zegart, 2005.
70. Ibid.; Falkenrath, 2001.
71. Kingdon, 1984.
72. Bailey, 2002; Hansen, 2002; Donley, Michael, and Neal Pollard. 2002. "Homeland Security: The Difference between a Vision and a Wish." *Public Administration Review* 62: 138–144.
73. Donley and Pollard, 2002.
74. Wise, Charles. 2002. "Organizing for Homeland Security." *Public Administration Review* 62(2): 131–144; Kady, M. II. 2003. "Homeland Security." *Congressional Quarterly Researcher* 13: 749–772.
75. Donley and Pollard, 2002.
76. Gordon, Vikki. 2007. "'The Law:' Unilaterally Shaping National Security Policy: The Role of National Security Directives." *Presidential Studies Quarterly* 37(2): 349–367.
77. Wise, 2002.
78. Wise, 2002.
79. Kady, 2003.
80. Brook, Douglas, and Cynthia King. 2007. "Civil Service Reform as National Security: The Homeland Security Act of 2002." *Public Administration Review* 67(3): 399–407.

81. Jacobson, Gary. 2003. "Terror, Terrain, and Turnout: Explaining the 2002 Midterm Elections." *Political Science Quarterly* 118(1): 1–22.
82. Brook and King, 2007.
83. Merolla and Zechmeister, 2009.
84. Stone, Geoffrey R. 2004. *Perilous Times: Free Speech in Wartime from the Sedition Act of 1798 to the War on Terrorism.* New York: W.W. Norton and Company, p. 545.

12

Conclusion: Madison Upside Down

The Policy Roots of Our Polarized Politics

Paul Pierson

This book's core theme is the centrality of policy contestation to modern American politics. Of course, policy has always been of tremendous importance. Contests for political office matter because the winners get to exercise (within constitutional limits) authority, allocating value among competing claimants. Throughout the nation's history, core political conflicts have been organized around competing views on policy. Yet Orren and Skowronek are right to stress the distinctive focus on policy as a marker of contemporary politics, and the contributors to this volume rightly follow that lead.[1]

The valuable contributions to this volume explore aspects of this transformation in some of the key policy sectors of modern governance. In this chapter, I take a step back from the narratives of individual policy areas to consider the broad consequences of this transformation – in particular its connection to the emergence of intense partisan contestation. As the chapters in this volume make clear, each policy area has its own distinctive features. Taken as a whole, however, they can help us see how the rise of the "policy state" has altered our politics in fundamental ways.

THE RISE OF THE POLICY STATE

What does it mean to say that the U.S. has become a policy state? The centrality of policy has grown in four key respects.[2] First, it has displaced alternative principles of political organization and contestation. Second, it has expanded tremendously in scale. Third, it has become much more centralized – the policy state in practice increasingly has come to mean Washington. And finally (as a consequence of the first three trends), established policies themselves have become a more central part of the institutional "terrain" on which American politics plays out.

Control over policy is now *the* prize associated with political victory. It has almost entirely supplanted previously important reward structures associated with patronage.³ In earlier eras, patronage created an important contending organizational basis for politics. Political contests were waged over policy, but many important participants in politics viewed "the stakes" that organized competing coalitions in terms of jobs to be filled rather than programs to be enacted or replaced. As scholars have long noted, the decline of patronage helped reorient the parties around programmatic competition.

A second aspect of the shift has been tremendous policy expansion. From the New Deal through the "long 1950s" initiatives explored by Mayhew in Chapter 2, and culminating in the extraordinary bulge of policy initiatives that marked the period from 1965 to 1977, the sheer scale of public policy expanded dramatically. Public spending is a crude indicator, but it provides some sense of the shift. In 1930, total federal outlays were 3.4 percent of gross domestic product. In 2012, they were 22.8 percent.

As the chapters in this volume make abundantly clear, spending is just the tip of the iceberg. The need for vastly greater revenue meant sharply higher tax rates. In turn, higher tax rates meant that every exemption ("tax expenditure") became an increasingly important, if often hidden, form of subsidy. The expanding contours of public policy in the United States took a distinctive path because of the heavy reliance on a tax-subsidized "private welfare state."⁴

At least as important, regulatory policy expanded tremendously beginning in the mid-1960s, with a wave of initiatives directed at consumer, worker, and environmental protection that simultaneously affected multiple sectors of the economy.⁵ The scale of this expansion can be seen in Mayhew's dataset of landmark legislation. Mayhew's data include 330 "major" laws passed between 1947 and 2002.⁶ Of those, fifty-two bills can be classified as mainly regulatory or deregulatory. Almost two-thirds of those fifty-two bills (thirty-four) were passed in just a thirteen-year period, between 1965 and 1977. Put differently, the rate of production of major regulatory laws was more than five times higher during the "bulge" years than in the non-bulge years.

As Farhang and Melnick's chapters discuss (Chapters 3 and 4, respectively), during the same period the "rights revolution" created another thick layer of centralized political authority over matters that had previously been treated as private or local matters. Now, national officials codified the basic structure of key social arrangements, on issues ranging from school integration to the sale of birth control devices to the treatment of criminal defendants and prisoners. Sometimes these public officials were legislators, sometimes bureaucrats. Often they were judges.

As the structure of the rights revolution highlights, it is not just that exercises of political authority became more extensive; they also became much more centralized. Almost by definition, once something is legally enshrined as a right, it becomes a national rather than local matter. Policies might differ between Mississippi and Massachusetts, but rights should not. Of course, many of the issues nationalized in this way concerned matters related to religion, sexuality, race, crime and punishment, and education, on which views were both intensely held and highly diverse across the nation.

Nor was the increasingly active arena of social rights the only area prone to nationalization. During this period, American federalism became much more heavily tilted toward Washington across most areas of policy. National author-ities expanded their role in more and more areas that had been local matters. Even where localities remained important, federal officials were often able to constrain local actions through statutory constraints or financial incentives. Federal grants accounted for more than one-fifth of state and local spending in 2012, compared to less than a tenth in the 1950s.[7]

Finally, a more subtle but fundamental aspect of this transformation is that these extensive new policies themselves became a key feature of the political landscape, a key part of the terrain shaping contestation.[8] Institutionalists in political science have generally concentrated on the formal institutions that establish rules for lawmaking and elections. They have paid less attention to how the extensive policy initiatives of modern polities themselves constitute important structures of rules. An important theme in the current volume is that these extensive new initiatives, once institutionalized, set the terms for future political action. What kinds of strategies made sense depended to a considerable extent on what established policy structures allowed or encouraged.

The rise of the policy state has had huge consequences for American politics – many of which remain underappreciated in a discipline that rarely takes policy as the starting point for analysis. The current volume highlights the manner in which increasingly salient battles over policy reform have spilled into the courts, executive branch, and states. Before exploring these results, however, I wish to highlight the underappreciated connections between the rise of the policy state and two fundamental political transformations – the stunning growth of national policy advocacy and the increasing polarization of the political parties.

OPPORTUNITY AND THREAT: THE INTEREST GROUP REVOLUTION

An explosion of organized advocacy has accompanied the expansion of policy. Causality clearly runs in both directions: advocacy produces policy and policy produces advocacy. Much has been said about the technological and organiza-tional innovations that facilitated increased advocacy, especially among the diffuse interests most vulnerable to the collective action problems famously highlighted in Mancur Olson's work.[9] The second process, however, is usually underappreciated. Public policies can confer substantial resources on specific types of groups, offering direct and indirect financial subsidies as well as organ-izational infrastructure and crucial information on which private actors can rely in their efforts to generate sustained collective action.[10] Terry Moe's study of teachers unions demonstrates the centrality of policy structures to group mobilization.[11] Teachers unions did not emerge naturally and automatically from some set of diffuse programmatic demands that fueled organizing. Instead, they rapidly expanded in the 1960s and 1970s as Democrats in various states (partly pressured by existing unions in other jurisdictions) enacted new collective bargaining laws that greatly facilitated organizing.

The rise of teachers unions is not an isolated case. Working independently, Theda Skocpol and Frank Baumgartner and his collaborators have demonstrated that the conventional story, identifying new group mobilization as the source of the major expansion of federal policy in the late 1960s and early 1970s, has a big part of the story backward.[12] As Skocpol summarizes her findings:

> [A] sudden "bulge" of important legislative enactments started in the late 1950s and peaked in the 1960s and early 1970s. . . . [T]he emergence of thousands of new nationally focused associations followed slightly after heightened federal legislative activism. . . . Tellingly, the same basic dynamic occurred across many specific policy areas, ranging from environmental policy to health care and expanded benefits and new services for older Americans. In each area, innovative federal measures tended to precede the bulk of voluntary group proliferation.[13]

For the most part, the policies came *first*, precipitating the massive expansion of organized citizen activism. They did so by providing resources that helped groups organize, creating greater incentives for groups to do so, and creating focal points for organized activity. Farhang makes the same point with respect to employment discrimination policy in Chapter 3. There, new policy arrangements restructured incentives for private actors, giving rise to a powerful new set of stakeholders and durably shifting the political dynamics of social regulation.

Important as this process of "stakeholder creation" is, it remains only part of the interest group story. Indeed, although this path-dependent dynamic is highly consequential, to see stakeholder creation as the principal story would be to miss the true political significance of the policy state's emergence. The impact of policy on group activity clearly extends well beyond the direct provision of resources to support group formation. As Leech et al. argue, "Government activity acts as a magnet, pulling groups of all kinds to become active."[14] Some of the most important processes involve countermobilization or backlash. New policies create new threats, leading previously dormant or under-organized groups to mobilize more energetically to fight back. As we shall see, a striking feature of contemporary polarization is the intensity of this countermobilization.

There is now strong evidence that this backlash dynamic was the main force at work in producing a vast expansion in the political activities of the business community in the mid- to late 1970s – arguably one of the most important developments in recent American politics.[15] Vogel stresses that the legislative onslaught of the early 1970s – especially the regulatory expansions just described – was critical in triggering a broad, multipronged mobilization on the part of business.[16] As I will discuss presently, other key additions to the organizational landscape of Washington – the National Rifle Association (NRA) and antiabortion groups – were also part of this backlash dynamic.

Thus, by 1980 Washington had been transformed, not just by the vast expansion of policy, but also by a greatly expanded interest group environment. Far more groups with far greater resources sought to influence outcomes in Washington. Crucially, this group expansion was not limited to beneficiaries, but extended to those who rose up to contest the contours of the new policy state.

THE POLICY REVOLUTION AND POLITICAL POLARIZATION

We are a long way from the policymaking style that prevailed during Mayhew's long 1950s, or even the more combative but highly productive legislative struggles of the 1970s, which often culminated in bipartisan compromises. Unlike the long postwar period during which the policy state developed, our more recent politics have been distinguished by frequent legislative stalemate and intensifying partisan conflict.

Political scientists have invested considerable energy in tracking the rise of partisan polarization. Surprisingly limited consideration, however, has been given to how the rise of the policy state may have contributed to the transformation of partisan conflict. I say surprising because the rise of the policy state is pretty obviously a big deal. Moreover, the timing is suggestive: the end of the big expansion period (mid-1970s) coincides with the takeoff of polarization. What I wish to suggest here – in an exploratory way – is that there are good reasons to think that the surge in policy activism played a considerable part in fostering and then sustaining the intense polarization that characterizes contemporary American politics.

The conventional narrative of rising polarization focuses on a single policy transformation: the civil rights initiatives of the 1960s. In capsule form the argument goes as follows. The civil rights movement eventually forced the breakup of the New Deal Democratic coalition, with national Democrats fatefully coming down on the side of racial liberalism. This policy realignment produced clearer signals about which party was the more liberal one. Over time this led elites and voters to "sort" into the appropriate party, producing two parties that were more internally homogeneous and differentiated from each other. Controversy now mostly rests on the extent to which (and reasons why) contemporary polarization is limited largely to political elites, or is driven more by changes in the broader electorate.[17]

The impact of the South's realignment, and the centrality of racial politics and policy to that transformation, are undeniable. Yet although there is much that is compelling in this narrative, a focus on the broader policy revolution – the rise of a more centralized policy state – adds significant elements to this account. It helps clarify why the parties have not just sorted but pulled apart from each other, as well as why these changes have not just endured but intensified over time.

Of critical importance is the role of groups in the broader political transformation. One valuable strand of recent work on polarization has advanced the idea that political parties should be conceptualized as coalitions of groups.[18] What distinguishes these groups is that they are "intense policy demanders." They care about what governments do, how political authority is exercised. Their preferences regarding policy are typically some distance (perhaps a considerable distance) from the median voter's. Thus, they face incentives to join with other groups in political parties, and exploit the limited attentiveness of ordinary citizens (what Kathleen Bawn and her colleagues term "the electoral blind spot"). Parties can use political authority to pursue strategies (such as agenda and procedural control, as well as clever policy design) that expand the electoral blind spot and grant policy rewards to reliable group supporters.

This view of parties should be of particular interest to students of American public policy and political development. It provides an elegant theoretical formulation with the potential to link many of the traditional concerns of American Political Development scholars – including regime dynamics based on particular coalitions and policy agendas – to mainstream political science's focus on electoral and legislative politics. It does so primarily by bringing groups and policy from the margins to the heart of discussions of political parties.

Seen from this perspective, there are obvious reasons for those interested in partisan polarization to take a hard look at the rise of the policy state. That rise, as I have just outlined, simultaneously involved an explosion of policy activity and a radical transformation of the advocacy group environment. The policy state promoted the growth of groups, and increased the stakes of politics. Although the chapters by Moe (6), Swain and Yetter (8) and Jacobs and Skocpol (7) show that the states play an important part in education, immigration, and health policy, respectively, what takes place in Washington is increasingly consequential. Parties are not the only vehicles for pursuing policy demands, and many groups continue to hedge their bets. But parties are a prominent mechanism for achieving policy goals, especially if those goals are large ones that are some distance away from the likely preferences of the median voter.

Moreover, the linkages between policy demanders and parties are potentially self-reinforcing. The more that groups choose to direct their investments to a particular party, the more central parties become to policymaking. Which party wins will substantially shift the set of likely policy outcomes. The more central parties become to policymaking, the greater the incentive groups face to invest in a particular party rather than hedging. In turn, this strengthening alliance between groups and parties feeds back into party polarization. Intense policy demanders become a major vehicle for recruiting, rewarding, and disciplining ambitious politicians.[19]

Abortion politics provides a particularly clear example of how these links between the emergent policy state and partisan polarization play out over time.[20] On the eve of *Roe v. Wade*, abortion had no particular partisan meaning in the United States. The issue was considered a local one, with varied policies across the country reflecting local political constellations. Knowing a voter's stance on abortion told you nothing about whether they were likely to be a Democrat or a Republican.

In an instant, *Roe* nationalized this policy domain. Abortion policy was to be identical across the country.[21] This new, Washington-centered policy regime was a catalyst for political organization on both sides of the issue. Women's rights groups strengthened, and made abortion rights an increasingly central concern. The same thing happened on the other side – another example of backlash mobilization. Along with fears about the tax treatment of (segregated) religious schools, abortion was the main development driving the political organization of Christian conservatives. This politicization, of course, is one of the most important developments in American politics over the past generation and a defining feature of the modern Republican Party.

Groups did not just organize around abortion policies; they picked a particular party. The core politics of the new national policy regime had a brutal simplicity: everything rested on the Supreme Court's pivotal voter. This meant that achieving one's policy demands required the election of a president (and senators) who would nominate (and confirm) the right kind of Justice. Powerful groups now organized their efforts not only to help "their" party win, but also to make sure that when it was victorious it selected the right candidates for the judiciary.

These increasingly important group attachments, driven to a considerable extent by the development of the policy state, in turn had big effects on the parties. In Karol's words:

[As] groups active on one side or the other of the abortion issue have become more central to each party, the pressure on politicians to conform to their demands has increased. ... [G]reater conformity ... has in turn sharpened the parties' images on abortion, further encouraging pro-choice and pro-life voters and activists to find a home in [the] Democratic and Republican parties, respectively.[22]

Karol's research reveals the centrality of groups to this process of polarization. Polarization initially reflected the increasing alignment of politicians' stances with those of group and party. In time, the new abortion politics filtered back down into the electorate. Voters who cared the most about the issue found it increasingly easy to pick the right party, and voters' tightening allegiances to a particular partisan team increased their likelihood of embracing the "appropriate" policy position. The electorate moved *after* groups and party elites had realigned. In sharp contrast to the situation a generation ago, views on abortion are now very strongly correlated with partisan attachments.

Gun control reveals a similar dynamic.[23] Here the initial policy triggers were the Gun Control Act of 1968, passed in response to the increasing gun violence of the 1960s, and the creation of the Bureau of Alcohol, Tobacco, and Firearms within the Justice Department in 1972. The Gun Control Act was the first significant piece of federal gun legislation since the New Deal. As with abortion, the role of intense policy demanders in generating partisan polarization is clear. Prior to the 1970s, the NRA had been essentially a sportsmen's club. Indeed, in 1977 the NRA leadership was making plans to relocate the association's headquarters to Colorado and consolidate its identity as a club for hunting and shooting enthusiasts. Instead, those angered by the new federal law and seeking to concentrate the organization's resources on gun rights and the repeal of federal gun legislation staged a successful revolt.

The new model was an enormous success, tripling the NRA's membership in a few years. In the late 1970s, the NRA became a much more formidable and aggressively political body. Its endorsement of Ronald Reagan in 1980 represented a sharp break with prior practice. As with abortion, it triggered a similar process of sorting. The GOP/NRA alliance first drew in prominent politicians, with gun control advocates moving in the other direction. The new alignment then gradually filtered down, at least partially, to the electorate. Again, however, a key indicator of polarization is that the positions of politicians come to comport more closely to those of party and affiliated groups, while mapping less well than they did before on the views of local constituents.

MADISON UPSIDE DOWN

Writ large, the dynamics described above represent a stunning reversal of Madison's famous predictions in *Federalist* #10. Madison's blueprint for limiting the mischief of faction turned not just on the establishment of a separation of powers, but on the establishment of an "extended Republic" embracing the thirteen former colonies. Scale was as central to his vision as institutional structure. A national polity, he suggested, would provide an institutional foundation for pluralism and diminish the prospects for the formation of broad and durable coalitions:

The smaller the society, the fewer probably will be the distinct parties and interests composing it; the fewer the distinct parties and interests, the more frequently will a majority be found of the same party; and the smaller the number of individuals composing a majority, and the smaller the compass within which they are placed, the more easily will they concert and execute their plans of oppression. Extend the sphere, and you take in a greater variety of parties and interests; you make it less probable that a majority of the whole will have a common motive to invade the rights of other citizens; or if such a common motive exists, it will be more difficult for all who feel it to discover their own strength, and to act in unison with each other. Besides other impediments, it may be remarked that, where there is a consciousness of unjust or dishonorable purposes, communication is always checked by distrust in proportion to the number whose concurrence is necessary.[24]

There are strong reasons to believe that the shift of political action to Washington – both because government is doing more and because more of what it is doing is being done centrally – has had the opposite effect. More and more of the money in political campaigns is national money, flowing from the wealth and large groups to wherever the action is, rather than reflecting local giving to local candidates.[25] Groups are increasingly organized, national in scope, and likely to be drawn into durable alignment with the party they see as most likely to advance their policy demands. Intensifying polarization increases the pressure on groups to pick sides. And the increasing centrality of party means that *more and more issues are drawn into the same political conflict.*

Of course, this is far from universally true. Many interest group communities resist picking sides – Wall Street is a good example. On the whole, finance has continued to "invest" in whoever is powerful at the moment and "hedge" by sustaining attachments to the other side. Understanding why partisan attachments vary across groups and policy areas represents a crucial research frontier for political scientists. Yet one of the clear markers of growing polarization has been a strengthening of attachments between parties and groups. Wand, for instance, observes a clear shift in business campaign contributions involving stronger bets on the Republican Party after 1994.[26] The Chamber of Commerce – far and away the biggest lobbying presence in American politics – has been increasingly open about its alliance with the GOP. Trial lawyers and environmental groups, by contrast, have moved closer to the Democrats.

THE POLITICS OF POLICYMAKING REVISITED

Another way to see the tightening connections between policy and polarization, and to begin to explore the implications for politics, is to briefly revisit three prominent frameworks deployed by political scientists to understand policymaking in the pre-polarization era, just as the policy state was in full ascent. The first is the literature on issue networks, associated with Hugh Heclo.[27] Heclo argued, persuasively, that "iron triangles" were giving way to "issue networks." The iron triangles of an earlier era involved a small inner circle of durable and insulated players, whose control over policy was barely disrupted by electoral tides. "Issue networks," by contrast, reflected the huge growth in organized activity *and* policy, which made for much more complex and fluid participation. By necessity, the policymaking "table" was much bigger.

Heclo emphasized a core area of consensus, grounded in expertise. An issue network was a "shared-knowledge group." "Increasingly," he argued, "it is through networks of people who regard each other as knowledgeable, or at least as needing to be answered, that public policy issues tend to be refined, evidence debated, and alternative options worked out – though rarely in any controlled, well-organized way."[28] In Heclo's somewhat technocratic depiction of how organized interests were connected to policymaking, political parties remained relatively unimportant, just as had been the case in the previous iron triangle framework.

However accurate this might be as a depiction of 1970s policymaking, few would describe the interest group environment today as organized around such issue networks. Given the scale of policy activity and the density of interest groups, the policymaking tables remain large. In most prominent policy domains, however, party-based coalitions operate *separate* tables. Every election reshuffles power. When it does, policymaking authority may shift from one party's table to the other's. Overlap in expert networks is minimal, because the experts are connected, loosely or tightly, to the party's dominant organized interests in the relevant policy domain.[29] This is perhaps clearest in areas such as environmental and energy policy, but it is true in a wide range of policy domains. Think about health care, most areas of regulatory policy, or the range of issues related to the administration of justice.

One can see the increasingly transparent team orientation of expertise in the evolution of think tanks. The Heritage Foundation was the earliest version of a prominent organization devoted to the development and promotion of partisan experts. The Brookings Institution, although it leans Democratic, remains an example of the older model organized around an imagined bipartisan consensus. On the left, the Center for American Progress is more in keeping with current realities. Its very strong links to the professional apparatus of the Democratic Party are not camouflaged. Originally founded by President Clinton's Chief of Staff John Podesta, it is currently headed by Neera Tanden, whose professional career includes high-level positions in the Clinton White House, on Senator Hilary Clinton's staff, on the 2008 Obama general election campaign, and in the Obama White House.

Revisiting John Kingdon's seminal analysis of agenda setting is equally revealing.[30] Like Heclo, Kingdon emphasized the "thickening" of Washington – more policy, more groups. Tellingly, his account – again, like Heclo's – stressed the diffuseness of authority and action within that increasingly densely populated space. Borrowing Herbert Simon's "garbage can" metaphor, Kingdon saw agenda setting as a decentralized process – or rather, a *set* of loosely coupled decentralized processes ("streams"). Agenda setting involved a wide range of actors who were largely uncoordinated and only became coordinated around the particular issue that emerged on the agenda. In Kingdon's framework elections could matter, but they were not emphasized. Party organizations played virtually no role.

Although aspects of Kingdon's analysis retain some relevance, agenda setting today is clearly a much more centralized and tightly coupled process. Moreover, party plays an absolutely central role. Party gatekeepers (themselves closely connected to the powerful organized interests in their coalition) are usually decisive in determining which issues will command attention. Occasionally a "focusing event" (9/11, the Enron and WorldCom scandals of the early Bush years) will be so powerful that it forces itself onto the agenda. Much more common is a controlled process in which party leaders set the agenda in accordance with strategic objectives of rewarding supporters, dividing opponents, and promoting electoral success.

Indeed, the powerful connection between party and agenda control has been a central contribution of recent work on party in Congress – the "conditional party government" literature. Parties centralize as they become internally more homogeneous. They use that centralized power to better control the agenda for partisan advantage.[31] In Van Houweling's novel formulation, agenda control and other legislative maneuvers can be used to pursue policy ambitions that are a considerable distance from the preferences of a representative's constituents – that is, these techniques expand the electoral blind spot.[32]

In a world of highly organized parties with strong and relatively stable interest group alliances, policy agendas generally do not emerge from a garbage can. They typically do not "bubble up" from below (although entrepreneurs retain a role in designing programmatic specifics); nor are they driven by the dictates of public opinion, although party strategists remain cognizant that the views of voters constitute a constraint on their freedom to maneuver.

The two most prominent domestic initiatives of our most recent presidents – the Bush tax cuts and Obamacare – are typical. These initiatives emerged, completely unsurprisingly, from each president's partisan coalitions. Substitute a different leader from the same party at the same time and arguably the policy agenda would have looked similar. Grover Norquist, whose Americans for Tax Reform is emblematic of the new policy advocacy world in which organized groups closely monitor their politician allies, explained why he was comfortable with the candidacy of Mitt Romney. He put the basic point with his usual bluntness:

> We don't need a president to tell us in what direction to go. We know what direction to go. We want the Ryan budget. . . . We just need a president to sign this stuff. We don't need someone to think it up or design it. The leadership now for the modern conservative movement for the next 20 years will be coming out of the House and the Senate. Pick a Republican with enough working digits to handle a pen to become president of the United States. . .His job is to be captain of the team, to sign the legislation that has already been prepared.[33]

If Kingdon and Heclo's formulations look dated, so does Anthony Down's famous analysis of how competition for votes would force the two political parties to the center.[34] Downs, of course, is one of the foundational texts of modern political science, especially for Americanists. As Morris Fiorina put it, "The proposition that two-party competition produces convergent politics *wherein the parties make overlapping appeals in an effort to capture the center* served as a kind of 'master theory' for American political scientists for most of the twentieth century."[35]

As the quote from Fiorina suggests, Downsian frameworks were deployed in American political science to explain convergence rather than its absence. True,

Downsian frameworks can be coaxed into consistency with symmetrical polarization (where the parties would gravitate into hostile camps, equidistant from the median voter) if primary electorates are sufficiently (and, crucially, equally) extreme and positions, once taken, are very costly to break. Group-based polarization around national policy disputes helps to explain how this kind of divergence could arise and be sustained.

Equally important, these Downsian frameworks are not consistent with asymmetric polarization (involving a significantly greater "off-center" movement on the part of one party). Up to now I have followed the conventions of much current scholarship by treating the policy-group-party configurations related to polarization as symmetrical while hinting at the greater intensity on the Republican side. Although a detailed discussion is not possible here, it is worth noting that there is substantial evidence suggesting that in fact the polarization occurring over the past few decades is actually better described as asymmetric, primarily reflecting movement on the part of the GOP.[36] In Mann and Ornstein's forceful formulation:

However difficult it may be for the traditional press and nonpartisan analysts to acknowledge, one of the two major parties, The Republican Party, has become an insurgent outlier – ideologically extreme; contemptuous of the inherited social and economic policy regime; scornful of compromise; unpersuaded by conventional understandings of facts, evidence, and science; and dismissive of the legitimacy of its political opposition.[37]

Seeing parties as national coalitions of organized actors possessing intense policy demands makes the development of asymmetric polarization easier to understand. The existence of sizable electoral blind-spots helps explain why the less centrist party may be able to successfully accommodate coalition demands without paying an overwhelming electoral price.[38] The parties are not mirror images of each other, but rest on distinctive coalitional structures constructed over time. One party may thus feel a stronger pull than the other to satisfy extreme policy demands. The factors that generate greater pressure toward the extreme within the modern GOP remain understudied. Among the possible causes are the greater size and radicalism of the GOP's activist base, the greater weight of politicized media in GOP circles, and the growing relative power of business in American politics, which plays a strong moderating role within the Democratic Party, while in many ways facilitating a sharp right turn within the GOP.

THE DYNAMICS OF POLARIZED POLICYMAKING

The frameworks political scientists used to analyze the development of policy prior to polarization now look antiquated. Highlighting the tight links between the policy state, organized groups, and our polarized parties helps illuminate some of the critical features of contemporary politics. It clarifies why particular political dynamics explored in a number of chapters in this volume now occur routinely. It can also highlight features of contemporary politics that are not easily discerned in studies focused on a single policy issue. Here I briefly discuss some of these characteristics of modern policymaking: tendencies toward legislative gridlock, heightened conflict over budgeting, and the dispersion of policy initiatives from Congress to alternative venues capable of unilateral action.

Legislative Gridlock

The most visible effect of growing polarization is increasing legislative gridlock. Polarization has made legislative action more difficult in at least three distinct ways. Most obviously, the parties are *farther apart*, which makes positive-sum policymaking more difficult. In many, many cases, the parties define policy progress in mutually exclusive terms. For instance, in the past few years Democrats have argued that immediate budget cuts in the current climate are harmful to employment growth, whereas Republicans argue that such cuts are required for job creation.

Polarization has also fueled gridlock by heightening the incentives for obstruction. It is no accident that the massive expansion of the filibuster – a fundamental reordering of American political institutions – has taken place during a time of rising polarization. As policy stances of the parties diverged, the cost of defeat in policy battles has grown; so have the rewards of obstruction.

Finally, polarization can render policy conflicts zero-sum, even in contexts where a zone of agreement on policy specifics might be found. Compromise, on which our institutions place a premium, typically requires the identification of mutually beneficial improvements to the status quo. As politics becomes more polarized, drawing more and more aspects of governance into the same broad struggle, mutually beneficial outcomes disappear because a win for one side becomes by definition a loss for the other. *Relative* advantage becomes paramount. Senate Minority Leader Mitch McConnell was criticized for publicly stating that his top priority was to "make President Obama a one-term president." Yet this stance makes good sense in the context of contemporary politics, where each party is strongly organized to pursue a very distinct policy agenda.

A major theme in this volume is that legislative gridlock does not imply inactivity. As discussed in a moment, it often produces displacement. Policy activity shifts to venues more capable of acting unilaterally, including the executive, courts, and states. It is worth stressing, however, that gridlock will often mean that the private sector becomes the main driver of policy change. Frozen policy in a dynamic society and economy implies *drift*.[39] Failure to update public programs means that the *effects* of policy will often change dramatically. Whether and how this happens will depend on the characteristics of a particular policy and how its structural effects are modified by changes in the social environment.

As Warren's chapter stresses, the increasingly antiquated nature of industrial relations law has been a catastrophic problem for private-sector unions. Gridlock has meant a form of drift that has been enormously favorable to labor's opponents. A similar analysis applies to the very important case of financial regulation. The weakness of public oversight of Wall Street in the years leading up to the 2008 financial crisis was not just a consequence of new deregulatory statutes, but of a failure to update old laws to grapple with radically new features of financial markets, such as the massive deployment of derivatives.[40] Industrial relations and finance are not small or isolated cases. The bigger implication is that gridlock-enhancing drift is not a neutral mechanism. It systematically favors the party (GOP) and aligned interest groups (mostly the business community) who benefit most often from a weakening of government's capacity to respond to social and economic change. The declining capacity of public authority to adapt in the face of private-sector dynamism is a major source of the rising inequality (especially at the top of the income distribution) that has characterized the United States over the past generation.[41]

Budget Wars

Much of the partisan battle waged around the policy state now runs through repeated conflicts over the federal budget. This is in part because the policy gridlock that makes breakthroughs in individual policy sectors difficult is at least somewhat attenuated in the case of budgeting. For many programs, spending decisions must be made. Moreover, reconciliation rules related to budgeting issues can reduce the Senate's sixty-vote hurdle to fifty votes, facilitating policy change. Not surprisingly, the two big policy breakthroughs mentioned before – Bush's tax cuts and Obama's health care reforms – relied on reconciliation for their passage. Most recently, the GOP learned that its willingness to jettison established norms regarding the debt ceiling potentially gave it added leverage over policy. As in many areas involving polarization and gridlock, gambits that allow a single set of actors to shift the status quo unilaterally have taken on a new significance.

Budget politics have also become more central as the GOP has determined, rightly, that some of its biggest opportunities to disrupt the policy status quo come from fights over taxation and deficits. Since the Gingrich revolution, the GOP budgetary playbook has been simple: push for tax cuts when they are possible, push for deficit reduction when they are not. Budget conflicts shift the framing from specific policies and expenditures (where voters tend to support the Democrats) toward a more favorable terrain centered on the scope and role of government. Although the GOP gives back some of that advantage because its position on budgetary issues (no new taxes ever) have shifted so far to the right, large-scale budget fights framed around an agenda of tax cuts or deficit reduction remain among the best options the GOP has for advancing its policy goals.[42]

The Politics of Unilateral Action

Partisan conflict is often most visible in Congress, but it is clearly not the only place where polarization is consequential. A theme in many chapters is the extension of partisan contestation to additional institutional arenas, including the executive, courts, and states. The intensification of partisanship throughout the separation-of-powers system is in part simply a reflection of the broad trends already discussed. The rise of party coalitions relentlessly focused on policy and vigorously opposed to each other means that these conflicts are extended to all sites where political authority is exercised.

As policy contestation becomes a kind of three-dimensional chess match, groups have expanded their capacity to engage in multilevel politics. The Chamber of Commerce, for example, is actively involved not only in national elections and lobbying, but also in critical state-level elections. Moreover, it has placed a very high priority on developing a litigation wing. The Chamber has enjoyed enormous success by incubating cases to be brought before an increasingly conservative and activist Supreme Court.[43]

Of course, the extension of partisan conflict throughout American political institutions also reflects the rise of gridlock in Congress. Politics, like nature, abhors a vacuum. The increasingly inertial qualities of the legislature means that policy advocates turn to where the action is. This may mean unilateral executive action, judicial activism, or initiatives at the state and local level. Both partisan teams mobilize to identify the best institutional venues to advance their policy goals.

In considering how this multi-venue combat operates in our polarized climate, it is worth highlighting the role of the judiciary. The courts have become a more important player in these intense policy disputes in part because they, too, have become more polarized, but unlike Congress, the Supreme Court is not vulnerable to gridlock. Over time, the nation's highest court has been incorporated into the broader political dynamic. Reflecting the growing strength of partisan policy coalitions, vetting of potential Supreme Court appointees has focused much more on their policy positions, and is much more carefully overseen by the two parties' organized allies. The strong partisan alignment of the Supreme Court is without precedent in modern American history. Decisions that are 5-4 are at an all-time high. So is the extent to which the voting alignments in those narrowly divided cases mirror the partisan divide.[44]

The Court's position also takes on added significance due to its expanding role as "traffic cop," allocating political authority among the venues of American governance. This is, in part, a consequence of the general institutional "thickening" associated with the extended policy state. More policy traffic creates more congestion, enhancing the need for someone to prevent collisions or sort things out when they inevitably occur. It is also a result of the diminishing capacity of Congress, the institution traditionally considered best positioned to break through a policy impasse.

With Congress is gridlocked, the Court's decisions about who has the freedom to pursue particular policy innovations becomes critical. In *Massachusetts v. EPA*, for instance, the Court ruled 5-4 that the EPA already possessed the authority to regulate green house gasses under terms of the Clean Air Act. This decision has had a profound effect on climate-change politics. Cap-and-trade legislation ultimately failed to gain a filibuster-proof majority in the Senate, but the legislative initiative only came as close to passage as it did because of the Supreme Court's decision. *Massachusetts vs. EPA* shifted the status quo, giving the Obama administration dramatically greater leverage with Congress than it had previously held. Moreover, the Court's ruling greatly enhanced the administration's capacity to pursue unilateral executive action in regulating carbon emissions.

The Court has also policed the division of authority between the federal government and the states. Indeed, the conservative Supreme Court's recent history could be seen as an extended exploration of how much to roll back the activist state by establishing new limits on Washington's authority. In a string of abortion decisions, the Supreme Court has chipped away at the national policy standard established by *Roe*, substantially expanding the variation in policy (and politics) across the states. Although this constitutes a form of decentralization, the polarization genie cannot be so easily returned to the bottle. Even a full reversal would not restore the status quo ante. Instead, nationally organized forces on both sides pursue trench warfare on a variegated state-level terrain.

Evidence of the court's increasing centrality to policymaking was obscured by John Roberts's unexpected decision to side with the court's liberals in upholding the Affordable Care Act's individual mandate. It is worth emphasizing, however, that the Court appears to have come within a hair's breadth of what would have been an extraordinary outcome: five GOP appointees, utilizing novel and extremely controversial reasoning, overturning the most important Democratic policy initiative in decades.[45] Roberts' refusal to join his colleagues in striking down the entire law overshadowed his willingness to join them in their restrictive interpretation of the commerce clause. He also engineered the substantial new restrictions on federal authorities that opened up the polarized politics of state Medicaid expansion discussed in the chapter by Jacobs and Skocpol (Chapter 7). If Roberts's opinion in *National Federation of Independent Business vs. Sebelius* was hailed for its moderation, this only signals the degree to which policy-focused polarization has successfully colonized the "least dangerous branch."

American Politics and the Activist State

At their heart, the deep schisms of contemporary American politics are connected to the rise of the activist state. As Robert Kagan and others have stressed, we now have an extensive array of government interventions operating within institutions that were not designed to handle so many initiatives.[46] And as I have argued in this chapter, the activist state has given rise to a second source of profound institutional tension. The increasing scope and significance of policymaking in Washington contributed to the rise of a highly organized, policy-focused partisanship for which our institutions were similarly ill-equipped.

American institutions were designed to necessitate compromise. That arrangement functioned reasonably well, in large part because our traditional checks-
and-balances system also facilitated compromise. Now, our institutions still
require compromise (with the rise of the filibuster, perhaps more than ever),
but they no longer facilitate it.

The policy contestation central to our modern polarized politics plays out on
this new terrain. A political science up to the challenge of making sense of it will
need to be more policy focused than has been true since the behaviorist and
institutionalist revolutions of a generation ago. This policy focus will give us a
more sophisticated sense of how program structures dictate political strategies,
opening or foreclosing opportunities to engage in unilateral action. Along with
this, it will draw our attention back to the role of groups, who have the
incentives, resources, and durability required to develop and pursue effective
strategies over time and across multiple venues. Finally, this policy focus can
help us make sense of the striking changes of the two parties, especially the
vigorous rightward march of the GOP. The two parties are not mirror images of
each other, but rather distinctive social organizations reflecting the history of
their development and balance of organized pressures within each coalition.

Notes

1. Although the specific formulations offered here are my own, this chapter draws in
   considerable part on joint work with Jacob Hacker and Steven Teles. I am grateful to
   the editors, along with Jacob Hacker, for comments on an earlier draft.
2. Paul Pierson, "The Rise and Reconfiguration of Activist Government," in Paul Pierson
   and Theda Skocpol, eds., *The Transformation of American Politics: Activist Government
   and the Rise of Conservatism* (Princeton: Princeton University Press), 2007, pp. 19–38.
3. By no means does this end the use of politics to deliver personal benefits to supporters.
   It means that the dominant vehicle for doing so is through the delivery of policies
   rather than political appointments.
4. Christopher Howard, *The Hidden Welfare State: Tax Expenditures and Social Policy
   in the United States* (Princeton: Princeton University Press), 1997; Jacob S. Hacker,
   *The Divided Welfare State: The Battle over Public and Private Social Benefits in the
   United States* (Cambridge: Cambridge University Press), 2002; Suzanne Mettler, *The
   Submerged State: How Invisible Government Policies Undermine American
   Democracy* (Chicago: University of Chicago Press), 2011.
5. David Vogel, *Fluctuating Fortunes: The Political Power of Business in America*
   (New York: Basic Books), 1989.
6. David R. Mayhew, *Divided We Govern* (New Haven: Yale University Press), 1991.
7. Office of Management and Budget, Historical Statistics, Table 12.1. Retrieved from
   http://www.whitehouse.gov/omb/budget/Historicals.
8. Paul Pierson, "Public Policies as Institutions," in *Rethinking Political Institutions:
   The Art of the State*, eds., Stephen Skowronek, Daniel Galvin, and Ian Shapiro (New
   York: New York University Press), 2006, pp. 114–34; Jacob S. Hacker and Paul
   Pierson, "After the 'Master Theory': Downs, Schattschneider, and the Rebirth of
   Policy-Focused Analysis," Perspectives on Politics, vol. 12, no. 3, 2014.

9. Mancur Olsen, *The Logic of Collective Action* (Cambridge, MA: Harvard University Press), 1965.

10. Terry M. Moe, *The Organization of Interests: Incentives and the Internal Dynamics of Political Interest Groups* (Chicago: University of Chicago Press), 1980; Jack Walker, *Mobilizing Interest Groups in America* (Ann Arbor: University of Michigan Press), 1991.

11. Terry M. Moe, *Special Interests*. Washington, DC: Brookings Institution Press, 2012.

12. Theda Skocpol, *Diminished Democracy: From Membership to Management in American Civil Life* (Norman, OK: University of Oklahoma Press), 2003; Theda Skocpol, "Government Activism and the Reorganization of American Civic Democracy," in Pierson and Skocpol, eds., *Activist Government and the Rise of Conservatism*, 2007; Frank Baumgarnter, Beth Leech, and Christine Mahoney, "The Co-evolution of Groups and Government," Paper Presented at the Annual Meeting of the American Political Science Association, 2003; Beth Leech, Frank Baumgartner, Timothy La Pira, and Nicholas Semanko, "Drawing Lobbyists to Washington: Government Activity and the Demand for Advocacy," *Political Research Quarterly*, vol. 58, no. 1, 2005, pp. 19–30.

13. Skocpol, "Government Activism," p. 48.

14. Leech, et al., "Drawing Lobbyists to Washington," p. 28.

15. Vogel, *Fluctuating Fortunes*; Jacob Hacker and Paul Pierson, *Winner-Take-All Politics* (New York: Simon and Schuster), 2010.

16. Vogel, *Fluctuating Fortunes*.

17. Morris P. Fiorina, *Culture War? The Myth of a Polarized America* (New York: Pearson Longman), 2005; Alan J. Abramowitz, *The Disappearing Center: Engaged Citizens, Polarization, and American Democracy* (New Haven: Yale University Press), 2010.

18. David Karol, *Party Position Change in American Politics: Coalition Management* (New York: Cambridge University Press), 2009; Kathleen Bawn et al., "A Theory of Political Parties," *Perspectives on Politics*, vol. 10, no. 3, 2012, pp. 571–97.

19. Seth E. Masket, *No Middle Ground: How Informal Party Organizations Control Nominations and Polarize Legislatures* (Ann Arbor: University of Michigan Press), 2009.

20. See Karol, *Party Position Change*, pp. 56–84, Greg D. Adams, "Abortion: Evidence of an Issue Evolution," *American Journal of Political Science*, vol. 41, no. 3, 1997, pp. 718–37.

21. Karol points to small hints that the issue was nationalizing prior to *Roe*, but his account is consistent with the widely shared view that the 1973 decision was a watershed.

22. Karol, *Party Position Change*, p. 57.

23. Karol, *Party Position Change*, pp. 84–101; Joel Achenbach, Scott Higham, and Sari Horwitz, "How NRA's True Believers Converted a Marksmanship Group into a Mighty Gun Lobby," *Washington Post*, January 12, 2013.

24. Alexander Hamilton, James Madison, and John Jay, *The Federalist Papers*, ed. Clinton Rossiter, with an introduction and notes by Charles R. Kesler (New York: New American Library, 1999), 51.

25. James G. Gimpel, Frances E. Lee, and Shanna Pearson-Merkowitz, "The Check Is in the Mail: Interdistrict Funding Flows in Congressional Elections," *American Journal*

of Political Science, vol. 52, no. 2, 2008, pp. 373–94; Adam Bonica, Nolan McCarty, Keith Poole, and Howard Rosenthal, "Why Hasn't Democracy Slowed Rising Inequality?" *Journal of Economic Perspectives*, 2013, 103–24.

26. Jonathan Wand, "The Allocation of Campaign Contributions by Interest Groups and the Rise of Elite Polarization," unpublished manuscript, Stanford University.

27. Hugh Heclo, "Issue Networks and the Executive Establishment," in Anthony King, ed., *The New American Political System* (Washington, DC: American Enterprise Institute), 1978, pp. 87–124.

28. Ibid., pp. 103, 104.

29. Arguably, there has also been a decline in the extent to which genuine expertise matters, although one can fairly ask if this was ever as true as Heclo's analysis suggested.

30. John Kingdon, *Agendas, Alternatives, and Public Policy* (Boston: Little, Brown), 1984. The following discussion draws on ongoing research with Steve Teles.

31. John H. Aldrich and David H. Rohde, "The Consequences of Party Organization in the House: The Role of the Majority and Minority Parties in Conditional Party Government," unpublished manuscript.

32. Robert Van Houweling, "Parties as Enablers," unpublished manuscript, UC Berkeley.

33. Quoted in David Frum, "Norquist: Romney Will Do as Told," *The Daily Beast*, February 13, 2012. Retrieved from http://www.thedailybeast.com/articles/2012/02/13/grover-norquist-speech-cpac.html.

34. Anthony Downs, *An Economic Theory of Democracy* (New York, Harper), 1957.

35. Morris P. Fiorina, with Samuel J. Abrams, *Disconnect: The Breakdown of Representation in American Politics* (Norman: The University of Oklahoma Press, 2009), XVII (emphasis added).

36. Jacob Hacker and Paul Pierson, *Off-Center: The Republican Revolution and the Erosion of American Democracy* (New Haven: Yale University Press), 2005; Nolan McCarty, Keith Poole, and Howard Rosenthal, *Polarized America: The Dance of Ideology and Unequal Riches* (Cambridge, MA: MIT Press), 2007; Thomas Mann and Norman Ornstein, *It's Even Worse Than It Looks* (New York: Basic Books), 2011; Sean Theriault, *The Gingrich Senators* (Oxford: Oxford University Press), 2012; Christopher Hare et al., "Polarization Is Real and Asymmetric," Project Voteview Blog, May 16, 2012, retrieved from http://vote view.com/blog/?p=494.

37. Mann and Ornstein, *Worse Than It Looks*, p. xiv.

38. Here recent behavioral research emphasizing voters' systematic biases and forms of myopia makes an important contribution that is complementary to the recent research suggesting parties will often be responsive to affiliated groups. For important examples see Larry Bartels, *Unequal Democracy: The Political Economy of the New Gilded Age* (Princeton: Princeton University Press), 2009; and Gabriel Lenz, *Follow the Leader? How Voters Respond to Politicians' Policies and Performance* (Chicago: University of Chicago Press), 2012.

39. Jacob S. Hacker, "Privatizing Risk Without Privatizing the Welfare State: The Hidden Politics of Social Policy Retrenchment," *American Political Science Review*, vol. 98, no. 2, 2004, pp. 243–60.

40. Hacker and Pierson, *Winner-Take-All Politics*; Simon Johnson and James Kwak, *13 Bankers: The Wall Street Takeover and the Next Financial Meltdown* (New York:

Pantheon), 2010; Nouriel Roubini and Stephen Mihm, *Crisis Economics: A Crash Course in the Future of Finance* (New York: Penguin Press), 2010.

41. Hacker and Pierson, *Winner-Take-All Politics*.

42. Jacob S. Hacker and Paul Pierson, "Presidents and the Political Economy: The Coalitional Foundations of Presidential Power," *Presidential Studies Quarterly*, vol. 42, no. 1, 2012, pp. 101–31.

43. Jeffrey Rosen, "Supreme Court, Inc.," *New York Times Magazine*, March 16, 2008. Retrieved from http://www.nytimes.com/2008/03/16/magazine/16supreme-t.html?_r=1&oref=slogin.

44. David Paul Kuhn, "The Incredible Polarization and Politicization of the Supreme Court," *The Atlantic Monthly*, June 29, 2012. Retrieved from http://www.theatlantic.com/politics/archive/2012/06/the-incredible-polarization-and-politicization-of-the-supreme-court/259155/. The Court's polarization also shows signs of asymmetry. A recent analysis by Landes and Posner suggested that four of the most conservative five justices on the court since 1937 are current GOP appointees. Of the four Democratic appointees, only one (Ginsburg) is in the top-ten most liberal, and none are in the top five. William Landes and Richard Posner, "Rational Judicial Behavior: A Statistical Study," *The Journal of Legal Analysis*, vol. 1, no. 2, 2009, pp. 775–831.

45. Jeffrey Toobin, *The Oath: The Obama White House and the Supreme Court* (New York: Random House), 2012.

46. Robert Kagan, *Adversarial Legalism: The American Way of Law* (Cambridge, MA: Harvard University Press), 2001.

Index

Abolition of Central Intelligence Act of 1995, 243–244
abortion politics
  partisan polarization concerning, 288
  Supreme Court rulings and, 295–297
Abu Nidal terrorist organization, 264–267
accountability for teachers. *See also* school accountability
  education reform and, 131–134, 153
  movement for, 136–137
Acker, Karen, 115
administrative guidelines
  school desegregation and, 91–93
  trade policies and, 217–220
administrative politics
  labor-management hostility and, 109–110, 126
  leveraging of state capacity for health care reform implementation and, 168–171
  liberal ideology and, 49
  policy reform and, 12
  in Reagan era, 59
  rulemaking process and, 51–53
adversarial legalism
  civil rights and, 10, 81–84
  federal regulation and, 97–99
  weak state paradox and, 80–81
affirmative action
  bilingual education lawsuits and, 95–97
  Title VII influence on, 85–86
Afghan War, terrorist incidents in response to, 254–256

AFL-CIO
  Employee Free Choice Act and, 115, 117–118
  immigration reform and, 183–185
  internal divisions in, 120
agenda-setting, policymaking and, 291–292
agricultural lobbyists
  free trade ideology and, 213
  immigration reform and, 183–185
Agriculture Act of 1954, 33
Agriculture Act of 1958, 35
AIDs, immigration reform and, 186–187
airline hijackings
  aviation security legislation and, 264–267
  policy reforms in response to, 262–264
Alexander v. Sandoval, 95–97, 98–99
Allende, Salvadore, 239–240
Alliance for Justice, 55–57
al Qaeda terrorist activities, 245–246
American Business and Public Policy: The Politics of Foreign Trade (Bauer, Pool, and Dexter), 34
American Civil Liberties Union (ACLU), 142
American Federation of Teachers (AFT), 130
  collective bargaining by, 131–134
  historical power of, 130–131
  politics of blocking reform and, 134–136
"American rule" on attorney's fees, 51–53
Americans for Tax Reform, 292
Ames, Aldrich, 243–244
amnesty programs, immigration reform and, 183–185
Angleton, James Jesus, 238–239

antidumping laws, 209–217, 225
  trade policy reform and, 208–209
Anti-Hijacking Bill of 1974, 262–264
anti-litigation reform, 48–49, 68–69
Arab populations, public attitudes concerning,
  256–257
Area Redevelopment Act of 1961, 36
Arizona v. United States, 179–181, 198–199
Ashcroft, John, 270–272
Asian immigrants
  immigration reform and, 182–183, 188
  immigration reform politics and, 194–196
Aspin, Leslie ("Les"), 243–244
Aspin-Brown Commission, 243–244
Atomic Energy Act of 1954, 32–33, 37
  political legacy of, 38–39
attorney's fees
  deregulation impact on, 59–62
  federal authorization for, 95–97
  private enforcement infrastructure and
    introduction of, 51–57
  proposed cap on, 62–63, 67–68
authority, distrust of, 6–7
Aviation and Transportation Security Act,
  272–273
aviation security
  legislation in 1980s for, 264–267
  politics surrounding, 259–261
Aviation Security Act of 1989, 264–267,
  275–276
Azcarate, Fred, 115

background checks, immigration policy and,
  179–181
backlash dynamic, policy reforms and,
  284–286
Bailey, Elizabeth, 264–267, 272–273
Baker, Nancy, 270–273
*Balancing the Sales of Justice: Financing Public
  Interest Law in America* (Council on Public
  Interest Law), 55–57
Balogh, Brian, 6–7
Barnes, Roy (Gov.), 139
Baumgartner, Frank D., 27, 284–286
Bawn, Kathleen, 287
Bazelon, David (Judge), 98
Beck, Nathaniel, 29
bilateral agreements, trade policies and,
  217–220, 224
bilingual education
  federal court-agency divisions over, 93–95
  Supreme Court rulings in, 95–97

bin Laden, Osama, 245–246
Black Chamber, 228–229
Bleich, Erik, 80–81
Block, Fred, 107–108
Bloomberg, Michael, 133
Blumrosen, Alfred, 86–89
Boehner, John, 3
Borah, William, 240–242
Border Patrol, immigration reform and,
  186–187
Borjas, George, 202
Bosniak, Linda, 180–181
Braden, Sprouille, 232
Brandeis, Louis, 10–11
Brannan Plan, 33, 43–44
Brewer, Jan, 15
BRIC countries (Brazil, Russia, India, and
  China), trade policies and, 218–219
Brook, Douglas, 274–275
Brookings Institution, 291
Brown, Harold, 243–244
Brown, Scott, 115
*Brown v. Board of Education of Topeka,
  Kansas*, 9–10
budget wars, partisan polarization over, 295
bureaucracy
  Anti-Hijacking Bill of 1974 and, 262–264
  Aviation and Transportation Security Act and
    role of, 272–273
  civil rights policies and, 10
  deregulation and role of, 59–62
  homeland security and terrorist policies and,
    257–259
  liberal disillusionment with, 50–51
  PATRIOT Act and role of, 270–272
  weak state paradox and, 80–81
Bureau of Alcohol, Tobacco and Firearms,
  288–289
Burger, Warren (Chief Justice), 86–89
Bush, George H. W., 186–187, 238–239
  aviation security under, 264–267
  Iran Contra scandal and, 242–243
Bush, George W., 7, 14–15, 17, 140–141
  Aviation and Transportation Security Act
    passage and, 272–273
  Homeland Security Act and, 274–275
  immigration reform and, 190–192
  intelligence reform under, 227–228,
    244–248
  PATRIOT Act passage and, 270–272
  post-September 11 support for, 256–257, 270
  trade policies under, 225

business interests
    capture of regulatory policy by, 50, 109–110
    educational reforms and role of, 136–145
    fee cap legislation and, 65–67
    globalization and tariff policies and, 217–220
    historical perspective on labor policy reform
        and, 110–113
    hostility to labor and, 109–110, 126
    immigration reform and, 181–194
    interest group politics and, 284–286
    private enforcement infrastructure and,
        59–62
    rise of policy state and, 289–290
    school choice initiatives and, 142
    trade policies and, 222–223
business necessity doctrine, anti-discrimination
    policy and, 86–89
busing issue, desegregation policies and, 91–93
Byrnes, James, 230

cap-and-trade legislation, 295–297
Carter, Jimmy
    intelligence reform under, 241–242
    labor policy under, 111–112, 118–119, 120
Casey, William, 242–244
Castro, Fidel, 240, 262–264
Center for American Progress, 291
Center for Consumer Information and
    Insurance Oversight, 169–171
Center for Individual Rights, 59–62
Central American Free Trade Agreement
    (CAFTA), 209, 220
Central Intelligence Agency (CIA)
    assassination targets of, 240
    Church Committee investigation of, 240–242
    establishment of, 227–228
    homeland security and terrorism policies and,
        261–262, 275–276
    Iran Contra scandal and, 242–243
    mission creep and, 233–236
    proposed abolition of, 243–244
    public opinion concerning, 228–233
    reform of, 12–13
    September 11, 2011 attacks and
        reorganization of, 244–248
Central Intelligence Agency Act, 234
Central Intelligence Group (CIG), 230–232
Chamber of Commerce, 289–290, 295–297
Change to Win, 120
charter schools, education reform and,
    131–134, 143–145
Cheney, Dick, 253

Chicago Tribune newspaper, 232
Chile, CIA operations in, 239–240
China
    immigration from, 188–190
    trade policies involving, 204–205, 214,
        220–222
Chinese Exclusion Act, 182
choice movement, emergence of, 136–137
Church, Frank, 230–232, 234–235, 240–242
city governments, school control by, 133
civil liberties
    Aviation and Transportation Security Act
        and, 272–273
    Homeland Security Act and, 274–275
    homeland security and terrorism policies and,
        253–254, 256–257, 275–276
    homeland security and terrorist policies and,
        275–276
    in PATRIOT Act, 270–272, 280
Civil Rights Act of 1964
    consequences of, 77–80
    litigation and, 53–54
    private enforcement infrastructure and,
        54–57, 70
Civil Rights Act of 1991, 88–89
Civil Rights Attorney's Fees Awards Act of
    1976, 53–54
civil rights policies
    adversarial legalism and, 81–84
    consequences of, 77–80
    courts and bureaucracy and, 10, 77–99
    enforcement mechanisms for, 77–80,
        282–284
    immigration reform and, 190–192
    inertia concerning, 242–244
    litigation's role in, 53–54
    partisan polarization and, 286–289
    private enforcement infrastructure and,
        54–57, 282–284
    private litigation and, 9–10
    public policy and politics and, 8–9
    strength of state institutions and, 80–81
"Civil Rights Turns to Gold Lode for
    Southern Lawyers" *(Washington Post)*,
    54–57
"Clark-Case memorandum," Title VII
    enforcement and, 85–86
Clarridge, Duane, 264–267
class size reduction, educational reforms
    including, 136–137
Clean Air Act, 295–297
Clifford, Clark, 234

Clinton, Bill
  educational reforms under, 136–137
  homeland security and terrorism policies of,
    267–269, 275–276
  immigration reform and, 188–190
  intelligence reform policies under, 243–244
  labor policy under, 111–112, 113,
    118–119, 120
  organized labor and, 104–106
Cohen, Wilbur, 77–80
Colby, William, 238–239
Cold War, intelligence reform and, 233–236
collective bargaining, teachers unions and,
    131–134
Commerce Department (U.S.), 207–208,
    209–212
commercial policy, trade policy and, 222–223
Committee to Re-elect the President (CREEP),
    238–239
Communications Satellite Act of 1962, 36, 37,
    38–39
Communication Workers of America,
    117–118
competition
  free trade ideology and, 213
  political polarization and, 292–293
  unfair trade statutes and role of, 209–212
conditional nonimmigrant status, DREAM Act
    legislation and, 192–194
conditional party government ideology,
    policymaking and, 291–292
conflict over policy, emergence of, 40–41
Congress
  absence of moderate Republicans in, 65
  Aviation and Transportation Security Act
    passage and, 272–273
  Homeland Security Act passage and, 274–275
  homeland security and terrorist policies and,
    257–259, 260–261
  immigration reform politics and, 181–194,
    198–199
  institutional reforms for trade policies and,
    205–209
  intelligence reform and, 227–228, 233–236,
    240–243
  National Security Act of 1947 and, 261–262
  organized labor and, 105–106
  partisan politics and unfair trade statutes,
    209–212
  PATRIOT Act passage and, 270–272
  Title VII enforcement and role of, 86–89
  trade and tariff policies and, 203–205, 224

conservative activism
  abortion politics and, 288
  immigration reform and, 188–190
  private enforcement infrastructure and,
    59–62
Constitution (U.S.)
  federalism and articles of, 179–181
  policy state and, 5–7
constitutionality issues
  bilingual education and, 93–95
  immigration reform and, 196–197
  school vouchers and, 143
  trade policies and, 217–220
Contractors v. Secretary of Labor, 86–89
"Contract with America," 188–190
Conyers, John, 83
Cooper, Mary, 264–267, 268
cooperative federalism, state powers and, 10–11
Corporate Average Fuel Economy (CAFE),
    19–20
corp pricing policies, reforms for, 33, 35
Council on Public Interest Law, 55–57
countervailing duty laws (CVD), trade policy
    reform and, 208–209
court system
  adversarial legalism and, 81–82
  civil rights policies and, 10
  federal agencies and, 59–62, 91–93, 93–95,
    97–99
  immigration reform constitutionality and,
    196–197
  policy reform and, 11–12
  school desegregation and, 91–93
  unilateral action politics and, 295–297
  weak state paradox and, 80–81
covert operations, intelligence reform and,
    233–236
Crenshaw, William, 262–267
"cry and sigh" syndrome, trade policy reforms
    and, 211
Cuban American National Foundation,
    257–259
Culper Ring, 228–229
currency fluctuations, institutional tariff reforms
    and, 205–206
curriculum standards, school accountability
    initiatives and, 138–139

Daniels, Roger, 182
Dark, Taylor, 112
"A Day without Immigrants" protest, 191
D. B. Cooper airline hijacking, 262–264

Defense Intelligence Agency (DIA), 236–239
democracy, policy reform and, 12–17
Democratic Party
  Affordable Care Act politics and, 161–164
  charter school initiatives and, 143–145
  decline of organized labor influence in,
    104–106, 122
  Democratic-liberal public interest coalition
    and, 50
  free trade ideology and, 212–217
  immigration reform and, 186–187
  intelligence reform and, 246–248
  labor policy reform and, 103–104
  Republican presidents and, 50–51
  teachers unions and, 135–136, 145–148
  trade policies and, 203–205
demographic change, immigration reform
  politics and, 194–196
Department of Health and Human Services
  (DHHS), Affordable Care Act and,
  159–160, 169–171
Department of Homeland Security. *See also*
  homeland security
  creation of, 12–13, 190–192, 274–275
  immigration reform and, 17–18, 19–20,
    192–194, 195
  PATRIOT Act provisions concerning, 270–272
deregulation
  legislative gridlock and, 294–295
  private enforcement infrastructure and,
    59–62
  in Reagan era, 59
Derfner, Mary, 55–57
desegregation
  adversarial legalism and, 81–82
  court-agency enforcement of, 91–93
  impact of civil rights policies on, 77–80
  of military, 81–82
Deutch, John, 244–248
developing nations
  homeland security and terrorism policies and,
    265–266
  trade policy reforms and, 224–225
Directorate of Operations (DO) (CIA), 244–248
Director of National Intelligence (DNI),
  246–248
Dirksen, Everett, 117
Dirksen-Mansfield substitute, Title VI revisions
  and, 90
discrimination policies
  civil rights legislation and, 77–80
  federal funding and, 82

federal judiciary and, 86–89
litigation strategies concerning, 53–54
partisanship concerning, 16, 25
private enforcement infrastructure and,
  54–57
reform proposals for, 85
Title VI revisions concerning, 90–97
dismissal rules of teachers unions, 131–134
disparate impact doctrine, anti-discrimination
  policy and, 86–89
diversity visa program, immigration reform and,
  186–187
divided government, polarization and, 50–51
Divided We Govern (Mayhew), 29–31
division of labor, Title VII enforcement and,
  86–89
Division of Military Intelligence, 228–229
documentation authentication, immigration
  reform and, 188–190
Doha Round, 204–205, 212–213, 219–220
Dole, Robert, 117, 190
Donley, Michael, 274–275
Donovan, William, 229–232
Downs, Anthony, policy frameworks theory of,
  292–293
Downsian frameworks, 292–293
Dream Act, 19–20, 192–194
due process issues, in PATRIOT Act, 270–272
Dulles, Allen, 235–236
Dulles, John Foster, 235–236
Duncan, Arne, 129, 145–148
Dunlop Commission, 107–108, 113

economic conditions
  factor endowments and, 215–217
  free trade ideology and, 212–213
  immigration reform and, 182, 188–190,
    194–196, 202
  institutional tariff reforms and, 205–209
  labor policy and, 103–104
  policy reform and, 20–21, 28–30, 38, 40–41
  trade policies and, 203–205
education effect, trade policy politics and,
  215–217
education reform
  academic scholarship and politics of,
    151–152
  charter schools and, 143–145
  endogenous change dynamics in, 145–148
  exogenous change and, 148
  future challenges in, 145–148, 149–150
  information technology and, 148

education reform (cont.)
  mainstream reforms, 136–145
  National Defense Education Act, 35
  politics of blocking, 134–136
  rent-seeking and, 11–12
  resistance of teachers unions to, 130
  school choice initiatives and, 141–145
  teachers unions and, 129–150
Education Trust organization, 138
Eisenhower, Dwight, 3
  economic policies of, 28–30, 32
  housing policies under, 33
  intelligence reforms and, 235–236
  Interstate Highway System and, 34–35
  policy reforms under, 28, 37–38
  space exploration policies under, 35
  tax policies of, 33–34, 36–37
"Eisenhower High," 4
electoral politics
  free trade ideology and, 212–213
  organized labor and, 104–106, 122
  partisan polarization and, 286–289
  teachers unions and, 131–134
  trade policy reforms and, 205–209, 215–217,
    223
Elementary and Secondary Education Act of
  1965 (ESEA), 91–93, 134–136
Employee Free Choice Act (EFCA), 109–110,
  113–116, 117–118, 120–121, 127
employer sanctions, immigration reform and,
  181–194
employment discrimination litigation
  labor policy politics and, 106–110
  monetary damages in, 95–97
  policy reforms and, 85
  private enforcement infrastructure and,
    54–57
  strategies for, 53–54
endowment effect, failure of retrenchment
  reforms and, 63
Energy Independence and Security Act, 19–20
energy policies
  under Eisenhower, 37–38
  Upper Colorado River Storage Project, 34
enforcement strategies
  immigration policy and, 179–181
  for No Child Left Behind, 140–141
  Title VII of the Civil Rights Act, 84–89
  for Title VI policies, 90
enlightened administration concept, adversarial
  legalism and, 81–84
entitlement reform, 3–4

environmental policies
  court activism and, 295–297
  Democratic Party and, 289–290
  legacy of, 38–39
Equal Access to Justice Act, 65–68, 69–70
Equal Employment Opportunity Commission
  (EEOC)
  adjudication authorization under, 53–54
  creation of, 81–82
  enforcement problems of, 77–80, 84
  labor policy politics and, 106–110, 125
  policy goals of, 86–89
Equal Protection Clause (U.S. Constitution),
  immigration reform constitutionality and,
  196–197
Erikson, Robert S., 38–39
ethnic groups
  immigration reform and, 186–187
  racial profiling and homeland security policies
    towards, 253–254
  terrorist incidents and, 254–256
European immigrants, immigration reform and,
  182–183
European Union (EU), trade policy reforms and,
  211–212
evaluation rules of teachers unions, 131–134
executive actions, policy reforms through,
  17–18, 19–20
Executive Order 11905, US Foreign Intelligence
  Activities, 241–242
existing rights, failure of retrenchment and, 63
externalities
  Anti-Hijacking Bill of 1974 and, 262–264
  aviation security legislation and, 264–267
  homeland security and terrorism policies and,
    254–256
  trade policies and, 220, 222–223

factor endowments, trade policy and, 215–217
fair housing legislation, administrative strategies
  for, 83
fair trade ideology
  trade policy reform and, 208, 220–222
  unfair trade statutes and, 209–212
false identification industry, immigration reform
  and, 188–190
"Family Jewels" intelligence reform initiative,
  238–239, 240
family reunification policies, immigration
  reform and, 182–183, 186–187, 189–190
Farhang, Sean, 7–8, 9–10, 12–13, 16–17,
  48–71, 82, 83, 84, 88–89, 282–284, 285

Farrier, Jasmine, 270–272
fast track procedures, trade policy reforms and, 209
federal agencies
    authority concerning health care, 161–164
    bilingual education initiatives and, 93–95
    civil rights policies and, 10
    deregulation and role of, 59–62
    education reform and role of, 134–136
    health care reform and role of, 157–161
    Homeland Security Act unification of, 274–275
    labor policy politics and, 106–110
    liberal disillusionment with, 50–51
    school desegregation and, 91–93
    Title VI revisions and powers of, 91
    weak state paradox and, 80–81
Federal Bureau of Investigation (FBI), 13–14
    intelligence reform and, 236–239
Federal Fair Housing Board, 83
federal funding restrictions
    budget wars and, 295
    impact on civil rights of, 81–84, 91–93
    policy reform and, 282–284
Federal Highway Act, 4–5
federalism
    Affordable Care Act and, 160–161, 176
    constitutional foundations for, 179–181
    future challenges for health care reform and, 171–175
    immigration reform politics and, 179–199
    national limits on state authority and, 162–164
    PATRIOT Act and issues of, 270–272
    policy reform and expansion of, 282–284
    politics of retrenchment and, 64
    progressive federalism in health care reform, 165–171
Federalist Papers
    Federalist 10, 13–14, 289–290
    Federalist 48, 5–6
    Federalist 51, 5–6
federal judiciary
    adversarial legalism and, 97–99
    bilingual education initiatives and, 93–95
    retrenchment initiatives and role of, 70
    school desegregation and, 91–93
    sexual harassment policies and role of, 80–81
    Title VII enforcement and interpretation and, 84–89
Federal Mediation and Conciliation Service (FMCS), 113–114

fee cap proposals
    failure of, 63, 69–70
    lack of moderate support for, 65
    lessons from failure of, 67–68
    one-sided interest group mobilization and, 65–67
    political costs of, 64
    retrenchment of private enforcement and, 62–63
Feeley, Malcolm, 179–181
fee shifting policies
    attacks on private enforcement infrastructure and, 62–63
    deregulation and, 59–62
    private enforcement infrastructure and, 54–57, 58
Feingold, Russ, 271
Fenty, Adrian, 133
Fielding, Fred, 64
filibuster
    increased use of, 18–19
    as labor reform barrier, 116–118
    policy reforms and role of, 37
Financial Modernization Act of 1999, 168–171
financial responsibility rules, immigration reform and, 188–190
Fiorina, Morris, 292–293
First Amendment, immigration reform constitutionality and, 196–197
fiscal policy
    partisanship over, 17
    politics of retrenchment and, 64
Forand, Aime, 224
Ford, Gerald, 239–240, 241–242
Ford Foundation, civil rights litigation report, 54–57
Foreign Affairs magazine, 230–232
Foreign Assistance Act of 1961, 239–240
foreign governments, trade policy reforms and unfair practices of, 208–209
Foreign Intelligence Surveillance Act of 1978, 241–242
foreign producers and consumers, trade policy reforms and, 209–212
Forrestal, James, 230
Fourteenth Amendment
    bilingual education initiatives and, 93–95, 96–97
    school desegregation and federal court rulings on, 91–93
Fox, Vicente, 190–192
Franken, Al, 114

Freedom Rides for immigration reform,
190–192
Freeman, Richard, 107–108
free trade
globalization and, 217–220
institutional reforms for, 205–209
public opinion concerning, 217–220
trade policy reform and ideology of, 212–217
Free Trade Agreements (FTAs), 209, 212–213,
220, 225
Friedman, Milton, 141
Frymer, Paul, 20, 80–81, 86–89

Galbraith, John Kenneth, 36–37
Gallegy Amendment, immigration reform and,
190
Gates Foundation, 133–134
gender issues, factor endowments and, 215–217
General Agreement on Tariffs and Trade
(GATT), 206–207, 208, 224
globalization's impact on, 218–219
geography, politics of health care reform and,
166
Gingrich, Newt, 3
globalization
labor policy politics and, 107–108
protectionist ideology and, 214
trade policies and, 204–205, 217–220
Global War on Terror (GWOT), 244–248
Goldstein, Judith, 7–8, 13–14, 203–223,
257–259
Goldwater, Barry, 3, 7, 22
Goss, Porter, 243–244
government institutions
civil rights policies and, 80–81
trade policies and growth of, 222–216
Graham, Hugh Davis, 86–89, 90
"Grand Bargain" (of Boehner and Obama), 3
Great Britain
civil rights law in, 80–81
trade policies in, 213
Great Depression, institutional tariff reforms
and, 205–206
Great Recession
health care reform politics and, 165–166
organized labor and, 104–106, 109–110
teachers union dynamics and, 145–148
Great Society programs, 4–5
legacy of, 6–7
Green, William, 111–112
Greenberg, Jack, 84
Greenstein, Fred I., 40–41

Greenstone, J. David, 103–104
Greve, Michael S., 59–62
Griggs v. Duke Power, 86–89
Grogan, Colleen, 167–168
Gross, James, 120–121
guest worker programs, immigration reform
and, 190–192
gun control
aviation security and, 264–267
partisan polarization over, 288–289
Gun Control Act of 1968, 288–289

H-2 workers program, immigration reform and,
183–185
Haass, Richard, 268
habeas corpus, PATRIOT Act suspension of,
270–272
Haldeman, H. R., 236–239
Hale, Nathan, 228–229
Halpern, Stephen, 91–93
Hamilton, Alexander, 213–214
Haney, Patrick, 257–259
Hansen, John Mark, 261–267, 272–273
Harkin, Tom, 113–116, 117–118
Hart-Cellar Act. *See* Immigration and
Nationality Act of 1965
Hartley, Fred (Repr.), 111
Hatch, Orrin, 67, 112–113, 117, 268
Health, Education and Welfare (HEW), U.S.
Department of
bilingual education initiatives and, 93–95
creation of, 83
school desegregation and, 91–93
health care reform. *See also* Patient Protection
and Affordable Care Act
budget wars and, 295
future challenges for, 171–175
institutional grafting and implementation of,
167–168
political polarization and, 292
progressive federalism and, 157–175
Heckscher-Ohlin trade theory, 226
Heclo, Hugh, 1–3, 6–7, 290–293
Helms, Richard, 236–239
Hepburn Act, 22
Heritage Foundation, 165, 291
Hersh, Seymour, 240–242
Hispanic immigrants, immigration reform and,
181–194
Hochschild, Jennifer, 77–78
homeland security. *See also* Department of
Homeland Security

in Anti-Hijacking Bill of 1974, 262–264
in Aviation and Transportation Security Act,
    272–273
aviation security legislation and, 264–267
external factors in policies of, 254–256
immigration reform and, 190–192, 195
intelligence reform and, 227–228
National Security Act of 1947 and, 261–262
overview of changes in, 259–261
in PATRIOT Act, 270–272
policy reform and, 13–14
political forces and policies of, 254–259
post-September 11 policy changes for,
    253–277
public support for, 7, 256–257
reform initiatives for, 253–277
summary of policy changes in, 259, 275–276
in Violent Crime and Law Enforcement Act of
    1994, 267–269
Homeland Security Act
    bureaucracy expansion in, 271
    passage of, 274–275
homosexuality, immigration reform and, 186–187
Hoover, J. Edgar, 232, 236–239
Hoover Commission of 1955, 230
Horowitz, Michael, 61–63
House Permanent Select Committee on
    Intelligence (HPSCI), 241–242
Housing Act of 1949, 31
Housing Act of 1954, 33
housing policies, fair housing legislation and, 83
Houston, Lawrence, 234
Howard, Christopher, 80–81
Huddy, Leonie, 256–257
Hughes-Ryan Act, 239–240
Humphrey, Hubert, 85–86
Huntington, Samuel P., 38–39
Huntington, Clare, 180–181, 195
Hussein, Saddam, 246
Huston, Tom Charles, 236–239

ideology, policy analysis and, 40–41
illegal immigration
    DREAM Act legislation and, 192–194
    immigration reform and, 183–185,
        188–190
Immerman, Richard H., 7–8, 12–13, 227–248,
    253–254, 261–262
Immigration and Nationality Act of 1965,
    182–183, 195
Immigration and Naturalization Service (INS),
    186–187

Homeland Security Department and,
    190–192
Immigration and Reform Act of 1986 (IRCA),
    183–185
immigration reform, 3–4
    constitutional authority concerning, 196–197
    federalism and politics of, 179–199
    historical background for, 181–194
    legal scholarship debate over, 197–198
    in Obama era, 192–194
    partisanship concerning, 18–19
    policy proposals for, 198–199
    public opinion on, 7
    September 11th, 2001 attacks and, 190–192
    state *vs.* federal initiatives in, 11
    statistics on immigrants and refugees and, 180
Immigration Reform Act of 1990, 186–187
Immigration Reform and Immigrant
    Responsibility Act of 1996, 188–190, 195
import competing interest groups, institutional
    trade policy reforms and, 205–209
incentives
    in education reform, 141–145
    in partisan polarization, 286–289
income distribution
    economic inequality and organized labor and,
        104–106
    state institutions and, 80–81
industrial relations law, organized labor and,
    50, 109–110, 126, 294–295
inequality, organized labor and, 104–106
information technology
    Affordable Care Act glitches in, 171–175
    education reform and, 148
    factor endowments and, 215–217
institutional fragmentation, failure of
    retrenchment and, 63, 69–70
institutional grafting, health care reform and,
    167–168
institutional reform
    of intelligence, 233–236
    of trade policies, 205–209
Intelligence Oversight Board, 241–242
intelligence reform, 12–13
    mission creep and, 233–236
    national aversion to intelligence operations
        and, 228–233
    politics of, 227–248
    post-Cold War inertia and, 242–244
    post-September 11 policies and, 269–275
    September 11, 2001 attacks and, 244–248
    Vietnam War and, 236–242

Intelligence Reform and Terrorism Prevention Act (IRTPA), 227–228, 246–248
"intense policy demanders," political polarization and, 286–289
"intent," Title VII enforcement and principle of, 85–86
interagency counterterrorism groups, 262–264
interest groups
  homeland security and terrorist policies and, 257–259
  one-sided interest groups, mobilization of, 65–67
  partisan polarization and rise of, 286–289
  policy reform and role of, 284–286
  rise of policy state and, 289–290
Intermodal Surface Transportation Efficiency Act ("Ice-Tea"), 4–5
international law, trade policies and, 217–220
International Security and Development Cooperation Act, 264–267
international trade
  partisan politics and unfair trade statutes, 209–212
  reform politics in, 203–223
International Trade Commission, 207–208, 209–212, 225
Interstate Commerce Commission (ICC), 22
Interstate Highway System, 2, 34–35, 38
  future issues for, 40–41
intervention bias, trade policy reforms and, 220–222
Investment Tax Credit, establishment of, 36
Iran Contra scandal, 242–243, 265–266
Iranian Revolution, terrorist incidents and, 254–256
Iraq War, intelligence reform and, 246
Israel state, terrorist incidents and, 254–256
issue networks, policymaking and role of, 290–293

Jacobs, Lawrence R., 8, 10–11, 15, 16–17, 104–106, 105–106, 109–110, 157–175, 222–216
Jacobson, Gary, 274–275
Jefferson, Thomas, 213–214
Jenkins, Jeffery A., 1–21
JJ Case v. Borak, 97
Johnson, Loch, 239–240
Johnson, Lyndon B.
  enlightened administration ideology and, 81–82
  intelligence reforms and, 238–239

labor policy under, 104–106, 112, 118–119, 120
  policy reforms under, 5–7, 37, 40–41
  space exploration policies and, 35
Jones, Bryan D., 27
Jost, K., 270–272
"judicial retrenchment," 70

Kagan, Robert, 80–81, 88–89, 297–298
Kahn, Anne, 236
Kaiser Family Foundation, 15–16
  Affordable Care Act analysis and, 168–171
Karol, David, 288
Kasich, John, 15
Kennan, George, 230–232
Kennedy, Edward, 189
Kennedy, John F., 4
  economic policies of, 28–30, 36, 38
  enlightened administration ideology and, 81–82
  intelligence operations under, 240
  policy reforms under, 28, 37
  space exploration policies and, 35
  tax policies of, 36–37
  Title VI revisions and, 90
  trade policies of, 36
Kennedy Round of trade talks, 208–209
Kerrey, Bob, 243–244
Kersch, Ken, 21
Keynesian economics, policy reform and, 40–41
Kim, Claire Jean, 267–268
King, Cynthia, 274–275
King, Desmond, 105–106, 109–110
Kingdon, John W., 27, 257–259, 272–273, 291–292
KIPP schools, 143–145
Klein, Joel, 133, 138–139
Know Nothing Movement, emergence of, 182
Kuzma, Lynn, 268

labels for policy reforms, pitfalls of, 27
Labor Law Reform Bill (1978), 112–113
labor policy. *See also* organized labor
  economic inequality and, 104–106
  factor endowments and, 215–217
  filibuster as barrier to reform of, 116–118
  free trade ideology and, 213–214
  globalization's impact on, 218–219
  historical perspective on reform of, 110–113
  immigration reform and, 183–185
  politics of reform of, 8–9, 11–12, 20, 103–121

public opinion concerning, 118–120, 128
union decline and politics of, 106–110
Laffer, Arthur, 7
laissez faire ideology, trade policy reforms and limits of, 220–222
landlord-tenant laws, immigration reform constitutionality and, 196–197
Landrum-Griffin Act (1959), 107–108, 118–119
Lau v. Nichols, 93–95
law enforcement, homeland security policies and, 274–275
Lawsuit Abuse Reduction Act of 2011, 48–49, 69
Lawyers' Committee for Civil Rights Under Law, 54–57
layoff rules of teachers unions, 131–134
League of United Latin American Citizens, 183–185
Lee, Richard C., 31
Leech, Beth, 285
legal immigration legislation
    Immigrant Responsibility Act of 1996, 188–190
    Immigration and Reform Act of 1986, 183–185
    Immigration and Reform Act of 1990, 186–187
legislative gridlock, polarization in policymaking and, 294–295
legislative statutes, table of, 29–31
Leighninger, Robert D. Jr., 40–41
Leventhal, Harold (Judge), 98
liberal ideology
    abortion politics and, 288
    administrative power and, 49
    Democratic-liberal public interest coalition and, 50
    educational reform and changes in, 145–148
    limits of bureaucracy and, 50–51
liberal law reform, private enforcement infrastructure and, 63, 67–68
Lichtenstein, Nelson, 104–106, 109–110
Lieberman, Robert, 23, 80–81
Liebman, Wilma, 113
Limitation of Legal Fees Awards Act of 1981, 62–63, 69
literacy tests, immigration reform and, 182, 186–187
litigation. *See also* anti-litigation reform; private lawsuits
    adversarial legalism and, 81–82
    civil rights model of, 53–54

emergence and spread in 1970s of, 53–57
policy reform and, 48–71
private enforcement infrastructure and, 54–57, 68–69
pro-litigation reform success and, 57
rates of, 58
regulatory reform through, 51–53
weak state paradox and, 80–81
The Litigation State (Farhang), 84
local government
    educational reform policies and, 90, 134–136
    immigration reform and, 180–181, 194–196
Lockerbie bombing disaster, 264–267
Logan, John, 120
"long-1950s"
    future legacy of, 40–41
    policy reform and, 2, 4, 27
    political legacy of, 38–39
Lowi, Theodore, 2–3, 12

MacKuen, Michael B., 38–39
Madison, James, 289–290
    on constitutional powers and responsibilities, 5–6, 10–11
Maier, Charles S., 28
Mann, Thomas, 292–293
Mansfield, Mike, 235–236, 241–242
market forces, trade policy reforms and limits of, 220–222
Markle Task Force on National Security in the Information Age, 246–248
Marshall, T. H., 107–108
Masci, David, 270–272
Massachusetts v. EPA, 295–297
Massey, Douglas, 187
Matusow, Allen J., 29
Mayhew, David, 2, 3, 4, 9–10, 23, 27, 282–284
mayor-controlled school systems, education reform and, 133
McCarran-Ferguson Act of 1945, 168–171
McCarthy, Joseph, 235–236
McConnel, Grant, 2–3
McConnell, Mitch, 294–295
McCormick, James, 262–264
McCormick, Robert, 232
McDonnell, Lorraine M., 28–30
Medicaid program
    Affordable Care Act and expansions of, 159–160, 171–175
    federal and state authority concerning, 161–164
    impact on states of, 166

Medicaid program (cont.)
institutional grafting in health care reform of, 167–168
politics over expansion of, 15, 20
private litigation over, 96–97
state's share of costs for, 165–166
medical loss ratio, Affordable Care Act policies and, 169–171
Medicare
future legacy of, 40–41
Part B premiums in, 166
prescription drug benefits and, 14–15
public support for, 7
Medoff, James, 107–108
Meese, Edwin, 61–62
Melnick, R. Shep, 53–54, 176, 282–284
on civil rights policies, 10, 77–99
on democracy and policy reform, 12–13, 16
on postwar policy reform, 7–8
on tax policy, 17
Merolla, Jennifer, 7–8, 13–14, 227–228, 253–277
Mettler, Suzanne, 80–81, 98–99
Mexico, U.S. trade with, 214
military
desegregation of, 81–82
intelligence reform and role of, 233–236
Milkis, Sidney M., 1–21, 81–82
Miller, George, 113–116
Mills, Wilbur D., 37, 224
mobilization, persuasion *vs.*, 15–16
Moe, Terry, 7–9, 11–12, 20, 63, 129–150, 284–286, 287
Mollenkopf, John, 31
Morse, Wayne, 37
Most Favored Nation (MFN) privileges, trade policy reforms and, 206–207, 224
Moynihan, Daniel Patrick, 2, 40–41, 243–244
multilateral agreements, trade policies and, 217–220
My Lai Massacre, 239

NAACP Legal Defense and Education Fund (LDEF), 54–57
Title VII suits filed by, 84
Naftali, Timothy, 257–261, 262–267, 267–268
Nathan, Richard, 11
National Aeronautics and Space Administration (NASA)
establishment of, 35
future issues for, 40–41
political legacy of, 38–39

National Association for the Advancement of Colored People (NAACP)
civil rights litigation and, 81–82
immigration reform and, 183–185
school choice proposals and, 142
National Association of Insurance Commissioners (NAIC), 169–171
National Association of State Attorneys General (NASAG), 65–67
National Commission on Terrorist Attacks Upon the United States (9/11 Commission), 244–248
National Conference of State Legislatures (NCSL), 179–181
National Defense Education Act, 35
National Education Association, 130
collective bargaining by, 131–134
historical transformation of, 130–131
No Child Left Behind opposed by, 140–141
politics of blocking reform and, 134–136
National Federation of Independent Businesses (NFIB) v. Sibelius, 96–97
National Foreign Intelligence Program, 241–242
National Institute of Municipal Law Officers (NIMLO), 65–67
National Intelligence Authority (NIA), 230
National Intelligence Council (NIC), 246
National Intelligence Estimate (NIE), 246
nationalism, terrorist incidents and, 254–256
National Labor Relations Act (NLRA), 8–9, 107–108, 113–114
National Labor Relations Board (NLRB), 21, 83
adjudicatory powers of, 53–54, 125
Congressional investigation of, 111
expansion of, 112–113
organized labor and, 106–110
National Mediation Board, 106–110
National Military Establishment, 233–236, 261–262
National Rifle Association (NRA), 288–289
National Science Foundation, creation of, 31, 38–39
national security
homeland security and terrorist policies and, 256–257
politicization of, 12–13
National Security Act (1947), 12–13, 229–232, 244–248, 259–261, 275–276
National Security Agency (NSA), 13–14, 236–239

National Security Council, 233–236
National Student Associate, 236
A Nation at Risk (report), 129, 130–131, 136
nation-based quotas, immigration reform and,
   182–183
Naturalization Act of 1906, 186–187
Nedzi, Lucien, 239–240
"negativity bias," failure of retrenchment
   reforms and, 63
Nelson, Ben, 162–164
New Deal programs, 4
   adversarial legalism and, 81–84
   labor policy politics and, 107–108
   liberal ideology and, 49
   organized labor and, 103–104
   rights revolution and, 8–9
"new federalism," state *vs.* federal authority
   and, 166
New Frontier programs, 4
New York Times, 236, 239–240, 246
Ngo Dinh Diem, 240
Nickles, Don, 117
Nixon, Richard M., 4–5
   civil rights policies under, 84
   divided government and presidency of, 50–51
   federal bureaucracy under, 53–54
   intelligence reform and, 236–239
   policy reforms under, 37
   security and terrorism policies under,
      262–264
No Child Left Behind Act (NCLB), 2, 134–136,
   140–141
nontariff barriers (NTB), trade policy reforms
   and, 208
Norquist, Grover, 292
North American Free Trade Agreement
   (NAFTA), 104–106, 209, 220
Nunn, Sam, 243–244

Obama, Barack
   educational reform and, 145–148
   homeland security and terrorist policies and,
      275–276
   immigration reform under, 192–194
   implementation of Affordable Care Act
      under, 167–168
   labor policy under, 103–104, 111–112,
      113–116, 118–119, 120–121
   national security under, 13–14
   policy reforms under, 17–18
   racial politics and, 16
   trade policy reforms and, 212–213

Office for Civil Rights (OCR)
   bilingual education initiatives and, 93–95
   enforcement problems of, 77–80
   school desegregation policies and, 91–93
Office of National Estimates (CIA), 237
Office of Naval Intelligence (ONI), 228–229
Office of Policy Coordination (OPC), 234–235
Office of Reports and Estimates (ORE),
   230–232
Office of Strategic Services (OSS), 229–232
Office of the Congressional Trade Enforcer
   (proposed), 209–212
Office of the Director of National Intelligence
   (ODNI), 227–228, 246–248
Office of the US Trade Representative (USTR),
   207–208, 209–212, 225
oil exploration and development, policy reforms
   concerning, 31–32, 38–39
Olson, Mancur, 284–286
O'Neill, Tip, 61–62
one-sided interest groups, mobilization of, 65–67
"Operation Blockade," 186–187
Operation ENDURING FREEDOM, 244–248
"Operation Gatekeeper," 186–187
Operation MHCHAOS program, 238–239
Operation Phoenix, 236
Oppenheimer, Bruce, 19–20
Orfield, Gary, 91–93
organized labor. *See also* specific unions, e.g.,
   teachers unions
   American inequality and, 104–106
   business hostility to, 107–108, 126
   Employee Free Choice Act and, 113–116
   factor endowments and, 215–217
   historical perspective on labor law and role of,
      110–113
   immigration reform and, 181–194
   industrial relations law and, 50, 109–110,
      126, 294–295
   opposition to Homeland Security Act from,
      274–275
   policy reforms sought by, 103–104
   politics and decline of, 106–110
   public opinion of, 118–120, 128
   right to work laws and, 111–112
   trade policies and, 222–216
   union density and division within, 118–120,
      122
Ornstein, Norman, 292–293
Orren, Karen, 1, 5–7
Outer Continental Shelf Lands Act of 1953, 32,
   37

Pacific Legal Foundation, 59–62
Page, Benjamin, 222–216
Palestinian Liberation Organization, 254–256
Paludo, Paul, 7–8, 16–17
"partial preemption" principle in federalism, 176
partisan polarization
    budget wars and, 295
    democracy and, 16–17
    divided government and, 50–51
    dynamics of, 293–297
    homeland security and terrorist policies and, 257–259, 275–276
    legislative gridlock and, 294–295
    policy reform and, 15–16, 282–298
    rise of policy state and, 286–289
    tariff and trade policies and, 209–212, 224
    unilateral action and, 295–297
Pastor, Robert, 211
Patashnik, Eric, 167–168
Patient Protection and Affordable Care Act, 2, 3
    administrative capacity of states and implementation of, 168–171
    "buying states" strategy for passage of, 165–166
    future challenges for, 171–175
    institutional grafting and implementation of, 167–168
    national and state authority concerning, 161–164
    politics surrounding, 14–15
    progressive federalism of, 10–11, 157–175
    Supreme Court rulings concerning, 295–297
PATRIOT Act, 270–272, 275–276
Patterson, Eleanor "Cissy," 232
Patterson, James, 6
Patterson, Orlando, 77–78
People for the American Way, 142
Peppers, Donald, 267
performance evaluations, educational reforms and, 139–140, 145–148
Perry, William, 243–244
persuasion, mobilization *vs.*, 15–16
Pierson, Paul, 3–4, 13–14, 16–17, 63, 162–164, 282–298
Pike, Otis, 240–242
Podesta, John, 291
polarization. *See* partisan polarization
policy reform
    activist state in American politics and, 297–298
    democracy and, 12–17

era of regulation and, 27, 282–284
expansion in postwar era, 7–12, 27, 282–284
future trends in, 40–41
legislative gridlock and, 294–295
litigation and, 48–71
partisan polarization and, 282–298
politics and, 2–5, 38–39
policy state
    Constitution and, 5–7
    evolution of, 1–21
    future issues concerning, 17–21
    legitimacy of, 3–4
    rise of, 282–284
politics
    of Affordable Care Act, 161–164
    intelligence reform and role of, 236–242
    of labor policy and union decline, 106–110
    organized labor and, 104–106
    policy reform and, 2–5, 38–39
    of retrenchment, 64
    teachers unions and, 131–134
    Title VII enforcement and role of, 86–89
Politics and Policy: The Eisenhower, Kennedy, and Johnson Years (Sundquist), 28
Pollard, Neal, 274–275
postwar era, policy reform and politics in, 3, 7–12
predatory trade practices, free trade ideology and, 214
presidential power
    homeland security and terrorist policies and, 257–259, 275–276
    intelligence reform and, 227–228
    organized labor and, 105–106
    private enforcement infrastructure and, 67–68
    trade policies and, 209–212
President's Foreign Intelligence Advisory Board (PFIAB), 243–244
President's Intelligence Advisory Board (PIAB), 243–244
PRISM program, 13–14
prisoner's dilemma, trade policy reform and, 220–222
privacy issues
    Aviation and Transportation Security Act and, 272–273
    Homeland Security Act and, 274–275
    homeland security and terrorist policies and, 275–276
    homeland security policies and, 253–254

in PATRIOT Act, 270–272
policy reform and, 13–14
private enforcement infrastructure
conservative attack on, 62–63
deregulation and, 59–62
failed attack against, 63, 67–68
federal agencies and, 90–97
growth of, 54–57, 68–69
implied right of, 97
legislative gridlock and, 294–295
monetary damages for plaintiffs and,
95–97
"regime politics" theory and, 70–71
private litigation
private enforcement infrastructure and,
54–57
pro-litigation reforms and, 57
as regulatory reform strategy, 51–53
private public interest law firms, emergence of,
55–57
private rights of action, bilingual education
initiatives and, 93–95
progressive federalism, health care reform and,
157–175
Progressive Party, formation of, 22
pro-litigation reform movement, 49
Proposition 187 (California), 188–190
protectionism
free trade ideology *vs.*, 214
globalization and, 217–220
institutional trade policy reforms and,
205–209
public opinion concerning, 217–220
trade policies and, 203–205
public interest groups
policy reform and, 50
private enforcement infrastructure and,
54–57, 59–62
public investment, legacy of, 40–41
public opinion
on airline hijackings, 262–264
of Aviation and Transportation Security Act,
272–273
of health care reform, 171–175
immigration reform and, 188–190
national aversion to intelligence operations,
228–233, 238–239
of organized labor, 118–120, 128
partisan polarization of, 15–16
on PATRIOT Act, 271–272
on terrorism, 268
trade policy reform and, 215–217

public sector unions, 20
establishment of, 130–131
growth of, 104–106
public opinion of, 119–120
public spending, policy expansion and, 282–284
Pucinski Committee, 109–110
Pulido, Paul, 13–14, 227–228, 253–277

Quarles v. Phillip Morris, 86–89

Race to the Top initiative, 141, 145–148
racial discrimination
consequences of civil rights policies on, 77–80
federal funding denial on basis of, 82
immigration reform and, 181–194
monetary damages for, court authorization
of, 95–97
partisanship and, 16, 25
PATRIOT Act impact on, 270–272
racial profiling and homeland security
policies, 253–254
school choice initiatives and, 142–143
Radin, Beryl, 84
Ramparts magazine, 236
RAND Corporation, 254–256
Read, Frank, 91–93
Reagan, Ronald, 22
aviation security legislation and, 264–267
conservative movement and, 3, 7
deregulation and administrative power
shifting under, 59
immigration reform and, 183–185
intelligence reform under, 241–242
Iran Contra scandal and, 242–243
NRA endorsement of, 288–289
organized labor and, 104–106
policy reforms under, 59–63, 70
terrorism policies under, 264–267
Real ID Act of 2005, 191
Reciprocal Trade Agreements Act (RTAA)
Extension of 1955, 34
Reciprocal Trade Agreements Act (RTAA)
Extension of 1958, 35
Reciprocal Trade Agreements Act of 1934
(RTAA), 206–207, 211–212, 224
"regime politics" theory, federal judiciary and,
70–71
regional trade agreements, trade policies and,
220
regulatory policies
business capture of, 109–110
era of, 27

regulatory policies (cont.)
  free trade ideology and, 213
  liberal ideology and, 49
  private lawsuits as reform strategy for, 51–53
  Reagan-era reform of, 59–63
  retrenchment attempts against, 59–63
  table of statutes enacted, 29–31
Rehnquest, William (Chief Justice), 95–97,
  98–99
Reid, Harry, 163–164
rent seeking behavior, free trade ideology and,
  212–217
Republican Party
  absence of moderates in, 65
  Affordable Care Act politics and, 161–164,
    167–168, 171–175
  anti-litigation reform and, 48–49
  business interests and, 289–290
  civil rights legislation and, 53–54
  Democratic legislators and Republic
    presidents, 50–51
  educational reform dynamics and, 145–148
  extremism within, 292–293
  free trade ideology and, 212–217
  immigration reform and, 186–187
  increased conservatism of, 3
  intelligence reform and, 230–232, 246–248
  school accountability initiatives and,
    137–141, 153
  trade policies and, 203–205
Republic Study Group (RSG), 3
retaliation, trade policies involving, 220–222
retrenchment initiatives
  attacks on regulation and, 70
  deregulation and, 59
  failure of, 63, 67–68, 69–70
  political costs of, 64
  private enforcement infrastructures and, 59–62
Revenue Act of 1954, 33–34
Rhee, Michelle, 133
Rice, Condoleeza, 246–248
Richardson, Elliiot, 93
Ridge, Tom, 253–254, 274–275
rights-based rhetoric, public policy and politics
  and, 9–12
right to work laws, 8–9
  historical perspective on, 111–112
  increased enactment of, 103–104
Roberts, John (Chief Justice), 98–99, 295–297
Roberts, Paul Craig, 7
Rockefeller, Jay, 246–248
Rockefeller, Nelson, 239–240

Rockefeller Commission, 240–242
Rodriguez, Cristina, 198–199
Roe v. Wade, 288, 295–297
Rohde, David, 267
Romney, Mitt, 292
Roosevelt, Franklin D., 6
  intelligence reforms and, 229–232
  trade policies under, 206–207
Roosevelt, Theodore, 22
Rubin, Ed, 179–181
rulemaking
  administrative process and, 51–53
  bilingual education initiatives and authority
    of, 93–95
rural poverty programs, Area Redevelopment
    Act of 1961, 36

safe harbor doctrine, EEOC enforcement and,
    88–89
Saguy, Abigail, 80–81
Saint Lawrence Seaway
  authorization for, 32
  economic impact of, 38
  political legacy of, 38–39
salary rules of teachers unions, 131–134
Schattschneider, E. E., 2–3, 203–205
SCHIP program, 166
Schlesinger, Arthur M., 38–39
Schlesinger, James, 236–239
Schneider, Bill, 15–16
school accountability, 137–141
School Aid Act of 1971, 53–54
school choice, education reform including,
    141–145
school desegregation
  enforcement problems with, 77–80
  monetary damages for plaintiffs under, 95–97
  Title VI revisions concerning, 91–93
school vouchers, proposals for, 141–145, 154
Schorr, Daniel, 240
Scott, Rick, 15
Scowcroft, Brent, 245–246
seasonal workers, immigration reform and,
    183–185
Sebelius, Kathleen, 157, 169–171
segregation, impact of civil rights policies on,
    77–80
Select Committee on Intelligence (SSCI),
    241–242
Select Committee to Study Governmental
    Operations with Respect to Intelligence
    Operations (Church Committee), 240–242

Senate, policy reforms and role of, 37
Senate Rule 22, changes in 1975 to, 117
separation of powers
    immigration reform and, 179–181
    national limits on state authority and,
        162–164
    policy state and, 5–7, 289–290
    politics of educational reform and, 134–136
    rights *vs.* policies and, 9–12
September 11, 2001 attacks
    homeland security/terrorism policy changes
        following, 253–277
    immigration reform and, 190–192
    intelligence reform following, 244–248
Service Employees International Union (SEIU),
    116, 120
sexual harassment policies
    federal judiciary role in, 80–81
    monetary damages for plaintiffs and,
        95–97
Shugart, William, 254–256, 277
Sierra Club, 117–118
Simon, Herbert, 291–292
Simpson, Alan, 188
skilled workers
    Immigration and Reform Act of 1990 and,
        186–187
    immigration policies and, 182–183
Skocpol, Theda, 8, 10–11, 15, 16–17, 157–175,
    284–286, 287
Skowronek, Stephen, 1, 5–7
Skrentny, John, 80–81, 86–89, 183–185
Sky Marshall program, airline security and,
    265–266
Smith, Howard, 111, 125
Smith, Lamar, 188, 194
Smith, Walter Bedell, 234–235
Smith, William French, 64
Smith v. Allwright, 9–10
Smoot-Hawley tariff, 203–206, 214
Snyder, Rick, 15
social citizenship, labor policy politics and,
    107–108
social justice groups, security targeting of, 277
social regulation
    private enforcement infrastructure and,
        59–62
    Reagan-era reform of, 59–63
Social Security, 8–9
    health care reform and, 158
    public support for, 7
Souers, Sidney (Rear Admiral), 230–231

Southern realignment, racial politics and,
    286–289
Souva, Mark, 267
Specter, Arlen, 114, 247–248
Spiro, Peter, 189–190, 202
stakeholder creation, interest group politics and,
    284–286
Staszak, Sarah, 70
state activism
    DREAM Act legislation and, 192–194
    immigration reform politics and, 179–181,
        188–190, 192, 194–196
    unilateral action politics and, 295–297
state-building strategies, adversarial legalism
    and, 81–84
state governments
    administrative capacity and implementation
        of health care reform under, 168–171
    authority concerning health care, 161–164
    "buying states" strategy for Affordable Care
        Act, 165–166
    charter school initiatives and, 143–145
    class size reduction initiatives and, 136–137
    educational reforms and role of, 136–145
    endogenous change dynamics and, 145–148
    future challenges for health care reform and,
        171–175
    health care reform and role of, 157–161
    immigration reform politics and, 179–181,
        198–199
    Medicaid expansion and, 15, 96–97
    national limits on powers of, 162–164
    policy reform and, 11–12
    policy state and, 10–11
    public school administration by, 134–136
    school accountability initiatives and,
        137–141
    Supreme Court rulings concerning, 295–297
state insurance commissioners, implementation
    of health care reform and, 168–171
statutory preemption principle, immigration
    reform constitutionality and, 196–197
statutory rules, administrative process and,
    51–53
Steelworker v. Weber, 86–89
Stern, Andy, 116
Stevens, John Paul (Justice), 95–97, 179
Stimson, Henry, 228–229
Stimson, James A., 38–39
Stockman, David, 61–63
Stolper-Samuelson theorem, 226
Stone, Katherine, 275–276

Stouffer, Samuel, 256–257
striker replacement legislation, 117
Submerged Lands Act of 1953, 31–32, 37
Sundquist, James L., 28
Super 301 legislation, 225
supermajoritarian rules in Congress
    budget wars and, 295
    filibuster use and, 116–118
    labor policy reform failure and use of,
        112–117, 127
Supplemental Security Income (SSI), 166
supply side economics, conservative embrace of,
    7
Supremacy Clause (U.S. Constitution),
    immigration reform constitutionality and,
    196–197
Supreme Court (U.S.)
    discrimination policy strategies and rulings
        by, 86–89, 98–99
    homeland security and terrorism rulings by,
        275–276
    immigration reform rulings by, 179–181
    monetary damages for civil rights authorized
        by, 95–97
    Patient Protection and Affordable Care Act
        rulings of, 157–161
    polarization in, 295–297, 301
Swain, Carol M., 3–4, 8, 11, 179–199, 287

Taft, William Howard, 22
Taft-Hartley Act (1947), 8–9, 103–104,
    107–108, 111–112, 118–119, 120
Tanden, Neera, 291
tariff policies
    free trade ideology and, 212–217
    future challenges in, 222–216
    globalization and, 217–220
    institutional reforms for, 205–209
    partisan mediation and unfair trade statutes
        and, 209–212
    public opinion concerning, 217–220
    recommendations for, 220–222
    reform politics in, 203–223
tax credits, school vouchers and, 141–145
tax reform, 3–4
    budget wars and, 295
    Kennedy tax cuts, 36–37, 38
    policy expansion and, 282–284
    political polarization and, 292
    Revenue Act of 1954 and, 33–34
teachers unions, 128
    charter schools and, 143–145

collective bargaining by, 131–134
contract provisions created by, 131–134
educational policy reforms and, 129–150
endogenous change dynamics in, 145–148
historical power of, 130–131
interest group mobilization and, 284–286
No Child Left Behind opposed by, 140–141
resistance to educational reform from, 130
school accountability initiatives and, 137–141
school choice proposals and, 141–145
school voucher systems and, 141–145
testing programs and, 138–139
Tea Party
    ambivalence about government in, 7
    conservative movement and, 3
Tenet, George, 244–248
Tenth Amendment, Medicaid program and, 15
tenure laws, educational reforms and, 139, 141
Terrorism Firearms Detection Act, 264–267
terrorism policies
    in Anti-Hijacking Bill of 1974, 262–264
    in Aviation and Transportation Security Act,
        272–273
    aviation security legislation and, 264–267
    external factors in, 254–256
    in Homeland Security Act, 274–275
    incidence of terrorism and, 254–256
    intelligence reform and, 244–248
    National Security Act of 1947 and, 261–262
    overview of changes in, 259–261
    in PATRIOT Act, 270–272
    political forces and, 254–259
    post-September 11 changes for, 253–277
    public support for, 256–257
    reform of, 253–277
    summary of changes in, 259–259, 275–276
    in Violent Crime and Law Enforcement Act of
        1994, 267–269
testing programs, school accountability
    initiatives and, 138–139, 153
think tanks, policymaking and evolution of,
    290–293
Thompson, Tommy, 142
Three Mile Island nuclear disaster, 38–39
Title IX of the 1972 Education Amendments, 84
    monetary damages for plaintiffs under,
        95–97
Title VII of the Civil Rights Act
    court-agency activism concerning, 98–99
    EEOC policy goals and, 86–89
    enforcement and interpretation of, 84–89
    litigation strategies and, 53–54

private enforcement infrastructure and, 54–57, 67–68, 69–70
Title VI comparisons with, 90
Title VI of the Civil Rights Act, 82
 bilingual education and, 93–97
 monetary damages for plaintiffs under, 95–97
 transformation of, 90–97
Tokyo Round of trade talks, 208–209
Toqueville, Alexis de, 20
Trade Act of 1974, 208–209
Trade Adjustment Assistance (TAA), 13–14, 213–214, 220
Trade Expansion Act of 1962, 36
trade policy
 free trade ideology and, 212–217
 future challenges in, 222–216
 globalization and, 217–220
 institutional reforms for, 205–209
 partisan mediation and unfair trade statutes and, 209–212
 public opinion concerning, 215–217
 recommendations for, 220–222
 reform politics in, 203–223
Trade Promotion Authority (TPA), 209
transfer rules of teachers unions, 131–134
Transportation Security Authority, 272–273
trial lawyers, Democratic Party and, 289–290
Trohan, Walter, 232
Truman, Harry S.
 intelligence reforms and, 229–232, 261–262
 labor policy and, 103–104, 111–112, 118–119, 120
 policy reforms under, 28, 31
Truman Doctrine, 233–236
Trumka, Richard, 114, 115–116
"two presidencies" thesis, homeland security policies and, 267, 269

Unabomber, 267–269
undocumented workers
 immigration reform and, 183–185, 188–190
 increase in, 194–196
unemployment
 policy reforms concerning, 29, 42
 trade policy politics and, 215–217, 220–222
unfair trade statutes, politics of, 209–212
Uniform Guidelines on Employee Selection Procedures and Guidelines on Affirmative Action, 88–89
unilateral action politics, partisan polarization, 295–297
unions. *See* organized labor

United Auto Workers, 103–104
United States Commission on Civil Rights, 83–84
United States Conference for Catholic Bishops, 183–185
United States Conference of Mayors (USCM), 65–67
United States v. Jefferson County Board of Education, 91–93
UNITE-HERE organization, 120
Upper Colorado River Storage Project, 3, 34
 political legacy of, 38–39
urban renewal projects
 housing policies and, 31, 33
 political legacy of, 38–39
Uruguay Round of trade talks, 208, 209
U.S. Court of International Trade, 209–212
U.S. Government Accounting Office, Affordable Care Act analysis and, 168–171
U.S.S. Cole, al Qaeda attack on, 244–248

Vandenberg, Arthur, 230–232
Vandenberg, Hoyt (General), 230–232, 233
Vanderbush, Walt, 257–259
Vietnam War
 distrust of public authority and, 6–7
 intelligence reforms and, 236–242
 terrorist incidents in response to, 254–256
Village Voice newspaper, 240–241
Violent Crime and Law Enforcement Act of 1994, 259–261, 267–269, 275–276
visa restrictions
 immigration reform and, 182–183, 186–187
 post-September 11 increase in, 190–192
 skilled workers and, 186–187
Vogel, David, 50, 285–286
Voluntary Export Agreements (VEAs), 209–212, 225
Voting Rights Act of 1965
 Amendments of 1975, 53–54
 consequences of, 77–80
 enforcement problems with, 77–80
 "preclearance" provision of, 83

Wagner Act (1935), 21, 105–106, 107–108, 110–113, 118–119
Walton, John, 142
Wand, Jonathan, 289–290
Warner, John, 243–244
war on terrorism, politics of, 13–14
Warren, Dorian T., 8–9, 11–12, 20, 21, 103–121, 222–223, 294–295

Washington Post, 54–57
Watergate scandal
  distrust of public authority and, 6–7
  intelligence reform and, 236–239
weak state paradox, civil rights policies and,
  80–81
Weapons of Mass Destruction (WMD),
  intelligence reforms and, 246
Weatherford, M. Stephen, 28–30
Welch, Richard, 242
welfare policy, state *vs.* federal responsibility
  for, 157–161
What Do Unions Do? (Freeman and Medoff),
  107–108
whistleblower protection, Homeland Security
  Act limits on, 274–275
Wiebe, Robert, 16–17
Wildavsky, Aaron, 257–259
Wilson, James Q., 2–4, 49
Wisdom, John Minor (Judge), 81–82, 91–93
Wisner, Frank, 234–235

Wittkopf, Eugene, 262–264
workplace regulation, labor policy politics and,
  106–110
World Trade Center bombing (1993), 267–269
World Trade Organization (WTO)
  domestic politics and, 214, 225
  globalization's impact on, 218–219
  Super 301 legislation and, 225
  trade policies and, 203–205, 209–212, 214
World War II, intelligence reforms and,
  229–232
Wright, Skelly (Judge), 98

Yalta Conference, 232
Yardley, Herbert, 228–229
Yetter, Virginia M., 3–4, 8, 11, 179–199, 287

Zechmeister, Elizabeth A., 256–257
Zegart, Amy B., 267–268, 272–273
Zelikow, Philip, 246–248
Zelman court decision, 143

47676442R00183

Made in the USA
Columbia, SC
03 January 2019